© Robert Yager

ED VULLIAMY was the New York correspondent for *The Observer* from 1997 to 2003 and spent many years as an international correspondent for *The Guardian*. The author of *Seasons in Hell,* Vulliamy lives in London and Arizona.

ALSO BY ED VULLIAMY

Seasons in Hell: Understanding Bosnia's War

AMEXICA

AMEXICA

WAR
ALONG
THE
BORDERLINE

Revised and Updated Edition

ED VULLIAMY

PICADOR

FARRAR, STRAUS AND GIROUX
NEW YORK

www.picadorusa.com

For book club information, please visit www.facebook.com/picadorbookclub or e-mail marketing@picadorusa.com.

Grateful acknowledgment is made for permission to reprint the following material: Lyrics from "The Road It Gives, the Road It Takes Away," words and music by Tom Russell and Andrew Hardin, copyright © 2001 by Frontera Music (ASCAP) and Alligator Farm Music (BMI), administered by Bug Music. All rights reserved. Used by permission. Lyrics from "When Sinatra Played Juarez" and "Where the Dream Begins," words and music by Tom Russell, copyright © 2001 by Frontera Music (ASCAP), administered by Bug Music. All rights reserved. Used by permission.

"Afterword to the 2011 Edition: Blood Money" was previously published, in a slightly different form, in *The Observer* (London).

Designed by Abby Kagan

Library of Congress Cataloging-in-Publication Data

Vulliamy, Ed.
    Amexica : war along the borderline / Ed Vulliamy. — 1st Picador ed.
       p. cm.
    Includes bibliographical references and index.
    ISBN 978-0-312-61061-6
  1. Drug traffic—Mexico. 2. Narco-terrorism—Mexico. 3. Drug control—Mexico.
4. Drug traffic—United States. 5. Narco-terrorism—United States. 6. Drug control—
United States. 7. Drug traffic—Mexican-American Border Region. I. Title.
    HV5840.M4V85 2011
    363.450972'1—dc23

                                 2011025013

First published in the United States by Farrar, Straus and Giroux

First Picador Edition: October 2011

10 9 8 7 6 5 4 3 2 1

THIS IS FOR MY FATHER, J.S.P.V.

1919–2007

CONTENTS

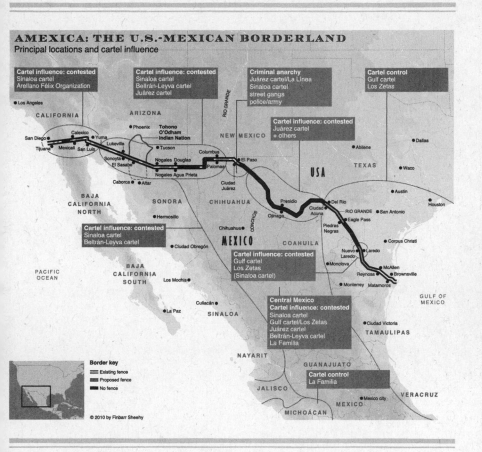

AMEXICA: THE U.S.-MEXICAN BORDERLAND
Principal locations and cartel influence

Cartel influence: contested
Sinaloa cartel
Arellano Félix Organization

Cartel influence: contested
Sinaloa cartel
Beltrán-Leyva cartel
Juárez cartel

Criminal anarchy
Juárez cartel/La Línea
Sinaloa cartel
street gangs
police/army

Cartel control
Gulf cartel
Los Zetas

Cartel influence: contested
Juárez cartel
+ others

Cartel influence: contested
Sinaloa cartel
Beltrán-Leyva cartel

Cartel influence: contested
Gulf cartel
Los Zetas
(Sinaloa cartel)

Central Mexico
Cartel influence: contested
Sinaloa cartel
Gulf cartel/Los Zetas
Juárez cartel
Beltrán-Leyva cartel
La Familia

Cartel control
La Familia

Border key
Existing fence
Proposed fence
No fence

© 2010 by Finbarr Sheehy

Los Angeles

CALIFORNIA

ARIZONA

RIO GRANDE

San Diego
Tijuana
Calexico
Mexicali San Luis
Yuma
Lukeville
Phoenix
Tohono O'Odham Indian Nation
NEW MEXICO

Abilene
Dallas

Sonoyta
El Sasabe
Nogales Douglas
Nogales Agua Prieta
Tucson
Columbus
Palomas
El Paso

USA
TEXAS

Waco

Caborca
Altar
Ciudad Juárez

BAJA CALIFORNIA NORTH

SONORA

CHIHUAHUA

CONCHOS

Presidio
Ojinaga
Ciudad Acuña
Del Rio
RIO GRANDE
Eagle Pass
San Antonio

Austin
Houston

Hermosillo

MEXICO

COAHUILA

Piedras Negras

Corpus Christi

Chihuahua

Ciudad Obregón

Nuevo Laredo
Monclova
Reynosa
Laredo
McAllen
Brownsville

PACIFIC OCEAN

BAJA CALIFORNIA SOUTH

Los Mochis

SINALOA

Monterrey
Matamoros

GULF OF MEXICO

La Paz

Culiacán

Ciudad Victoria

TAMAULIPAS

NAYARIT

GUANAJUATO

JALISCO

MICHOACÁN

MEXICO

Mexico city

VERACRUZ

AMEXICA

INTRODUCTION: AMEXICA

As dawn breaks over the vast desert, the body is hanging from a concrete overpass known as the Bridge of Dreams. It has been there for two hours—decapitated and dangling by a rope tied around the armpits. The sun begins to throw its rays across the busy intersection with its rush-hour traffic and former American school buses carrying workers to sweatshops. And it is still there an hour later, this grotesque, headless thing—swaying, hands cuffed behind its back—in the cold early morning wind that kicks up dust and cuts through the Mexican border town of Ciudad Juárez, the most dangerous city in the world.

Next to their prey this morning—left hanging just as the factory shifts were about to change—the executioners, or *sicarios* as they are called, have hung a sheet, on which they have painted a message: YO LÁZARO FLORES, APOYO A MI PATRÓN, EL MONTE PERROS—I, Lázaro Flores, serve my boss, the dog-fucker. ATTE. (ATENCIÓN) LA LÍNEA—Look out, the Line—it concluded. A crowd assembles to watch in unsurprised silence. The straps underneath the corpse's armpits creak, and its feet flap in the wind, but the crowd remains gawping at this hideous, buckled thing, perhaps fearing, if they leave, they might take with them the curse of that which was done. So that before we can go, it must be dealt with, erased from view and from the morning. Finally, after three hours, firemen arrive and erect ladders in order to take the carcass down, wrap it in canvas, put it in a red van, and drive it away to the morgue, to be examined and "read" for any message contained in the mutilations—allowing Juárez to get on with a day that will see another four narco murders before it is out. Which was an unusually low count: a month into the year of publication, 2010, 227 people have been killed in this city on Mexico's border with the United States.

La Línea is a recent mutation of what was once the Juárez narco-trafficking cartel run by Amado Carrillo Fuentes, known by the nom de narco "Lord of the Skies," so called because of the fleet of Boeing planes that was at his disposal for smuggling cocaine from Colombia. But La Línea is now just one of the myriad factions and interests—cartels, street gangs, corrupt police units, military detachments—fighting with ever more inventive twists of violence for the plaza, the river of drugs running north through Juárez into El Paso and from there across the United States. Fighting too for the resultant plazas of Juárez and northern Mexico themselves: for where the river runs through, people will drink, and as a direct consequence of the Mexican cartels' near monopoly of narcotics to the United States, northern Mexico is ravaged by crack and methamphetamine addiction, and by the bloody battles for terrain on which to sell these drugs. The sheet, known as a *narcomanta*, and its message, a *narcomensaje*, are common features of the executions, designed to charge the slaying with menace or even opacity: Lázaro Flores was not the dead man's name, but that of a prominent local businessman—something for the city, and indeed Mr. Flores, to ponder.

This macabre, barbaric execution, in November 2008, took the number of murders in the anarchic city of two million people propped right up against Texas to about 1,300 that year. The toll would cap 1,700 before the end of December. The national figure of those killed across Mexico reached more than 5,400 in 2008. In 2009, despite successive waves of military reinforcements and a promise by Mayor José Reyes Ferriz on January 1 that Juárez "cannot have another year like that," the toll was even higher: 2,657 people murdered, making Ciudad Juárez the world's most murderous city, with 192 homicides per 100,000 citizens. The total of those murdered across Mexico in 2009 reached 7,724.[1] This means that by the end of that year, more than 16,000 people had been killed since President Felipe Calderón launched a military offensive against the cartels in December 2006, with many of the victims mutilated, like this man, horribly and carefully, then exhibited to convey some message or threat. By summer 2010, an even bloodier year, the total killed since December 2006 had exceeded 23,000 and by February 2011, 34,000. The killing is everywhere across Mexico but concentrated along the border with the United States—twenty-one hundred miles long, the busiest border in the world and a place that belongs to both countries and yet to neither.

Ciudad Juárez lives cheek by jowl with the United States and its "twin city," El Paso, on the other side of the frontier. Sometimes the proximity is surreal: from the campus of the University of Texas at El Paso, one sees, in the foreground, the diligent enjoyment of life— students strolling to and fro. In the middle ground, less than half a mile away, runs the border in two forms: an articulately harsh wall decorated with barbed wire, and the trickle of the Rio Grande. And beyond the boundary, one of the poorest barrios—or *colonias*, as they are called here—in Mexico: a bleached, ramshackle shantytown called Anapra, crawling across the high desert, thrown up out of wood and corrugated iron on the edge of a burgeoning city. The desert dirt and dust on which it is built is crisscrossed by outlaw electricity supply cables to the barrio huts. El Paso and Juárez form the heart of, and midway point along, this singular strip of land conjoining two countries. The borderland is a place of paradox: of opportunity and poverty, promise and despair, love and violence, sex and church, beauty and fear, sweat and family. Even the frontier itself is a dichotomy, simultaneously porous and harsh. The U.S. Border Patrol itself recognizes the contradiction in its recruiting billboard on Interstate 19 north of Nogales, Arizona: A CAREER IN BORDERS, BUT NO BOUNDARIES.

The frontier itself can be brutal. In 1994, the United States initiated Operation Gatekeeper in San Diego, Operation Hold the Line in El Paso, and another similar operation in the Rio Grande Valley. Since then, under five administrations (Bill Clinton's twice, two led by George W. Bush, and now Barack Obama's), the border has become, and continues to become, a military front line, along which run more than six hundred miles of fence enhanced by guard posts, searchlights, and heavily armed patrols.

In places where there is no fence, there are infrared cameras, sensors, National Guard soldiers, and SWAT teams from other, specialist law enforcement columns, like the Drug Enforcement Administration and Bureau of Alcohol, Tobacco, Firearms and Explosives, plus the newly empowered Border Patrols and their own special forces, called BORTAC and BORSTAR. From the other side, apart from the tidal wave of drugs and migrants smuggled across the border, there are the killings: the Border Patrol agent Robert Rosas in Southern California in August 2009, shot when he tried to interdict an armed incursion; and the rancher Robert Krentz near Douglas, Arizona, when he chanced upon what were believed to be smugglers.

There is a striking contrast between the asphalt of the United States and the jumble and tumble of Mexico. When you fly over the border, you see streets arranged in a grid on the U.S. side give way suddenly to those arranged, if at all, like a crazy quilt. And an even greater discrepancy between poverty on the U.S. side and poverty on the Mexican side. One is struck by a stark, brazen inequality of wealth and power as one crosses the line, whether through the busy *click-clunk-click-clunk* of turnstiles between sprawling Mexicali and tiny Calexico, or along the remote desert road between Lukeville, Arizona, and Sonoyta, Sonora; or over the trickle of the Rio Grande from El Paso into the cauldron of Juárez; the lustier flow between Eagle Pass and Piedras Negras; or the last remaining cross-border ferry, between Los Ebanos, Texas, and Díaz Ordaz, Tamaulipas.

But the border is, as I say, porous. The more the United States builds its fence, enhances its technological stockade, and empowers its patrols and customs officers, the more the number of people crossing the border legally increases—currently about a million of them every day. Families live astride the frontier; workers, shoppers, relatives, and schoolchildren commute across the line. It takes twenty minutes to walk from downtown El Paso to main street Juárez, from what is supposed to be the first world into what looks like the third, yet is not. More commercial traffic crosses the U.S.-Mexican border than any other in the world, currently worth some $367.4 billion a year.[2] Five million trucks cross the border annually, and thousands of freight-train wagons each day, carrying goods from across the Americas into the United States, and from China via the Mexican port of Lázaro Cárdenas—as well as southward, bringing exports from the United States. A necklace of thousands of sweatshop assembly plants, called maquiladoras, has been established all along the border especially to provide the United States with cheap labor, along and just across its own frontier. American and Mexican fire services answer each other's calls, and during 2008, more than fifty victims of the drug violence in Ciudad Juárez were treated for multiple gunshot wounds at Thomason Hospital in El Paso. The border country has its own music, *norteño*, and its own Spanglish slang spoken on both sides of the frontier, a lexicon that sometimes just jumbles the two languages together, as on the door of a bar in El Paso: MINORES AND PERSONAS ARMADAS STRICTLY NO ENTRADA. Friends may address each other as "Mano!" mixing "hey, man" with *hermano*—brother. Across Mexico, a bicycle is a *bicicleta*, but on the border it can be a *baica*. Someone's wife can be his *waifa* rather than *esposa*. In the United States, a Chicano gangbanger is a *vato*, but on the border he's a *cholo*.[3] Then there's the word for diarrhea: *turista*, tourist, for obvious reasons. Perhaps the most useful border term of all is *rasquache*, or *rasquachismo*, defined by the writer Tomás Ybarra-Frausto as "to posit a bawdy, spunky consciousness, to seek to subvert and turn ruling paradigms upside down. It is a witty, irreverent, and impertinent posture," and if it doesn't define the borderline, there is certainly no shortage of it.[4]

The borderland is a territory in its own right, astride the line, estranged from both Washington and Mexico City, the centers of power whence decrees about its daily life are issued often without much understanding of how the borderland works or fails to work. There is as much seamlessness across the border as there is contrast. There is as much that bonds the two sides of the frontier as there is that divides them, though these points of commonality and adhesives are being tested and strained by the narco war. Gloria Anzaldúa, who revolutionized the Chicana writing of her generation, called the border "*una herida abierta*—an open wound—where the third world grates against the first and bleeds. And before a scab forms, it hemorrhages again, the lifeblood of two worlds merging to form a third country—a border culture."[5] The borderland has an identity and a flavor of daily life that span the frontier, and I call this land—twenty-one hundred miles long and about fifty miles wide, from the Pacific to the Gulf—Amexica. Now, because of the flood tide of narcotics running through and along it, Amexica is a battlefield, but a battlefield wrapped in everyday life. And for all its inquietude, the border is every bit as charismatic, complex, and irresistible as it is fearful and terrifying.

Amexica is not just a play on words. The original and proper term for the Nahuatl-speaking Aztec people who migrated south to build their great city at Tenochtitlán—later Mexico City—and found their empire is *Mexica* (pronounced "Meshica"), and they came from just north of the border, around the so-called Four Corners where New Mexico, Colorado, Arizona, and Utah meet. The Chicano consciousness movement in the United States during the 1960s resurrected the notion of a cradle land of the Mexica people—in the northern (or southwestern, to the Americans) deserts—called Aztatlán, or just Aztlán. This land was important to Mexica creation mythology, based, like the border today, upon a concept of duality and complementary opposition. The creator god Ometeotl incorporates both male and female, and his/her children, Quetzalcoatl and Tezcatlipoca, are both allies and adversaries, representing harmony and conflict, balance and change.[6] According to some accounts, it was from Aztatlán that the primary god, Huitzilopochtli, led the Mexica south to what would become their imperial capital.[7] It was in what Mexicans now think of as the northern desert borderland that Huitzilopochtli was born to his mother, Coatlicue, primal mother and principal goddess of fertility and destruction, womb and tomb, who wore a skirt of serpents and a necklace of human hands and hearts.

The Spanish word for a border is *frontera*, with all the intended connotations of the word *frontier*—as in the American last frontier. While the southwestern United States is the frontier in American parlance and nineteenth-century folklore, so El Norte—the same terrain, through Mexican eyes—has always struck a similar chord of mystique in the lore

of both Spanish conquistadores and Mexicans after them. Before it actually became a border, what is now the borderland was a territory charged
with the myth of exploration, risk, opportunity, outlaw glamour, and
danger. El Norte is symbolically charged in ancient Mexica legend: according to the Aztecs' colored system of the flat world's four directions,
north was white: its stone was white flint, and the white ceiba, the tree of
abundance, was said to grow there. But north was also associated with
death and winter, and was the way to the underworld. More recently,
while the Americans had Billy the Kid, Mexicans had el Zorro; to Americans, the cowboy is in the Southwest; to Mexicans, *el vaquero* is in the
North—they are the same personage in the same place, on la frontera.
Miguel Olmos Aguilera, a quietly spoken musicologist who directs the
Cultural Studies Department at the Colegio de la Frontera Norte in Tijuana,
posits, in conversation, that the "frontera has always had an imaginative
and emotional meaning, as well as a geographical one. Since pre-Hispanic
days, it has been a place in the imagination of death and fame, suffering
and heroism, as well as a reality which kills people."[8]

It is usually to citizens of the United States that "America" refers
only to that country. To the rest of the continent, it refers to the entire
continent—as well as to Mexico City's most famous soccer team, Club
América. Mexico's powerful and ubiquitous symbol and icon, the Virgin
of Guadalupe, is the Mother of God and Queen of Mexico—but she is
also Empress of the Americas, all of them. There is, furthermore, academic debate about how and whence the masculine word *Mexico*
emerged—*Mexica*, like *America*, having initially been feminine.[9]

The border was created by the Treaty of Guadalupe Hidalgo in 1848,
which ended the Mexican-American War, after which the Gadsden Purchase of 1853, known in Mexico as the Venta de la Mesilla, or "Mesilla
Sale," pushed what is now Arizona and New Mexico south of the Gila
River to the present frontier.[10] Ever since, people have kept arriving
on the border, not just to cross it but to remain by it. The more the
populations grow, the more each pair of twin cities binds together,
the closer the two countries become—an adhesion now challenged
by the narco war. The demographics of migration across the border

are, meanwhile, astounding: one in five Mexicans either visits or works in the United States at one time or another in his or her life.[11] But *Amexica* is not about (to use that dreaded shorthand expression) "the Hispanicization of the United States" or that moment in 1996 when salsa overtook ketchup as America's favorite condiment. True, the Hispanic population of the United States now takes Amexica to and beyond the Canadian border, and especially to such places as Los Angeles (of course) and thence Chicago, New York, and the Carolinas. But this book is not about the estimated twelve million Mexicans and twenty-eight million Mexican Americans living legally in the United States nor (probably) another twenty-eight million illegal Mexican residents. It is about the quintessence of Amexica, the borderland itself.

Amexica found me as much as I found it. For years, I have worked along the borderline: narratives about international trucking and sweatshop factories, abducted women and the breathtaking desert, all set against a backdrop of adventure and hard grind, love and lust, achievement and tribulation, scintillescent light and occult shadows. This is a place of impenitent heat by day and bitter winds cutting through the darkness of night. I have been a reporter on many battlefields, yet nowhere has violence been so strange and commanded such revulsion and compulsion as it does along the borderline. War deepens the dichotomies, intensifying Amexica's magnetic field. It darkens the already opaque shade, making the colors even more lambent. The edge gets edgier but the ready smile more winning; the danger deepens but the welcome becomes warmer. The perversion of values makes the everyday more valuable; the feral physical cruelty of the slaughter accentuates the borderland's sensuality and libido. The narco war has a suffocating claustrophobia about it, in counterpoint to the unique beauty and infinite scale of the landscape—the eternity of desert and sky that forms its backdrop. The distances are all the more liberating but they are deceptive, and savage also: something is always about to happen in Amexica, hence the dread and expectation, the tenterhooks of every moment.

This is not a history with a beginning, middle, and end; it is a slice of very recent, unfinished history. Or, to take from Brian DeLay's introduction to his greatest of all books written about the border, *War of a Thousand Deserts*: "This is a shared story. This is American history, Mexican history, and Indian history." This book is not so much about a war as it is a view of a singular place in time of war. It is about the ways war impacts Amexica, but it is also about how the war is a consequence of other—mainly economic—degradations and exploitations, quite apart from drugs, from which the border's people suffer. A suffering due not least to the fact that narco cartels are corporations like any other, applying the commercial logic and following the same globalized "business models" as the multiplicity of legal enterprises that have wreaked their different kind of havoc along the borderline. Indeed, the drug violence is in many ways a direct result of this depredation caused by the legal globalized economy. The cartels are not pastiches of multinational capital—they are pioneers of it, integral to it, and apply its rules and logic (or, rather, lack of rules and logic) to their marketplace just as does any other commercial enterprise.

The book is also a journey from west to east, Pacific to Gulf. It begins in Tijuana, opposite San Diego, where two cartels are locked in battle. Thence into the deserts of Sonora and Arizona, and the deadly trails followed by half of all illegal migrants into the United States across the border—a business being commandeered by the narco cartels. The kernel of the voyage is Ciudad Juárez, where the idea of a war between cartels collapses and implodes into criminal anarchy and terrible suffering from violence, addiction, and deprivation. The road then winds through breathtaking country in Texas on the U.S. side and, on the Rio Grande's right bank, into cities like Ciudad Acuña and Piedras Negras, utterly transformed by the arrival not so much of drug cartels as maquiladoras. Next is the border's main trade corridor and temple of its commercial porosity, from Nuevo Laredo into Laredo, Texas. This is the truck route between Mexico and the United States, which is also where the latest drug war began, for the trade is contaminated by a river of smuggled drugs. The journey ends in the border's most complex and richest territory in terms of history and identity: Tamaulipas on the Mexican side and the Rio Grande Valley in Texas, between which the cartels' drugs flow north—and the guns run south across the borderline to the terrifying Zetas, a paramilitary cartel and the voyage's climax.

The journey will not be only a geographical one. It will afford a glimpse behind the insistently glamorous associations that the drug business enjoys. When the narco trafficker looks in the mirror, he sees not a criminal but a romantic bandit. As Roberto Saviano, author of the remarkable book *Gomorrah*, about the Neapolitan Camorra syndicates, put it in conversation: "They love to think of themselves as Scarface; it's their favorite movie."[12] But because of the singular product in which the *narcotraficante* deals, the media and society also see in the narco more than a little bit of Scarface, thanks to the packaging of drug culture by our mass culture. We have become voguishly obsessed with "fair-trade" consumerism to the point that supermarket chains compete with each other about where and how mange-tout peas are grown by happy African villagers. Multinational coffee shop chains strive to make consumers feel good about the "sustainable" Andean or Indonesian plantations their particular brand of latte comes from. But this pop-moral advertising lexicon does not apply to the origins of drugs: public fascination with celebrity drug addiction has exempted drugs from the touchy-feely vocabulary of "ethical" consumerism. For all the concern, however laudable, with the lives ruined to make cheap clothes or an unethical cappuccino, few ever stop to ask how many lives just went up a supermodel's nose—the opposite, indeed: the same media that pontificates about ethical consumerism treats celebrity drug taking as fodder for tittle-tattle gossip, laced with a giggly—and only slightly disapproving—waggle of the forefinger. Or even excessive sympathy for the stars in rehabilitation, or admiration for gutsy appearances on reality TV. *Amexica* offers a backstage pass, access all areas, behind the celebrity gossip and those glittering cocaine nights in Los Angeles, New York, London, and Madrid.

There is another way the narco war belongs to, and fits into, our contemporary modus vivendi that makes it very much a war of its time. It is the first real twenty-first-century war, because it is about, in the end, nothing. Mexico's war is a conflict of the postpolitical era. It is being fought in an age of belligerent hypermaterialism as an ideology in itself, the leading exponents of which run their corporations or banks with personal greed as their sole credo, and their brands as icons of this postmodern religion. Until this hypermaterialist era, the human race had been, and in places remains, an inhabitant of a world where, unfortunately, Muslims and Jews fight each other, communists and fascists, Serbs and Croats, Tutsis and Hutus, American or British soldiers and Islamic insurgents, and so on. We may all have different readings of why they do this, but they do so—at least nominally—for a cause, faith, or tribal identity, however crazy.

But Mexico's war (some do not like calling it a war) has not even the pretense of a propelling cause. Mexicans are mutilating, decapitating, torturing, and killing each other ostensibly over money and the drug-smuggling routes that provide it. Some argue that all wars are fought indirectly over money and resources—whether wars of empire fought from the nineteenth century until 1918, or of ideology or religion in the twentieth century. But most of the savage violence in Mexico is for the smaller profits of the domestic market and local street corner, meted out for its own sake. There is no financial gain in killing a street addict. There are regional and clan identities, to the states of Tamaulipas, Michoacán, or Sinaloa, but they are fluid and subject to too many whimsical alliances and betrayals for the war to be defined as tribal as the way it is in, say, Rwanda. Mexico's war has no ideological pretensions or window dressing—its only cover is that it was originally fought, like other, lesser Mafia wars, over the now diversified product lines that get America (and Europe) high. But the casus belli is now even more vacuous than that. The narco war is fought for the accoutrements—brands, accessories, applications, and other possessions—of postmodern social kudos, social performance, the ability to show off the right labels, brands, and products in accordance with advertising; to wear the right clothes, to be accompanied by the appropriately desirable partner, chatter on the latest mobile phone with the latest so-called applications, own the right gadget, and drive the right SUV. For these definitions of status, thousands die. The narco war is fought on YouTube and mobile phones as well as in the streets and backroom torture chambers: cartels use YouTube to threaten rivals and public officials, boast of their killing, set up rogue "hot spot" digital sites to broadcast their savagery and invite comments. One such site hosted from El Paso received more than 320,000 hits and posted more than 1,000 comments.[13] Murders, mutilations, and executions are exhibited on the Internet, themselves a blend of cyber-sado-pornography. Unlike the cyberstrutting of Al Qaeda, from whom it is sometimes argued they got the idea, the narcos use digital communication not as a weapon of insane holy war but with something approaching a sense of humor with which to goad and boast across cyberspace—gift-wrapping their real-life bloodlust in the electronic ether of titillation and nonmeaning.

One striking feature of the postpolitical war is that neither the political left nor right has managed to muster the slightest resistance. There is no significant trade union, or any revolutionary or overt workers' movement against the narco cartels (though civil society organizations doing their level best tend to be loosely of the left). Similarly, there is no sign of a rightist, fascistic, or vigilante movement for law and order (at least not on the Mexican side of the border); the army's role is a mercurial one, and no Mussolini figure to the right of President Calderón has come to the fore. Instead, and interestingly, a war that is quintessentially materialist and largely male meets resistance from two quarters that do not belong to conventional politics. The postpolitical, materialist war meets resistance from the prepolitical clergy and church groups more than any other constituency of society—both Catholic (though not entirely from the organized church) and reformed. And the male war meets resistance from strong women, as individuals, as organizations—and in the home. That these social quarters provide the only measurable, let alone cogent, counterweight to narco violence at street level is something with which a secular mass media, forever seeking policy options and conventional political or military "solutions," is deeply and visibly uncomfortable, not least because they all, serially, fail.

I am writing this at the end of 2009, over Christmas. This was the kind of war being fought by the cartels during the two weeks over Christmas last year, in 2008:

- A man masquerading as a fisherman, calling himself Enrique Portocarrero, is arrested in Colombia for designing and building twenty fiberglass submarines to bring cocaine ashore in Mexico. He is known as "Captain Nemo."[14]
- A sudden escalation of declamatory "narco banners" in public places, usually naming and warning local police officials, reaches a zenith in every sense, hung from a Monterrey cathedral and ominously denouncing President Calderón himself for favoring the Sinaloa cartel over its principal rival, the Gulf cartel.[15]
- A member of President Calderón's personal and permanent bodyguard is arrested and charged for being in the employ of—and feeding secrets about the president's policies and movements to—the Beltrán Leyva brothers' narco cartel.
- After five men are arrested and charged in El Paso for procuring firearms in Texas and smuggling them into Mexico, U.S. Secretary of State Condoleezza Rice insists that the lifting of a ban on semiautomatic weapons had nothing to do with the vast quantities of such weapons seized in Mexico.[16]
- The decapitated bodies of twelve federal army soldiers are found in the southern state of Guerrero, the most audacious single execution of serving military personnel since the Mexican Revolution of 1910. Their arms and feet were bound, with a message reading: "For Every One of Mine You Kill, We Kill Ten."[17]

During the first two weeks of 2009:

- Twenty-one people are killed within forty-eight hours in and around Ciudad Juárez.
- Twenty-seven people are killed within one week in Baja California.
- A television station in Monterrey is attacked with grenades after reporting on narco murders.[18]
- General Mauro Enrique Tello Quiñones, who left the army to work as a security consultant for the mayor of Cancún in his efforts against the narcos, is abducted, tortured, and executed along with

two adjutants. Among those arrested in connection with the murder are Cancún's police chief and several of his senior officers.[19]

- In Tijuana, Santiago Meza López is arrested, charged with disintegrating three hundred bodies in acid.
- Four decapitated seventeen-year-olds are among twenty-one people killed in Tijuana during the first week of the year.[20]
- Twenty-one senior law enforcement officers in Tijuana are arrested for protecting the Arellano Félix Cartel. There is speculation as to whether authorities are genuinely trying to clean up corruption, or they are working for the rival Sinaloa cartel.
- The National Drug Threat Assessment report for 2009 declares that "the Mexican drug-trafficking organizations represent the greatest organized crime threat to the United States."

The transition from December 2009 into the New Year 2010 went thus:

- During the first four days of December, twenty-five are killed in Ciudad Juárez, as the city is blanketed by a rare snowfall, bringing the annual total of dead to 2,390 for a single city.[21]
- It emerges that only 2 percent of the much-vaunted $1.4 billion Mérida Initiative of aid from the United States to Mexico to help fight the cartels has arrived, due to bureaucratic problems, contracting rules, and difficulties getting helicopters to Mexico.[22]
- Thirteen Zeta gangsters are killed as Mexican marines burst through the gates of a narco compound outside Monterrey. Several passersby, including a twelve-year-old girl, are injured by intense fire. Los Zetas call for help, which arrives in the form of a dozen armed vehicles that engage an army patrol they meet on the way.[23]
- An American teacher and school district councillor from Southern California, Bobby Salcedo, is abducted and killed in Durango while visiting his wife's hometown of Gómez Palacio during a twinning celebration between his town and hers. Four others are also kidnapped and killed.

- The Inter-American Court of Human Rights rules that Mexico failed to investigate the deaths of young women abducted, tortured, violated, and murdered in Ciudad Juárez. The ruling applies to three test cases.

- Antonio Mendoza Ledezma, a member of the Azteca street gang that acts as an enforcer for the Juárez cartel, is charged with involvement in the murders of two hundred people.[24]

- The journalist Bladimir Antuna of Durango, who bragged to his colleagues after serial death threats that he wouldn't mind being killed but was terrified of torture, is found strangled and tortured to death. A note beside his mangled body reads, "This happened to me for giving information to soldiers and writing too much."[25]

- Six decomposing bodies are found at the seaside resort of Puerto Peñasco in Sonora, two hours' drive from Tucson, Arizona, beloved by and known to American tourists as Rocky Point.[26]

- Naval Special Forces mount the most successful raid ever against a leading cartel drug lord, killing Arturo Beltrán Leyva, head of the rebel cartel pitched against Joaquín "el Chapo" (Shorty) Guzmán's Sinaloa cartel and the Mexican government, at his home in the smart Mexico City suburb of Cuernavaca.

- A Special Forces ensign, Melquisedet Angulo Córdova, is killed during the shoot-out that eliminates Beltrán Leyva. But two days after his official funeral, gunmen burst into the home of Angulo Córdova's family, killing four of his immediate relations, including his mother.[27]

- The body of thirty-six-year-old Hugo Hernández, abducted in Sonora on January 2, turns up in Los Mochis, Sinaloa, though not in one piece. His torso is in one location, his severed arms and legs boxed in another place, and his skull found in another. His face has been flayed, left near the city hall of Los Mochis, sewn to a soccer ball.[28]

- The death toll in Ciudad Juárez for only the first week of 2010 reaches the abominable figure of fifty nino.[29]

The last day the body of this book was being written, January 30, 2010, began with the receipt of the following e-mail from Molly Molloy, at New Mexico State University in Las Cruces, who keeps the most reliable tally of drug violence in Ciudad Juárez. Molloy's introduction to today's bulletin is assiduous, as usual: "*Diario* reports 12 people were killed in shooting incidents yesterday . . . Or it could be more. I checked stories in *Diario* before I went to bed at about 10:00 and several women and a baby were also injured in these incidents. Below is a post from Lapolaka [a Juárez website] posted at 23:10 last night that says 10. Then, another at 1:03 that describes another massacre after midnight in the Oasis neighborhood that left 3 more people dead. The tally yesterday [for the year so far, one month old] was at about 183, so with these the toll is now at least 195 or 196. It would seem that an apparent lull came to a very violent end on Friday night. Molly."[30] The following night, sixteen teenagers were shot dead as a unit of gunmen stormed a party of young people. Thirteen months and hundreds of bulletins later, Ms. Molloy is still counting and still in touch with her "fronterizos" on the list, more than once daily. The introduction to her report for February 17, 2011, as this paperback edition goes to press, reads: "I do not know what the final tally for today, February 17, will be, but as of about 10:00 pm, there are 12 or 13 dead. This is the rundown of the reports in *El Diario* today. The video at the link of the article from 18:48 says that this couple were victims 12 and 13 for the day. I'll try to post the tally tomorrow morning. Molly."

On New Year's Eve, a week before Mr. Hernández's face was discovered sewn to a soccer ball in Los Mochis, the bound, beaten, and tortured bodies of two men had also been found nearby, with their hands tied behind their backs. A message beside them read: "This Territory Already Has an Owner." But the twist was this: these last deaths of 2009 were hanging from an overpass, just like the headless man from the Bridge of Dreams in Juárez.[31]

1

LA PLAZA

My friend Jorge Fregoso and I were drinking a beer at a bar in a labyrinth of quiet alleyways away from central Tijuana one Saturday afternoon in September 2008 when the latest shooting started. It targeted an art deco mansion in the sedate Misión del Pedregal suburb. Federal army trucks arrived to its left, state police shock troops to the right. Few shots were fired from inside the building, it seemed, but a deafening fusillade of fire was aimed at the villa. Only the next day was it revealed to have procured, for the authorities, Eduardo Arellano Félix—"the Doctor"—chief of the clan trying to defend the plaza of drug traffic between Tijuana and California for his Arellano brothers' syndicate from the raiding Sinaloa cartel. Misión de Pedregal is clearly marked, on a sign adjacent to Arellano's house, as a "*Vecinos Vigilando*," neighborhood watch zone. Yet, says a woman cleaning her porch opposite Arellano's, "I didn't think there was anyone living in that house." What followed the announcement were seventy-two hours of carnage, extreme even by Tijuana standards, which took the year's death toll for the city to 462 and caused even the local *El Sol de Tijuana* newspaper, accustomed to such things, to run the headline BAÑO DE SANGRE, bloodbath.

Fregoso, a reporter for the local Síntesis TV news channel, and I receive our first alert shortly after 3:00 p.m. on Monday, when we are called to Colonia Libertad, where a corpse lies slumped in the dirt beneath steps made of tires. A crowd of young people arrives to observe the busy forensic aftermath in a disconcertingly knowing silence, punctuated by the odd giggly joke or mobile phone call, while some thirty yards away is the border with the United States, the old fence made of metal landing sheets used by the U.S. Air Force from Vietnam to Iraq.

Three young women from the forensic team (wearing identical gray shirts, black jeans, and ponytails) take careful photographs and notes, but like the accompanying trucks full of balaclava-covered federal police, they are soon ordered to speed off to a different location, Mariano Matamoros, and a major artery on the city's outskirts where another corpse lies, visible by the green light of a PEMEX gas station. The windshield of the victim's Ford Explorer (with California plates) is pitted with three bullet holes, and he seems to have made a run into the street, followed by twenty-five more shots, each shell casing marked by a blue number on a yellow card. Before the forensic women have even finished here, we are summoned across dirt tracks—zigzagging between cement buildings—to a crossing of backstreets in the Casablanca district, and a lifeless body beside the doorway of a corner shop painted with yellow flowers. When the ninja-clad cops pull back the sheet, we see a teenager shot at point-blank range in the face, blood oozing onto the flagstones, and a girl watching turns away to weep into her mobile phone. But now the night really begins.

Fregoso, with his access to police communications, receives the news so fast that we hurtle our orange Volkswagen between the fourth and fifth jeeps of a machine-gun-toting police convoy (to the hooting fury of jeep number five) heading for the next slaughter. The cordon of plastic tape reading PRECAUCIÓN is not even in place yet outside the 9/4 minimart in Villa Floresta, in theory selling "*Vinos y Licores*," where a blanket covers the remains of the security guard, with two more dead inside. There is wild wailing from the womenfolk as this body outside is revealed. His flesh has been grated into something like raw kebab meat by fire at point-blank range from a Kalashnikov, or *cuerno de chivo*, goat's horn, as an AK-47 is known around here. Further screams follow the sight of those killed inside the store, brought out on stretchers and loaded into the white DFI forensic department truck now carrying five former people. The shop, says the rustling whisper through the crowd, was a stash for drugs being loaded for export aboard two cars, presumably intended to join the sixty-five thousand that cross from Tijuana into San Diego every day, but that the police now tow away. Meanwhile, heavyset men in sharp suits arrive to look from a slight distance, embracing each other in a way that suggests burdensome comradeship and solace, but little sadness. Any attempt to speak to them is rebuffed with menacing silence and a glare. One of them goes over to console a young woman clutching a baby, in paroxysms of grief, beneath a mural advertising Viper auto alarms.

Yonkes—repair yards for fixing up cars with secondhand parts—are a hallmark of Tijuana's byways, and next morning another group of sicarios—or maybe the same squad—returns to Villa Floresta in brazen, broad noonday light, past the murals of a girl in a bikini sprawled over an SUV and into gate number one of Yonke Cristal, killing one man whose body, wearing a red shirt, is visible through the bars of a red gate. Two other corpses are hidden behind a white van, the skeletal metal frames of the vehicles all around, detached wheel hubs like prying eyes, and JESUCRISTO EXCELSIOR carved into the hillside above. This is now Tuesday, and on Wednesday morning Tijuana awakes to the news that while the city slept, three bodies were found in an abandoned van and one in a car. The van has been dumped in a quarter called Los Álamos, at a meeting point between ramshackle hillside colonias, a smart gated community, and an electronics factory, and the dead men have been tortured, mutilated, and strangled—one of them handcuffed. People killed and dumped in vehicles are known in this war as *encajuelados*, literally entrunked. The body in the car is that of a police officer called Mauricio Antonio Hernando Flores. It is his personal car, and the officer had parked beneath a great statue of an open-armed figure of Christ, presiding over Tijuana in imitation of Rio de Janeiro, with its engine running, just past 1:00 a.m., apparently awaiting someone. Whoever shot him, leaving his body to be discovered slumped in the blood-soaked driver's seat, knew him and was apparently expected at the scene.

There are two kinds of cop killings in the narco war. One was illustrated in January 2008 when the narcos crossed some line in the etiquette of drug warfare. The sicarios' car pulled off a main road onto the dirt track into the wretched Colonia Loma Bonita. They would have parked next to the "Swap Meet" hangar and walked to what is now a vacant lot for sale, marked by white wooden cross, where Officer Margarito Zaldano lived. They entered the house and executed not only Zaldano but also his wife, Sandra, and twelve-year-old daughter, Valeria. Zaldano's crime? Being a cop and doing his job trying to arrest criminals who were protected by his own police force.

The other kind of slaying of police officers—*la chota*, as it is known on the border, the fuzz—involves those who become embroiled with the narcos, working for them or adding to the income of their day job by moonlighting for the cartels, often with the same uniforms and weapons. These officers get caught out if they charge too much for their services, oversights, or information; renege on a deal; or if their work for one cartel becomes irksome to another. Mexicans joke that a police officer is offered a simple career choice: *plata o plomo*, silver or lead, and many, while they can get it, inevitably opt for the former. After the killing of Officer Flores, the authorities, in contrast to their outpouring of tribute to Zaldano back in January, refused to fuss much over this latest execution of one of their colleagues by a single *tiro de gracia*, a mercy shot to the head. In Tijuana, as elsewhere, the municipal police can be working for one cartel, the state police with another, and the Federales with yet another. None of this happens in a vacuum.

Like every war, this carnage has a history, and we need to understand the history of the narco cartels' business lest the war appear to be the senseless bloodletting it is not. Or, at least, was not at first. Indeed, one needs to know one's Mafia history as much as that of any major player in the global economy and polity, because the syndicates are more powerful, more astute, and handle higher turnovers than most multinational corporations, as well as fuel our society with their products. The drug cartels were prototypes and pioneers of globalization; the Neapolitan Camorra was the first multinational into postcommunist Eastern Europe, harvesting Kalashnikovs produced under Soviet license. The Camorra was also among the first capitalist enterprises to penetrate Communist China, dealing in textiles and drugs coming into the port of Naples. Now that the "legal" global economy is in crisis, narco cartels respond to their own crisis within that economy in their own—but by no means separate—way.

Unlike their Italian counterparts, the Mexican cartels cannot trace their origins to the eighteenth century, but they were dealing drugs before the Italians. The smuggling syndicate based in Ciudad Juárez was not only the first narco syndicate run by a woman, Ignacia "la Nacha" Jasso, but also was among the first to trade in heroin to the United States, after the market for supplying America with alcohol, during Prohibition, came to an end in 1933. The Mexican heroin-growing and opium market in Sinaloa gained impetus during World War II, when the United States signed an agreement to buy opium to meet its wartime medical needs.[1] The Mexican narco smugglers did start dealing in drugs on a major scale at the same time as the Italians, toward the end of the 1960s, when it became clear that demand from the United States and Europe was insatiable. "The narco economy," wrote Guillermo Ibarra, an economist at Sinaloa State University, "and family remittances from the United States actually keep our state on its feet."[2]

At first, Mexico's role was that of producer, of Mexican Mud heroin, poppies for which were ideally suited to the climate of the Pacific coast state of Sinaloa, home of the "classic" narco cartels—then and now. Two initiatives by the U.S. government during the 1970s and '80s changed this, and in part laid the foundations for the modern cartels. First, during the 1970s, the United States steered the Mexican government through Operation Condor, which succeeded in all but destroying indigenous Mexican heroin production, incinerating and defoliating the Sinaloan poppy crops in dichotomous partnership with the same Mexican political apparatus that had ruled in close coexistence with—protected by and protecting—the *gomeros*, or heroin barons, so called because of the gummy texture of their merchandise.

Second, Washington embarked on its covert backing of right-wing contra rebels against the Sandinista government in Nicaragua.[3] The contras would be armed with weapons secretly transported from the United States, with the criminal underworld as supplier and mediator, to Central America. But the arms had to be paid for in "currency" that would not call attention to itself, and they were: in cocaine from Colombia. Luckily for all involved, narcotic science and narcotic fashion both coincided with Washington's interests, as well as those of the cartels in Colombia and Mexico. Just as the United States needed Colombia's natural currency to procure and pay for arms to the contras, cocaine was becoming the drug of choice: in powdered form for American entertainment and other smart circles, and in its chemical derivative form, crack, on the street and in the ghetto. According to a fictionalized account in *The Power of the Dog* by Don Winslow, the Mexicans became the courier service for arms in one direction and cocaine in the other—a service that became known as the Mexican Trampoline. Mexico's cartels combined three things to act as conduit in flooding America with crack and cocaine: their knowledge of smuggling routes as old as the border itself, the unofficial acquiescence of the Reagan administration, and their conviviality with Mexico's Institutional Revolutionary Party (PRI), which had ruled since 1917. In so doing, they realized, as Winslow put it, "that their real product isn't drugs, it's the two-thousand-mile border they share with the United States . . . Land can be burned, crops can be poisoned, people can be displaced, but that border . . . isn't going anywhere."[4]

As masters of the border, Mexican narcos were in a position to assume control of the hemisphere. Cocaine supply routes through the Caribbean and Miami were strangled by U.S. authorities still earnest about fighting a "war on drugs." That only increased the flow through Mexico, which it was impossible to throttle. The Mexican traffickers demanded that their Colombian suppliers pay not in cash for the necessary transportation but in kind, and the percentage of cocaine payable as commission for the delivery service increased, and increased. Colombians trying to penetrate the Mexican groups themselves were promptly killed. So now, according to the U.S. Drug Enforcement Administration, 90 percent of all drugs entering the United States do so as part of Mexican cartel business. The major imports are still cocaine and marijuana, though recent Mexican mass production of methamphetamine accounts for most consumption of the drug in the United States, as it does across Latin America. The bust of a methamphetamine factory in Argentina in September 2008 involved predominantly Mexican nationals. Drug enforcement agencies also blame Mexican cartels for the sudden spike in heroin availability and the precipitous fall in street prices, from $5,000 per ounce in 2004 to $1,000 per ounce in 2008.

But when we talk about "the Mexicans" we talk not about a homogenous organization; quite the reverse. We talk about cartels operating, during this period, under license from the authorities. Franchised by Mexican municipal, state, and federal government officials and police forces, the system was based, through an organized network of corruption until the fall of the PRI in 2000, on what is called the plaza—a place of gathering, whether a square in the center of a town or the *plaza de toros* (a bullring) or the jurisdiction of a police or military force. Apart, crucially, from its eastern stretch toward the Gulf, the border was strategically carved into drug-smuggling plazas, each considered the territory of a subdivision of the original Sinaloan Mafia, which paid the authorities for protection and cooperation—with percentages shaved off at every level, to the top—on its turf. In return, the Mafia fingered freelance or rival operators so that the authorities could give the impression of an authentic enforcement operation.[5]

Even if it sometimes feels a bit like trainspotting, we need to be familiar with the names and heritage of the major trafficking organizations that operate the trade worth an estimated $323 billion a year[6]—pushing drugs into the veins of the wretched, up the noses of the rich, and frying the brains of the young. People refer to the Mafia as though it were some amorphous alien force or, worse, a romantic brotherhood operating according to some code of honor laid down by Godfather Corleone, a Marlon Brando don. We are all familiar with the Sicilian Mafia (Cosa Nostra) because of its history and mythic presence in mass culture. In Mexico, the dramatis personae of the mafia is more complicated, and we need to know the cast.

The pioneer of Mexico's narco-trafficking mafia was Pedro Avilés

Pérez, from Sinaloa, who escalated the smuggling of marijuana and heroin into the United States during the late 1960s. But the original Mexican Godfather was Miguel Ángel Félix Gallardo, a protégé of Avilés's who took over his operation after Avilés was killed in a shoot-out with the police in 1978. Félix Gallardo founded the Guadalajara cartel and became perhaps the biggest narco trafficker in the world during his zenith. In 1985, however, a calamity changed the cartel, the Mexican government's conviviality with it, and U.S. complicity with that relationship. An undercover DEA agent, Enrique "Kiki" Camarena, was fingered, kidnapped, and tortured to death in Guadalajara. (There is evidence that the CIA knew and may even have trained the people who did it, to a point that relations between the two agencies have never fully recovered.)

The truth behind Camarena's death has eluded all attempts at excavation, but whatever that truth, Washington demanded that Mexico do something—and that something was to arrest Félix Gallardo. In 1989, Gallardo was convicted of ordering Camarena's abduction and murder, but from jail he sought to keep his organization together, allocating the various clans their plazas in which to operate. There was even a council, held in an expensive Acapulco hotel, to which the jailed Gallardo sent messengers to clarify the plazas, exhort the cartels to cooperate against their common enemy, U.S. law enforcement, and offer advice on how to negotiate with the Mexican authorities and impose discipline.[7]

Gallardo's vision was one that in Italy is called a Pax Mafiosa, whereby criminal syndicates know their place with reference to each other, law enforcement knows its place in the same scheme of things, the product keeps flowing, and politicians understand that this kind of quiet comes at a price—protection. A Pax Mafiosa can guarantee the politician votes, and a power base, in return for nothing more than the tranquillity of a blind eye at least, or cover for, even adherence to, a particular cartel. But this is not how the criminal mind works. If the cartels are greedy, why should they not become even greedier? If their modus operandi is to break laws, why would their modus vivendi be to keep them? When things become bloody in the world of narco trafficking, and the peace is blown apart, this means power is shifting, disintegrating, or resisting disintegration and being claimed across the ordained plazas. When Cosa Nostra famously blew up the anti-Mafia judges Giovanni Falcone and Paolo Borsellino in 1992, it was taken wrongly to be a sign of the Mafia's strength. Cosa Nostra was reeling from what the judges had achieved against them, and—crucially—the tables were turning across the plazas of Italy. Cosa Nostra was being overtaken by new—leaner and meaner—operators: the Camorra of Naples and 'Ndrangheta of Calabria. The old guard was in trouble, the plaza unquiet. Nor, in Mexico, could such a momentous event as Gallardo's arrest occur without leaving a vacuum, any more than any of his lieutenants could resist trying to fill it. The Guadalajara cartel split, different branches claiming its mantle: one, led by Gallardo's nephews and nieces, established the Tijuana cartel, while another, led by Avilés's nephew Joaquín Guzmán Loera, founded the Sinaloa cartel, and a third formed the Juárez cartel.

But the shattering of the Pax Mafiosa did not result in a reduction in the flow of drugs. Control of the flow, of the plazas, was simply up for grabs. And now, in Mexico, unfettered greed and an enormous surplus have created a new plaza on home turf, contaminating Mexico itself. And so a draft map of the present war came to be drawn.

The most famous plaza, that between Tijuana and California, was featured in Steven Soderbergh's film *Traffic*. It was run by the Tijuana cartel, or the Arellano Félix Organization, the AFO, but is now contested. The Tijuana cartel is the only one to claim a direct (but disputed) family connection to Gallardo: Gallardo had five nephews, the Arellano Félix brothers, of whom Eduardo, arrested that Saturday in Misión del Pedregal, was the last to remain at large. Joachín Guzmán's first round of offensives on the border followed the borderline itself, west to east, starting in the early 1990s in Tijuana, soon after Gallardo's arrest, when Guzmán claimed the *padrino*'s (godfather's) mantle and the heritage of his own uncle, Pedro Avilés Pérez. In those days, the AFO kept Guzmán at bay: the early 1990s were the days of the "Narco Juniors" in Tijuana, who flaunted a style that the recent violence has only recently forced out. The brothers and their entourage would cruise the city and its nightlife, dressing outrageously on their motorcycles or in SUV *trocas*. In many ways, they invented a narco style of yuppie razzmatazz. The AFO perpetrated the highest hit against the Catholic church by any crime syndicate when its hit men killed Cardinal Juan Jesús Posadas Ocampo, on May 24, 1993, at the Guadalajara airport.

The AFO can be said to be prime movers in changing the rules of engagement to include women and children as well as clerics—something the old-guard narcos prided themselves on avoiding. In August 2008, Jesús Rubén Moncada—aka "el Güero Loco," the Crazy Blond—was arrested in Los Angeles for a famous massacre in 1998 of nineteen people, including a baby clutched in its mother's arms, on a villa veranda near Ensenada, down the coast south of Tijuana. He had been living illegally in LA for ten years.[8] In 2002, the cartel's leader, Ramón Arellano Félix, was shot and killed by federal police. And in the latest round of violence since 2006, the AFO has been subjected to a battering by Guzmán's cartel, which abated only recently when his man in Tijuana, Eduardo García Simental, known as "el Teo," was arrested in January 2010. The arrest that Saturday afternoon in 2008 of Eduardo Arellano Félix leaves his sister Enedina as commander of the Tijuana clan (a first for a woman since "la Nacha" Jasso in Ciudad Juárez), while Eduardo's nephew Fernando Sánchez Arellano, "the Engineer," runs the AFO's street operation. Enedina is an important figure. Now that more and more women are entering the business, drug trafficking is seen as a more dignified profession than prostitution. Women serve as smugglers, with a better chance of passing border controls and checkpoints than men. There have been some major arrests of women, and the body of María José González, a singer and winner of the Sun Festival beauty pageant, was found by a road in Culiacán in spring 2009 near that of her drug-trafficking husband and a sign reading DON'T THROW TRASH. The authorities believe she had become involved with the Sinaloa cartel—one of the many beauty queens to become cartel mascots, then victims of the cartel's rivals.[9]

A stretch of land between Tijuana and Ciudad Juárez is variously controlled by an organization that switches allegiance to bigger cartels in order to operate. It was once run by the brothers Arturo and Alfredo Beltrán Leyva, who come from the same range of mountains as Joaquín Guzmán, near the town of Guamúchil, in Sinaloa. For years, the Beltrán Leyva brothers operated their stretch of frontier on behalf of the Sinaloa cartel, to which they were allied. They acted also as a security wing for Guzmán, overseeing squads of sicarios and protecting Guzmán's lieutenants and their families. But two things happened in rapid succession: in December 2007, while Guzmán's cartel was fighting the Gulf cartel and its military wing, Los Zetas, leaders from the Beltrán Leyva cartel held a treacherous meeting with Los Zetas in Veracruz, purportedly to discuss opening a space for the brothers in central Mexico, independent of Guzmán. The meeting fitted into a series Los Zetas were said to be holding, offering their services as hit men for a "supercartel" comprising anyone prepared to challenge Guzmán.[10] In January 2008, a month after the meeting, the elder brother, Alfredo, was arrested, and suddenly there was a turning point in the war. Guzmán is said to have commented that Beltrán Leyva's meeting with Los Zetas necessitated his having to "cut off that arm of the organization." The Beltrán Leyva clan deserted Guzmán, convinced that he had delivered Alfredo to the authorities in order to court, or even secure, their favor. The younger Arturo Beltrán Leyva, "el Alfa," exacted revenge on senior public officials, including the federal police commissioner, and on Guzmán's son Edgar Guzmán López, whom his sicarios gunned down in a shopping mall in May 2008. As head of security for Guzmán, Arturo had the home addresses of the families of his senior affiliates, and the violence unleashed by Beltrán Leyva against his former protector's entourage accounts for some of the worst recent killing in Sinaloa.

Over Christmas and New Year 2009–10, a government offensive against the Beltrán Leyva cartel reached high drama. On December 16, a unit of Naval Special Forces, backed by helicopter cover, stormed Arturo's dwelling complex in Cuernavaca and shot and killed him—the highest narco drug lord to be assassinated by the military since President Calderón's offensive and the first since Ramón Arellano Félix in

2002. Beltrán Leyva's bloodied corpse was subjected by his military assassins to an official rite associated with the narcos themselves. Photographs showed his jeans pulled down to his knees and his torso adorned with rows of bloodied $100 bills, and in another shot with spiritual accoutrements. This display angered commentators, such as Jorge Chabat of *El Universal*, who called the rite "the typical modus operandi of narcotraffickers,"[11] but that paper, like others, eagerly published the images.[12]

During the December 16 raid, an ensign from the commando unit, Melquisedet Angulo Cordóva, age thirty, had been killed as Beltrán Leyva's bodyguards exchanged fire. He was buried with full military honors, and the response of Beltrán Leyva's supporters was immediate. The day after the commando's hometown funeral in the state of Tabasco, gunmen burst into his grieving family's home, killing his mother, sister, brother, and an aunt.[13] By targeting the immediate family of military personnel serving in the war against them, the narcos had escalated the stakes in Mexico's war by another notch, but the authorities' response was equally swift. With both senior Beltrán Leyva brothers removed, leadership of the cartel fell to the younger Héctor Beltrán Leyva. He remains at large, but on January 2, 2010, another brother, Carlos, was taken by a bloodless swoop in the Sinaloan capital of Culiacán. The government could not have made itself clearer: the war was being cranked up still further. But who stood to gain? The president, of course; but also, according to the *susurro*, as it is known on the border, the rustle of leaves, the Sinaloa cartel, which had everything to gain from the government's war against its rivals, as the government well knows.

Ciudad Juárez was always the core of Amexica, formerly "El Paso del Norte"—Portal to the North—a trading route long before the border and a smuggling route as old as the line itself. "La Nacha" Jasso was the unchallenged heroin and then marijuana queen of Juárez from the legalization of alcohol until the 1970s. But the modern Juárez cartel was forged by Amado Carrillo Fuentes, who emerged as a force after he attached himself to the most powerful drug lord of the central border area, Pablo Acosta Villarreal, during the 1980s. Acosta operated out of the isolated town of Ojinaga, opposite Presidio in Texas, and in an unparalleled series of interviews with the writer Terence Popper, he detailed how his syndicate enjoyed the protection of the state and federal police, politicians, and army.[14] But, spotting his chance, Carrillo arranged for his mentor to be killed by federal officers during a raid on his home village of Santa Elena in 1987, which involved cooperation with forces from the U.S. side. In his excellent account of Carrillo's building the Juarez cartel, *Down by the River*, Charles Bowden relates that Carrillo paid a federal commander $1 million to mount the raid and ensure Acosta's death.[15] Carrillo Fuentes then shifted the cartel's power base to Juárez itself and strengthened it. In the mid-1990s, according to the DEA, the Juárez cartel was the biggest drug trafficker in the world, shifting more than 50 percent of all narcotics consumed in the United States. In 1996, Carrillo died during facial surgery—or did he? Mystery still surrounds his alleged passing, with all four surgeons engaged for the operation subsequently murdered. Violence in Juárez followed his death as Carrillo Fuentes's heir and brother, Vicente, tried to secure the terrain, but even that bloodbath was moderate compared to the present savagery in the city, which is supposed to have begun when Joaquín Guzmán's Sinaloa cartel laid siege in 2007. Whether the Juárez cartel remains a force in the labyrinth of competing interests that are killing across the city today has yet to be ascertained, but one can only presume that its present incarnation, La Línea, retains potency in the maelstrom, alongside some five hundred street gangs, the Sinaloa cartel, different strata of corrupt police forces, and the armed forces. How fitting, and gruesome, that *la línea* is also a common term in everyday parlance for the border itself.

As a man who perceives himself as heir to the Avilés/Gallardo empire, and as Avilés's nephew, Joaquín Guzmán—known as "el Chapo," or Shorty—saw the plaza of his Sinaloa cartel as a national one, almost a birthright. The moment Gallardo was arrested, Guzmán, who had built solid alliances with cocaine exporters in Colombia, declared war on those whom he disdained as pretenders in Tijuana and, with time, on every other criminal organization in Mexico. Guzmán was captured, however, early into his leadership of the cartel, in 1993. It was from jail, in luxury confinement at El Puente Grande maximum security prison near Guadalajara, that—U.S. intelligence sources believe—Guzmán adapted his tactics to build alliances in public office and high politics. Perhaps because of those contacts, Guzmán escaped spectacularly in 2001, just before he was due to be extradited to the United States, thus becoming poster boy for the latest wave of cult narco folk heroism. "Breakout of the Millennium" was the title of one *narcocorrido* ballad commemorating the escape. Another, by Los Buitres (the Vultures) and broadcast across radio airwaves, jukeboxes, the Internet and on YouTube goes: "He sleeps at times in houses / At times in tents / Radio and rifle at the foot of the bed / And sometimes his roof is a cave / Guzmán is everywhere." Guzmán is semiliterate, but issues communiqués boasting that he pays out $5 million a month to corrupt officials, and makes sudden, brazen appearances like that in May 2005 at a restaurant in Nuevo Laredo (on Gulf cartel terrain he was contesting at the time), when some forty diners found the doors suddenly locked by his gunmen. The clientele was asked not to use cell phones while Guzmán and his entourage enjoyed their meal and drinks, after which el Chapo pulled out thousands of dollars in cash and paid for everyone in the house.[16]

From jail, Guzmán had directed successive assaults on the border plazas, which chronologically followed the frontier from west to east. After Tijuana came Juárez, following Carrillo's death. But it was after Guzmán had escaped that he launched the offensive that detonated this latest phase of the war by unleashing his forces, unsuccessfully, against the Gulf cartel in 2005, in pursuit of the prize: Nuevo Laredo, the busiest commercial border crossing in the world. The offensive in Nuevo Laredo was both an end and a beginning: it was the last of Guzmán's first round of attacks but also the onset of the current war, taking the violence to another level altogether. Some expert observers believe that Guzmán has become something of a figurehead, a symbolic narco monarch who wields less power than notoriety, and that the cartel is now run by others with lower profiles but greater ruthlessness: Ismael "el Mayo" Zambada— who in 2010 gave a unique interview to *El Universal*, boasting about the cartel's prowess. It is often speculated that if it was part of the Mexican government's strategy to restore a Pax Mafiosa by backing one cartel in its bid for a monopoly, then that cartel would be the Sinaloa. But it is now too late to pursue such a goal, because of the ferocious power wielded by Guzmán's main rival, the Gulf cartel.

Until 2005, the drama was mainly among and between Sinaloans moving up to the border, which initially excluded the only syndicate to which Gallardo had conceded its own indigenous terrain, the Gulf cartel, based in the northeastern state of Tamaulipas, opposite deep south Texas. At the time of this writing, it is too early to discern any specific outcome to the offensive launched by President Calderón in December 2006, but one partial result is clear: the Gulf cartel and what was formed as its military wing, Los Zetas, have held their terrain against both their rivals and the army. While el Chapo Guzmán remains Mexico's most powerful drug lord, and his cartel appears to remain closest to political power, Los Zetas' insurgency and resilience make it the Mexican government's gravest problem, along with the very different nightmare of the anarchy in Ciudad Juárez. For this reason, the Gulf cartel and Los Zetas warrant special attention.

Unlike the other syndicates, with leaderships from Sinaloa, the Gulf cartel grew out of—and is fiercely proud of—its territory and home state, which runs along the border from Nuevo Laredo to the mouth of the Rio Grande. The cartel was founded by a whiskey bootlegger from the 1930s, Juan Nepomuceno Guerra, when he moved into the marijuana and heroin business during the 1970s. He is said to have had the only rival on his terrain, Casimiro Espinoza, killed. That murder, in 1984, was reportedly organized by Guerra's nephew Juan García Abrego and marks the birth of the modern Gulf cartel. By moving the cartel into cocaine, García Abrego became the first drug trafficker to make the FBI's Ten Most Wanted list and was duly arrested and extradited to the United States in 1996, leaving the leadership contested but easily won by Osiel Cárdenas Guillén. Cárdenas, who hailed from a poor ranch on the outskirts of Matamoros, consolidated his power within the cartel by killing his rival, Chava Gómez—earning himself the nickname "el Mata Amigos," the Friend Killer—and led it from his home city until being arrested during a gun battle in 2003. He was subsequently extradited to the United States in 2007 and sentenced to twenty-five years in prison in February 2010, after a trial held in secret.

Cárdenas, in his way, defines the present narco war: from a very humble background in the police force, he sought not to manipulate high politics but to secure his position within the cartel and against its competitors by recruiting an enforcement wing trained by former members of special service military units, which Cárdenas named Los Zetas, after their leader Arturo Guzmán's call sign in the police, Z1. Los Zetas emerged to take over the cartel as a syndicate in their own right (a position now facing a challenge from within the cartel). They are one of the most terrifying and formidable drug-trafficking organizations in the world, with a paramilitary army estimated by the DEA to number four thousand highly trained soldiers. Arturo Guzmán and his deputies Rogelio González, "Z2," and Heriberto Lazcano, "Z3," enticed former members of Mexico's special airborne antidrug military unit, the GAFE, to defect and train others. Some of Los Zetas' troops were reportedly trained by the United States at Fort Benning in Georgia, but this has not been proved. After Z1 Guzmán was killed in 2002 and Z2 Rogelio captured in 2004, Lazcano, a former commando in the GAFE, took on the leadership. The recruiting continues: Los Zetas, calling themselves a *grupo operativo*, hung a narcomanta from a bridge in Nuevo Laredo in 2008 calling for men with "military experience" to phone a displayed number. "We offer a good salary, food, and medical care for your families," it taunted. The Gulf cartel and Los Zetas claim as part of their territory the most lucrative smuggling point on the border, a prize coveted by any cartel: the freight road and rail bridges that cross the Rio Grande between Nuevo Laredo and Laredo, Texas. In 2005, the Sinaloa cartel attacked, in pursuit of a share of the contaminated traffic that crosses the frontier every day. The assault was the beginning of the current war, the latest and most vicious phase not just in the long history of narco violence but in Mexico's history since the revolution of 1910.

Meanwhile, Los Zetas have all but secured their goal of a route down the Gulf Coast and into Central America, affording direct access to the traditional cocaine-producing country of Colombia and to new export markets for the drug opened up by Los Zetas in Peru and Venezuela. The advantages of coastal supremacy were illustrated by a novel haul on June 16, 2009: dozens of mysteriously dead sharks in two containers brought ashore by the marine authorities at the Gulf port of Progreso turned out to have had their bellies stuffed with bags containing almost two thousand pounds of cocaine.[17] In order to secure a clear route to the cocaine-producing countries, Los Zetas are combating the Sinaloa cartel in guerrilla warfare in Guatemala. Los Zetas are the cartel with the best connections to markets in Britain and Europe, aligned with their opposite numbers, the 'Ndrangheta of Calabria. When in September 2008 some 175 operatives for the Gulf cartel were arrested by U.S. authorities—to whose intelligence services the cartel is known as "the Company"—ten were in Calabria.[18] The alliance is important in light of remarks made by Mexico's attorney general, Eduardo Medina Mora, in March 2009, that the crackdown against cross-border traffic was forcing Mexican cartels to shift their attention and potentially their operations, and "focus more closely on Europe."[19] The alliance is equally cogent in the wake of recent briefings by the Mexican diplomatic service indicating that a slight decline in cocaine consumption in the United States creates a surplus in Mexico needing to be shipped somewhere else—which may partly explain why Britian, Spain, and other European countries serviced by the 'Ndrangheta have now overtaken the United States in the per capita consumption of cocaine and its "cooked" derivatives. There have been recent reports of direct contact with drug gangs on Merseyside in Britain.[20]

An alliance between Los Zetas and 'Ndrangheta is logical also in terms of narco social style, as well as economics. Although the parallels are not exact, some similar progression can be traced in the decline of the classical Sicilian Cosa Nostra as matching that of the Félix Gallardo federation during the 1980s, as both were overtaken by more ferocious syndicates emerging from poorer backgrounds and without pretensions to become "Godfather" figures—epitomized by Los Zetas from Tamaulipas (challenging Sinaloa) and 'Ndrangheta from Calabria (challenging Sicily). In Mexico as in Italy, there is a ubiquitous nostalgia, however misplaced, for "old-time" gangsters with almost aristocratic pretensions for their codes of "honor," debonair style, and political connections. But they have been superseded, both generationally and in terms of savagery: in the Italian instance by the 'Ndrangheta, and in Mexico by the also leaner and meaner Zetas, who came from a background of rural slums, urban street gangs, and the police or military academies. In both cases, the old fedora or Stetson has been replaced by a shaved buzz cut and tattoos; the appointment with a politician by that with a personal martial arts trainer. Osiel Cárdenas Guillén was an auto mechanic before joining the police, and as a modest dresser is seen as the style guru of this transition to what one could call Generation Z in the genealogy, without end, of drug dealing. In February 2010, however, there was a sudden and violent rupture between the Gulf cartel and Zetas, and infighting which cut a swathe of murder across Tamaulipas. The syndicate had become a victim of its own success: its grip on that section of the border too strong, it had led to a calm in which the Zetas' enforcement role left them with little to do beyond becoming a cartel in their own right. The might it then claimed to wield was too much for the Gulf cartel old guard that had resisted Cárdenas, and which the Zetas in theory served.

Los Zetas are, moreover, leaving an ever-heavier footprint in the United States. Apart from their deep penetration of the most important border hub city of Houston, Los Zetas have been linked to appalling violence in the Deep South. In August 2008, five men were found with their throats slit in Columbiana, Alabama, after being tortured with electric shocks. The FBI claims the victims owed a debt of $400,000 to the Gulf cartel. During the big raid against the Gulf cartel in September 2008, twelve of its operatives were arrested in Atlanta, where authorities reported an increasing level of cartel-related violence. In 2001, a haul of $4.1 million in Gulf cartel cash was uncovered in Atlanta, and another $2.3 million in Houston. In the United States, the battle for distribution is now essentially between Guzmán and the Gulf. After the swoop against the Gulf cartel in September 2008, 750 affiliates of the Sinaloa cartel were arrested in another famous roundup across the United States, Operation Xcellerator, in February 2009. Some $460 million in cash was seized, along with twenty-four thousand pounds of cocaine and twelve hundred pounds of methamphetamine.

In its essence, Mexico's cartel war is becoming a three-way battle between the army, Guzmán, and Los Zetas—but there is a recent addition to the list, La Familia. La Familia emerged during the 1990s as a syndicate entirely indigenous to Sinaloa's coastal southern neighbor, the state of Michoacán. It was devoted to claiming drug trafficking from and across the state for itself against a subsidiary of Guzmán's, the Milenio cartel, run by a family called Valencia. According to some reports, the rift was due to rivalry over a woman between a member of the Valencias and the man who founded La Familia, Nazario Moreno González, known as "el Más Loco"—the Craziest One—killed by the Mexican army in 2010. La Familia "came out" with a famous incident on September 6, 2006, when twenty masked men burst into a low-rent discotheque, the Sol y Sombra in Morelia, the state capital, and bowled five decapitated heads across the floor, accompanied by a message that is bizarre even by the wayward standards of narco communication: "La Familia does not kill for money. It does not kill for women. It does not kill the innocent. Only those who deserve to die. Know that this is divine justice." El Más Loco prosletyze from a book mixing quotations from the Scriptures with his own excruciating mantras, such as: "Don't View Your Obstacles as Problems but Accept Them and Discover in Them the Opportunity to Improve Yourself."

To fight off its Sinaloan neighbors, the emergent Familia had elected to be trained by Los Zetas. In 2007, however, La Familia decided to carve out an identity for itself alone, throwing off Los Zetas, who were getting closer to their goal of dominating La Familia. The response from Tamaulipas to the rebuff was a brazen act of terrorism against civilians: a bomb was thrown at crowds of families celebrating the Grito—the Cry of Independence—on the night of September 15, eve of Mexico's Independence Day. It killed eight people and injured more than one hundred in the president's home city of Morelia. La Familia sent a flurry of messages to local media disavowing the attack and hung narcomantas accusing Los Zetas of responsibility. After the swoops against first the Gulf cartel and then Guzmán, the U.S. authorities targeted operatives working for La Familia, with 305 arrested during mid-October 2009 by a sting known as Project Coronado. The concentration was around Dallas, where 77 were arrested for operating a distribution network feeding Illinois, Minnesota, and Mississippi.

As the year 2006 drew to a close, some two thousand people had been killed in violence between the cartels, mostly in Nuevo Laredo and Michoacán. Against this mayhem, on December 11, only ten days after he had been sworn in, the newly elected president of Mexico, Felipe de Jesús Calderón Hinojosa, mobilized forty thousand troops. Calderón, a Harvard-trained lawyer and devout conservative Catholic from Morelia, was the second president to be elected as a leader of the National Action Party (PAN), of which he had been a cofounder, succeeding Vicente Fox, a former executive of the Coca-Cola Company in Mexico. For the previous seventy-two years, Mexico had been ruled continuously by the Institutional Revolutionary Party, which had become more institutional than revolutionary by building and managing a byzantine system of government by patronage, thereby exercizing political power or influence in every pore of the social fabric to a degree unknown elsewhere in the West. Fox's victory in 2000 was seen at the time to have broken with a stifling epoch, liberating Mexico into the Elysian fields of free-market capitalist meritocracy. His victory was an overwhelmingly urban one and especially resounding along the border. Fox won every border state and sixteen of the nineteen electoral districts adjacent to the United States.[21]

Commentators in the United States and Mexico consider it unfortunate that the narco violence coincides with the transition to a genuinely capitalist free market in Mexico; but my essential argument is that the violence is not, however, a counterforce against what the title of one learned account of this mutation in the country's history calls "opening Mexico."[22] The violence occurs not despite but, in large part, *because* of these changes; it is at best an inevitable side effect of "opening Mexico," and at worst integral to it. La plaza is a marketplace like any other, and narco cartels are not criminal pastiches of contemporary, multinational "late" capitalism—they are part of it and operate according to its values—or rather lack of values—and logic.

It would have been almost impossible for the narco cartels to operate without the help of the PRI; they mirrored and were part of the party's pyramidal, monopolistic system of patronage. But a newly competitive economic environment and the defeat of the PRI obliged the cartels to look again at their own operations, tighten international alliances, and diversify their merchandise beyond the cocaine line that had been the main product of their boom years, the 1970s and '80s, during cohabitation with the PRI. Now, a new generation of cartel leaders, typified by Osiel Cárdenas Guillén, have expanded their catalog range and strengthened their production and supply of synthetic drugs like methamphetamine, or crystal meth. And with cocaine consumption declining in the United States, they also returned to the best seller of yore, heroin, researching new permutations suitable to the latest taste—such as the craze for "cheese heroin" in Texas, mixing heroin with over-the-counter drugs to make it cheaper, stronger, and longer lasting. These are products of "open" Mexico's Fox-Calderón era.

President Calderón's foursquare spokeswoman, Alejandra Sota Mirafuentes, meets me at Brasserie Lipp (the one in Mexico City, not Paris, and part of an international luxury hotel complex) to insist, over mineral water, "We cannot turn a blind eye to criminality. The power of the cartels has become a very real threat to the security of the Mexican state—the ability to buy off local and state authority, even federal government. For years," she says of the PRI epoch, "the authorities just gave in." But, "this is very important: Mexico has changed politically. If in the past, the government was greedy and wanted to take advantage of the cartels, that is no longer the case." The initial intervention in Michoacán, she says, "opened the body, and once the body was opened, we could see that it had contracted severe cancer: Juárez, Sinaloa, Tamaulipas, whole regions were controlled by the cartels."

It seems odd that this bright young woman—let alone Calderón's government—had not known that all along. President Calderón has, after all, needed to purge his own apparatus of corruption in an initiative he called Operation Clean House. His former acting police chief, Gerardo Garazy, was arrested for protecting the Beltrán Leyva brothers, and his "drug czar," Noé Ramírez, for taking a $450,000 bribe from the Sinaloa cartel. Both are awaiting trial; both have denied wrongdoing. Operation Clean House, however, had failed to net another of Mexico's apparently trustworthy drug czars, José Luis Santiago Vasconcelos, who was warmly embraced by Washington and had extradited Osiel Cárdenas Guillén. Vasconcelos was killed in a mysterious plane crash over Mexico City in November 2008, and six months later, in May 2009, a DEA report named Vasconcelos as being on the payroll of the Beltrán Leyva cartel.[23]

The thrust of the offensive, says Sota, is to challenge the cartels militarily while "aggressively" reforming the legal system and institutions, starting with the federal structure. The task, she says, "begins with the military, but by the end of the presidential term, we aim to have established an honest and well-structured federal police. We start with the military because we cannot count on the municipal and state police. In a number of places, the traffickers control the police." So that is official, at least. As is this: "The military is going to stay in there for as long as it takes." As long as what takes? "So long as it takes for the state to fulfill its basic obligations: public security and the collection of taxes, which are currently threatened by and even subverted and imitated by levies imposed by the cartels." Strangely, and with estimable honesty, Sota adds, "The president is clear: the fight is not against drugs, it is against the violence and the ability of criminal organizations to subvert the state. The president knows that drugs will not disappear."

That is the map at the outset, the template of the cartel war, to bear in mind as one explores the border, although there is no predicting how the lines on the map will blur or demarcate the narco topology. However, a journey along the map as it stands entails, loosely, three stages. First, the road from Tijuana to Ciudad Juárez, across the terrain of warfare among the Sinaloa, Tijuana, and Beltrán Leyva cartels. Then a meltdown in Juárez, as the cartel pyramids collapse into a murderous anarchy. Finally, from Ciudad Acuña and Nuevo Laredo eastward, the road leads into a land where there was, between 2005 and 2010, relatively less fighting but that is the most terrifying stretch along the border. Until early 2010, this terrain was subject to an iron reign consolidated by Los Zetas and the Gulf cartel. Only now they are no longer synonymous with each other: the "classical" and military wings are at internecine war.

With the election of Barack Obama, the map has also changed at the level of U.S. government. After decades of the United States seeing the narco-trafficking problem as essentially an all-Mexican one, there is now, for the first time, a sense of officially acknowledged coresponsibility over crucial areas of policy. During visits to Mexico City by Secretary of State Hillary Clinton and the president himself, the matter of arms trafficking from the United States to Mexico, previously taboo, has been addressed. There has been acknowledgment of the fundamental fact that the cause of the crisis is addiction to drugs in American society. In March 2009, President Obama announced a package with two themes: man the border defenses and attack the roots of addiction. He increased the budgets of all federal agencies along the border, with $700 million that year toward personnel and technology, and more to come. President Obama said he would upgrade intelligence gathering and improve cross-border interdiction, and also "redouble" efforts to diminish demand for drugs in the United States and stanch the flow of weapons from the United States to Mexico. "It's really a two-way situation here," said the president, speaking a language never before heard from the White House. "The drugs are coming north, we're sending funds and guns south."[24]

The reality on the ground is elastic, mercurial, and in places much worse than the map suggests. The map shows a war caused by fighting among cartels for smuggling routes and a consequent government crackdown, but it does not show another, monstrous, reason for the war: the Mexican side of the borderline has become accursed by addiction to hard drugs. This seems of little consequence to the United States, and is virtually never mentioned in Mexico, but it is the cause of most of the killing and the most wretched circumstances in the drug war. All warfare creates resultant "sideshow" horrors. And the consequential sideshow of America's addiction to hard drugs supplied by Mexico and both countries' war against the traffic is twofold: first, the ravages of hard drugs along the border, and subsequently, the feral war for control of this domestic plaza, which is just as savage as that for narcotic exports, if not more so. Fundamental to both Mexican government strategy and the thinking of the DEA is that fragmenting the cartels would weaken them, thereby damaging drug traffic and reducing violence. "We want it to be disorganized," says Eileen Zeidler, spokeswoman for the DEA in San Diego, of the cartels' fragmentation since President Calderón's offensive. "If they're not organized, they don't function. We want it to fall apart."[25] Ms. Zeidler's boss, the DEA's chief of intelligence, Anthony Placido, went so far as to call the violence a "sign of success," and to speak of "wounded, vulnerable" cartels.[26] But fragmentation does not guarantee a weakening of narco traffic, it simply adds nuance to the market: the domestic plaza is fought over by the plethora of gangs that serve the big cartels when drugs cross the frontier, but they fight one another when dealing on home turf, bringing death and misery to the colonias. Like any other corporation, the cartels nowadays outsource much of their business to subcontractors who tender for a slice of the profits. Narco outsourcing even has a name: *el derecho de piso*—the right of tender, of passage, and it is a murderous business, as street gangs and other interests vie and kill for the contracts.

Our journey begins where the desert sun sets in the Pacific at Amexica's western edge, the frontier between Tijuana and San Diego. The latter is not really a border town—it is too big, too Californian. But one can already feel the frontier at the Twelfth Street and Imperial transit center, where early mornings there is a two-way rush hour through the mumbling homeless pushing their belongings in supermarket carts: of people arriving for work from Tijuana, and people leaving for work in Tijuana. The blue line trundles toward the railway yards and dockland base of the U.S. Pacific Fleet, frigates and masts thick with radar, and painted murals illustrating the "History of Our Community" at Barrio Logan (a Hispanic settlement named after an Irish pioneer), featuring a Mesoamerican Indian blowing into a conch shell, fishermen hauling their catch, and dolphins at the SeaWorld theme park. Through factories and the lights and smoke of dawn, Rosebud Law Enforcement services and Tactical Assault Gear are right next door to Rosa's Mexican diner just as they would be anywhere else in America. But anywhere else is not the suburb of Chula Vista, five miles north of Tijuana, nor San Isidro, end of the line—and of the United States. Thirty minutes south of downtown San Diego, on the platform teeming by seven thirty in the morning, the two-way rush hour is in full swing, as is a McDonald's that is a border hub of its own: customs agents, girls laden with huge packs of diapers, Mexican businessmen who have fled to Chula Vista but return each day to work in Tijuana, and Mexican ladies on their way to clean American toilets are all eating breakfast. And there it is: the concrete barrier, the footbridge, and beyond it, Mexico. *Aquí Empieza la Patria*—Here Begins the Homeland—is Tijuana's municipal motto, and a Mexican flag, defiantly and desperately giant, with its eagle clutching a snake on a cactus, which legend has it predicted the birth of the nation, flies in America's face, at the border.

2

AQUÍ EMPIEZA LA PATRIA (HERE BEGINS THE HOMELAND)

Tijuana's image north of the border was always that of a festive party town. And for the Americans who poured into TJ by the thousands every day, and by the tens of thousands every weekend, it was. YOU ARE IN THE MOST VISITED CITY IN THE WORLD claims the sign above Avenida Revolución, and whether statistically true or not, people thronged here to savor Mexican exotica, buy souvenirs, drink margaritas by the jug (at an age younger than the United States permits), get teeth fixed cheaply, invest in a spare pair of eyeglasses, and, latterly, buy Viagra and Prozac and other medications for a fraction of the price back home. Tijuana grew during the nineteenth century, after the loss of Alta California to the United States in 1848. The downtown area acquired its reputation for selling an ersatz Mexico to North Americans in 1915, when Tijuana decided to echo that year's great Panama-California Exposition in San Diego with a fair of its own called the Feria Típica Mexicana, to lure visitors across the border. Since then the city has specialized in sombreros, reproduction Aztec bric-a-brac, ponchos, and other trinkets that actually have nothing to do with the country's sixth-largest city of 1.5 million people. Every Mexican border city and town divides itself among indigenous *norteños*, *sureños* from the South, and *chilangos* from the capital. There is even a constituency that calls itself *fronterizos*, from the border itself. These are crucial points of identity.[1] More than half the population of Tijuana comes from "traditional" southern Mexico, not to live according to some folklore kitsch but to work in maquiladoras or eke out some other living in desperately poor colonias on the city's outskirts.

For the southerners, or those from El Salvador, Honduras, and Guatemala, Tijuana can be harsh, unwelcoming, dangerous, and violent. Attacks on Mixtecs, Mayas, and Zapotecs are routine. Until recently, when vast estates of uniform housing were built around the city, whole communities from South and Central America lived on the *dompes*, or landfills of domestic and industrial rubbish.[2]

Tijuana's reputation for naughtiness grew during Prohibition, soon after the *feria*, when the city became a magnet for those seeking not only off-the-peg Mexico but also alcohol, gambling, and the go-go good-time vices that accompanied them. The existence of the biggest naval base on the Pacific at San Diego guaranteed off-duty customers in addition to civilian tourists. But the narco war has changed all this, so that now, says Enrico Rodríguez in his empty shop full of unbrowsed jewelry, trinkets, and Western wear, "I cross myself every time I make a sale and have not crossed myself for two days." No one wants a Polaroid picture taken of himself wearing a sombrero next to an old donkey painted black and white like a zebra, and the strippers pole-dance pretty much to one another. Except, perhaps, the odd scurvy vagabond from California, too stoned to care about any potential danger, and, of course, the local backsliders, equipped with a limited supply of greenbacks. The famous district around Avenidas Revolución and Constitución is now more about sleaze than aphrodisia. On its uppers, the Mermaid's Club and Hotel, with Western-saloon-style swing doors, is forced to offer "Two Massages for the Price of One." The Adelita Bar (est. 1962), with the Hotel Coahuila situated conveniently next door, has seen better days, now hoping to attract guests with neon signs of girls wearing *bandolero* bullet belts and brandishing Kalashnikov machine guns. A passing gringo, I am ushered inside with desperate insistence and quickly introduced by a heavily tattooed doorman to comely Gabriela in a glittering, fluorescent turquoise bikini and train of plastic feathers like a peacock's. She asks if I would like to buy her a drink while the doorman, whose height reaches as far as Gabriela's articulate bust, runs down a list of offers—including stiff alcohol, sex, and a card game—all easily refused. The cavernous depths are not quite empty: a group of Mexican men share a bottle of tequila while their female company sip sodas, and a lone, pallid American with a goatee and skin that has not seen daylight for a good while watches the writhing pole dancer. But that's about it for the night, concedes the doorman. The narco "Juniors" themselves, once cocks of the walk, have disappeared too. Since war broke out, the modern narcotraficantes, out of prudence and self-preservation, keep a low profile, partying at the villa and entertaining ladies through home delivery rather than brazenly in public—as they did not long ago.

How well she remembers those days. How could she ever forget—when the Juniors, as they became known, were in their prime: flashing their wealth around Tijuana, dripping gold with a scantily dressed beauty hanging from each arm? Cruising in their SUVs, taking over nightclubs in which they would drink only champagne. Cristina Palacios Hodoyán, lighting ultrathin cigarettes with a gold lighter held in her ultrathin fingers, remembers them with a sorrow in her eyes that even her polished demeanor cannot hide. How could she forget the Juniors, when two of her three sons were among them? The eldest, Alejandro, was kidnapped twice—once in 1996 and again the following year, since when he has never been seen again. The youngest, Alfredo, became known as "el Lobo," the Wolf, and is serving 176 years in a Mexican jail, convicted of multiple murder and criminal association. "I had wanted them to become lawyers, or go into their father's business as civil engineers," their mother reflects. After finishing her cigarette, she picks at a smoked salmon sandwich, at a table in the Merlot restaurant, near the Tijuana Country Club, where the better class of people go. Mrs. Palacios turns sixty-nine the day after we have dinner, and says she plans a quiet meal with close friends, nothing extravagant.

Her boys had had the city at their feet. As heirs to the Palacios Hodoyán family, they enjoyed automatic membership in and access to the *club campestre* (country club) and the so-called Instituto Set, alumnae of the elite Tijuana Institute. There was an auspicious future in their father Ramírez's legitimate businesses if they wanted it. Alfredo was confirmed into the church by the bishop of Tijuana, a family friend who would become Cardinal Posadas Ocampo, assassinated by the very cartel Alejandro and Alfredo later joined. "Ocampo was very dear to us," recalls Cristina, "known and loved by Tijuana." Born in the United States, the boys could cross the border any time and set up in business there if they preferred, with their father's Rolodex of clients at their disposal. And the Hodoyán brothers were heading that way, until Ramón Arellano Félix arrived in town from Sinaloa.

"I remember Ramón," says Cristina with a shudder. "He always wore a mink coat, even on a hot day, and shorts—with a big golden cross against his bare chest. There was a place by a tree where children had always played with tricycles and bicycles, and later they might meet up there in the evening, chatting up the girls or boys. Alex was in college studying law, age about twenty-five, Alfredo was eighteen or nineteen. And Ramón Arellano Félix and the boys from Sinaloa used to come up to the tree, presenting themselves as interesting and exciting, flashing their money, and the girls wanted to be seen with them."[3]

"So that the people who would start bringing drugs into my house—only I didn't know that at the time—were children I had known since kindergarten," she continues. "Ramón would take them to the clubs. He would walk in and commandeer a table, even if it was taken, just send the people away. He would buy champagne for his company all night, but if you talked to anyone else, you were considered a traitor. At any time, they could take someone out and kill them, and they did. Once you were in, you were in, and there was no way out. My sons had become part of it all, they were among people who would laugh while cutting someone's fingers off, or chop someone into pieces for fun. All this I learned later, when Alex had been captured and Alfredo was in prison."

On September 11, 1996, "Alejandro disappeared in Guadalajara. Until February, he was in custody, held by General Jesús Gutiérrez Rebollo of the Mexican army." During this time, in December, General Gutiérrez Rebollo was appointed to the top post as Mexico's drug czar, leading the government's effort against the cartels, not least because of his success in capturing Alejandro Hodoyán. Alejandro was "singing," telling the general all he knew about his AFO cartel.

It emerged when Alejandro talked to his family, says Cristina, that the confessions were coerced, and that the general had played a vile game with his quarry: "The soldiers," she recalls, "used electric shocks on his eyes and feet, and burned him with cigarettes and lighters to get him to talk. Gutiérrez Rebollo," she says, "had arrived later, after others had tortured him, so that Alex felt beholden to him and would tell him everything." In late November, Gutiérrez Rebollo, once he had softened his prisoner, called in prosecutors from Mexico City, who videotaped a confession in which Alejandro, between gulps of water, recalls how his partners in the cartel would "laugh after a murder, and go off and have a lobster dinner." Killing, he told his captors, "is a party for them, it's a kick." Alejandro admitted that he had started running errands for the cartel, progressed to running drugs across the border, and then joined a unit of sicarios. After they had the information they needed, the Mexican Department of National Defense handed Alejandro over to the Americans, who were preparing an indictment against the AFO. "We also now know," Mrs. Palacios adds with a shudder, "that the Americans were aware this was how he was forced to talk.[4]

"On February 10, 1997," she continues, "Alejandro was flown to San Diego, he told me, and put in custody by the FBI and DEA. At that point, both my sons were in San Diego, in different prisons, because Alfredo had been arrested too. But Alejandro was not arrested; it was worse than that: he was to become a protected witness. 'I know a lot of things,' he told me, 'and I need protection.' But he had no protection. They did not tell Alex that everything he had said in Mexico City had been leaked by the Ministry of Public Security to the Tijuana cartel, and that General Gutiérrez Rebollo was working all along for the Juárez cartel." Only two months into his new job at the apex of Mexico's supposed anticartel offensive, General Gutiérrez Rebollo was convicted of collaboration with Amado Carrillo Fuentes—the general even lived in a villa owned by the Lord of the Skies.

After ten days in DEA custody in San Diego, "Alfredo was asked to testify against his brother," says Cristina. Her younger son had been charged with two counts of murder and was about to be extradited to Mexico for trial. He was in an impossible position between the rock of family loyalty and the hard place of his own survival. At the same time, "Alejandro [escaped and] ran back to Tijuana. By then, he was a condemned man: by the AFO for having squealed to Gutiérrez Rebollo, and by the Juárez cartel for belonging to a rival." Alejandro hid at home. Two weeks later, Cristina was driving her son in the family's SUV. "We were in a parking lot, when a truck blocked our way. Men surrounded us, with guns, and told us to get out of the car. I said no. They didn't have masks or anything. Then they pulled Alex out and drove away. I never saw him again." She lights another ultrathin cigarette, draws in the smoke with a deep breath, and says, "It all made sense. They're all working for one cartel or another. When I went through a police album of intelligence officers, I found the face of the man I saw in the van, who kidnapped my Alejandro. But I still have Alfredo. He is in jail in Matamoros, and we are trying to get the sentence reduced."

All this is in the past, she insists. Cristina now works with parents or family of people kidnapped and probably killed by narco traffickers, trying to pressure the authorities to track their lost loved ones and do something that only very rarely happens: go after the kidnappers and killers. "The problem is, though," Cristina continues in a matter-of-fact way, "most of these people, once kidnapped, were dissolved in acid."

We are joined by Fernando Ocegueda Flores, whose son, also called Fernando, was taken from the family home, he says, on February 10, 2007. "The police were so uncooperative, even obstructive, that at first I thought they themselves had taken my son," he says. "Then the whisper from neighbors told me that it had been the Arellano Félix Organization. From the authorities, all this time, I have had nothing, zero, no investigation, not even a reply. I went crazy and decided to conduct my own investigation. For two years, I searched—I went to everyone I knew in the cartel and asked them point-blank to tell me. I went to their houses, I knocked on their doors in rage." "We were worried," says Cristina, "that he would not survive this line of investigation." "Someone did this, and I had to find out who," retorts Fernando. Finally, he says, "I went to a very dangerous place, and they put me in a car and I talked to this man. My request had gone high up the chain, and they told me my son had been killed and the body dissolved in acid."

On January 24, 2009, federal police raided a narcotraficantes' party at a ritzy seaside resort on the coastal highway from Tijuana to Ensenada, and arrested one Santiago Meza López, universally known and wanted in Tijuana as "el Pozolero," the Stew Maker. *Pozole* is a popular stew made of pork, vegetables, and seasonings, but this is not what Meza was brewing. He confessed to having disposed of some three hundred corpses by dissolving them in vats of lye or hydrochloric acid, initially at the service of the AFO but defecting to the Sinaloa cartel, for which he was paid $600 a week.[5] Meza's confession was straightforward: he would fill a vat with water and two bags of lye, don protective gloves and goggles, boil the pinkish brew, and dispose of the bodies delivered at his lair by truck, one by one.

Accordingly, Fernando Ocegueda came to know that the answer to his and hundreds of other distraught families' questions lay along the road southeastward from Tijuana to the satellite colonia of Florido, a place of shriveled orchards and ramshackle houses, home to the Silza propane gas terminal. Up a dirt track into the desert lies the hamlet of Ojo de Agua, the Eye of Water, above which are two small graveyards nestled into the hillside. El Pozolero's lair is surrounded by a blue tarpaulin and guarded by an encampment of bored Federales. It is a square of ground, about thirty by thirty yards, enclosed by walls of gray cinder blocks, open to the sky, with a little hut in the corner. For a tip of 400 pesos ($32), the Federales open the padlock and slide open the heavy white gate for a guided tour. Across the compound, earth is piled in mounds, and there are blue plastic barrels here and there. Two steel containers stand beside a cistern at the top of the slight incline on which the lair is built. "This is where he put them into the acid," says the police captain, in a plain-speaking, unadorned way, but with something between a grimace and a smile.

The unofficial tour is economically informative. "They would have been brought by truck and unloaded over here," says the captain, striding around, "then taken here, probably on wheelbarrows, put into the vats, and there you go, no more bodies!" But a potent smell rises through the afternoon heat: the inimitable, sickly sweet, putrid smell of death and decomposition, of human remains. "It's always stronger when it gets hot, around this time of day," observes the captain, as though by way of apology. So el Pozolero was not as thorough in executing his task as the public was led to believe, nor, clearly, were the police investigators whose duty it is, in theory, to collect any remaining DNA on the site, seal it, endeavor to identify the dead, and seek out their relatives. In fact, here we are, stomping around a crime scene that is abandoned but littered with evidence. "We haven't noticed any sign of the detectives for three months—no one, nothing, we're just told to stay here and . . . well, watch for anyone who arrives," complains the bored captain. This was August 2009, eight months after the arrest and confession. The captain points into the cistern, from which an especially pungent stench ascends into the afternoon. "There's still plenty down there," he informs us, kindly but unnecessarily. And not only "down there"—we take a look inside one of the blue plastic barrels, and there is the gum of a lower jaw, with teeth still attached, that somehow escaped dissolution. At the bottom of one of the steel tanks, there is raw flesh and jellylike human tissue.

There are also quite a few remnants from the recreational life led by the Stew Maker and whatever apprentices he needed to practice his craft: a barbecue, several dozen empty Tecate beer cans, bits of seafood in the dust, and a thriving marijuana plant. The arrest was made in January, and in the little hut in the corner of the settlement, el Pozolero's Christmas tree remains, complete with decorations made of festive red velvet ribbon and sparkly tinsel.

During the recent war, the killing has become qualitatively, as well as quantitatively, more grotesque—savage mutilations, decapitations, tortures to a point of perverse cruelty. All this requires a deviant sense of innovation, a twisted creativity: "bone tickling" involves scraping the bone with an ice pick sunk through the flesh. Doctors are employed to ensure that those being questioned or tortured do not lose consciousness or die too soon. Methods of execution are of calculated atrocity: one of the Arellano brothers' victims was left tied to a chair and his hands chopped off, so that he bled slowly to death, alone. The killing has been extended to include families and children among the victims. This is not entirely new. At one point during the 1980s, Félix Gallardo needed to deal with an encroachment into his Guadalajara business by an interloper called Héctor Palma. Gallardo tasked one of his operatives to seduce Palma's wife and run off with the woman and her children. One day, the cuckolded Palma received a package by courier. It contained his wife's severed head. He learned later that Gallardo's man, Clavel Moreno, had pushed his children to their deaths off a bridge. Palma built a special little chapel in their memory.

The children of some lesser narcos attend Valentina Farias Gómez primary school in Tijuana. The school is kept beautifully clean, and the children, wearing red uniforms, chirp around the playground before settling in for lessons with orderly discipline. One morning in March 2008, however, the children arrived to find a message for them to bear in mind as they prepared their futures in the community: twelve festering corpses piled across the road from the school gates, naked, tortured, and with tongues cut—people who talked too much. It was a lesson to the pupils not to do the same, says the principal, Miguel Ángel González Tovar, simultaneously courteous and exhausted as he describes running a school attended by "the children of narcos, children of police officers, and children of ordinary workers. The situation is very delicate. There are evil people in our area, but they still send their children to school.

"It was terrifying," he says of that morning in March. "The children were terrified, the staff were terrified, and I had to pretend not to be terrified, but everyone knew what was happening. It was a warning, and it means what it means. We try to teach here, to teach against that message, like an island of education and peace and security for the children, but we are fighting a form of barbarism here and cannot be isolated from what is going on outside. That is not easy, however. They gave me a CCTV camera, but it doesn't work. They gave me an alarm button, but that's broken. It's terribly sad, a situation we despise, are scared of, but fight against."

Dr. Hiram Muñoz, a forensic pathologist assigned to the Baja California state prosecutor's department in Tijuana, talks about how "each different mutilation leaves a clear message. They have become a kind of folk tradition. If the tongue is cut out, it means they talked too much—a snitch, or *chupro*. A man who squealed on the clan has his finger cut off and maybe put in his mouth." This is logical, a traitor is known as a *dedo*—a finger. Sometimes fingers are stuck up the rectum. "If you are castrated," continues Dr. Muñoz, "you may have slept with or looked at the woman of another man in the business. Severed arms could mean that you stole from your consignment, severed legs that you tried to walk away from the cartel. Decapitation is another thing altogether: it is simply a statement of power, a warning to all, like public executions of old. The difference is that in normal times, the dead were 'disappeared' or dumped in the desert. Now they are executed and displayed for all to see, so that it becomes a war against the people."

At another school, in the deserted resort of Rosarito Beach down the coast from Tijuana, an official visit is being put together on the tarmac basketball court. A fifteen-year-old pupil called Víctor Hugo at the Abraham Lincoln Secondary School No. 32 was gunned down in a narco shoot-out earlier this year, for reasons that are still unclear. And today, the recently appointed state prosecutor of Baja California, Rommel Moreno Manjarrez, has chosen the school to make a speech reassuring teenagers that there is a force out there trying to hold the traficantes to account. There are speeches to the children about how "the police are now with us, and there is new hope against violence," says the prosecutor. And the pupils applaud; "*¡Viva México!*" shouts one.

Moreno stepped into a difficult job when he became state attorney general in 2007. His predecessor, Antonio Martínez Luna, had stepped down after a video released in May of that year by a known drug dealer accused Martínez of protecting the Sinaloa cartel; he even had a nickname: "el

Blindado"—the Bulletproof. The trafficker in the video was found dead soon after it was released, so the veracity cannot be tested. Mr. Martínez, now reported to be living in the United States, has denied all connections with the Sinaloa cartel, but he stepped down and Moreno was appointed nonetheless to clean up the image of a pivotal office during a drug war.

It had seemed worth giving Moreno the benefit of the doubt. When we first met in 2008, he was immediately engaging, not least because he had studied law at Sapienza University in Rome and taken many trips to Sicily to learn from his mentor, Giovanni Falcone. He has an affable if somewhat vague manner, and we enjoyed sharing recollections of the great Falcone and speaking Italian in Tijuana. He remembered the campaign of another mutual acquaintance, the brave Leoluca Orlando, who mobilized a mass popular movement against Cosa Nostra called "la Rete," the Network. "This is what I want to see here in Mexico," said Moreno. "A culture in the magistrature similar to that in Italy, committed to going after the Mafia, supported by movements in the civil society like that organized by Orlando." It all sounded good, and I was hoping to talk on, toward an elusive point in the discourse, the bit about efficacy, arrests, and convictions. But Moreno did not make himself available for a follow-up conversation for weeks afterward.

Most mornings, I hovered about like a courtier at various official engagements that featured Moreno and a rolling dramatis personae like an acting troupe in repertory, also featuring Mayor Jorge Ramos and José Osuna Millán, governor of Baja California. The format was always the same: the panel sat in the shade of a large open-sided tent and applauded one another's speeches about combating the cartels, after which its members were served cool drinks by waitresses in high heels and miniskirts. On one occasion, launching a fleet of high-tech vehicles for use by the state police, that morning's edition of Tijuana's newspaper *El Mexicano* carried a front-page story about the murder of lovely Adriana Alejandra Ruiz Muñiz, a model and cheerleader for the local soccer team Xoloitzcuintles de Caliente.[6] The horrific scene of her death had been found filmed on the mobile phone of one José Carlos Meza, known also as "el Charlie" in narco circles, who had been detained and put under investigation by Moreno's department. Meza protested his innocence, claiming that Alejandra was an informant for the police, furnishing the authorities with information on Guzmán's man in Tijuana, Eduardo "el Teo" García Simental. Meza implied that Alejandra had been el Teo's lover, and provided what he claimed to be the name of the man who duly kidnapped and killed her. Alejandra's fingernails were pulled out and the bones in her fingers were broken during the interrogation, after which she was decapitated.

Meanwhile, Dr. Muñoz is inspecting Adriana's corpse on his slab. He is eager to oblige my request to join him while he conducts his autopsy, in order to develop and illustrate his decoding of mutilations with a visual aid. But Prosecutor Moreno's assistant says this is impossible, beyond the prosecutor's authority, a matter for the courts. Dr. Muñoz is annoyed, for he is considering this case carefully, weighing the various hypotheses, "that it could be the big narcos, as they say, or that this is a crime specifically against a woman, a so-called crime of passion by a common criminal, for what passion is more wrathful and violent than that of a man toward a woman he is obsessed with and cannot have? And this is, actually, my inclination in this case. I've looked very carefully at how the fingers have been broken, and it has not been done very well— you could almost call it careless, or reckless, and when the narcos are torturing an informant, the tracks they leave are never careless. They would have sliced the fingers off at the joints, not merely crushed them, maybe so as to send them to someone. But my job is not to pass judgment of this kind. I'm not a police officer, and the police do not ask me who I think did it, or why. My job is to make a report, and the rest is up to the prosecutors and investigators, and—how can I say this?—that's where the farce begins. The authorities don't look at any of this socially or forensically." Dr. Muñoz produces a bullet from a plastic bag and brandishes it between his thumb and forefinger. "If I find bullets from the same weapon in different bodies that are brought to me, and put this in my report, no one takes any notice. The narcos give us signs, they leave unique marks, like fingerprints, only the authorities do not heed them.

They have the files, they have the register of weapons, but they will not make an inventory, bullet by bullet."

Dr. Muñoz gets out a pen and draws four boxes, labeled "Me," "Prosecutor's Office," "Judge," and "Jail." "For every hundred bodies sent to me, twenty [killers] go to the prosecutor's office, ten go before the judge, and one ends up in jail—no, fewer; in less than one percent of cases do they ever get the real killer. And that one percent is probably not a criminal boss, it'll be the little guy. Meanwhile, they convict people for things they couldn't possibly have done." There are not many people in Mexico, or anywhere, brave enough to speak so freely and boldly from inside the system about their employer, but there is no stopping Dr. Muñoz. "There is a woman called Jacinta, from the South, a Mixtec lady, who is supposed to have kidnapped six armed federal agents all by herself. The strategy of the authorities is show business. They need to make a spectacle out of these cases—you can see, whenever they do catch a narco, they parade him, with all the drugs and guns. It is pure theater, to impress the president like I as a child tried to impress my father. To the press, they feed the phrase *presunto responsable*—presumed responsible. What on earth does that mean? Is that conviction by a court? It's a lot of rubbish. And all the while, I have these victims of torture and mutilation brought before me, knowing that they will never catch the people who did this. But I love my profession, I love my job. It combines medicine and law in practice: the corpse is my patient, and my job is to interrogate the corpse, to ask it questions. Because the dead cannot speak, I have to find ways of getting them to tell me what happened."

Tijuana is a strong city, and after all, the local Mexicans are still here even if the tourists are not. A "Fab Four" Beatles tribute is sold out. Taking your lady for a skinny-vanilla-frappuccino at a branch of the D'Volada chain—a Mexican Starbucks—is a cool date, especially if it has Wi-Fi so one need not actually talk. Sanborns is a landmark institution that characterizes any Mexican city, combining a restaurant and rendezvous with a small department store, and Tijuana's is no exception, brimful every Sunday lunchtime, its waitresses in their hallmark "traditional" costumes with wings on their shoulders. The Cinepolis is packed for the latest movie glorifying violence—fantasy violence—made in Hollywood up the coast. After reading so much Hemingway and D. H. Lawrence, I decided I really must sample a *corrida* at the bullring near the border fence by the sea, only to be reminded how little I admired either writer, failing utterly to feel any macho-libido rush as yet another bull is slashed according to plan and his carcass hauled off with ropes. But couples cheer, the band plays, and ladies wave handkerchiefs at the matinee idol matador clad in the regalia of Old Spain.

Far more authentic is the Sótano Suizo pub, which was heaving on the Sunday that Eduardo Arellano Félix was being flown to the capital, but not because of him. There was another, different arrival in Mexico City that day: the Chivas soccer team from Guadalajara, for the match Mexicans call El Clásico, against Club América. On screen in Tijuana, both teams unleash attack after attack in a tremendous game to the death, Chivas winning 2–1. A joyful Guadalajara fan in the bar, Adán, likens snatching victory in the capital and seat of power to "robbing your boss's house and fucking his wife on the way out." But the temperature of El Clásico was nothing compared to that eight months later for Mexico's make-or-break World Cup qualifying match against none other than its neighbor, the United States: the transborder Amexica derby. Quite apart from its complex piquancy on the border, there is history to this fixture. Mexicans find it hard to admit that Americans play very good soccer nowadays, and it is a deeply held belief that while the gringo subjugates Mexico, there is one thing that the boys in green do better than their northern neighbors: play soccer. Or so they thought, until a terrible night during the 2002 World Cup in Japan, when the United States dismissed Mexico 2–0 in a knockout round. The wound cut deep, and right to the top. Before the game, President Vicente Fox proposed to George W. Bush that the two might watch the game together at a venue on the border, as a gesture of friendship between the two nations. But the dismissive answer came back from an aide: since the game was being played in Asia, the president would be asleep at that time of night. America slept through its historic victory while Mexico was wide-eyed with anguish.

Now, with Mexico trailing the United States in the 2010 World Cup qualifying table, defeat today in Mexico City would entail a serious risk of shameful elimination from the finals in South Africa while the gringos sailed through. The Americans score first: Mexico 0, United States 1, in Mexico City. Adán from last time cracks the inevitable sullen joke about the boss robbing *your* house this time, and fucking *your* wife. But then Israel Castro equalizes with a glorious shot from twenty-seven yards, and with minutes to go, Miguel Sabah controls a perfect cross to score the winner for Mexico. Then one of those things happens, as they do, by word of mouth from bar to bar, colonia to colonia: head for the border. Which they do, by the thousands, on foot and in hooting, flag-waving motor-cades. They paint their faces, stick fingers through the fencing, and sing their songs. Finally, the whooping crowd blocks the frontier traffic cross-ing and six are arrested. "Look," says my friend Delgado, trying to ex-plain, "we clean their toilets, we pick their fruit and water their lawns. But we can beat them in soccer."

The gaiety in Tijuana even has a certain surreality: at the height of the killing in winter 2008, couples and excited parties of schoolchildren in pressed uniforms lined up to see a museum exhibition of mummies with preserved skin like parchment that stare hauntingly across the cen-turies from pre-Aztec Guanajuato. The crowds make no connection be-tween these cadavers and other events in town, somehow affirming that Mexican cult of death.

The Sunday crowds fill Tijuana Cathedral, outside which market stalls sell unmistakably Mexican devotional accoutrements: it may trouble the Vatican, but it is of deep meaning to many devout Mexicans that the Virgin of Guadalupe, national symbol and Empress of the Americas, can also represent Coatlicue, mother of the Aztec primary god. Such dichotomy—ubiquitous in the "folk Catholicism" practiced in Mexico—is incomprehensible to dogmatic Christians, just as the ambivalence of the

Mexican gods themselves was incomprehensible to the conquistadores, whose religion the Mexica incorporated into their own. During the Credo, in which the congregation proclaims its faith in "One God," a text message arrives to say that Eduardo Arellano Félix was arrested during that shoot-out at the villa. After administering the Host, Archbishop Rafael Romo gives an interview, despite having only just been briefed on the arrest himself by a whispering aide, on his way to the sanctuary. "It is a time of challenge for us, as Christians and as citizens whose quality of life and lives themselves are in real and immediate danger," he says. "The violence is now strategic, against all society, and this is the difference. Not to mention the problems that the drugs cause in our diocese. What we can do is offer resistance, and an affirmation of hope." Most of the narco aristocracy, and more than a few of the sicarios, though, are devout Catholics, or at least they go through the motions of devotion— baptism, church marriage, cash donations, and confession. There is even an unofficial narco "saint," Santo Jesús Malverde, a bandit with a Robin Hood legacy to whose shrine in Sinaloa devout traffickers pay homage with devotional pledges, *mandas*, in return for the holy outlaw's blessing. During the 1980s, the narcos actively aligned themselves with the church's conservative wing against priests advocating liberation theology.

Archbishop Romo is direct for a man of his austere authority. "They expect to come to us and talk about what they do. Our word to them is clear: we will talk about these things, these dangers. If they think they are religious, we will debate them, urge them to leave behind this evil and these activities against God. They are like those 'ultra' soccer fans who come to the stadium—they support your team but the club doesn't want them there to behave like that, but it is still your team and you are not supposed to turn them away. Moreover, it is not easy in the barrios for priests dealing with them face-to-face."

This was October 2008. Perhaps the bishop would have replied more severely had we spoken some months later, after a terrible narco execution in July 2009. Father Habacuc Hernández and two seminarians training for the priesthood were ordered out of their pickup truck on the road into Ciudad Altamirano, 180 miles south of Mexico City, and repeatedly shot. Hernández had traveled by horseback and truck for hundreds of miles across mountainous terrain to serve his scattered community. He was one of ten children from a poor family who had worked awhile, illegally, in Texas. Villagers believed he must have fallen afoul of instructions by the narcos not to meddle in their affairs.[7]

On the Day of the Dead, November 1, 2008, the daily *El Sol de Tijuana*'s front page looked like a heavy-metal album cover, with a hooded skeleton brandishing a scythe and a headline quoting a carefully timed pronouncement by the bishop: ROMO: LA SANTA MUERTE NO EXISTE— Holy Death does not exist. The archbishop was taking a public swipe in a popular paper at the cult in which the borderline is steeped, on both sides. Santa Muerte adorns car windshields, T-shirts, and mobile phone holders, and hangs as a silver pendant on chests all along the border. To the uninitiated, they look like trinkets from a Goth shop at Camden Market in London or the Lower East Side of New York, but they are not. Most cogent, wayside shrines to Santa Muerte, also called "la Señora de las Sombras," the Lady of the Shadows, have been erected on the outskirts of most cities skirting the border on the Mexican side. In these shrines, built as little temples, the hooded skeleton holds the orb of the world in one hand and her scythe in the other. She usually wears a crown or miter, and her cloak is often white, but sometimes it is painted in the colors of the rainbow. In some shrines, the skeleton is a real one, draped in fabrics. And around her, offerings are made: cigarettes, fruit, photographs of the deceased. Candles are lit to her, which bear her image on glass around the wax. Messages and petitions are written, asking for protection. Sometimes she is adorned with flowers.

This cult has its origins in the syncretism between Catholicism and pre-Columbian faiths and the cult of death, and has been dated to the eighteenth century. In the 1960s, the first public sanctuary to Santa Muerte was built in the poor Tepito neighborhood of Mexico City. In 2005, the cult was removed from the Mexican government's list of religious rites licensed to practice, and only since then has it captured the imagination of the criminal young, winning a rapidly expanding number of devotees among narco traffickers and the street gangs affiliated with them. Santa Muerte has become an icon to which drug dealers and killers plead for protection against their own death, a talisman and mass cult accompanying the war. Though Santa Muerte is regarded outside the country as yet another exotic piece of Mexican mumbo jumbo, the cult can make one's flesh crawl as one watches others pull over their cars and whisper their devotions to her at these shrines. Santa Muerte has a calculated didactic iconography. In mystical Catholicism, the figure of the Antichrist—the notion of Satan in the guise of the returned Messiah—is more terrifying than the devil himself, because of the deceit. Perhaps that is why the Antichrist is so rarely portrayed in Christian art (among the few portrayals is Luca Signorelli's very unsettling depiction in the Orvieto cathedral of Satan preaching to the prayerful masses, wearing a mask of Jesus). The point is this: all the accoutrements of Santa Muerte echo exactly the iconography of devotion to Mary in general, and the Virgin of Guadalupe in particular—the shrines, offerings, prayers, flowers, and candles decorated with her image. Santa Muerte is not, like satanism, an inversion of the faith. Rather, she wears the garb of faith—like the Antichrist, she is not an inversion but a masquerader.

In conversation, most priests are afraid to fathom the cult and its potency, while authorities are afraid enough to attack it both legally and physically. In Tijuana, almost all the roadside chapels that stood in 2008 had, by the summer of 2009, been demolished—by the army, said Mayor Jorge Ramos, though the military will not accept official responsibility. Demolished, but not gone. One especially prominent shrine had been erected above the concrete sweep of the Abelardo Rodríguez Dam. I remember the shrine, high above the reservoir: painted white, with low front walls through which one could enter into a space for offerings and pleadings for intercession—the "saint" looking out from behind a real human skull, adorned with a head shawl of rainbow colors and wearing a miter over which necklaces of beads were strewn. The hideous figure usually clutched a bunch of fresh flowers, regularly laid. The shrine is now demolished, jagged masonry and broken bricks, but there remains a defiant shrine within the rubble, crammed with candles bearing the image of Santa Muerte, a few of them still burning. The butts of cigarettes given in offering are lined up in neat rows, wedged in the broken stonework. Cigars have been left, and personal trinkets. To the side is a mound of empty glass votive candleholders, most of them decorated with the familiar figure, evidence of the hundreds of people who have been this way since the destruction. And there is more: messages painted on the shrine's toppled walls, now scattered across the terrain: "Though they destroy you, I still believe in you." "They have taken my child, my parent, my penance, my condolence." Watching us all this while, guarding the rubble of the shrine, is a black Ford F-150 truck with darkened windows and a CD hanging from the rearview mirror. The next day, I return to find a different vehicle, a Toyota truck this time. I wander over, cheerily, dumb gringo complimenting the shrine. The truck's passenger window is open, and there are two men sitting inside. The younger looks straight ahead, out the window, at the shrine. The older man turns toward me, stares, nods twice, and stares again. *"Vete a la chingada"*—go fuck yourself—he says nonchalantly, and without further word flicks the electronic switch to close his window.

The Day of the Dead in Mexico is syncretism in action, a profoundly charged entwinement of ancient faiths with imported Christianity, of Aztec communion with the underworld with the Catholic days of All Saints (November 1) and All Souls (November 2). Elaborate meals are cooked, and special breads baked to share with the departed in cemeteries. Musicians are hired to sing them ballads and laments, toys are brought for dead children, special prayers are whispered and rites observed. Most feasts across the country are held in cemeteries, but in Tijuana this can be the occasion for a family reunion astride the border itself, by the beach where California and Mexico meet. This may sound more idyllic than it is. The turquoise ocean looks distantly seductive, but this is a scrappy piece of land divided by a mesh fence, which is the border—across and through which families sit down for picnic lunch, one half on the American side, the other in Mexico. This is the last stretch of fence along the whole border as flimsy as this, and during earlier visits to Tijuana, it was an evening pastime to come down to the *playa* and watch people climb over and run for it. In the past, boys sometimes posed atop the fence, balancing, while family members or tourists took pictures, before darting into the United States, knowing that the Border Patrol, the *migra*, would catch some but could not catch them all. Another favorite crossing point was a dry cement canal running between Tijuana and the United States, along which so-called roadrunners would hurtle at dusk, timing their sprint across the *territorio de nadie*, no-man's-land, between passes by the migra patrols and helicopters above.[8] These days, fence hopping as a spectator sport at sundown is over; it ended after the Clinton administration mounted Operation Gatekeeper in 1994, overseen and enforced by the U.S. attorney in San Diego, Alan Bersin, now border czar for President Barack Obama. But the crossings continue and so do the picnics as a matter of weekend ritual, especially on the first day of November.

The Giovanni family assembles: Salvador Giovanni on the Mexican side with his daughter-in-law, Jessica, holding her baby, Jorge, so that the child's father, her husband, Ricardo, can play a game of finger tickling through the mesh (the international frontier) with his son and catch up on his wife's weekly news from the southern side of the border. Salvador's daughter, Chantelle, a student of criminal justice at San Diego University, has also come to the U.S. side "for the first time, when I heard that my brother could meet his wife and baby at the fence," along with her boyfriend, Luis—so it becomes quite a Sunday reunion, only with an international border running through it. "It sure is a picnic with a difference," says Salvador in perfect English, cutting his son a slice of watermelon to a size that will fit through the fence. Dollar bills as well as tamales get passed to and fro through the border. "Some of us can't get across at all, and others who did cannot go back again if they return to this side, like my son-in-law. He made it over, got a job, earns money, and sends most of it back—what father of a girl and grandfather of a little baby in this town is going to have a problem with that?" Salvador "spent a while over there myself, working in Los Angeles. But they were different times. We used to come and go as we pleased. For ten years, I worked in an auto shop and came home every two weeks." Not any longer. Jessica and her husband kiss through the wire, she lingers a moment, sadness flickers in her eyes, Dad tickles his baby, and it's time to go. "I gotta work," says Ricardo, and slouches back across the parking lot. However, says Salvador Giovanni, the United States will soon end these traditional Sunday picnics and replace the mesh fence with the reinforced version that already runs for more than seven hundred of the twenty-one hundred miles of border. It is concentrated at and around urban centers, so that these family assemblies become a vulnerable point in America's defenses. "But the thing is," says Salvador, "there's always a chance," and he gestures toward a no-man's-land at the fence's edge, near the ocean. "Every six or seven days, a big group just makes a run for it and the Americans know as well as the Mexicans that they can't catch everyone—there's always a few who'll dodge the cameras and infrared lights, and God bless 'em."

Some make it, others are caught and deported—after hours, days, sometimes years in the United States. An afternoon at the border dump for deportees, fenced off from the *click-clunk-click* of the turnstile through which thousands of pedestrians cross the border every hour, shows most of the deported to be like Natalia González, age thirty-eight, who lived for twenty-two years in Los Angeles making batteries before a check on documentation by the immigration authorities. "There's work here in the maquilas," she says, "but my son's in LA, so I don't know what to do next." There is another small constituency among the deportees, whose numbers, says Victor Clark Alfaro, for years a campaigner for human rights in Tijuana, conceal a minority extremely useful to the cartels: "They speak English, they have contacts across the USA, many have been in gangs like the Latin Kings and Mexican Mafia, one-third have been in prisons, they know about drugs and how to use weapons. They cover up their gang tattoos when they cross, are dumped without work, but quickly find it."

A man with teardrop tattoos arrives, the kind of tattoos you get as a gang member or in prison. Julio César is a confident and friendly, if intimidating, alumnus of the Huntsville prison in Texas, America's capital of capital punishment, where he served time for dealing in amphetamines. "You're looking at my tattoos, ain'tcha?" He speaks the obvious with a blend of menace and amusement. "Yeah, I got 'em, and you know what for, don't you—ha ha." César is not going to elaborate, but that's all right. It was explained to me in a scary quarter of East Los Angeles by gang members with teardrop tattoos that for each person you killed, a teardrop was filled in. They were a form of initiation into and protection by the Mexican Mafia or some other gang inside and outside jail. César sheds many tears of ink, two of them filled in. He says that in the three jails in which he served time in America, "I got looked after by the *raza*" (the race, as Mexicans call themselves by way of assertion in the United States), "by the brotherhood." By which brotherhood? Mexican Mafia? Latin Eagles? Latin Kings? I ask. "Now that'd be telling," says César, but he concedes, "one of those." It is a conversation I probably could not have had were César not in the compound and overseen by the police— and that he cannot continue for the same reason. César was due to be deported in 1993, but the prison lost his records, he says, so he re- mained inside until 2001, got deported, slipped back into California for five years, and was caught again: "just because I like to smoke." Now back, "I'm going to get whatever work I can find here in TJ that'll get me the money to get back there," he says. "I have some contacts. TJ's cool, only there's no way for an honest man to make a living, if you understand what I'm sayin'."

Others who cross the border are never seen again: they are never greeted by the relatives to whom they were headed, nor are they received back home, unless it is aboard a plane, in a coffin paid for by the Mexi- can government. For some in Tijuana, el Día de los Muertos 2008 has a special purpose, which is to pay homage to those who died in the deserts of America on their way to what they had intended to be a better life— the theme that dominates and defines the next stage of this book's jour- ney along the border. The procession of homage in Tijuana is by those who survived the journey but were deported, and assembles at the Scal- abrini hostel, which receives deposited, homeless deportees from the United States. Each marcher carries a white cross bearing the name of a compatriot who died attempting to make it to the United States—of ex- posure in the desert, heat or cold, thirst or hunger, attack by bandits or

venomous snakes, even suicide. The deportee marchers walk as far as
the Mexican side of the fence, onto which, after saying prayers beside a
little shrine of flowers and candles, they affix the crosses. "Lord, hear
our prayer," chants the Reverend Luis Kendzerski, "for the migrants and
the poor, the abandoned and the dead, of the border." Of every ten who
die, he says, two are women or children.

East of Tijuana, through Tecate, along Mexican Highway 2, there is the
first of many heart-stopping moments on this journey. The heat of early
afternoon rises from the land below the road and across the desert,
stretching into Southern California and on, it seems, for eternity. Hues of
red, pink, and burnt sienna wrap the distance, ascending into the smoky
blue haze of sky as it meets the horizon. There is complete stillness in
the apparently boundless landscape. On the Mexican side, the road
leaves Tecate onto a high mountain ridge and on the Californian side a
parallel border road winds through leafy glades to a lonely but hospita-
ble little town called Jacumba with a spa motel, and into the cauldron of
Imperial Valley. Here, the crossing into Mexico connects two towns with
names that place both of them didactically in Amexica: called Calexico
and Mexicali, California and Mexico spliced and shared. Much of the
Imperial and Mexicali valleys lies below sea level, and the twin cities
cohabit in a geological bowl in which air is trapped, so that neither the
pungent stench of livestock, feedlots, and fertilizer on the U.S. side, nor
the waft of chemicals drifting on the breeze from Mexicali, can escape.
Though this is a desert, Imperial Valley boasts some of the most produc-
tively fertile farmland in the western United States, thanks to the All-
American Canal, running from the Colorado River and benefiting farmers
on both sides of the border, due not only to intended irrigation but also to
an unforeseen life source in the Mexicali Valley: seepage.

Water seeping from the canal created wetlands in the desert that
have been pumped from the ensuing aquifer by farmers on the Mexican
side and used to grow crops. Until, that is, April 2009, when the rebuild-
ing of the canal along twenty-three miles of watertight concrete was

completed, saving an estimated 3.1 million acre-feet of water per year.[9] The canal lining was seen by Californians as a popular environmental and economical recovery of lost water for use by farmers in the Imperial Valley Irrigation District and domestic taps in the Metropolitan Water District of San Diego. Except on the border, in Calexico, which sided with the outraged Mexican farmers. Former mayor Alex Perrone argued that "economically, if Mexicali loses, we will watch Calexico die. We're near totally dependent on the development and spending power of more than a million people on the other side. If the water goes, the farms suffer and the industries suffer. And if they suffer, Calexico suffers." And so, concludes Perrone, who was born in Mexicali, "We opposed the lining of the canal. Water is scarce, and our joint community has been developed around what has been available. Now the farmers are losing land over there, because the water is limited. This'll stop creating jobs, which means you contract the economy. It impacts on the agribusinesses, the people who sell the seed and fertilizer, or supply and maintain the machinery, and then it will impact us."

But in this sweltering valley, and across the land to the east, water—*agua*—has a significance way beyond matters of irrigation and farmland. For something else, more urgent, is afoot: along Highway 98, the road from Interstate 8 down into Calexico, the temperature rises higher above 100 degrees with every mile, and blue plastic tanks have been placed along it at regular intervals. Above them fly blue flags, and each is marked AGUA stenciled in white paint. There is a connection between these water posts and a plot in the cemetery at Holtville nearby, where those who died in the desert without a name are buried. This road takes us out of California now, into Arizona and on to the narrative that lies behind both the water stations and the cemetery—that of the desert as graveyard. What is happening here has nothing to do with the canal, and even a few drops of agua can make the difference between life and death.

3

EL CAMINO DEL DIABLO (THE DEVIL'S HIGHWAY)

There was a northern road, cut wood-blackened and flower-sided;
wing feather bowstring, down feather bowstring-sided. On that
side, north, bad were my thoughts. And I uprooted it, broke it,
threw it down, stamped on it. Thus you may wish and plan, vari-
ous kinsmen. —*Opening speech in preparation for war,*
Tohono O'odham tribal ceremony

The hinges of hell would cool this land; it is a pyrexia and breathlessly still. Not a zephyr to disturb the simmering air. The desert has a vast indifference to it—insouciance, in the grandeur of heat and silence—which has to do with its extremity and its timelessness. The perpetuity of this land has infinite unconcern toward anything or anyone with the audacity to try and survive. And yet even the immutable desert abounds with defiant life. Beneath the mesquite trees, creosote bushes, and agaves with blades like drawn swords are thousands of holes in the dust, some burrowed by kangaroo rats to escape the sun. These animals have kidneys that can reabsorb water and concentrate urine so as not to lose fluid; their nasal passages have evolved to recycle any moisture from breath they exhale. Also invisible until the impenitent heat has abated are kit foxes, whose dens are so ubiquitous that it seems there must be hundreds of them in just two square miles. Not so: this animal changes dens frequently, and changes vixens with every season, but never leaves its terrain and always rests underground during the day.[1] The spindly branches of the ocotillos appear like a fan of parched, dead sticks—only they are alive, hibernating, feigning dry death. They would spring to verdant life with the slightest fall of rain or during a desert storm, for weeks if not months, storing the water, then return into their disguise of mummified kindling. And when its leaves do grow, and flowers that look like flames blossom from the stems, there is a spike behind each tiny leaf, to punish and warn off any thirsty animal tempted to steal its moisture with a refreshing bite. The teddy bear cholla cacti, backlit, look as cuddly as furry toys, but their spines are barbed and stick to anyone who brushes against them. Their big cousins, *Cylindropuntia fulgida*, aka the jumping cholla, have treacherously weak joints that can dislodge themselves and, it appears, fly into the skin, implanting their spikes within it. Then there is the Arizona barrel, with fishhook spines that can bury themselves into your flesh and cannot be removed. At dawn and dusk, rattlesnakes appear along the pathways, flicking their forked tongues, and the wilderness echoes with the haunting range of howls, yaps, cries, and growls of the coyotes—songs of the trickster in Native American lore, one of the most resilient, cunning, and adaptable of all animals on earth, even in this barren land. In the legend of the Navajo, north of here, the First Coyote flipped a blanketful of stars into the heavens, creating the Milky Way.[2]

In this xerosis of the land, anything left to desiccate in the dust cracks underfoot like old parchment. Discarded snakeskin lies by the wayside, dry as burned paper. The stillness itself is immense, broken only by the occasional dart of a lizard across a rock, or the flight of a black-and-white-backed woodpecker through the cavity it has excavated into the wall of a mighty saguaro within which it nests and whose fluids it extracts. The only persistent movement is on high, circling eagles on the fly, ready to dive at any chipmunk or jackrabbit with the audacity to move across country at this time of the afternoon. Or else vultures, seeking those who could not make it. In the distance lies a boundless world and a constant drama of color and light, of predator, prey, and survival. The immensity stretches into the Cabeza Prieta, or Dark Head, mountain range of western Arizona—black volcanic peaks laid bare by millennia of erosion, and colored a smoky indigo as evening considers its options. There are other dark colors, from granite and mica, which beneath the unrelenting sun create a haze of navy blue across the wild: the Diablo Mountains, Growler Valley, Scarface Mountain, Black Mountain, Gunsight Hills, Alamo Wash, John the Baptist Mountains . . . As Luis Alberto Urrea writes, "the poems on the map read like a dirge."[3]

The esteemed Mexican naturalist Exequiel Ezcurra writes that his "work in the Gran Desierto changed my stereotype image of a competitive nature, where killing and conquering was the rule for the survival of selfish genes, into a different and somewhat opposing view: Life is driven not by contest, but by symbiosis and a drive for reproduction. It is not so much about supremacy as it is about co-operation of organisms and passion of the senses."[4] And that is all very well, but for an animal or plant to evolve and endure this terrain takes millennia of natural selection and mutation. To be a frail human in this land is quite another matter, for over all this presides the sun. There are some scattered signs of *Homo sapiens*. Off a hiking trail running through the Buenos Aires National Wildlife Refuge in southern Arizona, abandoned: empty plastic five-liter water canisters, grimy shoes, soiled fake Nike tracksuit zip-tops, school backpacks with pictures of Hannah Montana, a shaving set, exercise books, used batteries. Most poignant of all, a pocket photograph album, the images bleached, just discernible, showing a group of people smiling at what appears to be a celebratory meal of mostly seafood. There are three men with mustaches, three big ladies in their best dresses, another man playing a guitar. These things are discarded slices from a journey being undertaken out there, in the baked distance.

This trail of dust—which winds south from Wellton, Arizona, over the Mohawk Canal, and out across the air force's Barry Goldwater bombing range and Cabeza Prieta National Wildlife Refuge—was named by Spanish explorers who used it as an exploratory route north from their mission at Caborca, now in Sonora, in the mid-sixteenth century. The name, marked in square Y-23 on the map of Yuma County you buy at the gas station, is el Camino del Diablo, the Devil's Highway.

El Camino del Diablo was an ancient trail first laid by Pima tribes native to the Sonoran Desert, but the route was pioneered for the historical record by order of Francisco Vásquez de Coronado, governor of Nueva Galicia, initially in pursuit of a mythical cluster of seven cities of gold called Cibola. The missionary and explorer Melchior Díaz is said to have set out from Coronado's encampment near Caborca, to seek Cibola and establish a route to the Sea of Cortez, into which the Colorado flows. The hardships encountered by Díaz's expedition earned the road its name. It was mapped more than a century later by the man whose memory remains ubiquitous across northern Mexico and southern Arizona: Father Eusebio Francisco Kino. Father Kino, a seventeenth-century missionary, philosopher, and astronomer, converted, but also defended the rights of,. the Pima and was the first to chart not only the Devil's Highway but also the water springs along it, called *tinajas*. Knowledge of the tinajas ensured the survival of the Pima, and the instinct for locating them separates real desert people from transient inhabitants and boarders even today. In 1775, a band of two hundred colonists under Juan Bautista de Anza endured the highway's hardships on their way from what is now Tubac, Arizona, to found the city of San Francisco.

The Devil's Highway won back its name in May 2001, when fourteen migrants recruited by criminal "coyotes" in the Mexican state of Veracruz were found dead from dehydration and exposure. Their smugglers, heading from a border crossing west of the Mexican town of Sonoyta for the Arizona town of Ajo, became hopelessly lost on a doomed meander across some of the most unforgiving terrain along the Devil's Highway.[5] The last stragglers were rescued in an operation no agent at Wellton's little Border Patrol station will ever forget, just south of a lovely palm-lined oasis and aquifer of water from the Colorado, and a service station on the freeway called Dateland that sells date milk shakes. They were just fourteen among the many who die, but in Mexico they were, absurdly, turned into folk martyrs by the country that exports people—through desperate poverty—across the border into America.

There are names for the players in this business of people smuggling: the migrants are known as *pollos*, chickens, and those who recruit them therefore *polleros*, chicken runners, working for *coyotes*, who control the networks. Bottom of the criminal ladder are the *guías*, the guides, who actually do the walk. To the Border Patrol, the migrants are "wetbacks," even if all they have crossed is sand, otherwise "bodies," "wets," or "tonkies." Mexicans use the word *mojados* themselves: literally, wetted. The Border Patrol, of immigration police, is of course *la migra*.

The causes of migration from Mexico into the United States—about which much has been written—are deep and many, but are all variations on the theme of extreme poverty in criminally unequal Mexico, the lure of the economic superpower along its northern border, and that country's demand for cheap labor. The first Mexicans came in flight from the revolution of 1910 and to fill jobs created by World War I, leading to the establishment of the Border Patrol in 1924. During the Great Depression, as now, opportunities for work shrank and migrants were made less welcome, only to return dramatically with World War II. Such was the demand for cheap labor after 1941 that the U.S. government devised the Bracero Program to regulate it (the name comes from the Spanish word *brazo*, arm), whereby employers could register immigrant workers and pay them specified wages for specific work over specific periods. The demographics and economics of the modern border began as many employers preferred to use it as cover to pay lower wages to illegal immigrants, while the migrants themselves would settle on the Mexican side of the border rather than return to the interior, in order to sign up again for further work in the United States. With the war over, migrants continued to flow north, so that the United States felt obliged to mount Operation Wetback in 1954, a roundup of illegal "aliens." The abolition of the Bracero Program in 1964 led directly to a second and even more momentous defining step in forging the border's population and economy: an agreement between Washington and Mexico City the following year to allow the building of the maquiladora assembly plants on the Mexican side of the line, "bonded" for duty-free export across the border. The scheme, a precursor to the North American Free Trade Agreement, was devised primarily so that American corporations could pay third-world wages just across the southern border, and in Mexican terms to find employment for *braceros* returning home en masse, but remaining on the frontier.[6]

The direct cause of the deaths along the Devil's Highway in 2001 was a sudden exodus of migrants from the time-honored border crossings into San Diego, El Paso, and cities along the Rio Grande Valley into the deadly wilderness, in response to the boldest offensive against illegal immigration the U.S. government had hitherto mounted. In 1994, the Clinton administration escalated Washington's perennial battle with Operation Gatekeeper in San Diego, Operation Hold the Line in El Paso, and Operation Rio Grande in the valley: three fronts that constituted a genesis of the process intensified by President George W. Bush after Al Qaeda's attacks of September 11, 2001. President Clinton's operations proceeded chronologically from west to east, with Gatekeeper overseen by the U.S. attorney for San Diego and Imperial counties, Alan Bersin, in spite of his favorite description of the transborder community as "San Tijuana." Gatekeeper brought the first stretches of the present-day border fence, night-vision cameras, infrared spy cameras, a reinforced Border Patrol, and high-tech sensors that could detect movement. And it worked: by the end of the decade, figures for arrested migrants had plummeted—in the cities. But from the point of view of those who smuggled migrants, as well as those being smuggled, Gatekeeper did not force them to suspend operations; they simply bypassed the concentrations of fencing, technology, and Border Patrol, and rerouted along el Camino del Diablo.

The fourteen pollos who died near Wellton were only a tiny portion of what Enrique Morones, founder of the humanitarian organization Border Angels, which placed those blue water stations along the road to Calexico, believes to be ten thousand people who have died in the desert since the inception of Operation Gatekeeper. But numbers are of as little use on the border as they are in the desert. There is no way of knowing how many have crossed and died, or how many have crossed and survived— how many corpses will never be found for each one that is. Or how many Mexicans or Central Americans are still illegally but busily working away in America for each one who is dead or deported. All we can know is what a friar called Francisco Salazar already knew in 1650 when he wrote that el Camino del Diablo was "a vast graveyard of the unknown

dead . . . the scattered bones of human beings slowly turning to dust."[7]
There is no sign of the exodus along this widened Camino del Diablo
abating—only of it becoming better organized, and exposed to different
dangers and cruelties, now that narco cartels are taking over the business end of things.

The Reverend Robin Hoover of the First Christian Church on East
Speedway Boulevard in Tucson leans back in his chair, feet on the desk,
soles in my face, and describes his many good works. He dismisses de-
scriptions of the efforts of others, like Morones and his Border Angels, as
"exaggerated." He points out that I "must be the thousandth journalist"
to interview him. "CNN were here only last week." But there is a reason
for his attitude. He has saved lives and gathered valuable information
that no one else in America has compiled about deaths in the desert.

During the 1980s, the decade of President Ronald Reagan's support
for military regimes and fascist militias in South and Central America,
an ecumenical cadre of clerics together with some five hundred congre-
gations based on the border, and in a network across America, organized
the Sanctuary Movement to protect political refugees from death squads
in El Salvador and Guatemala, and the murderous U.S.-backed regimes
in Chile, Argentina, and elsewhere. After his time with the Sanctuary
Movement, Reverend Hoover went on to establish and run another organization, Humane Borders, which agitates on behalf of migrants and organizes the placement of lines of water stations throughout southern
Arizona, and especially along what Hoover's data shows to be the new
corridors of death. One is across the land of the Tohono O'odham Native
American tribe, their "reservation" across which the border now cuts
like a gash, cutting off its people on the U.S. side from Mexico, and vice
versa. The other is a corridor running either side of Interstate 19 between Nogales on the border and Tucson, seventy miles north. These two
corridors account for 42 percent of recorded deaths in Arizona, says
Hoover, which in turn account for half the total deaths along the entire
border. The clusters of corpses on Hoover's screen show, he says, "that

although we had an overall reduction year over year until 2007, the numbers of migrants dying is now on the rise again. If the Border Patrol and new security measures were effective, the numbers dying would be dropping. But they are not. In the mid-2000s, we were seeing one hundred deaths a year. Over the last three years [to 2009], that figure has increased to two hundred, and the reason is that, as we can see from this diagram [he flicks to another chart], the more the roads are patrolled, the more the migrants cross more remote and dangerous terrain. The deaths occur farther from the roads, where you may be less likely to get caught but also less likely to make it." The collation and analysis are estimably thorough: maps from 2005 show that the majority of deaths occured about three miles from paved roads. The latest figures show them at least five miles away. "The distance from the roads where people are perishing has nearly doubled," says Reverend Hoover. "We are the authority for mapping this shit out—the government doesn't do it." In August 2010, details of the work by the Pima County Chief Medical Examiner's office were published, showing the migration crisis to have totally transformed its work, with 20 percent of its examinations performed on border-crossers. The office had "admitted" 1,700 corpses over the preceding decade, and 81 for the months of June and July 2010 alone.

Hoover calculates that "up to twenty-five percent cross using contacts they know—relatives or cousins—people concerned with the well-being of everyone in the group, should anything go wrong. That leaves a huge majority, about seventy percent, in the hands of the coyotes, whose only interest in getting you there is a bit of extra pay, but who will not wait if something goes wrong, walking across country where a twisted ankle is a death sentence."

The fourteen dead on the Devil's Highway in May 2001 had used as their point of departure the border town of Sonoyta. At that time, Sonoyta was abuzz with human traffic, the main square bustling with movement. Coaches from the interior disgorged load after load of people from the South, ready for the journey. The town was full of flophouses where itinerants could stay cheaply and be picked up by prowling polleros and coyotes. Now Sonoyta is quiet—uncannily quiet. The town seems to have shut. El Chapo Guzmán chose Sonoyta as the location right on the border to deliver an order, according to U.S. intelligence, that operatives for his cartel "use their weapons to defend their loads at all costs" while crossing into Arizona.[8] Guzmán was said to have convened an inner circle to deliver his morale-boosting rap right here, fifteen minutes' walk across the border from Lukeville, Arizona. So, observes a dentist in Sonoyta, "the polleros have gone. This is now a place for another kind of crossing. You will see them only at night, and it is a good thing not to see them. From here, the bad guys now transport drugs, not other people." The *Ajo Copper News* on the U.S. side gives a weekly update on shootings in Sonoyta, while the sheriff's log is a litany of drug seizures. For the pollos, says the dentist, "you need to go to Altar."

Altar, some thirty miles southeast of Sonoyta and sixty miles back from the frontier, is by no means the most dangerous town in the borderland, but it is one of the eeriest. There is no way of arriving in Altar without being thoroughly checked out, heart in mouth, for there is no reason why a gringo like me would be in this place other than to pry into its main trade. Altar is the new hub, in the western half of the borderland, for the arrival of migrants in transit from southern Mexico and Central America. In the heat of late morning, stalls along the sides of the square and up the backstreets are selling the equipment needed for the crossing and ordeal ahead: black backpacks, black T-shirts, camouflaged combat pants, flashlights—and, of course, the necessary spiritual protections: key rings, prayer cards, and purses for change bearing the image of the Virgin of Guadalupe and San Judas Tadeo, cousin of Jesus Christ and the patron saint of lost causes, to whom one turns in time of difficulty.

Throughout the town are flophouses of the kind found a while back in Sonoyta—shelters where migrants pay between $3 and $5 for a bunk bed made of wood, used blankets, and the possibility of a mattress stained with dried semen and sweat. There are dormitories like those on Panteón Street, into which we are not admitted by an administrator apparently nervous about the men lounging around the reception area—polleros plying their trade, preparing to bake chicken in the desert.

There is one shelter, however, that is free and where there is a welcome, the Centro Comunitario de Atención al Migrante y Necesitado (CCA-MYN, the Community Center for Assistance to the Migrant and Needy), supported by the diocese of Hermosillo, the state capital. The center, clean and wholesome, is run by Marcos Burruel, who was once a quality control supervisor at the brewery in Tecate, using his sense of smell to pick out a substandard brew, but who now uses similar instincts to prevent anyone who has been drinking alcohol to sleep here, or a pollero disguised as a migrant but looking for customers by conniving his way into the dormitory. At CCAMYN, there are clean mattresses and linen. Outside is a carved plaque and dedication: A LOS CAÍDOS EN LOS DESIERTOS DE LA MUERTE—To the fallen in the deserts of death. EN MEMORIA DE AQUELLOS QUE POR BUSCAR UNA MEJOR VIDA / LO ÚNICO QUE ENCONTRARON FUE LA MUERTE—In memory of those who searched for a better life / But the only thing they met was death.

We sit and talk while the shelter is closed during the day. "How different it was when I was a boy here," recalls Burruel. "There were no fences, and people would cross and come back, cross and come back. Which they still do—there's much more coming and going than one hears about. Most get taken straight off the bus; the coyote is waiting there. They're cunning. The migrant may say, 'I'm looking for Roberto, or el Tigre,' and the coyote will say, 'I'm el Tigre's friend,' and make a fake phone call: 'Hey, Tigre, your people from Chiapas have arrived.' And if they don't want to go, they're sometimes taken with violence and held until they pay. The authorities don't give a shit, and do nothing. Besides, there's always a deal between the police and the coyotes: the police can get one hundred pesos for each migrant, which is more than they earn working for the police."

Burruel estimates that "about eighty percent of the people who cross know of the dangers, but the rest don't have a clue. From here to Tucson or Phoenix can take them four to five days, but the coyotes tell them it'll take three to four hours. It's become a dirty business. Not just the heat, but kidnapping. Every day there's kidnapping, here in Altar and the desert. They kidnap the wetbacks [Burruel uses the word *mojado*, although he is Mexican and though there is no river here] and ask for ransom. They hold them for days, weeks. I have no way of knowing how many just disappear. They kidnapped and held a crowd of them in that house just across the street there." He gestures behind him, through the window.

Burruel, a slight man wearing a beige shirt, talks about his work and his charge with a certain detachment, as though such an attitude may protect him from the many people in Altar who disapprove of him and of whom he is clearly afraid. "The migrants are here because they're eager to cross, but know nothing apart from what they heard back in the villages, where they see the coyote as someone important. In some ways, I'm here to help them in this madness: I feed people, give a bed to a few—but I must also make them aware of what's about to happen. I warn them about kidnapping, show them videos about the dangers. And some do change their mind. They see the films and decide to go back. One time a man kept asking to change the video, and that's how I knew he was a coyote infiltrating the shelter. That's how my trouble begins.

"What I do here," he continues, "angers the coyotes. If I talk about the dangers, this upsets them." But, as he has implied, it is more serious than that. "Here in Altar, other people have come who are part of organized rackets, to kidnap people—criminals who are not coyotes but related to the drug-trafficking cartels. The drug smugglers use Altar too, to stash and transport drugs and to tax the polleros. And this is very dangerous for me. They insult me, threaten me, tell me they're going to kill me." Burruel is suddenly haunted, loses his detachment, and confides, "Since I got my job here, I've been terrified of the night."

Most of the narcos and coyotes working Altar are from Sinaloa, says Burruel, as are the *bajadores*, bandits who come with guns and rob people before they cross. What his conversation drives toward is a recent development: the traffic in migrants between here and the border-crossing town of El Sásabe is being taken over by the cartels. "The narcos control the frontier," says Burruel. "From here to Sásabe, the coyotes have to pay a tax to the Mafia, which they collect from the poor pollos, between seven hundred and twelve hundred pesos [$55–$95] for each. If they don't pay, the narcos stop the truck and beat the hell out of the driver, maybe beat the migrants and burn the bus.

"So why do I do this job? I must be crazy, I know. It's not because I think it matters, because it doesn't. Actually, what I try to do is pointless, against their business. It's because I believe in God, and because the priest is a friend of mine. But I'm only human, and of course I'm afraid. I'm also, by the way, a postman, and must do my rounds now." These rounds delivering mail, he says, afford a break, a breath of air beyond the stifling claustrophobia of this deceptively sleepy town, apparently calm but saturated with the movement and violence of which Burruel speaks.

But there is more to learn. In the thicket of backstreets behind the square is a shop selling clothing, aimed like every other at the migrants' needs, but a little less like a military surplus store than the stalls: there are children's clothes and sun hats that are not black or camouflage. The shop is run by Amanda Ortiz Reina, wife of a man I had met briefly when he was mayor of Altar a decade ago, Francisco García Atén, a schoolmaster who had warned then that drug dealers would move in on the smuggling of migrants. In 2009, Mrs. Ortiz herself campaigned to win the office her husband occupied until 2003, on a ticket challenging the power of organized crime in town, but she was beaten by her rival, Rafael Rivera Vidrio, who refuses to see us.

Mrs. Ortiz, by contrast, admits two unannounced strangers rolling up on her doorstep—after a brief but visible sizing up—and makes sweet tea, to drink with cakes served on a tray with a paper doily. She came to Altar when she was twenty, to marry, in a city "where everyone knew each other and supported one another." Most of the population "worked in the fields, like my father, and no one got rich from the collective farms, but they fed us. It was companionable, and we lived in symbiosis with the desert." But now, "incomers from Sinaloa have taken over the town and subjugated the local authorities and police. This has escalated even over the past two or three years; things have changed even since the government began the offensive." So far as the cartels are concerned, Mrs. Ortiz posits tentatively, the terrain is contested between Guzmán and those loyal to the Beltrán Leyva clan, now allied to the Gulf cartel. "While they fight each other for the plaza, they both extort from the migrants up to one hundred dollars per head smuggled, I understand." But there is a twist to the cartels' involvement. As they swing their organizational muscle behind migration, so "it becomes more efficient. And safer, in some ways, though not in others. Our indications are that there is less rape by the coyotes, less robbery by bandits, less harassment on the way to the drop houses, less of anything that will attract the authorities' attention to the drugs or get in the way of the money. But there is a terrible price to pay for this. Once they reach safety, the migrants are at their mercy."

Then Mrs. Ortiz reverts from this distant menace to what is before her. "My greatest worry for our town is that children along the border are growing up with this as their world. My sons used to play in the streets; now that is simply too dangerous. We're terrified of the kids from Sinaloa, but the criminals become role models for the young people. When I ran for mayor, the old people wanted me, but the young people voted against me. When we used to go into town campaigning, there would be kids twelve or thirteen years old, with walkie-talkies, reporting on our movements—to whomever. The truth no one wants to admit is that the young don't want to take a stand against what is happening. They're happy with this new culture, these new opportunities; they're growing up with it. Many parents have left, leaving us who remain scared, alone, and frustrated. We're afraid to talk to our neighbors, because we're unsure who we are talking to." As we look around her shop, minibuses heave by, up the little street and out across the land where the buckhorn cactus changes color in response to stress, turning purple in times of severe drought or cold, then blooms in the many colors of fire during spring—the desert's mixed messages to those about to cross it.

They sit in what shade they can find around the main square and wait, plan, figure out the next move. They are people in flight from what they have left behind and in fear of what lies ahead. Some are on their way out, others on their way back. The latter have less to lose now and are readier to talk. "We knew the risks, and we took them," reflects Ramón from Tabasco, who has now crossed twice and been deported twice, "and that's enough." Ramon has spent $1,200 paying coyotes since he left home near Villahermosa four months ago, "and there's nothing left. I have nothing for it but to go home, where there is nothing." There are a lot of "nothings" in that sentence, *mucho nada*. Ramón has a tooth missing and wears a pale blue shirt and a smile incongruous to his lot. He worked the land back home, "where it's very beautiful, but I couldn't feed my family, I could hardly feed myself." The second crossing was the worst, says Ramón's friend Víctor from Chiapas, with whom he teamed up on the bus from Villahermosa. "The first time we crossed we were picked up by the migra as soon as we found the main road. We were back in El Sásabe within three days. But the second time, it was hotter, we walked longer. The first guides knew their way, it was just bad luck the migra spotted us. But the second pair were useless, a pair of *pendejos* [idiots]. They thought they were the real thing, but in the end they were *cobardes* [cowards, weaklings] who argued between themselves. After two days, we were still on the Indian reservation, they said, when we should have been near the freeway services where the bus would take us to Phoenix. We were spotted by helicopter, and this time all the migra were Mexican, real *sábelotodos* [smart-asses]—kids like I would walk past in the street back home, but they called us all kinds of shit."

People in Altar embarking on their first journey across, on which they have staked their life, are edgy and some do not want to talk at all. Groups of boys with tattoos and cropped hair switch their conversation to an indigenous language as soon as we approach. But one man, Rodolfo, manages a joke. He is traveling with two cousins to join his eldest son in Minnesota, where, he says, "I've heard about the cold in winter and how it'll kill me, but now I'm more worried about the heat." The bridge home, to Jalisco, is burned: "All I own I have put into this journey," he says. "I sold my house and my animals to pay the coyote and to buy clothes and things we need for the trip. Yes, I know the risks, but we have to take them; I cannot sell even the little I grow anymore. The prices for produce are so low I'm paying to grow it, so we'll pray all day and leave before dark."

The road from Altar to El Sásabe, across a spectacular landscape called the *sierrita*, is a route to take during daylight. A sporadic flow of rickety white minibuses crammed with migrants and open-backed cattle trucks with wooden slats to contain the human load account for the only traffic to speak of. Minibuses kick up dust and our Arizona plates get us waved down and pulled over by men in bomber jackets and jeans. There is no demand for money, no sign of weapons, but there are plenty of questions, nods of disapproval, and partial belief at the answer that we are researching migration patterns—one does not mention drugs or trafficking around here. And there are stories told, whether true or false, with menace: about a hamlet called Los Molinos where a car full of people was "shot off the road, with everybody killed." Ten miles on, approaching El Sásabe, the incinerated skeleton of a minibus adorns the roadside. During 2010, swathes of the land across the horizon of buttes visible from this road became "no-go" areas, in to and out of which people could not travel, with access routes barred by roadblocks manned by gunmen from either the Sinaloa or Beltrán Leyva cartel—and villagers completely cut off.

The town of El Sásabe is set slightly back from the border, giving the migrants a diagonal line to walk before they cross, hoping to avoid the concentrations of agents around the town of the same name in Arizona. It is low-slung, a main drag of buildings made of bricks or hastily applied cement, including the Super Coyote café selling fresh water. The migrants line up at a makeshift hut to register with a branch of the Mexican public safety ministry called Grupo Beta. These men and women wearing orange T-shirts and driving orange jeeps have a peculiar role, a kind of migrant services branch of the government's social welfare administration, the Desarrollo Integral de la Familia. Grupo Beta agents take the names of those crossing, lest they be needed or never heard of again. They fill the migrants' water canisters and even provide maps of the U.S. side, where there is disquiet among the authorities as to whether Grupo Beta is helping to save lives or facilitating, if not encouraging, illegal immigration. One agent, called Alemán, remarks that "we are doing the best we can. We're not encouraging them; we just try to stop them from dying." He says that "the flow of migration has slowed down, because it's getting much harder. We all know now that just over there, not only are the Border Patrol waiting for them, but even the National Guard." And waiting in numbers recently increased by the Homeland Security secretary, Janet Napolitano, who was, until summoned by President Obama, governor of Arizona, the promised but parched land, receding up the Devil's Highway. A group of migrants hunker down in the dust, wearing black hoodies and carrying their backpacks, and joke that it is in the interest of Grupo Beta to help them, because if they make it, the government benefits from the money they send home. But if they die, the government has to pay for the coffin and the plane to carry it. "That would be the first time the government did anything for me," cracks Jorge, a young man from Chilpancingo. "If only they had given me that kind of money when I was back home!"

Only one trafficker is prepared to mumble a few words. Introducing himself reluctantly as Mario, he is a lean youth with spiky hair and a T-shirt reading METAL ROCK ON. He says between cigarettes that he had been doing this for two years, after losing his job in Ciudad Obregón in the south of the state. "I'm good," he assures us, but adds nervously, "You can write that all these people will make it to Phoenix," as if he could know. One's mind runs back to the famous guide Antonio López Ramos, who accompanied those who died on the Devil's Highway in 2001. He was identified by all the survivors as having a thatch of dyed red hair, for which he was nicknamed "Red Rooster," and was apparently as cocky as this young man in El Sásabe now, who even echoes López's reported dress sense. Eleven miles of wall are under construction here: steel poles that mark the frontier as it disappears through scrub and creosote, being filled with concrete and standing four inches apart, a dust service road along the American side—nothing but desert grass to the south. Suddenly, about four miles west of the hamlet, it stops, and the border continues as a line of squat metal posts, around and over which the migrants will go, into the furnace.

The journey had been easier than Vicente Sánchez Morín feared.[9] A bus arrived as promised to take him and a cousin from Cintalpa in the west of Chiapas to the airport in Tuxtla Gutiérrez, from where a charter plane flew them to Hermosillo. "I had never flown," says Vicente. "That was the only time I was scared, before we crossed the border." From Hermosillo, another bus drove them to Altar, though there had been a breakdown and short delay at a place called San Agustín—Vicente remembered the name because it is the same as his brother's, whom he was to join in Denver. Agustín had a good job, or jobs, in Colorado: working fields and orchards during summer, fixing cars and casual shifts packing meat in winter. The crossing at El Sásabe had been "easy," said Vicente. "We went at night, the guide knew where he was going." By now, they were in a party of ten, including a man from Apizaco, in Tlaxcala, who said nothing and whom Vicente did not trust. "He wore a black T-shirt and camouflage pants, he was always watching people, he never talked or seemed worried." A minibus duly appeared, Vicente could not remember where, but we worked out it would have waited for them at Arivaca, twenty miles from El Sásabe, with a connection to Interstate 19. Vicente saw the lights of Tucson at dusk, "and I thought it was Phoenix already. They told us in Altar that's where we were headed and I'd told Agustín to pick me up there." The van arrived in Phoenix during the heat of afternoon in May 2009—Vicente did not know where, although "I know where it is now," he says, safely in the care of a church group. "I've been back to look at it a couple of times."

When the van arrived, the group of men were corralled into the back of a building in the outskirts of town. "There was a group of four people waiting for us, and they were scary to us. By now, I had been separated from my cousin, at the place where the bus picked us up in the dark. The mood had changed. It wasn't like they were trying to get us to our relatives; it was like we were going to jail." Weirdly, "the man from Azipaco, who we had thought was one of us, knew them, like he suddenly switched sides." The windows of the house were blackened, the door locked, the men left alone. "Everything had gone wrong. I had no idea what was happening. Some hours later, more men came, with guns. These were completely different people. They were wearing masks, while the other people we had dealt with until now showed their faces, though they never told us their names. They'd had nicknames; the one who took us through the desert was called 'la Flecha,' the arrow. Now I was really scared. Then they took all our papers, our money. Two days passed, maybe one night and a day. I tried to keep count with a man from Campeche. It was only when I finally found Agustín by telephone that I realized what was happening. It was almost more terrifying for him." Agustín had been contacted by telephone and asked for $3,000 to buy his brother's freedom. "He panicked completely. He hadn't expected anything like it. He'd sent me a thousand dollars for my trip, and hadn't anything like that kind of money. He was running around, asking anyone he knew. They told him that if he didn't find it within a week, they'd kill me. I knew nothing about all this."

Vicente is a rugged man who looks older than his age of thirty-two, though he is physically fit. He tells his story in the office of a church as though it were happening to someone else. He wears a clean shirt, pressed slacks, smart shoes with buckles on them. Vicente is one of more than one thousand people from Mexico and Central America whom Phoenix police have freed from captivity—in the city becoming known as the "kidnap capital of America."[10] Out of 368 kidnapping cases handled by the Phoenix Police Department in 2008, says spokesman Tommy Thompson, 78 were calls to migrant drop houses. During the first six months of 2009, another 68 had been identified or raided after emergency calls. In a raid on another drop house in the suburb of El Mirage, conditions had been even more frightening, some thirty men kept half naked and pistol-whipped, their relatives shaken down for $5,000 before the property was raided in June 2009.[11] This is the delivery end of the narcos' takeover of the migrant business, using their contacts in the drug distribution network, based on street gangs and family associations, to recruit those prepared to hold migrants for ransom. Phoenix, now America's fifth-largest city, has long been a destination for Mexican migrants, especially those from Sinaloa. According to the police department, Sinaloan gang members cruise the bars in Phoenix frequented by people from their towns back home, Culiacán and Los Mochis, recruiting for migrant kidnap operations, offering to pay cash advances with the balance payable upon receipt of the ransom money. As the mortgage market crashes, so the work is made easier by the number of properties to rent, which has increased by 75 percent since 2000.

"We waited, and after a day they brought us some food," says Vicente. "They had provided water, but no food until now. A woman came to help the men give it out. She told us she was 'cooking for them,' but I think I know what that means. This time a man showed his face. They needed more money, he said, and they asked us for the names of the relatives waiting for us. A man said he wouldn't give it, and they hit him, and told him, 'If you want to live, give us the name and number.' I gave them Agustín's number in Denver, which I had learned by heart."

After four days, police stormed the property, without major incident. "It happened quickly and suddenly. They took our names and arranged for our relatives to be contacted. I didn't know how the police found us; I know now, but I'm unable to say." Vicente, which I do not think is his real name, avoided deportation by agreeing to testify against the man from Tlaxcala. For the moment, Vicente is safe in Salt Lake City, protected by his church and U.S. law enforcement. Vicente will probably get deported, says the pastor looking after him at the evangelical sect to which Vicente belonged back in Mexico. And if so? "I'll try again," says Vicente. In October 2010, the cost of the cartels' takeover of migration could be counted by the single worst massacre of the entire war to date: the summary execution of seventy-two migrants, mostly from Honduras, held at San Lorenzo in Tamaulipas, at the other end of the border. Believed to have been kidnapped by the Zetas, the group apparently refused to pay the extra levies demanded and paid with their lives, apart from sole survivors who lived to bear witness to the atrocity.

The agricultural center of Caborca, ten miles west of Altar, is regarded as the Spaniards' point of departure along el Camino del Diablo. The histories have it that the expedition set out from an Indian village near Caborca, leaving the possibility that this may have been Pitiquito, where the loveliest church in the area nestles between the backstreets of town and fields beyond. The cool and the damp, musky scent of plaster and stone inside the chapel of the Misión San Diego de Pitiqui, give relief on a baking hot afternoon, especially when the walls speak, as they do. Built in 1687, the aisles were decorated in 1719 with frescoes depicting Death and Glory, a magnificent eagle's head representing St. John the Evangelist, a bull's head for St. Luke, a majestic Virgin of the Apocalypse, and a skeletal figure of all-conquering death, pointing the way toward the Resurrection by prophesying the exact month and year of Christ's crucifixion, as in the Book of Daniel.[12] "All the bikers want their photo taken underneath it," laughs the priest, Father Claudio Murrieta. He is in his midforties, handsome, energetic, forever at work around the fields or at his computer writing a history of this corner of Sonora. Pitiquito was an Indian village, where a mission farm was established, run by the church, while Altar was a military garrison—different foundations which led to very different histories. Altar became a city of commerce, legal and illegal, while Pitiquito remained agricultural, a place of orchards and crops: cotton, wheat—and, eventually, asparagus. But this last was emblematic of what has happened here since the government of President Carlos Salinas de Gortari ended the system of village landholding, privatizing communally owned lots of farmland known as *ejidos* during the 1980s and allowing agribusinesses to take over the peasants' plots. "Asparagus is new here; it is the big-business crop that takes the nutrients and leaves the land barren. It is typical of the system we now have, exploiting the land and the people, bad production for quick profit and low wages."

We set off in the priest's truck to survey the scourge of poverty that followed President Salinas's privatization of the ejidos—and the ensuing arrival of narco ranches on the land. The initial buyers were big landowners who turned the self-sufficient peasants (who were also small traders in their produce) into serfs or the rural unemployed. It is about this process, and its devastation of Mexican agriculture, along with NAFTA, that Father Murrieta is writing his book. "This is a route I do every day," he says, "to keep an eye on what's happening." Which is, he says, "that the average Mexican salary in the fields is fifteen pesos

[about $1.20] a day," in a country where prices are not far below those in
the United States. We pull up at a hamlet called La Estación, beside a
disused railway line in the shadow of the spectrally beautiful Cerros
Mountains. Another of President Salinas's rickety ideas was to privatize
Mexico's railways, selling thousands of miles of track to American freight
rail companies and ultimately closing the entire passenger network. Behind us is the old station, once a bustle of meeting and greeting, arrivals
and departures from this now still and subjugated community, the building in ruins.

Father Murrieta greets a woman putting her washing through a man-
gle, chickens clucking around her ankles on the scrap of land surrounding the shack that is her home. "She once farmed this land herself, when
it was communal," says Father Murrieta. "But the privatization was
a precondition imposed by the Americans for entry into the free-trade
zone. The peso collapsed around the same time, and none of the peasants could afford even a slice of land. So first came the big ranchers with
political connections, then American agribusiness, buying up vineyards
like that one, owned by a winery in California." He points to rows of
vines climbing the hillsides. Dogs lie in the shade of the mesquite trees;
in a yard, a girl gets ready for a date, washing and applying makeup beside a tub of water with a cracked mirror balanced against a rusty pump.
Along the dirt road adjacent to the railway line, posters have been
erected by the rival political parties, the PRI and PAN, for an upcoming
election. The candidates' faces beam out at the hamlet. "They're just
messing with the people," scoffs Father Murrieta. "There's no difference
between them, so they agree to fight it out with each other for the right to
steal from the village." We agree that this is hardly a phenomenon
unique to Mexico. In the yard of a bigger house with acacia trees in front
of it is parked an incongruously brand-new SUV with tinted windows.
Father Murrieta shrugs. "It's not hard to spot the ones who are working
for the narcos, but these are just the foot soldiers. After the landowners
and the Americans, the narcos came, needing to clean money and stash
drugs. They may keep horses, but obviously they don't farm."

In late October 2009, an agricultural union leader called Margarito

Montes Parra, who had tried to defend the rights of peasants, was ambushed by gunmen and killed while visiting Sonora. The Worker, Peasant, and Popular General Union of which he was president is based in Oaxaca, but Montes Parra was trying to organize fishermen off the Sonoran coast and arbitrate disputes involving the Yaqui Indian tribe. He had repeatedly criticized the authorities for protecting narco traffickers, and his son Adrián had also been shot here in Sonora in 2007, a murder the authorities said was linked to narcos buying land. On October 30, Montes was leaving a ranch with a party of families when a convoy of three trucks sped by, firing AK-47s at the small crowd. In all, fourteen people were killed, including four children.[13]

This war has butchery for its badge, or cachet, and it was also not far from here that a massacre of unimaginable brutality took place. A white SUV was found abandoned, and inside it a stew of mutilated bodies—hacked, chopped, castrated, decapitated—literally cutlets of severed head, arm, leg, and torso crammed into the vehicle with no relation one to the other until they were matched by the forensic police. Unpublishably gruesome pictures of the discovery and its aftermath were taken by the authorities, showing the deeply disturbing sight of human pieces laid out on a tarpaulin across the floor of a hangar. It is a scene from hell from which even Hieronymus Bosch in his most vividly imaginative moments of pious terror would have flinched.

We drive through this terrain with Father Murrieta, the Cerros cloud-capped in mid-distance, and pass a compound by the old railway fenced off by chain link topped with barbed wire, with a gas cylinder and trucks and trailers parked up on the gravel within. "That's them," Father Murrieta says, "transferring and loading up drugs; they don't even bother to hide it." He accelerates, for this is not a place to be caught snooping. Soon, there's a fine-looking ranch with a wide gateway and horses visible behind a fence along the driveway lined with cypress trees. "That's another," says Father Murrieta almost nonchalantly. "You're now driving past quite a big operation. They have some fine stables there, but that is not their line of business." He confirms Amanda Ortiz's diagnosis: the warring factions here are the Sinaloa and Beltrán Leyva cartels, the latter representing Los Zetas' western front. We tell the priest that we slept a second night in Caborca, wary of Altar, to which Father Murrieta retorts, with laughter, "You fell for the appearance of things, did you? For sure, you're more likely to get kidnapped in Altar, or your car hijacked. But there's a much greater chance of getting killed in Caborca, even if it looks quiet. It's far more dangerous, because that's where the infrastructure the narcos need is located, distribution centers, support industries— packaging, transport, that kind of thing." He points past a burned-out cotton mill, American owned now but deserted. "There's an important archaeological site over there, which no one can visit now since a narco bought the land."

Father Murrieta is now livid and needs some refreshment. The advantage of being a parish priest in Mexico is that the old ladies of the village are delighted to cook lunch for he who nourishes them with Communion each Sunday. Father Murrieta registers no objection as we are welcomed into María Bonilla's little house for a hearty meal of pasta, seafood, and beans, with a bottle of Tecate for the priest, over which he tells a funny story. The father had always wanted, he relates, to go for a beer-drinking holiday during the Munich Oktoberfest, and recently he made it. There had been a convention in the Veneto, after which most of the faithful wanted to go to Rome, "apart from the priests!" he jokes. So Father Murrieta and a friend headed for Bavaria, "and we lived on beer and potatoes for a few days. They had glasses *this big*!" He raises a hand above the lace tablecloth to illustrate the height of a stein. "But, oh dear, the hotels were so expensive. We used to go up to the airport and sleep there, on the seats, then back to the *bierkeller* in the morning. Which was fine, but if I go again, I'll save up for a bed."

Of the two "corridors" along which Reverend Hoover's charts showed people dying in the largest numbers, the more deadly was the land of the Tohono O'odham—Desert People. For this Native American tribe, smuggling, and the U.S. government's war against smuggling, constitutes just the latest chapter in a history of striving against—and living with—

subjugation and persecution ever since the white man, first Spanish, then American, stepped on its ancient land. The O'odham were a people from what the Spanish called the Pimería Alta region, unified by traditions and the O'odham language, but for centuries the tribe lived in groups without tribal government or centralized secular leadership. The O'odham had no formal laws; individuals and families were expected to maintain "order and proper decorum, and people who went against customs were asked to leave," writes the historian of the tribe, Winston P. Erickson.[14] They farmed with no idea of private land ownership but were constantly raided for goods, food, and women by people they described with the O'odham word for "enemy"—"Apache." Their land was crossed by the Coronado expeditions, missions were established by the Spanish, and colonization accelerated after the discovery of mines in Sonora. The O'odham were quick to show an interest in the growth of wheat as a crop, and European tools with which to grow it, which led the Spanish to think they might be potential converts to Catholicism. In the last years of the seventeenth century, the tribe was caught between the Spanish military's abuse and the favor of Father Kino, whose shrine at Magdalena in Mexico remains a pilgrimage route for many O'odham Catholics. When the Spanish moved permanently onto their land in the early 1700s, in search of gold and silver, the O'odham came to distrust them, hiding their sources of precious metals—and the Spanish responded ruthlessly and violently toward the O'odham and their neighbors, the Yaqui. In 1821, both tribes exchanged Spanish for brief Mexican rule, and in 1848 the border between the United States and Mexico was drawn across O'odham land. "The splitting of O'odham land between two countries inconvenienced the O'odham somewhat, but it would be many years before strong enforcement of border policies would occur," writes Erickson, with understatement. Under U.S. law, he continues, "the O'odham had few or no rights as intruding Anglos took what they wanted and ignored the rights of the native peoples."[15] By the turn of the century, the killing and destruction of the O'odham and their ways had begun in earnest. The reservation was designated across forty-eight hundred square miles, as cut off as it was expansive, and the cash economy ravaged the O'odham and Yaqui ways of living, as many native people migrated to Tucson in search of employment as construction workers, railroad laborers, or domestic servants, or to the copper mines of Ajo. During the 1930s, the first border fence was erected, although the O'odham remained—and remains—the only tribe in the United States that enrolls Mexican citizens and allows them to vote in tribal elections. The tribe is one of the poorest in the southwestern United States, with an average annual family income of $8,000 and about one-third of its citizens unemployed.

When the world's press descended on southern Arizona after the deaths of the "Yuma 14" in 2001, the Tohono O'odham tribal authorities greeted visitors with pride and courtesy. The chairman, officials, and employees of the tribe discussed education and the dilemma of retaining the native Uto-Aztecan language and culture while giving young O'odham a chance in modern America. Now, attempts to contact the tribe officially disappear down a black hole—messages to its gatekeeper, Pete Delgado, hit a brick wall. America's most respected and tenacious reporter on Native American affairs, the indefatigable Brenda Norrell, through an estimable website called Censored News and others, is constantly hammering at the door in search of answers to questions about abuse of land, heritage, and people by construction of the border fence, and about where profits go from casinos operated by the tribe, most of whose members live in extreme poverty. The generous inference is that tribal affairs are private, and privacy must be respected. The less generous interpretation of the stonewalling is that things are happening of which the tribe is aware but that are unfit for prying eyes. "I'll say it on the record," Robin Hoover had said back in Tucson, "because I can and I have, and few others would. There's a degree of complicity in the smuggling of drugs and people." In the eyes of some tribal members, their authorities have, ironically, done something even more serious: having vowed to oppose yet another invasion by the white man in his attempt to reinforce the border with fences and hundreds of agents, they have instead cooperated with the militarization of their own land. The tribe is again exploited, caught again between a rock and a hard place, between smugglers exploiting the poverty of its people and U.S. authorities trying to stop them.

People cannot be silenced, however, and where there is grievance, the courageous talk, whether out of rage, pride, despair, or all three. Mike Flores is one such person. "Who are you?" he asks by way of introduction, in the inimitable way Native Americans ask the question, with an implied inquiry after one's ancestry. Flores is a Native "Amexican" in the deepest sense. He lives in a trailer on a patch of land behind the roadside café on the main highway through Sells, but his father comes from Quitovac, across the border carved through his tribe's ancient land, and migrated north to Ajo in the United States—just west of the reservation—to work in a copper mine. Flores's mother was born beside a natural spring in what has since become the Organ Pipe Cactus National Monument park, adjacent to the border on the U.S. side.

Flores is a true son of this land we are calling borderland, but with an identity that precedes any borders and transcends Spanish colonization, Mexico, the arrival of the white man, and the United States. Spiritually, he feels close to the Mexica, calling himself a "traditional," which is one who follows the ancient belief of his ancestors, as opposed to what are called "progressives," who converted to and still adhere to the Catholic faith. "My grandfather told me: this is our way, the four directions, the four winds and what we call the him'dag, the way, the journey. When I went [to Teotihuacán] to see the pyramids, I felt part of *that*," he insists. "Those people were looking at things the way I do, they saw it the way we see it, and that's not surprising, they came from here." I foolishly mention the journey to Tenochtitlán of the Mexica from around here, but Flores scoffs. "Oh yeah, people have all these anthropologies and sociologies and all kinds of 'ologies,' but I'm an O'odham, not an 'ologist.' All I know is what I was told by my father and grandfather, which was what they had been told by their fathers and grandfathers: that I can rub the dirt on my face anywhere between Alaska and Mexico City, and call it me, because that's where I come from." The uniquely complex and beautiful emblem of the Tohono O'odham tribe portrays the human journey within the scheme of the him'dag: a small figure, representing birth, stands atop a circular maze that winds, via an ultimate point in the far corner of the pattern, to a "dark center" of eternal life, in which one is cleansed and reflects back on knowledge gained during the journey. The O'odham paper *The Runner* reports that him'dag is now a popular subject taught in school on the reservation. Pupils are said to look forward to the special day of the week when traditional food replaces the usual junk served at lunchtime.

Flores learned how the creator god I'itoi led his ancestors from the underworld up into this land. He would call months *masads*, or moons, the first being the "eda wa'ugad masad," backbone month, beginning with the winter solstice to commence an annual cycle divided into halves, with its midpoint the summer cactus-wine feast on the longest day.[16] During the 1970s, Flores recalls, he became involved in the militant American Indian Movement. "I still feel the war, like it never ended," he says, wearing an AIM hat when we meet for breakfast in Sells. "Right behind my trailer is where the U.S. army set up its first base on our land. And sometimes at night it's like I can hear our warriors preparing for battle. The past is very close by around here, you know—it's with us all the time. And the ancestors are watching to see how we deal with this latest situation. The land has fallen sick from being raped over and over. First the white man, then the border, now ninja guys prowling around, helicopters flyin' over making the people and the horses scared." Flores spits words of fire but with an expression of deep calm that is disarming and compelling, his vocabulary ablaze, but his eyes wide, his voice soft.

The Border Patrol has Flores's unmitigated contempt. "They come from Texas, South Carolina, upstate New York, and they don't know jack shit about this land. They act the tough guy, but if you put any of 'em out on the land under the sun without their toys, they'd be dead in two days. I can walk for weeks across this land, light and dark, 'cause I know it, I know where the springs are and what to eat. We've been close to the land for all time, we understand these things—how the birds hatch, how the water flows, how lizards stay cool in one hundred and ten degrees, so we can imitate them. But these guys, they think they're big boys but they ain't nothing on this land." Which makes it even more offensive to Flores that "they're interfering with him'dag, the way itself. We can't get the elders from the Mexican side to perform the sacred rites because they don't have the papers. Last year, we held our traditional ceremony, and it's the custom for our warriors to hunt a pronghorn deer; it has to be caught, cooked, and eaten in the correct way. But last year, the Border Patrol drove up on the warriors, handcuffed and detained them for eight hours, for having a weapon on their homeland." Such audacity is "overstepping the line," fumes Flores. "It's part of the same shit that gets these kids in gangs who are twenty-one, twenty-two years old, using drugs and alcohol, and I get on my soapbox and tell 'em that's not the way, that's the way the white man sent us. He taught us that to get anyone's attention you gotta show 'em a thousand dollars, and that's what it's come to on the rez. Whoever offers the money gets their way." This affects the tribal authorities too, says Flores. "There's a switch in tactics. At first, the tribal leadership opposed the border fence. But they feel more confident now, against us of the old way, 'cause they've seen a little money in it. Now they're happier about cooperating with anyone who wants to trample on this land, whatever they're messing in."

We drive south, off the main highway running parallel to the border and down the road toward the frontier, marked with an arrowhead as INDIAN 19, leaving behind the shacks and trailers, the land rising so that we are surrounded by agave, chollas, mesquite, and creosote. To the east, a conic mountaintop rises above the other desert peaks along the ridge and pierces the horizon like the tip of an arrow itself. Flores says, "That's Baboquivari, which our ancestors considered the center of the universe," and one feels a strong sensation from the passive but passionate way he says this, and from the mountain itself. "It's the land that keeps us going," he says again. "We and the land are the same." We pass a compound of buildings and a holding pen for people, labeled LAW ENFORCEMENT AREA, out of which a bus bearing the name and insignia of the Wackenhut security company tears toward and past us. This is one of the vehicles that commute between the law enforcement area and the border, taking illegal immigrants apprehended in or rescued from, depending on how you look at it—the expanse, corralled and now shipped to the border and dumped on the other side to make their way back to Altar whence they came. "One time," says Flores, "the tribal police stopped one of those buses and found the guards had stolen a tortoise from the desert. You know, to keep as a pet, a beautiful desert tortoise. That's how they see our land."

After nineteen miles of Indian Highway 19, the paved road veers left toward an outpost community of trailers called San Miguel, clinging to the border, while we take a dirt track to the right, at the end of which is a clearing in the desert scrub, containing a Border Patrol van, an electronic surveillance tower, fence made of steel poles of alternating heights, and a heavy electronic gate. This is a pedestrian thoroughfare that is not an official "port of entry" but a passageway for members of the tribe only, upon production of ID. Behind it is an old fence made of sticks linked by two strands of rusty wire, intended—with little success, usually—to stop cattle wandering between the United States and Mexico. This latter was the border until recently. And beyond both these frontiers, across earth identical to that on which we stand, lies a place with two names: Flores calls it the continuation of ancient Tohono O'odham tribal land; the world beyond the tribe calls it Mexico. "On the weekend," says Flores, "there used to be a market here. People would bring stalls and line them up along the border and sell tacos and clothes and stuff over the fence. That doesn't happen anymore." The markets, recalling those Day of the Dead picnics at Tijuana Beach—themselves soon to be a thing of the past—are hard to imagine in the empty silence under the gaze of the Border Patrol and, no doubt, its quarry of smugglers on the other side.

On the edge of Sells is Poltergeist Lane. No one seems to know its real name. It was baptized by the gangs that patrol it and tag the empty houses: POLTERGEIST NORTHSIDE reads one graffito. This is the newer housing on the reservation, considered better than the trailers or shacks in which many O'odham live. One of the local gangs, explains a boy putting up a flyer for a tribal rock poetry event in the café, is called the Dream Walkers, because "they can kill you in your sleep, by spiking your dreams with curses and stuff."

"There's a lot going on out there at night," says Angelita Ramon, who lives at 18 Poltergeist Lane, pointing past the creosote bushes. "A lot of people coming through the wash right there, a lot of drugs coming through. I hear them, and it keeps me awake." But Mrs. Ramon's sleeplessness and struggle arise from the impact of all this movement on her own family. In the living room of her house, two daughters busy themselves with housework, cooking, and television, but her three sons are present only as portraits on the wall. One "committed suicide after the police took him into the desert one time and gave him a hard time. He was so mad at them, he killed himself; he was sixteen," says Angelita. A second, Joseph: "He's in jail, in New Mexico . . . they say he shot . . . you know . . . oh, I don't know . . . He's very protective of me now, always calling to see if I'm okay." And there's the third, Bennett, who died a death so strange and unexplained "it's driving me over the edge."

At four thirty in the morning of Tuesday, April 9, 2002, Bennett Patricio, Jr., age eighteen and known as BJ, was walking home to Sells from a party following a baseball game. He turned from a dirt track onto the main road near a village called Cowlic, where he was struck by a Border Patrol vehicle and killed. Ever since, his mother and his stepfather, Ervin Ramon, have insisted that Bennett stumbled upon a drug transfer involving members of the Border Patrol, and was killed after making a getaway run. It would not be so far-fetched: the FBI's Operation Lively Green in Arizona and the associated Operation Tarnished Star in Oklahoma resulted in ninety cases being brought against serving soldiers and government agents for drug smuggling in this region; among them were thirteen guilty pleas entered during a single trial in Tucson in 2005, including a National Guard sergeant, Robert Bakerx, jailed for smuggling cocaine and getting other soldiers to do so.[17] Between 2001 and 2004, sixty-nine members of the military, Border Patrol, prison guards, law enforcement, and other public employees were convicted of accepting bribes to help smuggle cocaine.[18]

After years of tribulations through the courts and the emergence of court papers naming two drivers behind the collision who were never called as witnesses, the Ninth Circuit Court of Appeals in February

2006 and May 2007 rejected the family's suit for unlawful death. The driver concerned was ruled not criminally responsible for killing Bennett Patricio. Applications to talk to the Border Patrol about the case, as well as the wider issues of migration and rescue, for this book were informally accepted during approaches made locally but later declined by Washington.

"Year after year, the pressures have eroded who we are as an original people," says Ofelia Rivas, organizer of O'odham Voice Against the Wall, a campaign against the means of fortification of the border. "Now, it's not just a border," she says, "it's a wall across our land. It stops people crossing, including our elders, and has already disturbed our burial sites. Some of our ceremonies are in Mexico, and I can't go. We've had tribal members on the American side arrested and deported while visiting relatives on their own tribal land, because they came from Mexico and didn't have the right papers. It's even disrupted the pathways of mountain lions, which have to find new areas of habitation because they can't migrate. This is our ancestry, not a kokopelli on someone's coffee mug! I'm fifty-three years old, and fifty-three is just fifty-three—but even I can remember when we got water out of water holes, and had to understand the land in order to eat and organize the year. I saw it all change during the eighties and nineties—the young people became lost, television took over our lives, then the militarization. Twenty years from now," Ms. Rivas predicts, "our children will look back and say, 'That is when it happened, the second destruction of our people.' And it's all happening at such speed, after so many thousands of years. For all time, we just went to what's now Mexico and visited families, and people would come here. The authorities don't seem to realize that we have the spirits walking before us when we have to do these things. You must understand that we feel the eyes of our ancestors upon us and have to explain to them that our history's being eradicated at this pace." On the road off the reservation, into Tucson, a sign with a picture of smiling young O'odham reads, WE LIVED AND SURVIVED THE DESERT FOR MORE THAN 500 YEARS. WILL WE SURVIVE THE NEXT 500?

Some twenty-eight thousand O'odham live on the U.S. side of the border and only an estimated two thousand on the Mexican side, most of whom prefer to be called by the name the Spanish gave them, Papagos. Toward their villages, through the Sonora desert, is some of the most majestic land in the Americas, over which tower the saguaro cacti, monarchs of the desert, and the organ pipes, with rounded ribs and fruit from which the O'odham make jelly, wine, and seed meal. As do the people of Quitovac, which lies up a track from the main road between Altar and Sonoyta. Quitovac is a village of fifty people, the largest single Papago settlement on the Mexican side, with a kindergarden that prepares children for "Mexican school" in Sonoyta. A woman called Leticia keeps the little village bodega, selling tortillas and household basics. She says that "teachers come from Sells to run special programs in O'odham traditions and culture, but the children tend to lose it when they grow older—and hardly ever go over to the American side because they get arrested if they don't have papers. They'll grow up as Mexicans, and go to Sells only if they need to see a doctor at the hospital . . . Most of our families are on the American side, but it's hard to visit them, and almost all traditional activities happen on the American side, apart from religious pilgrimages. Most of us here are Catholic and make pilgrimages to Magdalena more than the traditional sites. Most of us still like to be called Papagos, like our parents called us, not O'odham." This is more significant than it may seem. For while Flores and Rivas feel quintessentially of the borderland in its most ancient sense, with their identity endangered by the white man, and now the materialism of the cartels and the fight against them, the O'odham on the Mexican side seem less discontented, even though their culture has been more thoroughly eroded by Hispanic culture and religion.

Sitting on a chair outside his home is Eugenio Ortega Velasco, age seventy-eight and the last man to speak the O'odham language in Mexico. "At least I think so," he says. "When I was young, I moved around the whole territory, both sides of the border. There was work on the U.S. side, and we used to go all the time, to and fro, and to visit family. Then, one by one, all my brothers and sisters went to work in the U.S. and never came back. Nothing much has changed since then, apart from the fact that it's very hard for most people to cross the border. I could if I wanted to"—he produces a pass with his photograph on it, valid for a year—"but I don't feel the inclination. It's so much trouble, all those guards." He folds his dog-eared letter from the Department of Homeland Security with a dismissive air, puts it back in his pocket, and adjusts the brim of his hat as the sun sinks low. Then he shifts his chair for no reason and continues staring out in silence across the desert, from the porch of the house in which he was born.

The Tohono O'odham's cash-cow casino, on an annex of the reservation called San Javier, south of Tucson, is packed this summer Saturday night. The song belting out beneath a full moon after a thunderstorm is "Contrabando y Traición"—Contraband and Betrayal—and it is the one the audience has been waiting for. The young people on the lawn behind the amphitheater whoop and sing along; the elderly folk and families in the more expensive seats "rattle their jewelry." The number, with its swaying accordion and rollicking bass line, is about a couple, Emilio and "Camelia the Texan," smuggling drugs from Tijuana into San Ysidro, their tires filled with "naughty grass." They cruise through a questionnaire at customs, make it to Los Angeles, and collect the cash, which they split, Emilio telling his partner that he is now proceeding north to meet the love of his life. Upon receipt of this news, "seven shots sound; Camelia kills Emilio," but when the police arrive, they find only a "*pistola tirada*," a fired pistol; "of Camelia and the money, nothing ever more was known." The song was an early hit for the band on stage, Los Tigres del Norte, recorded in 1972, when the now middle-aged men were teenagers. Though not the first narcocorrido, it was the first to become a hit on every jukebox and across every dance floor in Mexico.[19] It was so popular that the band recorded two sequels: in the first, Camelia is tracked and gunned down by rival traficantes in Guadalajara; the second, "The Son of Camelia," is about her offspring killing five members of the Tijuana cartel and hunting down others to avenge his mother's murder. Los Tigres—three brothers and a cousin—are the kings of the genre they created, the undergrowth of which now provides a sound track to the narco war. They are the originals who have gone glitzy and international while the seeds, or some would say weeds, they planted grow thick and healthy, for the glorification of criminals.

Tonight, Los Tigres are dressed in flagrant red silk emblazoned with shameless gold, their pants are skintight to show their bulging efforts to best advantage, their heels are high and their posturing lusty, for these are the pinup boys of narcocorrido, from the state of Sinaloa, of course, but playing to a home crowd in the Arizona desert. Tucson—a name derived from the O'odham phrase "Chuk Shon," at the foot of a black hill—is seventy miles from Mexico and not strictly a border town, more like a border hub. It is a heartwarming place: scrappy but funky; sun dried, vibrant, and eclectic—comprising a university, a thriving bohemian art and music scene, gated suburbs in the northern foothills, horse heaven toward Saguaro National Park, and a downtown through which railroad trains hoot and thunder on their way from Yuma to El Paso and beyond, past the Hotel Congress, where John Dillinger hid out before he was arrested. The south side of the city, including a separate entity called South Tucson, lies on what is regarded as the wrong side of those tracks: a burgeoning and mettlesome Mexican-American community, umbilically connected across the border. During 2008 and 2009, the city saw a sudden rise in drug-related crime and home invasions resulting, in most cases, said the police, from unpaid debts due to cartels smuggling people and narcotics.[20] But tonight it's all bandannas with the Mexican flag and LOS TIGRES DEL NORTE GIRA USA 2009 emblazoned upon them. For all Los Tigres' bravura as the godfathers of narcocorrido, this is a family outing. The entire Mexican-American spectrum is here: elderly couples with their children and grandchildren, boys in baggy shorts with tattoos on their shins, a scary-looking man with a long black coat and a fedora, and gaggles of girls pressed up against the fence at the front of the standing area. Jorge Hernández, the bandleader, raises his Stetson with a debonair bow to the crowds and presents the musicians: "*mi hermano Raúl, mi hermano Hernán, mi primo Óscar,*" my brother, my brother, my cousin.

Next up is a blustering number called "El Avión de la Muerte"—The Airplane of Death. It is a true story, supposedly, compiled from news reports, featuring the narco Manuel Atilano, captured and tortured by the Mexican army into flying them to his cartel's hideaway landing strip in Sinaloa. Atilano, however, seizes control of the plane and broadcasts details of his treatment over the radio: *"Con pinzas machacaron partes nobles de su cuerpo"*—With pincers they crushed the noble parts of his body. The song ends with an act of heroism. Atilano changes his plan to crash the aircraft into a police compound when he sees a schoolyard full of children next door, and instead plunges himself and his captors to their deaths against a hillside, bidding fond *"adiós a sus amigos camaradas de aviación"*—farewell to his friends in the landing strip's control tower.

Los Tigres have no connection to any cartel, but one is left uncertain whether the brazen inclusion (on a tape, of course) of rasping, rapid automatic machine-gun fire that carries along their next song, called "Pacto de Sangre," Pact of Blood, is being faithful to their roots or offensively tasteless. There is no uncertainty, however, about how much the audience relishes all this gaudery: the gunfire, which sweeps in stereo from stage left to stage right, gets 'em dancing with even more splash and splurge.

Jorge Hernández puts it this way: "Poor people idolize the narcos: they admire their bravery, and they want to be like them. When you sing the songs, the audience feels that they're living through the characters, as if they were watching a film. That's why people love the *corrido*. It lets them dream."[21] Within weeks of tonight's concert, Los Tigres would become involved in their share of controversy. The band pulled out of an appearance at the prestigious Las Lunas music awards show because its organizers refused to allow them to play their latest song, "La Granja," The Farm, a critique of President Calderón's offensive against the narco cartels, accompanied by a video showing pigs representing politicians getting rich on the backs of the poor.[22] This peacockery is the razzmatazz side of this genre. More recently emerged narcocorrido bands are sometimes recruited to sing the glories of one particular cartel over another, a hero against a villain or, more usually, against the army. This, of course, makes them fair game for a rival cartel.

In a separate but chilling incident, the most famous murder of a musician occured in Matamoros, the easternmost city on the Mexican side of the border, on December 1, 2007. Twenty-eight-year-old Zayda Peña, the raven-haired singer for Los Culpables—the Guilty Ones—a best-selling band, sang the famous hit "Tiro de Gracia"—a single "mercy shot" to the head. She was staying at a motel in Matamoros after a concert the previous evening when gunmen came to the door and opened fire, killing a male companion and the hotel manager. Peña was taken to the hospital and given emergency surgery, but as she emerged from the operating room a squad of sicarios was waiting in the corridor to deliver a tiro de gracia through her heart. "Nothing, nothing, nothing," was the response of the Tamaulipas state prosecutor's office when asked for possible trails in search of Peña's killers.[23] Her mother has been working for the prosecutor's office since 2007, the year of her daughter's murder.

The Spanish word for walnuts is *nogales*, and there are two towns of that name, facing each other across the border south of Tucson, so called because of the walnut trees that grew wild and in orchards across the verdant slopes that rise into Mexico from the thirsting desert of Arizona. On the southern edges of Nogales, Sonora, is a new building, opened to great fanfare, called Camino a Casa—the highway home—another border project of the government's Desarrollo Integral de la Familia, or DIF. The brief is simple: to gather children who have been smuggled north across the border, caught, and deported, and to get them home. But the process is complicated. In the clinically clean reception area, a couple, César and Yvet, waits. He wears a white T-shirt and tattoos, she wears lines of exhaustion and her cheeks are tearstained. They are in their thirties, from Acapulco, where, says César, "there is nothing for a family." They had crossed just east of Nogales, into the desert, and were caught near the town of Patagonia, having paid one coyote $1,000 in Acapulco and a further $400 in supplements in Altar and along the way. They had been caught, then deported separately, their daughter, Francisca, brought to Camino a Casa. César signs a last piece of paper, and the security guard retreats through a magnetically locked door. Sometime later it opens, emitting a chorus of high-pitched, young farewells— "*Adiós*, Francisca!"—and the couple's daughter, age twelve, runs into her weeping mother's arms. "There's nothing more to say really, thank you," says César, sweeping his womenfolk toward the door. "We're going to find the bus home." Across the road, other children chirp and run around an urban schoolyard. Francisca shoots them a glance of envy, takes her mother's hand, and disappears back to Acapulco.

At first, the imposing María Mayela Alessi Cuevas appears as a set of long, painted fingernails with a woman and shoulder-padded jacket attached. She is the impeccably dressed director of this branch of Camino a Casa and runs the place with a mixture of no-nonsense authority and compassion. She took the job when her husband moved his business to Nogales. Mrs. Alessi explains the situation with straightforward clarity. "We get about five hundred a month," she says, "of whom twenty percent are fetched by their families and eighty percent are sent home." When they cross into the United States, most have both parents living there and are forwarded by relatives who put them in the care of coyotes. "Some cross the desert, some through the official ports of entry with false visas or fake documents, with other families. They are asked what their name is, questions about things on the papers, get confused and get caught. A child's instinct is to tell the truth, and if the customs ask, 'Is that your mom?' they give the game away. Often they're drugged to sleep when they cross, but the customs wake them up, and when they're drowsy they make even more mistakes. We sometimes get girls who have had their hair cut to look like boys in the fake papers." They, however, are the lucky ones. "For the ones who cross the desert, things are harder," says Mrs. Alessi. "We get girls who have been raped, as young as twelve, and some are pregnant after having been raped on the way north. Others sustain physical injuries: we had a group deported after they had been in a car crash, a chase by the Border Patrol—one boy was in a wheelchair, his bones broken from his feet to his hip. Often we'll get one left behind by their brothers or sisters—two who made it and one who didn't, with everyone traumatized and parents trying to get in touch from the USA. They sometimes think when they come here they're being arrested and going to jail. When children are introduced to their parents or, more often, grandparents, they usually burst into tears. A few have so little to go back to that one or two older ones want to stay and work here. But most, by the time they get here, all they want to do is go home. So much that they often try to escape, break the windows at night to try and run for it."

Most of the children, Alessi explains, come from the South. Then the bombshell: "Most of the kids from Sonora, from around here, are being used by the cartels as *burros*—donkeys—to carry drugs, some as young as thirteen. They cross over, know the territory, and deliver the drugs, then try to hitchhike their way home and get caught. The Americans don't arrest them because they're minors, and the cartels know that. And some of them are doing and selling the drugs they run—it's a way of paying them." Mrs. Alessi leaves us, with permission to talk without supervision to the children.

Two large recreation rooms off the courtyard house boys and girls separately. In each, about a hundred faces traverse the spectrum of youthful emotion. Some are puckish, full of mischief; some are melancholy, even lachrymose. Some of the boys wear their courage—or their fear—behind a mask of steadfastness, even aggression. Some of the girls wear theirs behind a mask of exuberance, while others wear their distrust out loud. The boys speak first, with César Magaña cursing the *pocho* (Mexican-American) migra agent who "kicked me in the back" when he was apprehended after two days of walking. His father in North Carolina had paid the coyote, who had taken him from Tabasco, and "things had been going well until we were chased by the migra, first in a truck and then, when we dived into the trees on the mountainside, they were on foot. They caught us, kicked and punched us, and said, 'That's for making us run, *mojados*!' They were all pochos, apart from one, and the gringo wasn't kicking!" Next to César is Marcos, age sixteen, from Campeche, with a heavier air, speaking more softly. "After three days, we were desperate," he says, his gaze far off. "By then, we were looking for the migra to get caught, looking for them to save us. My father had paid the coyote. I was told to do everything the man called Zepeda said; I had to meet him off the bus in Altar. But Zepeda was a liar. He didn't know the way and got lost. They got us on a night it rained so hard you couldn't see in front of you. One day, nothing to drink; another day, wet through. When the Border Patrol caught us, they were kind—they knew we were pleased to see them. The older men ran, but we walked toward the Border Patrol, because all we wanted was to go home."

Two boys sit silently, more shy than taciturn, it turns out, not because of us but because of the others. Xochitl, sixteen, and Itzel, a year younger, are not the usual Mexican mestizo: they are pure Aztec, from Veracruz. Everything is *más o menos*, they say, more or less. Do they want to go home? More or less. Was it frightening in the desert? More or less. Then Xochitl adds, "It was okay, until our friend was gone. Then the guide was gone. There were eight of us left, and we didn't know where we were, in the dark, in the night. After they found us, they brought three of us here, but I have no idea what happened to the others." "I don't care about Texas anymore," says another boy, Adán, age fourteen, from San Luis Potosí. "I don't want a rich blond gringa from Dallas. I thought I did—it's what I imagined, that and my mamá and papá, but I was wrong. I don't care about anything else now, I don't even want to see my parents in Texas, I just want to go home."

A show of hands is hardly a scientific way to gauge opinion, but sometimes it suffices, and when asked whether they wanted to go home or try again, only one hand out of about eighty is raised in favor of the latter. This is Gabriel, from Cacahoatán in Guatemala, with no return ticket. It is strange he is here; the DIF in theory administers only to Mexican citizens, those from farther south being regarded with greater contempt than Mexicans in the United States. "I came on the train," he says. "All the way, with my uncle. In the South of Mexico, they robbed us, and again in Nogales. The first time was Mexicans, the second time was Salvadorans. This town was our last chance, my uncle said. And after a day, the helicopter came over us—we scattered. I lost my uncle and ended up here. The lady who processed me said not to tell anyone where I am from, and that I could leave with some others and try again. I have to try again." He is seventeen, but seems either twelve or thirty-five; he is so strong-willed but so poignantly and utterly alone, and a child.

"This place is the middle of nowhere," says Arturo from Hidalgo. "I hate it. They give you two tortillas a day and some water. That's it. They don't let us play soccer in case we try to escape. And we wait—wait for them to find our relatives and for our relatives to raise the money to get us home." I had naïvely assumed that because the poetically named Camino a Casa was a government agency, the government might pay bus fare to send these children home. "Of course the government doesn't pay," scolds Magdalena from Chiapas, and with a wisdom and humor she really should not possess at fifteen, she adds, "The government only pays if you're in a coffin." And at last, everyone laughs, a hollow but badly needed laugh, and we talk about soccer and the inevitable rivalry of El Clásico—felt as keenly by the girls as the boys—between Chivas and Club América.

"America" is a beautiful word, especially when it is the name of a child. And the group marooned in the purgatorial care of Camino a Casa in Nogales is sustained by its collective fascination with, and care for, the shelter's most heart-searing resident, four-year-old América. In any other life she would be headed for the stage; as it is, heaven knows what awaits her. The little girl's parents are living in Florida, and she was sent across the border by relatives in her native Acapulco, ostensibly to join them. However, Mrs. Alessi had explained, "The coyotes took her to the border with two others, age five and six, in the middle of the night, sent them through the fence, and pointed to a house, saying, 'If you follow the lights and go into that house, your parents will come and pick you up.' They walked up to the door, and the Americans called the Border Patrol. They were dumped at four a.m. in the deportation pound on the Mexican side, alone, with no explanation or adult present. They're not supposed to deport minors after six p.m., but in practice they don't care. So we went to get them, and América is still here while we try to locate her family." This has taken two weeks so far, without success.

There is a teenage boy called Francisco and a girl called Lizabeth who are very proud of their special role in minding América. "Things can happen to a little girl that she cannot understand," says Francisco, horribly perceptive. "And we cannot let you talk to her without our presence," affirms Lizabeth, thirteen, with authority. "I want to go back to Acapulco," cheeps little América, "because there is a fairground there, and my mother [that would be her grandmother] has my lovely pair of boots there, in the Calle de Chile." The child starts blowing kisses down the corridor. "Then I got trapped," she says suddenly. "I went through the gate to play, and the men came. But now I'm going and after the fair my mother and me will sit and watch Amy on television."

There is a sudden frisson along the corridor, the sun glinting through the frosted glass ceiling and firing a ricocheted shaft of light across the tiled floor. Amy is a character in a TV soap the children know from home, and they want América to sing, as she does. One of her favorite songs is by Danna Paola, who plays Amy in the hit telenovela *Amy la Niña de la Mochila Azul*. América walks toward the shaft of sunlight and stands for a moment, gathering the words in her head, eyes closed. Then she opens them, takes a deep breath, and sings:

> *Fiesta, fiesta, la vida es fiesta, escucha tu corazón*
> *Fiesta, fiesta, qué poco cuesta, dar un poquito de amor*

How little it costs to give a little love. Then América stops and everyone claps. She smiles a big, sunny grin, claps too, and bursts into tears.

INTERMISSION: THE BUSINESS END OF A 12-GAUGE— BARRETT AND MORGAN'S WAR

The Gadsden Hotel in Douglas, Arizona, is grander than it probably needs to be nowadays. But that doesn't stop one catching one's breath walking into the lobby, to behold the marble columns, the imperious winding stairway, and walls echoing with the sounds of Wild West war along the borderline. Built in 1907, the hotel bears the name of Lieutenant James Gadsden, president of the South Carolina Canal and Rail Road Company, rabid southern nationalist, advocate of states' rights and slavery. Later, he became U.S. ambassador to Mexico and secured the purchase in 1853 of all land, including southern Arizona, south of the Gila River for the United States from Mexico. The Gadsden Purchase was a territorial postscript to the Treaty of Guadalupe Hidalgo of 1848, which ended the Mexican-American War, though some around here would say that the war is still being fought, for the borderline here is fraught with tension. In late March 2010, a respected rancher called Rob Krentz was shot dead by Mexicans coming through his land, fueling rage as well as grief, and strengthening the hand of a growing antismuggling, antimigration vigilante movement. A month later, Arizona's governor, Jan Brewer, signed into law a measure, enabling police to stop and demand that anyone produce documents proving his or her legal immigration status, on pain of arrest and deportation if there were none. The measure was eyed by other border states with a view to similar legislation, and polarized Arizona. Thousands of protesters took to the streets of Phoenix and Tucson, and sheriffs for two counties, Pima and Yuma, said they would not enforce the new law. The sherriff of Pima, Clarence

W. Dupnik, would become an international figure after the Tucson shootings of January 8, 2011—adored by supporters and despised by critics for his outspoken tolerance and liberalism.

But the border road has now led us east of Tucson and Pima County, into hard-line Cochise county, via the gun stores and bike repair shops of Sierra Vista, a vigilante stronghold, in the wild southeast of Arizona, where the rancher Krenz was shot dead. Here lie two neighboring towns, both of them former copper-mining centers: Bisbee, a hip, liberal outpost and arts center, and gritty Douglas with its Gadsden Hotel, built before Arizona became a state on St. Valentine's Day 1912, and while Geronimo was still leading Apache troops against both Americans and Mexicans. For all the quick-draw legends and pomp of the surroundings of the hotel, Butch Barrett dresses casually in the searing heat for our appointment in the lobby. Barrett was for decades a customs special agent in this corner of Arizona, riding horseback and fighting regular hand-to-hand shoot-outs with narco traffickers from Agua Prieta over the border. During his time patrolling this land, the territory between Nogales and Arizona's eastern border with New Mexico had become known as Cocaine Alley.[1] But to Barrett and his partner Lee Morgan, this country was both home and castle.

Not many stories like those of Barrett and Morgan's war get to be told firsthand anymore, in the days of high-tech border policing, with sensors and virtual fencing. But Lee Morgan set it out in a memoir called *The Reaper's Line*, which tells it like this: "The outlaw took aim with his Blazer and went for Miller's plump, round silhouette. The agent dropped the spikes and took aim at the driver with a 12 gauge pump shotgun. Looking down the business end of the 12 gauge convinced the smuggler he was about to commit a grave mistake."[2]

Morgan's book is the best action movie never made about the border: a latter-day high-noon Western set largely at midnight, because Morgan was in the thick of the nascent years of the narco war, which he saw coming a decade away. After graduating from the Border Patrol Academy in 1975, Morgan was stationed in Douglas, but he worked across America and the Caribbean in the immigration service's antidrug task force before returning as a customs special agent in 1987. After that, he and Barrett fought perpetual total war on two fronts: against their quarry, the smugglers, and against what he calls REMFs—rear-echelon mother-fuckers, who get paid by the taxpayers to push pens in Washington and throughout the bureaucracy. "What did I learn from my first gunfight as a federal agent?" Morgan asks rhetorically. "Well, I learned that as usual the REMFs are wrong and the grunts know what they need in the field to get the job done."

For this book, access to the current Border Patrol was, sadly, de-clined by Washington—so what better than to hear it like it was? As a special agent out of uniform, Morgan teamed up with Barrett and an-other agent called Allan Sperling on horse patrol. Both Morgan and Bar-rett were Vietnam veterans, though, says Morgan, while "I've seen my share of hell when the shit hit the fan in the jungle, Butch saw some re-ally *bad* shit. Try to imagine floating in a body of water so thick with bloated bodies that you actually had to lance the corpses with a bayonet so they would sink." After Morgan and Barrett returned from fighting the Vietcong, their enemies were the Agua Prieta cartel, allied to Ciudad Juárez, and Morgan's favorite horse was called Cougar. Through the turn of the decade, they rode against the bareback narcos, fought shoot-outs against them, and apprehended them in unarmed combat. It is a late-twentieth-century Wild West desert war as thrilling as it is portentous of what is to come: "I yelled to the asshole that I would blow his face off if he brought the barrel of his rifle up . . . I hate to cap a guy if I don't ab-solutely have to . . . God-fearingly correct in his decision, the outlaw dropped his assault rifle to the floorboard and raised his hands above his head." During an incursion by Mexican soldiers protecting the cartel: "Let me be perfectly clear about this. These armed black uniforms were not patrolling in Mexico. They had invaded our country and were con-ducting military combat maneuvers on U.S. soil!" As for the narcos, Morgan respects the mules carrying *la merca*, the dope. "You know how those mountain-climbing pro dudes use the picks and pitons to ascend a rocky mountain bluff that goes straight up? Mickey Mouse crap! We've seen mules go up the same incline using only their bare fingers and tennis-shoe-covered toes." On the narco bosses themselves, however: "Being the chickenshits these behind-the-border back-shooters are, any show of equal or superior force causes them to run like scared jackrabbits being chased by coyotes." And: "But the Mexican outlaw wasn't quite done yet. The son of a bitch fought Butch tooth and nail while he kept hitting the accelerator with the tip of his cowboy boot. The truck kept surging and spinning in a tight circle like a wounded duck with one wing shot off."

Not only did Butch Barrett's son get married on the magnificent staircase at the Gadsden Hotel, he also joined the Border Patrol recently "and I'm mighty proud of that," says his father, for all Barrett's misgivings about the service these days. His were "days when you had to provide your own horses and saddles," he recalls, "until the REMFs were persuaded by a couple of successes we had that we deserved us a team of four. But it worked—tracking 'em down on horseback proved very successful. We knew the terrain, we knew how to get 'em and we got 'em. It was another world back then: pre-9/11, pretechnology, pre–Generation X and Generation Me before it—but more heroes, I'm tellin' ya. Yes, they'll laugh at you now, but we did it for God and country. Some did it for the highs and the adrenaline, but they likely pulled out from the sheer terror of having someone carrying a load and trying to kill you to get it through." We sit in armchairs at an old, low wooden table. There is no tea, coffee, or beer, just talk and a big empty lobby around us. "The kids now, they do it mostly for the money, and because it's a job. I don't blame them, but it's just an existence nowadays—in our time, you had to prove yourself, produce bodies, getcha hands dirty, and take 'em on. The dope smugglers project this image of being the macho men, but they cry like babies when you've got 'em in handcuffs."

But, says Barrett, "I still talk to some of the young agents. They're no fools, and they get into situations when they need a little old-school advice, particularly when it comes to dealing with the people with their feet under desks. That was the only mistake I made, to get promoted behind a desk! The problem is what it always was: the REMFs in Washington, D.C. They'd come down in my day, look around for fifteen minutes with the press secretary, and we'd offer them a tour out with us once, good to go. But they never even sat in a car with us."

Butch is proud of Douglas but unsure about what the frontier has done to Douglas of late. "If you go to City Hall and look at the portraits of the mayors, you'll find that the white guys suddenly stop, and after a certain time, around 1980 when Phelps Dodge [the copper-mining company] up and went, they're all Mexican. Well, I don't say I have a problem with that, except if the town is Mexican, then there's going to be a lot of them in the smuggling trade, you know, part of the picture. There's going to be a situation where you have a guy in law enforcement and his cousins are across the border. And he's going to get a call saying, 'Hey, we'd like you to join the customs service and do as you're told,' let this car through or turn a blind eye there. And that's gonna be said by your cousin on the other side, and it's going to be an offer you can't refuse. And that has happened, I know it has." There was a customs officer, says another agent, who was passed by the same pretty girl every day. *"¡Hola!"* she would say, smiling and waving, until, to script, he asked for her number. After a little rendezvous and one or two drinks, a carload of men arrived at the supposedly discreet bar with a briefcase containing $250,000 in cash, put it on the table, and made a suggestion: take the money, or we call your wife—now. All he had to do is what he'd always done: wave back, and wave her through, only now he was in, and once in, there's no way out.[3]

Long before the Obama administration finally found a buzzword to admit the United States' "coresponsibility" for Mexico's drug war, Lee Morgan wrote, "Maybe we, as the decadent, arrogant Norteamericanos, should start questioning our own insatiable appetite for drugs." He was also on top of the smuggling of guns to the South, when the matter was taboo: after one terrifying "surreptitious excursion" to Agua Prieta, a man whom Morgan was trailing was arrested with "enough ammo to start a small war," which indicated, along with Morgan's progressive seizures of weaponry from China, that the business ends of 12-gauge shotguns would soon be superseded by those of AK-47, AR-15, and TEC-9 machine guns. No one saw the narco war coming, writes Morgan, because "we have an entertainment and media industry that thrives on keeping our vegetating minds stuffed with compost . . . so there's no real need to think for yourself in America." His conclusion: "The border is a line of barbwire and spiked pillars that seems only to serve as a symbol of one man's futile lifetime endeavors, his attempts to define Mother Nature's boundaries, as well as man's national claims to a piece of what no human can ever call his own possession. Men will always be willing to fight and die in follies of nationalism, but they will never be able to continually control their own borders."

Morgan and I meet farther along the road, in San Antonio on the River Walk opposite the Alamo, which, we note with amusement, has become Texas's leading tourist attraction and icon of the Texan revolution against Mexico despite having fallen to the Mexican army during the famous battle of 1836, with all but two of its defenders killed. Morgan looks younger, and certainly trimmer, in smart casual than the rugged desert rat on the inside cover of his book, clutching binoculars.

"We were wild," says Morgan. "We were outta control, socially unacceptable. But we were effective. Now, it's all just policy, policy, policy and orders from the top. The good people are getting thrown out, pushed aside—'Do it our way or get out of our way'—and it's been like that ever since we told 'em this was coming, that the drug lords were getting serious. These people in Washington don't want to be told the truth. They don't understand the drug lords, they don't get it that you can't deal with them—look at the things they do to people! You can't offer 'em a better job because they don't want to be in any other business unless it's another form of crime."

There is a surprise by the Alamo. Morgan and Barrett had a mentor in the customs service, a man called James Rayburn—the team leader, a slightly older man who knew every grain of sand in the desert and taught Morgan a few of the tricks in the book. Rayburn has joined us for a chat by the river. They are two of the best special agents their service ever had but have trouble figuring out the silly computerized machine that distributes timed tickets in the parking lot for display on the dashboard of the truck they have driven into town from hill country. These men don't like to be controlled, and good for them. Both men smoke and enjoy their cigarettes. Morgan and I order Dos Equis; Rayburn wants a Bud Light. Rayburn's expertise, among many things, was in running informants in Mexico, people regarded, says Morgan, by defense attorneys as "Judases" and by prosecutors as "a painful but necessary black plague."

On July 2, 1998, the Clinton administration signed an accord with the Mexican presidency of Ernesto Zedillo that became known as the Brownsville Agreement. This obliged U.S. law enforcement agencies—principally customs, the DEA, and the FBI—to notify, through the embassy in Mexico City, the Mexican attorney general's office of their undercover investigations and informants. Intelligence agencies, markedly the CIA, were exempt. "For us border narcs, it was like being the only blind son of a bitch at a poker table," objects Morgan. "Everyone is reading your cards but you!" In practice, the accord meant that a Mexican government deeply infiltrated by narco cartels was being informed who the snitches were, to disastrous effect in Douglas alone, and on informers run by Morgan. One of them was infiltrating a syndicate manufacturing and smuggling methamphetamine at a series of meetings at the local Motel 6. But after being informed by their government who the informer was, the smugglers avoided a sting Morgan had prepared. The informer became one of three undercover spies working for Morgan across the border in Agua Prieta to be gunned down soon after the Brownsville Agreement.

The events recalled the cornerstone murder of DEA agent Kiki Camarena in 1985, to which James Rayburn, sipping on his Bud, has a connection. Rayburn had controlled an informer, Benito Suárez, who was commandeered to look for Camarena after he had been kidnapped on instructions of the Godfather himself, Miguel Félix Gallardo. But when Suárez arrived in Sinaloa, the Gallardo clan appeared suspicious of his timely return from Arizona. He and a fellow Mexican informer based in Phoenix were taken to a private house in Jalisco where Suárez was tortured and beaten, and believed he heard Camarena's voice in an adjoining room. Afterward, the two men were driven to a cliff. Suárez was put in the driver's seat while his friend's face was crushed by the butt of an AK-47 and Suárez was whiplashed at the base of his skull. But as the car was pushed over the cliff to the bottom of the canyon, Suárez was miraculously thrown from it and survived. Rayburn did all he could to have his man rescued and carried across the Bridge of the Americas from Ciudad Juárez into El Paso. "The last time I saw him was when he went hunting for Camarena," says Morgan, who took turns with Rayburn driving Suárez to physiotherapy, he had been a "healthy young man with fire in his eyes and a zest in his heart for life. But what met me at his apartment door on my first visit was the pitiful remains of a man I didn't recognize." Suárez died of AIDS in 1998, a secret he preferred to keep rather than be treated, after being repeatedly sodomized during torture.

"It was the beginning of the end," reflects Rayburn. "After the Brownsville Agreement, it became almost impossible to do an effective undercover operation. It became harder to deal with Washington than to fight the criminals. When you go undercover, the REMFs hate it while you're doing it, then go on TV and claim all the credit when you pull the outlaws in. Nothing substitutes for human intelligence and infiltration, and that's something we're losing, just as the drug lords are gaining it. While it gets harder for us to infiltrate them, they'll use relatives and friends to infiltrate us, they'll call a cousin on the U.S. side and tell 'em, 'Hey, we need you to work in border law enforcement—for the U.S.,' and there ain't no saying no to them. We've seen it happen; we arrested one of our own customs people smuggling cocaine for a drug boss called Yolanda Molina. We were told years ago, by a man I arrested, 'If we can't beat you with weapons, we'll infiltrate you.' We reported this, but no one listened. And sure enough, next we knew, the assistant special agent in charge of Nogales had been working for them all along." They were referring to Richard Padilla Cramer, another decorated Vietnam veteran who served three decades in law enforcement, locking up corrupt officials and busting drugs, and was promoted to attaché for immigration and customs enforcement at the U.S. embassy in Mexico City. According to the prosecution case at the time of writing, as Cramer awaits trial, Cramer was selling his knowledge to the cartels, a treachery dating back to his days as head of ICE in Nogales, Arizona. "This," said Rene Andreu, former assistant head of the ICE customs division in Tucson, "is impossible to grasp."[4] "We didn't believe it," hoots Morgan. "Must've talked with him a thousand times—all that time, he was one of them." Cramer has yet to stand trial and has denied all wrongdoing.

"When they called us cowboys," Morgan ponders, "it was intended as an insult. I was told I had a John Wayne attitude—well, what in hell's wrong with that? Dammit, the smugglers sure have a John Wayne attitude. They live like smugglers and expect to die like smugglers, and we were the same. You gotta know your enemy, you gotta know his terrain better'n he does. The way we did the job was to get inside the smuggling organization and hit it head-on. We were working with the inside view of how they work, who they are, what they do—got to know the basics, and the pressures they're under. That's what I try to tell the young guys now: get to know 'em, don't look down on them—but we could never do it now. I wouldn't be allowed to work the way we did [then]. We were in the right place at the right time."

Since it is a beautiful afternoon by the river, another round of beers seems in order, and we turn the conversation to a favorite subject: reading tracks, or "cutting for sign," as it is known in the trade, a skill that precedes even mankind's presence in the desert, where covering—and detecting—tracks is everything. The red fox walks the desert in such a way that its hind paws fall near or directly onto its fore prints—known in zoology as a "direct register"—obliterating the forepaw tracks. It changes coat with the seasons for both insulation and camouflage, taking on what is called a "dark morph" when necessary.[5] The art of covering and cutting sign was perfected by Native Americans for hunting animals, and latterly by law enforcement for hunting humans. There is a special unit of the Border Patrol on the Tohono O'odham reservation called the Tracking Wolves, cutting for sign. And of course, sign cutting was perfected by men like Morgan, Rayburn, and Barrett. You need to know, says Morgan, the difference between a chevron and a starburst imprint, when a mat of some kind has been attached to the shoes, when footprints have been swept away by the last person in a convoy, walking backward and brushing the terrain, as tribal raiders had done ever since this arid land was inhabited. And to read the sign that tells you exactly when these movements occurred, for your quarry may be near, or too far—the kind of thing you learn from whether the track of a bug runs over or beneath a footprint.

Back in the lobby of the Gadsden Hotel, Butch Barrett had recalled the romance of sign cutting. "It was something handed down to us country boys," he said. "My father used to take me hunting animals when I was twelve years old, and the first thing I learned was how to read their tracks. So I took that knowledge and applied it to hunting people. The real hunt starts when you get off the roads, working out when a footprint isn't a real footprint, when they've made a mistake trying to lay a false trail—that's something the best of the young 'uns who are interested in getting results love to ask us about. 'Back in your day,' they say, 'when you used to cut for sign . . . ,' and they ask us how it was done."

By the river, Morgan confesses, "I'm still always looking for tracks, habitually, every time I go for a walk. Fact is, it worked. All these sensors and gadgets, they break, they malfunction. [He imitates a dumb voice on the end of the phone:] 'I'm sorry, the system's down.' And they can lie. But the ground can't lie. A piece of fiber caught by a cactus can't lie. The smallest shift in the sand on terrain you know can't lie. Just like a border fence can hold you up for twenty minutes but it can't arrest you—it don't have no John Wayne attitude. Unlike the drug lords, watching all this and laughing." They might also be laughing at a report by the General Accounting Office filed in August 2009 finding the Secure Border Initiative launched by President George W. Bush in 2005 to be running seven years behind the schedule it set for putting the latest gizmos in place, and running millions of dollars over budget because of maintenance bills. The "virtual fence" system designed by Boeing had "fallen prey to weather and mechanical problems," said the report by the GAO's Richard M. Stana. The total bill will come to $6.5 billion over twenty years, he estimated. During the same week as the report's publication, the government extended Boeing's contract for another year.[6] In 2010, President Obama conceded that the "virtual fence" was an absurdity, and cancelled it.

The cartels will also, says Morgan, "be wondering how all this'll enhance their ability to infiltrate us deeper, corrupt the system, and keep the money flowing around." He pauses. "Kinda strange, ain't it, how Washington got all this technology but never goes after the money— billions of dollars of it? Billions of dollars moving around the U.S. banks and going back into Mexico. They never go after it. That ever strike you as strange?"

The heresy has been spoken. Morgan, who saw the war coming, now wonders about the money-go-round that circles between Mexico and the United States, just as the late sun aims its last, deep rays against the Alamo. There are hundreds of billions of dollars in drug profits swilling around the U.S. banking system, and U.S. Customs veteran Lee Morgan II would like to know a hell of a lot more about who is moving it. Farther along the border road from Morgan, Barrett, and Rayburn's terrain of eastern Arizona, a sociologist at UT El Paso, Howard Campbell, suggests that we should try relabeling the narco cartels because of the money-go-round, calling them the Sinaloa-Phoenix-Denver cartel, the Juárez–El Paso–Chicago cartel, or the Gulf-Houston-Atlanta cartel so as to more accurately reflect their sphere of influence. It is out across the desert toward El Paso and its twin city of Ciudad Juárez that the road now beckons. But first, one last round with the horsemen of the John Wayne attitude, a toast to the reaper and his line in the sand.

4

URBAN FRANKENSTEIN

*If Juárez is a city of God, that is because the Devil is scared to
come here.*   *—street* dicho, *or saying*

Ciudad Juárez: right now I'd say it's the safest city in Mexico.
                  *—Lt. Col. Jorge Alberto Berecochea, on taking over
                            the Sixth Police District, March 2009*

Of all the enthralling landscapes in America, none is more complicated
in its awful beguilement than that southward from the balcony outside
room 262 on the upper floor of La Quinta motel on Geronimo Avenue in
El Paso, Texas—with a six-pack, a lime, hot salsa, and a bag of tortilla
chips for company. In mid-distance runs the border. And beyond the
boundary lies the factory smoke, the sea of lights, the lure and menace of
this most charismatic and daunting of cities: Ciudad Juárez. While El
Paso is the second-safest U.S. city of its size, with only sixteen homicides
in 2008, Juárez is currently the most dangerous city in the Americas
and, by some counts, the world. The scene is especially striking at dusk,
when fleets of cast-off American school buses have done their rounds
taking home the day shift in the maquiladoras, so that a layer of gray
dust stirs around and settles on the lanes and the labyrinth of outlaw
electrical wires supplying the colonia shacks.

To get here, the road from eastern Arizona has crossed the border
state of New Mexico on the U.S. side, and western Chihuahua on what
many Americans living on the frontier still call "Old Mexico" when

wishing to convey a rugged affection. The small town of Columbus, New Mexico, faces Palomas, Chihuahua, across an expanse of otherwise wild and empty land populated by ghosts from the Mexican Revolution—Pancho Villa State Park is nearby. Alima McMillan lives in remote Columbus and enjoyed her work across the border at a medical center in Palomas, where Mayor Estanislao García was kidnapped and shot dead the week after she and I met in September 2009. Ms. McMillan had already decided that the eruption of violence in the town a short walk from where we had lunch in a café should prevent her from carrying on her regular surgeries there. Often, victims of the violence appeared at the border crossing in need of help, like a teenage boy the previous week who had been beaten, shot, doused with diesel fuel, and set on fire. Palomas had been a place to which visitors from New Mexico went regularly to get teeth fixed and buy cheap medicine until new arrivals in town, says McMillan, "put the fear of God into everyone and started clearing the territory." Palomas was turned almost overnight into a three-way battlefield among the army, the Juárez cartel, and the Sinaloa cartel. Now it's a place in which one family remains dominant, among the silence, the emptied houses, new narco villas, and army Blackhawk helicopters overhead, "flying their noses right up to the line," says McMillan, "to blow a bit of Mexican dust into Columbus." From Columbus, the road clings to the border through a village called Malpais—bad country—a suburb of El Paso called Sunland Park, which is nonetheless still in New Mexico, then across the Texas state line, but cheek by jowl with the rusting iron fence, the barbed wire, and the colonia of Anapra that tumbles down into Ciudad Juárez, just yards away from the highway into downtown El Paso.

The scene from El Paso across the border is all the more surreal on the night of the Grito, commemorating Mexico's independence from Spain in 1810. This is the United States, but on a stage at the northern end of San Jacinto Square, a full mariachi band launches a night of festivity to precede the day commemorating that on which the Mexican nation was born 199 years before. "¡Viva la independencia!" shouts the singer, in a long, very tight cocktail dress from which she bursts. "¡Viva!"

answers back the crowd of several thousand families, cuddling teenagers, and old ladies with Indian faces from Mexico's deep South, wrinkled with hard work, smiling beneath the round brims of their hats. *"¡Viva México!"* shouts the singer, the Grito, the cry itself. *"¡Viva!"* replies the crowd as the band strikes up the national anthem, whereupon the crowd stands still, hands across the chest, clutching the heart, here in Old El Paso. Long lines wait for food served from stalls—sweet fried churros, tacos, and shredded beef, though the longest queue approaches the sign promising TURKEY BREAST, BRATWURST, HAMBURGERS. Other stalls have games: pop the balloon and win a three-foot-high plaster cherub for the garden or a big cuddly gorilla.

Down a side street, a lone van with flashing lights advertises SODAS, AGUAS, GATORADES and plays a tune more disturbing than jolly. As well it might, given what is happening over the border in Ciudad Juárez. The crowd of some ten thousand in El Paso can hear its counterpart four times the size, across the river, the whooping and music that happens only rarely in a city that lives under a self-imposed curfew. At eleven o'clock, fireworks fill the skies on both sides of the border, bursting with a sound like gunfire—concealing the fusillades of murderous, real gunfire across Juárez at exactly that moment. In fact, some of the witnesses to the killing of ten people in a drug rehabilitation center in Barrio Azul thought the rasp of AK-47s was a part of the celebrations.

The killers burst in through the gateway of the Anexo de Vida, annex of life, a rehabilitation center in the heart of Barrio Azul, a poor colonia of little streets, and threw a grenade into the first room on their right, occupied by a sixteen-year-old guard. Inside the room the next morning, a mattress is splattered with blood, the floor next to it saturated, but the teenager seems to have made it through the door before falling to the ground where his workout weights still lie. The killers have soaked his blood into the soles of their heavy boots and stamped it around in horribly clear footprints that anyone who cared to solve the crime might examine, only no one ever seems to solve the crimes.

The cement and whitewashed walls of Barrio Azul are staked out with the blue graffiti tag of the local *pandilla*, or gang, the BAZUL, to claim the colonia and remember: IN MEMORIAM, ZAIKO Y NORDIANO, presumably two street-fighting "brothers" who died "defending" it. A dog rests in the stinking trash strewn along Vía Juan Escutia. A burned-out building is likewise tagged by the BAZUL, next door to which a neat pink house with flowerpots on the windowsills flies the flag for Independence Day. Turning into Vía Jaime Nunó, there is the entrance to the Anexo de Vida. PARA ENFERMOS DE DROGADICCIÓN Y ALCOHOLISMO is written on the white paint, for the sick from drug addiction and alcoholism. There is no vida in this place the morning after Grito, only chains on its padlocked gates and a black tarpaulin hiding the aftermath of the horror unleashed just as the mayor of Juárez, José Reyes Ferriz, rang the bell and shouted the Grito last night. The previous week, seventy-five people had been killed in Juárez, including one man beheaded and another hung to die by handcuffs from a chain-link fence. And this was only a few weeks since September 3, when eighteen people were killed at another rehab clinic, El Aliviane, a few blocks from city hall and the downtown bridge to El Paso. Black-clad gunmen had burst into El Aliviane, lined up the young men against a wall, and summarily executed them. The father of one of the dead said that his son had completed his rehabilitation, but went back to El Aliviane for prayer meetings.

We clamber onto the roof and down into the courtyard of the Anexo de Vida, still a mess thirteen hours after the killing, hiding, and flight. Sneakers are discarded in piles, crates are upturned, and furniture is scattered across the ground—following the painted signs to the RUTA DE EVACUACIÓN. Off the courtyard are the rooms that were death chambers overnight, which still emit the sickly sweet stench of blood, which congeals in pools around us—wrapped in the other scents of what was until last night a rehabilitation center run by poor people for people below poverty: stale sweat, rotting broccoli piled up in boxes, and the ashes of a fire on which dinner was being cooked. It does not take a policeman to work out what happened, only there is little sign of any police work and no question of guarding the crime scene, or preventing us from contaminating it, nor the young boys who follow us inside, scavenging for souvenirs and things left behind to sell—drugs, tools, pairs of shoes, packets of cookies.

The carnage divides into two directions, along each side of the court-yard. After killing the teenage guard, the killers went left to the room of the center's director, who seems to have made it outside, where a pond of his blood putrifies on the cement. Next were the quarters of the vice director, a woman whose room is a pitiless sight: blood spattered across her floral bedspread, and rushing to the floor beside it where she seems to have been raked with bullets, then horrible smears where she appears to have collapsed onto her sofa beneath the window. Now, two boys cast their eyes over the ransacked drawers, taking two baseball caps. The dead woman's handbag lies on an armchair—it contains Christian magazines and a paperback guide to sacred sites in the Holy Land. Her CD collection is scattered on the floor—*Metal en Rosas*, a compilation of Guns n' Roses and Radiohead. Curiously, only a single bullet casing lies on the floor; perhaps the children have taken the rest. Or maybe even the police.

The assassins moved past the main dormitory, in which mattresses still lie and posters line the wall announcing that LA ADICCIÓN ES UNA ENFERMEDAD. And in this room a man now appears, wearing a Dallas Cowboys cap, returning to pick up the set of tools and shoes he left behind in the flight last night. "I used to sleep over there, at the end. It happened about eleven o'clock," he testifies. "We were watching the boxing on TV. We heard the explosion, then the shooting, and hid under the mattresses at the end there. The whole thing took about two minutes." How were they dressed? He doesn't remember. Why did they do this? "I have no idea. The people who ran this center did it just by themselves, and we came by ourselves, after they had taken us off the streets. We never received any threats, and we never threatened anyone. We hid nothing from the narcotraficantes—we had nothing to hide from the narcotraficantes." He breaks open a packet of biscuits and eats. No, he will not give his name—"*anónimo*," he insists—and no, no photograph. The death squad proceeded to the room at the far left-hand corner, where two beds are now empty, in between which is a pool of blood so thick that it is still sticky underfoot, its darker coating over the still congealing red glistening in the shaft of sunlight that penetrates the doorway.

Meanwhile, another squad of executioners continued on from the entrance up the courtyard's right flank, past a storage area, the smoking area, and a cooking yard, where blackened pots hang in which soup would have been cooked, and a metal tub for washing clothes. The grate of the fire that warmed the last supper is still full of ash. The scene in the next small room suggests that the killers were looking for something—a mattress overturned and shot to shreds, but no sign of murder. In the far right corner, however, there is a brutal scene, in and outside the *enfermería*. In the courtyard is another pool of blood, and the wall is pitted with bullet holes. Whoever came to investigate the scene has scrawled CUERPO I, corpse I, on a piece of paper placed on the ground. Inside the infirmary is a fearsome sight: a cupboard of medicines has been ransacked, with much of its contents left, and a closed door shot through with a bullet. There is a pool of blood by the door, but someone seems to have forced a desperate way out like a trapped beast, for his blood is splattered all over the bullet-riddled wall outside, and the metal door—ajar—is gnarled at the base, as he staggered and fell outside to become CUERPO F.

This room must have been a sanctuary of sorts: there are sports trophies and a bookcase with several editions of the same paperback Bible. This collection belonged to José Ángel Torres, who obviously read, maybe even taught, English, for he had several copies of a volume called *Famous Christians*. He had potted cactus plants and a CD/cassette player, and had just sipped at a plastic bottle of Diet Coke when his murderers arrived: it is almost full. To the rear of this hospital reception area are a bunk bed, more blood, and a label reading CUERPO H next to a cabinet behind which is the doctor's stethoscope, on the floor. As we rummage around trying to re-create the crime, an SUV with blackened windows pulls up in the otherwise empty street outside the gate. Having climbed in, there is no quick way out—we're trapped. While it remains there, motionless, the flesh creeps with goose bumps for all the 100-degree heat, and one's vision blurs with fear. Then the car purrs away.

Oddly, there are cuerpos F, H, and I, but no A, B, C, D, E, or G.

Maybe the kids took the labels as souvenirs. It doesn't matter—no one is going to look for the men wearing the boots that left further bloodied marks here in this corner. Although that is not what they are saying at the press conference in the Chihuahua state offices. "We continue in our unrelenting work against the criminals," affirms Patricia González, state prosecutor, with as little menace as hapless Rommel Moreno in Tijuana. "We have shown the world that the struggle against organized crime is resolved and determined." The new police chief is "confident in our continuing investigations" into this latest carnage in yet another rehabilitation center. Being the police chief of Juárez is work on a high wire. In February 2009, the narco traffickers decided that Chief Roberto Orduña, a retired army major who had been in office since May 2008, should go. After the purging of three hundred police officers accused of working for the cartels, the narcos vowed to kill a police officer every forty-eight hours until Orduña resigned, starting with his operations director Sacramento Pérez Serrano and three of his staff. On February 20, Orduña—who had lived in the police station for several months—quit his post and fled the city. He had replaced another chief who had also fled to live in El Paso. The mayor of Juárez, José Reyes Ferriz, has also received death threats, one in spring 2010 written on a severed pig's head, and keeps houses on both sides of the border. Interviewed in El Paso, he vows, "I am not going to give in." After inviting me to attend a summer cultural festival in Juárez, the mayor lists the things he needs, including an encrypted radio network so that he and the police do not have to constantly listen to the knocking sound followed by a narcocorrido with which the cartels hack in to announce that another officer has been or will be shot. Reyes Ferriz has been menaced by communiqués threatening to kill and decapitate him, even in El Paso, if he "continues to help you know who," as one message put it.[1] The mayor and authorities decline to speculate on what the message—implying favor toward one cartel over another—could have meant. The governor of Chihuahua, José Reyes Baeza, was also the target of an assassination attempt: a car in his convoy was hit by machine-gun fire in February 2009. This time, one of the five gunmen, an ex-soldier, was arrested.

These people preside over a city that in January 2010 was confirmed as having the world's highest homicide rate by a group based in Mexico City called the Citizens Council for Public Security. The organization calculated Juárez as killing 191 citizens per 100,000, way ahead of second-place San Pedro Sula in Honduras with 119, New Orleans with 69, Medellín with 62, and Cape Town with 60.[2] What characterizes the killing in Juárez—or what fails to characterize it—is that no one really knows who the killers are, or what they seek to gain from the killing. There is no reason why a "drug lord," as newspapers call the cartel leaders, would want to liquidate ten wretched addicts in a rehab center.

A week after the mayor shouted the Grito of independence, the black plastic sheet covering the gate of the Anexo de Vida in Barrio Azul has been removed. Inside, the blood has been whitewashed away with lime; all that is left are bullet holes, mattresses, a Toronto Blue Jays cap, and a newspaper from the day of the massacre (which would itself become the next day's front page). Its cover carries vividly illustrated coverage of the previous day's atrocity, but the paper is open at the pinup spread of a girl wearing a studded leather bikini, gagged at the mouth and bound in chains.

I had first crossed the Rio Grande into Juárez in 1981 for the same two reasons as anyone else: the opening line of Bob Dylan's "Just Like Tom Thumb's Blues" ("When you're lost in the rain in Juárez / And it's Easter-time too"), and to gawp at the salaciousness and audacity with which anything and everything was for sale, most of it carnal. And although the fleshpot, the dope den, and the Kentucky Club in which Marilyn Monroe celebrated her divorce from Arthur Miller are certainly not the "real" Juárez, they are not entirely deceptions either. Not because Juárez was superficially a playground of danger and vice for visitors but because it was above all, and remains, a marketplace of the purest, unfettered kind. Juárez is a pioneer of, and monument to, economic deregulation. When I returned two decades later in 2001, Ciudad Juárez was ready to implode, and has now imploded. The implosion was not sudden, and its

roots are deep. Juárez is at once a singular city and also one that encap-
sulates many things common to most other cities, though in extremis.

Juárez lies, so they say, *"entre algo y la nada"*—between something
and nothing. It is, and always has been, a city of transit: a military, then
road, then railway junction. A pivot of Spanish colonization, it is the old-
est settlement along what is now the border, established as Misión de
Nuestra Señora de Guadalupe de los Mansos del Paso del Norte in 1659,
as Spanish explorers and then traders and missionaries prepared to
cross what they called the Río del Norte—what Mexicans now call the
Río Bravo and Americans the Rio Grande. (*Mansos* was a loaded and
thoroughly unpleasant Spanish colonial word applied to those indigenous
to the area, equivalent to the "tamed" or "meek"—the subjugated.)[3] El
Paso del Norte was a commercial junction and entrepôt for trade between
New Spain and its province of New Mexico, then between independent
Mexico and its northern reaches.

Until the international border was drawn across Juárez's face in
1849, along a line following the river as it takes a sharp eastward turn,
there was little on its northern, left bank. Only after the frontier was
etched was the city of El Paso established on the U.S. side. The metropolis on the Mexican right bank expanded as a market center for the surrounding cotton fields, but toward the end of the nineteenth century had
become urbanized by the arrival of the Mexican Central northbound
railway from Mexico City, which connected El Paso del Norte to the railroad network that had woven an industrial infrastructure across the
United States. The railway brought hundreds of thousands of Mexicans
to the doorstep of the United States and the siding yards of the new
American sister city and transport hub, so that a flow of goods and human traffic now connected the border city to the industrializing United
States. Letters sent from El Paso by a German immigrant, Ernst Kohlberg, describe the border city on the U.S. side as "nearly the end of the
world, and the last of creation," while in El Paso del Norte on the Mexican side, after a reinforcement of cavalrymen, he had "never seen so
many cut-throats together at one time." The businessmen of the city, he
noted, were each extorted $160 for the military's stay. "The money will

not be lost if no other party gets control," he wrote, but "if another crowd gets the upper hand, they will declare the levying of the tax as illegal and make us pay again."[4] Whether Kohlberg's remark was a more apposite prediction of the arrival of the PRI and PAN, or of the drug cartels, is a matter of subjective judgment in hindsight.

In 1888, El Paso del Norte changed its name to Ciudad Juárez, in honor of Benito Juárez, president of Mexico during the 1860s, who had used the city as his headquarters. For a short while, the city even acted as Mexico's provisional national capital, while Juárez's republican forces fought French intervention in Mexico. Juárez became a capital city of a different kind during the Mexican Revolution of 1910, of which it was the cradle. In the years of reconstruction that followed, it grew into a manufacturing base in its own right, making copper wire. But the city's economic recovery from the revolutionary violence was also due to a thriving trade in smuggling during America's Prohibition between 1919 and 1933. Juárez meanwhile opened its doors to anyone wishing to come and consume banned firewater rather than have it illegally delivered. And so the city's reputation for opportunism in illicit markets was born, enhanced by the shift, orchestrated by Ignacia Jasso, from alcohol to heroin once the former was legalized over the river. La Nacha was dope queen of Juárez until the 1970s, by which time another wave of commerce was about to engulf the city with far greater impact: the maquiladoras, industrial assembly plants. Hundreds of thousands of Mexicans would arrive in Juárez from the interior and desperately poor South, not to cross the border but to work on it, in the proliferation of assembly plants that suddenly spread throughout the borderland like an invasion of bland low-rise Lego bricks. Initially, and for complex reasons of exploitation and demographics, the majority of those employed in these soul-destroying factories were young women. Juárez attracted more maquiladoras than any other city along the border and, therefore, more workers, but it did not create an infrastructure to house or shelter them, let alone keep them warm, light their shacks, or school their children—or protect them from the nightmarish kind of metropolis that resulted from this smash-and-grab of cheap labor. For the big landowners, markedly the Bermúdez family, after whom Juárez's biggest maquiladora park is named and by whom it is owned, the industrial explosion was a boon beyond their wildest dreams. As the photographer who has captured this city's descent, Julián Cardona, puts it, "The rich of the city had paid the politicians to raise taxes from the poor, in order to turn the place where they lived into an urban Frankenstein."

I met Cardona long after first seeing his work: he had curated shocking, striking pictures for a book called *Juárez: The Laboratory of Our Future*, with a text by Charles Bowden, which I had bought in 1998. The volume proved even more pessimistically prescient than it dared presume when published. Juárez has indeed become the laboratory of our future: it remains a prototype for the postpolitical global economy and is now also the arena for postpolitical war that that economy has produced in the city. A decade after *The Laboratory of Our Future*, Bowden would reflect, in another book about the city, "Juárez is not behind the times. It is the sharp edge slashing into a time called the future . . . This is not some breakdown of the social order. This is the new order."[5]

Off the road leading southeast from the city, past road bridges built by the big landowners to connect their properties to the industrial parks, a dirt track turns into the scrub, toward the main cemetery. The concrete gateway and cinder-block walls are tagged by gangs when they come to bury their casualties: RIP HULK and RIP OXXY. RIP ONZA refers to someone named after the Spanish word for ounce. In one corner is a section marked with white paint on a yellow wall: FOSA COMÚN, the common grave, stretching into the desert—mound after mound of earth beneath which lie those unidentified who died in Juárez. Some have blank wooden name boards, and some have crosses and name plates; those are bare too. Some, oddly, have flowers placed in memory—perhaps by a fellow patient at a rehab clinic, a fellow addict, or a family member who dare not give the murdered loved one a name. Traffic from over the horizon sends a distant hum of life from the road running through the army checkpoint and out into the desert, and a northerly wind scatters stray garbage and rustles the petals left in memory of the anonymous dead.

Hugo de León, proprietor of Marmolería Hugo, one of the sellers of funerary monuments and flowers at the entrance of the cemetery, watches the funeral corteges come and go, and reckons that "about eighty percent are to do with fighting over drugs—and too many of the dead are young. But some of the funerals still bring the mariachis and have a party." For some of those without names, he suggests, "the family couldn't afford to get the body from the morgue" or "no one dared come forward to claim the body in case they got killed as well." Of course, many of those buried in other parts of the cemetery do have names: "We've had eighty bodies in the last five days, most from the violence, and most of them went over there, to the regular cemetery," says de León. The walls to the "regular cemetery" are tagged like those at the entrance: RIP FLOZO 2008 and SAD DOG. There are photographs on some of the headstones, like that of Miguel Ángel Juan Pavilla, who turns his firm, almost belligerent gaze out across the cemetery, having been killed the night of the Grito in 2009—possibly one of the victims in the Barrio Azul rehab center—just before his nineteenth birthday. He had a strong jaw, close-cropped hair, and a blue zip jacket with ROCKET emblazoned across it. Someone has put a pink teddy bear on the grave of Luis Ramos Vega, killed on June 20, 2009, age twenty, and written TQM in pebbles—Te Quiero Mucho, I love you so. She has also left a bottle of Coca-Cola in which yellow and white flowers are placed, struggling to drink the soda into their stalks. Beyond the latest headstones, the gravediggers have done their hefty workload well: deep, fresh holes dug, mounds of earth beside them, ready to welcome tomorrow's harvest.

"If Juárez is a city of God, that is because the devil is scared to come here," goes the old saying. But Julián Cardona, braver than the devil, remains in Juárez and is building himself a new home here, which his German shepherd guard dog Caesar is only just getting used to. In November 2008, Cardona and I had embarked on a forensic tour of the scene around the decapitated body suspended from the Bridge of Dreams that same morning. The narcomensaje was itself a puzzle. "I, Lázaro Flores, serve my boss, the dog-fucker," but that was not the dead man's

name. Lázaro Flores is a prominent businessman with no connection to the killing who owns an event palace, and narrowly escaped kidnapping, allegedly by police officers working for La Línea. There was also written a threat to a named senior police officer whose son was rumored to have defected from La Línea to another trafficking cadre. Around the time of the execution, La Línea took to publishing the names of police officers it was about to execute on public narcomantas. A list of twenty-six officers was posted at a dog-racing track just before Christmas 2008, above the bodies of four civilians, one of them wearing a Santa Claus hat.

The Bridge of Dreams overpass is officially called Puente Rotario, after the Rotary Club whose cogwheel emblem it bears, right next to where the body was hanged. It is one of the city's busiest junctions, so there would have been no shortage of witnesses, especially at 4:30 a.m., with the morning tide of shift workers just then heading for the maquiladoras. Hundreds of people must have seen it done. How quickly and surreptitiously can a vehicle or possibly a small convoy of vehicles pull up on an overpass, unload a bloody victim, suspend him between billboards advertising Frutti Sauce and Comida Express fast food, tie and fasten the ropes, and hang the sheet bearing the message—all during rush hour? The killers would have driven their getaway vehicle past a sports bar, open late, called Hooligans; the GMC car concession; and a maquiladora belonging to Honeywell, which would have changed shifts while the headless body was being hung there.

The severed head of the victim, from Sinaloa, was found days later in the Plaza de Periodistas—Journalists' Square—at the foot of a statue of a boy hawking newspapers, a celebration of old Juárez's pride in itself as the cradle of a free press during the Mexican Revolution. The message to journalists could not have been more articulate: a few days later, on November 14, 2008, one of the leading crime reporters in Juárez, Armando Rodríguez of *El Diario*—who had reported on both the execution at the Bridge of Dreams and the discovery of the head beneath the statue—was shot dead while warming up his car. His eight-year-old daughter, whom he was taking to school, was in the passenger seat.[6]

"There's a lot of world-class business here," says Cardona, as we pass the maquiladoras along the executioners' getaway route. "And these worlds entwine, they're inseparable," he explains. "Young families come north, the girl gets a job in the maquila, and the man is sexually potent but economically impotent. But he can earn money working for the narcos, part of a waiting labor force, and if he has a habit himself, which he probably has, he turns to crime and drug dealing to maintain it. So his addiction becomes an economic activity in the marketplace. If you keep things separate," counsels Cardona, "you will not understand what is happening in this city. Narco-maquiladoras-migration, that's the triangle, they're all related. And of course, there's narco money in the construction you see everywhere." We pass the iron girder skeleton of a building that never seems to get finished; it was under construction when I was here seven years previously. "Narco installation art," says Cardona. And later, a car with its windshield shot out: "the new Juárez window design." In the waggish parlance of Juárez, recent architecture is categorized as being of the "early narco," "mid-narco" or "high narco" period. A series of arches proclaim the entrance to the upscale Rincón San Marcos, or St. Mark's Corner, a gated community of villas inevitably rechristened Rincón de San Narcos on the street. Around a pleasant green is arranged a quiet retreat of mansions, each more garish than the next, and advertisements for facial and cosmetic surgery. Here is a metaphor for the economy of power in Juárez. Outside some villas are vehicles marked with maquila corporate logos, and in the forecourt of those belonging to well-known drug barons are powerful four-wheel drives with blackened windows—which are now illegal in Juárez, but what the hell.

In Juárez, the map of the cartel war frays. Any preconceptions about combat between narco-trafficking structures dissipate into a delta of violence. The chains of narco command have, apparently, collapsed. Something new is happening, something terrifying and more murderous. Before proceeding, there is a cautionary word from one of the more renowned Mexican journalists who call Juárez their home, Alejandro Páez Varela, editor of *El Universal*. Paez is back home from Mexico City to greet a group of friends at a cultural center called the Cafebrería—coffeebookshop—and launch his novel, *Corazón de Kalashnikov*, about two women who become involved with narcos. The Cafebrería is an agreeable space, an oasis in Juárez, frequented by a slice of life in the city whose existence is scarcely acknowledged outside it: a beleaguered intelligentsia with tortoiseshell spectacles and ponytails that gathers to talk on white sofas beneath an ironwork staircase. But even this is considered worthy of the cartels' attention. The Cafebrería is run by José Pérez-Espino and his wife, Claudia. José is a former reporter with *El Universal* and runs the Juárez alternative news website Almargen. In January 2010, he posted this message on his Facebook page: "I am afraid for my life. I've been a journalist for twenty years and I've overcome many threats. A person . . . has threatened me with death. I know that he could be an extortionist as there are very many of them. I just wanted to post this information here."

Red wine is served after Páez's reading from his book. Then Páez tells me, "Juárez has been ruled by the Juárez cartel, it is true. But forget what you have read and heard about who controls what. Whoever the controllers are, they leave those who remain in the city to fight a battle to the finish that involves the extermination of rivals, and others. This has become crazy warfare, not even necessarily between the Sinaloa and the Juárez cartels; it is anarchy. Yes, they are all there, Juárez, Sinaloa, and Zetas trying to get in. But the pyramids have collapsed, and not one of the big bosses in the battle for Juárez has been touched, not one—they are far away. This is a fight between the groups and gangs on the ground that used to work for them, and it has become a massacre."

Julián Cardona cautions that "it simply doesn't make sense, as the media and government think, to draw lines between cartels in Juárez. Along the smuggling corridors into the U.S., maybe, but not on the streets. The cartels cannot even see those lines themselves here anymore. Of course the drug cartels exist, they are players, but they are no longer the main reason for the violence here. Look at this as a factory. You have a product and a production line. There are bosses, managers, middle management, line workers, accountants, bankers, shippers—

they are all part of the process, but they never meet each other and most of them are not directly employed by the corporation. We'll have counted seventeen hundred dead in this city by the end of the year [he predicted, rightly, in September 2008] and in most cases, the executioners don't even know which cartel, if any, they're working for. If they change sides, from someone far from here who is part of the Juárez cartel to someone far from here in the Sinaloa cartel, they won't know it. All they have is their assigned task, their piece of turf, and maybe an order to do this, do that, or kill someone. Not why, or who for. They have no idea about the big money, or who their bosses are."

This comes as a partial surprise (if anything surprises in Juárez), subverting the official "map" of the cartel war. But it is utterly convincing. The notion that the cartel war has imploded and no longer explains the bloodshed in Juárez is a heresy against the versions of what is happening as expounded by the U.S. and Mexican governments and many of the media in both countries. It fundamentally challenges the notion of a carefully staged cartel war on a narco Monopoly board, as well as that of a government "offensive" against drug dealing in the city. The heresy was formulated by two reporters, Cardona and his friend Ignacio Alvarado Álvarez, who ran the investigative Almargen media service now run by Pérez-Espino from Cafebrería, but who has since been persuaded by his cocitizen Páez to work at *El Universal* in the capital. "I have a family," Alvarado says, explaining his decision to leave Juárez.

But we had first met when Ignacio was still living in Juárez, with Cardona, later in the morning after the decapitated corpse was hung from the overpass, in the inimitable and inevitable Sanborns coffeehouse, for what was for me an unforgettable briefing. The cartels, explained Ignacio, have "substituted the old pyramidal chain of command for the same concession or franchising system as any other corporation marketing any product or service in the globalized economy." It takes a moment to realize how sarcastically funny Alvarado is being about the legal economy around us. "You know how a corporation will not do its own detailed work anymore—no!—that's not cost effective, that's monopolistic. So like a good capitalist, the cartel outsources, puts contracts out to tender, gives other people a chance to compete in order to reduce its own costs. Why should drug traffickers be any different? They're a business like any other. The cartels have gotten much more democratic in the capitalist sense: outsourced, meritocratic, and opportunistic," he says, half laughing, his eyes widening in mischief, disgust, and fear. "There really are far more opportunities for the small investor nowadays, with of course a higher risk, and more people getting killed. But think of the freedom to operate! The small guy pays a commission for the cartel's control over corrupt officials and the border, and occasionally it'll tell you whom to kill, though not necessarily. The cartels don't need to control the streets—they cannot—so they franchise them, they get other people to kill and die. The problem is: What happens if they have outsourced so much that they lose control completely? Do you see outsourcing making modern capitalism any more efficient? Of course not, it's a complete mess! So the cartels find that it's not so much that they need not control the streets, but they *cannot*." "What wealthy drug lord," adds Cardona, "would want to try and control *this*?

"I used to call my town a city of two economies," Cardona continues, ordering huevos rancheros, "one legal, the other illegal. But now that both are globalized, the dividing line has gone. Both the maquilas and the drug plaza are based on the same notion that the market will find its proper balance, and the market alone will dictate how Juárez will do business. And that is exactly what has happened. The 'legal' economy brought hundreds of thousands of people to Juárez, me included, to work in maquilas as I did, and offers to pay them three dollars a shift. The illegal market needs people and offers better opportunities: double that money for street dealing, multiply it by ten for a carrier, and by a hundred for killing. The maquila job market can't support what it created, so it sends you to get sucked into the parallel drug market, where you get paid in kind, you become an addict, you cut the drugs to sell, so that your addiction becomes an activity in the market, and you become an economic agent. When the recession comes, the maquilas find cheaper labor in Asia, so more people lose their jobs and turn in even greater numbers to buying, taking, and selling drugs. And killing."

Long before Juárez became the economic model for an inflation of killing, it was often a place of tussling between smugglers of goods into the United States. But now, this late-capitalist, postmodern battlefield is for a plaza that did not show up on the previous "map." A plaza that is more fiendish in its violence than any war over trafficking into the United States: the battle for the internal drug market of Juárez—indeed, of Mexico itself. In the aftermath of the cartel war and the throes of this new conflict, Juárez is blighted by drug addiction, markedly to heroin, crack, and methamphetamine. Indeed, one reason Ignacio Alvarado gave for the erosion of cartel structures and boundaries, especially in Juárez, is that "Mexico has become a country with a vast internal consumer market for drugs that is deliberately underestimated by government lies, and too anarchic for the cartels to control, even if they wanted to." "If we divide the drug market into eras," says Cardona, "we can see the smuggling era as that of the cartels—the monopoly capitalist era, if you like—and the explosion of domestic drug taking as that of the free market, of criminal anarchy. Before, in the monopoly era, everyone knew their place: drug lords, the politicians, state police, local police, mid-narcos, and gangs. Now, Juárez has become a formless, horizontal hierarchy, responding to the free market—some become very rich, most go into the trash." Juárez is a city of five hundred colonias, or barrios, with no municipal facilities to keep up with (until the recent recession) its eight thousand weekly arrivals. In each colonia, wasteland is drug-dealing territory for one of the five hundred colonia gangs, apart from big spaces in the outlying barrios like Anapra. There," says Cardona, "the waste spaces are controlled by a gang called the police."

Each colonia also has what in Tijuana are called *tienditas*—little shops, outlets for cocaine, marijuana, synthetic drugs, and heroin—which in Juárez are called *picaderos*, usually marked by a shoe tied to a nearby telegraph wire. As the cartel pyramids collapse, they lose control of the burgeoning domestic market for drugs, with each picadero claiming and operating its own plaza, protected by the local gang. The more the domestic plaza expands, the looser the grip of the cartels, and the need for them to operate not so much a chain of command as an affiliation system of outsourced gangs. As a result, Juárez is now being fought over by a labyrinthine Pandora's box of warring interests. Some of them are street gangs collated into a federation called Los Aztecas, which in turn serves La Línea, a street-level resurgence of the old Juárez cartel thought wrongly to have been shattered by el Chapo Guzmán. Another federation of gangs is Los Artistas Asesinos, which are affiliated to the Sinaloa cartel's siege of Juárez, as are Los Mexicles, also at the pleasure of Guzmán, who will kill anyone they can find who had business with La Línea. An especially vicious animosity exists between La Línea's Aztecas and Los Mexicles, since the latter defected from Los Aztecas to join Guzmán. This betrayal led to a riot in Juárez prison in March 2009 in which twenty-one Mexicles were killed by Aztecas, reportedly with official sanction.

Then there are the various police forces. In January 2009, the police chief tasked with gang busting, Francisco Ledesma, turned out to have himself been a coordinator for La Línea and was murdered. Partly as a result, the rogue element in the Chihuahua state police, formerly a wing of the Juárez cartel, is now believed to be an independent force of its own. The municipal police has meanwhile been liberated by the domestic market from its attachment to politicians and cartels, and can operate as it wishes. The army and federal police, supposedly in town to quell this murderous farrago, we shall consider later.

There is some idea abroad that the killings are contained within one sector of society, or in the shanty barrios, but not in town or the exclusive quarters. Not at all: we drive to a smart villa currently "under administration," where nine bodies were found recently, just opposite a fancy hall called La Cite, a venue for weddings and functions. Then along Avenida Rivera Lara, past Desperado's disco and rodeo, into Calle Sierra del Pedregal, to arrive at a white, gated property where up to thirty-six bodies (depending on which account one heeds) were found buried beneath the patio in March 2007. At another house, at 3633 Parsioneros, known as the House of Death, twelve bodies were found buried. These were killings over which controversy raged, with reports that an informant for the U.S. government was part of the cell that carried them

out, and that those who ran him in the customs service were warned in
advance of most murders and knew that the massacre—in which state
police officers on the Juárez cartel payroll took part—was ongoing.[7] In
the yard behind the House of Death, the picture of a mysterious and
beautiful woman has been attached to the wall and "shot" in the mouth,
as though she were used for target practice. "The general pattern was,"
says Cardona, "that if you exhibit the bodies, you are not killing for the
police. If you hide them, you are either killing for the police, or you are
the police." On the roadside around the corner from the House of Death,
a police recruitment poster features a ninja cop in a balaclava, and the
words ¡JUÁREZ TE NECESITA!—Juárez needs you.

Only guesswork could explain why the satellite town of Riberas del
Bravo is where it is: about an hour's drive from Ciudad Juárez, clinging
to the borderline on the city's eastern edge. According to the susurro,
these communities of relentlessly identical little houses—in which to
install maquila workers previously living in cardboard shacks—were
built here to suit landowners acquainted with politicians making the
decisions, with both set to gain financially from an agreed deal over
some far-flung location. Or maybe it is just that the city authorities somehow thought it a good idea to hurriedly throw up this maze of streets on a
swamp by the river, on what were previously paddies and cotton plantations, cut off from the city, with no attempt at transport connections apart
from a single bus route downtown. There has apparently been some idea
for a park in which children could play: the remains are still there of a
rusting merry-go-round, half submerged in the swamp water seeping
from the Río Bravo. And anyway, to build all these houses during the
maquiladora boom appears now to have been optimistic. Since the emergence of cheaper labor in Asia and the onset of recession, row upon row
of them have been abandoned and ransacked after their owners were laid
off and returned home to the South. The PFK gang—whoever they are—
seems to have made a crack den in most of them, tagging the walls or
else incinerating them. On one street, four houses in a row are burned

out, whether as a result of gang warfare or just pyromaniac recreation. Another posse in town is, apparently, the MK 18, which has taken over a row of empty houses leading down to an open sewer, so that the stink of excreta wafts on the breeze through its territory. At the end of Rivera de Zempoala, two lookout guards stand watch with a walkie-talkie. Ten years ago, this was a city of cardboard boxes growing out of the mire; now it is a showcase for the urban Frankenstein.

As so often, the only respite or sign of resistance emanates from the church, surrounded by a high fence with a locked gate ever since the priest's computers were stolen. Here, children abandoned all day while both parents work at the maquilas can find a meal and company, lining up in shifts—girls, then boys—chatting over polystyrene plates divided into three sections of beans, pasta, and a tortilla, before adjourning to the common room to watch Michael Jackson videos. When the priest is out doing his rounds, the center is run by Alfredo Aguilar, once a gang fighter on these streets, now a recent father and guardian of the next generation. "Here, they are left alone," he says, by way of opening our conversation. Left alone by whom? "By their parents, older youths, their families. We deal with trauma from sexual harassment by fathers and elders; the most common form is violation of girls by their stepfathers, and in some cases a man will kill the children of the woman he takes on, if she has them from a previous marriage." Next to his desk, Aguilar's computer has a screen saver showing a tropical scene—waterfalls, birds, and lush vegetation.

"The little ones," says Aguilar, "are abandoned when their parents go to work, and they fall prey to everything imaginable. We try to give them shelter, some glimpse of other values. It's not easy—we have ten-year-old boys trying to hit on girls who are even younger, because it's what they see at home. There's so much violence in their lives, so many drugs, and that too starts in the home: five to ten people living in a tiny house, on top of one another, with abuse, violence against the children, no privacy, and no one able to sleep. So most of the gangbangers are fifteen or sixteen years old, some as young as thirteen. I was one of them, not serious, but I grew up among these people, girls raped, boys joining gangs and getting killed; I lived with them." Aguilar, twenty-eight years old, wants to make a point rather than deliver a confession. "The main point," he argues, "is that these are people spat out by the maquiladora factory system, and out of that come the gangs and the drugs. These people arrived from Veracruz, Tabasco, Oaxaca to work in the maquilas and when the maquila spits you out, drug dealing becomes a way of staying, a way of living. You stay and survive the best you can, or you leave and your house becomes a crack den. But not only the maquilas: the city has spat these people out too. No wonder truancy is a problem if you have six small primary schools for seven thousand families and no secondary school." To get to secondary school in Ciudad Juárez can be a two- to three-hour crosstown journey each way because the bus routes are arranged like a fan from outlying places like this. Every retired American school bus converges from the colonias on the city center as its destination; there is no transport between one satellite and another, so pupils must travel via what is considered by most to be a no-go downtown zone before daylight in the morning and after dark at night.

Father Roberto returns a few days later and tells me, "When I first came here, I was doing many children's funerals, children who had died after accidents at home. Well, I say accidents, I mean they were killed by their stepfathers, raping them and killing them. I found that in order to have a lover, a woman had to agree to kill the child to get the man. I had six of those funerals in my first two years." Then Father Beto, as he is universally known, relates a few statistics. "There are twenty thousand houses in this district, of which eight thousand are now abandoned," leaving more than sixty thousand people living in twelve thousand tiny houses. The proportion of empty houses is high, even for Juárez, though the figures for the city itself make terrifying reading. A report by the Colegio de la Frontera del Norte, published in January 2010, found that there are 116,000 vacant houses across the city, out of a total housing stock of 416,000 units. The empty dwellings, says the report, "result from the economic downturn that began in 2001, and the depopulation has increased greatly in the last two years because of the recession, violence and insecurity. Many migrants who came from southern Mexico to work in the maquiladora industry have decided to return to their places of origin. Others have migrated to the United States. Various neighborhoods contain mostly deserted and vandalized houses. In addition, statistics from the tax administration offices show that since 2008, more than 10,670 businesses have closed, the majority, according to the business leaders, due to the economic crisis and the insecurity. There are many factory buildings vacant and these cannot be sold for any price to manufacturers due to the current conditions. The vacancy rate in industrial real estate is now at 14 percent. Many of these businesses have abandoned Juárez." The author of the report, COLEF researcher César Fuentes, told *El Diario* newspaper, "The economic, public security, and social crises in the city have important repercussions in terms of economic and social viability. It is difficult for someone to invest in the city if they know that they will become victims of extortion, robbery, and kidnapping."

"The border is all about trash," says Cardona. "Think of Juárez as perpetual motion by different kinds of trash: someone else's trashed fridge or car recycled, turning human beings into trash in the maquilas, dead human trash in the rehab centers—though you can't refit the dead people in a yonke and put them up for sale like you can the trashed cars." We hold this conversation on a ridge of precarious housing above the sprawling colonia of Poniente, to which Cardona originally came himself, from the state of Zacatecas, to work in a maquila. Brought up by his grandparents in the country, he has stayed ever since, apart from a spell back home during which he tried to organize resistance to the breakup of communally held and farmed land, after privatization. But neither the campaign against big landowners grabbing the little holdings nor a love affair worked out. So he headed back north, settling into the miasma of little dwellings spread beneath us. Cardona surveys the panorama, with its views of downtown El Paso in one direction and, to the south, burgeoning cinder-block and cement housing crawling down into the valley and up the other side, dogs and children scattered across the maze of streets and radio antennas piercing the sky. "More than half a million people," says Cardona, "and only a single high school. Anyone who can't make it, throw them on the trash heap."

In the eye of this storm, and at the far corner of Sandborn's Café in the business district of Juárez, Sandra Rodriguez sips a cup of green tea. Even more striking for her courage than for her beauty, Ms. Rodriguez is one of the senior reporters on the principal local paper, *El Diario*. Rodriguez is direct about the peril in which she lives and works, and she speaks with a bravery that is utterly humbling in its dignity and resolve. But she is not without a sense of irony. Born in Chihuahua, she came back to Juárez from Mexico City, she says, after being threatened in the street— she returned because she thought the capital was too dangerous, and affords herself a hollow laugh at the thought.

To do her work, Rodriguez must drive by night through zones of the city few dare penetrate, to listen to people who may know the answers to questions that seem unanswerable. She recalls an evening on which she had to abruptly end a conversation with a man who calmly announced he was informing on the cartels to the authorities—not someone to know in Ciudad Juárez. Although the job is becoming increasingly dangerous, Ms. Rodriguez remains tied to the city and to her work here. But, she acknowledges, "I am very, very concerned for some of the reporters who have young families. There was a colleague of mine, a young woman with a child, who was going to do a story, and I said, 'Let me do it—I don't have children.' But this woman said, 'I have to, like a duty, because it is my job.' She wasn't looking for fame, because we don't have bylines anymore. She just knew we all have to carry on with this task to expose what is going on."

But what is going on in Ciudad Juárez, Sandra? "Above all, we are talking about a culture of total impunity," Rodriguez says. That word— *impunidad*—is the title of a book on which she is working. "Impunity starts at the top, with the people like those who arranged for the building of Riberas del Bravo where it is, on a marsh, who created the monster of a city purely for reasons of personal gain. The entire urbanization of the city is a criminal enterprise." And it goes all the way from those in power to the very bottom, and everyone in between; right down to the kids growing up in this criminal city, who never go to school, who instead go over to the narcos. All the way down to the sixteen-year-old boy I wrote a story about who killed his mother and father and little sister. When I asked him why, he said, "Because I could."

The message to reporters in this city implicit in the murder of Armando Rodriguez, after the head of the victim hanging from the Bridge of Dreams was found in "Journalists' Square," could not have been more articulate. But in Juárez—while newspapers elsewhere in the country have been silenced by the cartels, and some fifty-eight reporters killed—*El Diario* continued to publish detailed, daily accounts of the bloodbath despite and since the murder of Armando Rodriguez (no relation to Sandra, though of course they knew each other as colleagues). The response of the cartels—or whoever the killers are—came on September 16, 2010, when a *Diario* photojournalist, Luis Carlos Santiago, and a young intern working with him were attacked by gunmen as they left the paper's office for lunch. Santiago was killed and the intern wounded. A week later, *El Diario* published a dramatic front-page open letter addressed "To the Leaders of the Different Organisations That Are Fighting for Control of Juárez" and titled "What Do You Want From Us?" The editorial, significantly, addressed the criminals as "the de facto authorities in this city," avoiding the word "cartel" so as to encompass all possibilities regarding who the killers might be—including politicians, police, gangs, and the army. "We ask you to explain what you want from us, what we should try to publish or not publish," wrote the editors, adding, with a chill, "so we know what to expect."

The open letter was wrongly reported in the United States as a sign that *El Diario* was going the way of newspapers like *El Mañana* farther downriver in Nuevo Laredo, which has agreed, very reasonably, not to report the slaughter in order to protect the lives of its own reporters after an editor was murdered and its offices attacked. But *El Diario*'s intentions in publishing its editorial were quite the reverse. "We cannot stop reporting what is happening here," Sandra Rodriguez says. "It is our duty, and we all of us feel it strongly—that we have a truth to tell, and we are committed to this first of all, because this is our community and because we know it better than anybody."

As importantly, but unreported in the United States, *El Diario*'s open letter went on to lambast the Chihuahua state secretary for education, Guadalupe Chacón Monarrez, who had accused the media of becoming "partners" in the violence by reporting it because, she said, "psychological terrorism is achieved through communication." "What is it she wants us to say with respect to that?" countered the paper. "That we will stop publishing?" Chacón Monarrez, the paper asserted, "has created a smokescreen, to hide the incapacity of the authorities who have not done their job." Unlike its journalists, who have done theirs beyond every call of duty.

Indeed, it is hard to imagine journalism as brave and dangerous as the kind Rodriguez and her colleagues practice in this murderous demimonde. The writer Charles Bowden urges that if the Pulitzer Prize is worth what it claims to be, it should be awarded with honors to the staff of *El Diario*, whose concerns are very much those of the United States as well as Mexico, and whose offices are, after all, only a short walk from Texas. "If the Pulitzer stands for publishing the truth against the might of governments and at risk of your life," Bowden says, "then this year [in 2011], the nabobs of American journalism have it easy: give all the newspaper prizes to the people of *El Diario*."

A spaghetti junction of slip roads connects U.S. Interstate 10, as it skirts within yards of the border fence and roars through El Paso, with the Patriot Freeway, which runs north from the frontier. Today, the cars are arrayed in all their glistening glory. No, not those above on the freeway, but in Lincoln Park below, where they are attended to with loving care by people from the tough barrios on the edge of town. A 1968 Impala Caprice convertible from the fourth generation of Chevrolet's iconic line is flanked by two Mexican flags and has the slogan VIVA LA RAZA emblazoned across the hood in palace script. Its interior consists of puffy cream-colored cushioning. A 1961 Impala, in burgundy, has the famous bubbleback roofline and bears the motto LOW-RIDING GIRL. Indeed, in front of the car is a child's doll dressed in a microskirt in the colors of the Mexican flag, next to which is a real live girl to match, subject of quite a few photos as she poses against the vehicle on the highest of heels, showing off the hair she combs, her legs, tattoos, and supposedly the car. The seats are upholstered in—what else?—green, white, and red with CHICANO POWER embroidered into them. The occasion is a heartwarming one: the Chicano Arts Festival—part car show, part family cookout, part girlie catwalk, part gang convention, part arts fair, part afternoon disco, part Mesoamerican costume parade for children. On the concrete stilts supporting the freeway are graffiti paintings of the pyramids at Teotihuacán and the assertion LINCOLN PARK: EL CORAZÓN DE EL PASO, the heart of El Paso. The pillars cast shadows in long straight lines along which rows of people, mostly extended families, align their deck chairs in order to eat barbecued picnics in lines that rotate like the shadow cast by a sundial, in order to stay in the shade. But the real matter at hand is the battle of the čar clubs, which loosely reflect neighborhoods and even gangs—or clans—and in which mutual respect and rivalry coexist in roughly equal measure: the Oldies Car Club of New Mexico pitched against the Imperials of El Paso, the Latin Pride Car Club against the Natural High Car Club, the Our Story Car Club against the Ekztazy Car Club. "It's about cars, it's about Chicano pride, and it's about your own pride in your own club, which is your brothers," says Alejandro Dávila from eastern El Paso, an imposing man with the Aztec calendar tattooed on his shoulder and the two-headed serpent on his shin below the cargo shorts. "It all started here, man—hot rods, zoot suits, that's our heritage here in El Paso and we're conscious of that. The chicas are part of that scene, they go with the cars. You got the car, you get the chica; if you don't have the car, you gotta find some other way, see what I mean," and he laughs, begging the obvious awkward question about gangland and drug dealing. Yes, he says carefully, there is a role for some *chucos*—people from El Paso—and what Alejandro calls "Segundo Juárez, which I guess means Juárez USA, you know—overspill of what's going on over there. There's a kind of connection between Juárez and a gang this side by the name of Barrio Aztecas."

But, Alejandro continues, "most folks aren't involved in the other side. That's gone way heavy now. We stay this side, just chúco clubs, car clubs. The crazy stuff don't come over here too much, and not at all on the car scene. The car scene is family, brothers, people who've been in jail maybe but come out again and cleaned out. We do heritage now, Chicano heritage. And I mean they're beautiful things, man, very beautiful objects, and a lot of work and money to get to that condition. It's all connected in the cars, you know—brotherhood, neighborhood, all kinds of connections, and sure it's a pussy connection too." A woman arrives and ends the conversation. "This is my mother," says Alejandro, introducing a cleaner for the school district, and they wander off together to admire cars and join the extended family for empanadas.

Alejandro has a point: the much-vaunted "spillover" of violence across the Rio Grande has not occurred (yet) other than as a series of episodes. Drug traffickers and their support systems in gangland—never mind the "legitimate" financial sector—seem reluctant, so far, to draw the authorities' attention on the border itself. Of course, there are exceptions that go beyond the daily routine of transborder carjacking and mugging. *El Diario* in September 2009 carried a grisly picture of a pair of severed arms folded and resting on the chest of their former owner, Sergio Saucedo, age thirty, kidnapped in the El Paso suburb of Horizon City one fine afternoon in May. Three men wearing black baseball caps and black gloves burst into his home and took him away in a maroon Ford Expedition, as recounted by his wife and a busload of schoolchildren who bore witness to the abduction. Saucedo had convictions in the United States for money laundering and cocaine possession with intent to distribute, and had been taken by his captors across the border to Juárez, where his mutilated body was found four months later, dumped in a busy street. Soon after the kidnapping, on May 15, José Daniel González Galeana was gunned down outside his hacienda-style villa in El Paso. He had been a lieutenant for the Juárez cartel turned informant for the customs service apparently rumbled and tracked down by his erstwhile compadres to become what the FBI in El Paso considers to be the highest-ranking member of a Mexican cartel to be assassinated in the United States.[8] One in eight El Pasoans is employed by the military and, in August 2009, the FBI arrested an eighteen-year-old soldier based at nearby Fort Bliss for being contracted by the Juárez cartel to carry out the execution.

The fate of informants, and those in flight to the United States from direct personal threat, is among the preoccupations of a tireless man who helped organize the car club corral and works from a little office on the low-slung Yandell Drive in El Paso: Eduardo Beckett, of Mexican-Irish descent, managing attorney at Las Americas Immigrant Advocacy. Most of Beckett's clients are families facing deportation, or those with citizenship and other problems of any large migrant or immigrant community—wife and the boys in Beckett's office, daughter staying behind in reception to take a nap. "Most people we see here," says Beckett, "have spent their whole lives in the United States, commit a crime, and get deported. They're not educated, and they end up taking odd jobs back in Mexico. A few get a break, others end up in whorehouses or committing another crime. Then you have the others, who have worked sometimes ten years for U.S. government agencies in Mexico—DEA, FBI, customs, police departments—on the understanding that if they give up information, they'll get a visa in return one day. It's called an S Visa, better known as 'Snitch Visa.' But in my experience, once they're found out, or after they've testified, they're just clipped off, they're garbage. The agencies I deal with won't even admit they were informants, and they're sent back to the wolves waiting for them." These special cases that demand Beckett's energy and motivation are people who face almost certain torture or death if they return to Mexico, having fallen afoul of the narco cartels for one reason or another.

Beckett surveys the paperwork, his caseload that looks like a truckload, with the air of an exhausted gladiator. This is a man who spent his student days knocking door to door for the United Mine Workers of America in Gillette, Wyoming, where "all these folks wondered, 'What's this *brown* person doing up here?'" He judges that "most of my clients are looked upon as trash by the system, and that's the starting point. With the informers, it's even worse—they were doing it for the money, and they're snitches. They know that if they cross back over, they're going to get tortured and killed. They have nowhere else to go, they're banged away before they get to court, and they're stuck. And still the feds just say, 'No, I never saw this man.' We argue that they're in danger and a hell of a situation, and they just wash their hands of them or say these things can't be decided in open court because it constitutes a danger to their operations and the way they do things. They argue for internal relocation within Mexico, but there's nowhere to hide in Mexico. And if you're an honest cop, put in an impossible position and in fear of your life, they argue that of course the criminals will be out to get you. They say that's not persecution. We're accused of imputing some kind of politics into what the narcos are."[9] So the law on asylum, persecution, and torture is not ready for postpolitical war, unable to recognize persecution unless it has a political color. The law of the United States is not ready for, and cannot cope with, the postpolitical nightmare of which the narco war is herald—organized terror by branches of the state whose only political color is white powder.

Among Beckett's cases is the extraordinary story of Martín Espino Ledezma. Espino was a mounted police officer in Juárez but left the force due to the strain of his division's duty digging up bodies of young women who had been kidnapped and murdered. He left Juárez in 1993 for his wife's native town of La Junta, to work as a singing teacher. La Junta lies at a strategic hub for the transportation of drugs into Juárez from the south, and there Espino was approached by the leadership of the local PAN party and asked to help in establishing order in "a lawless town." Then Espino found out, he claims in an affidavit filed in a federal asylum case in El Paso, that his sponsor in the PAN "was a puppet for [the narcos] in La Junta." One day, "two individuals came to my office and said they came on behalf of Pepe Estrada [the local municipality president] to put me at his disposal, for me to work for organized crime, and for this they offered me a substantial amount of money . . . My job would consist of distracting the federal police officers at the checkpoints near La Junta. I would also have to put the officers under my authority at their disposal. When I refused, they went from being kind people as they had presented themselves at the beginning to being very overbearing and threatening. On March 3, 2008, Mr. Estrada sent some men to kill me. This occurred that day, which was my birthday," he says. His wife answered the door, outside which two SUVs had parked and "at least six individuals with high-caliber weapons had surrounded the house and pointed their guns toward it. They told her I should watch out, and wherever they found me, they would kill me, that it didn't matter where I went, that they could find me anywhere because they had connections all over Mexico." It was later "confirmed," claims Espino in the same affidavit, that Estrada was working for La Línea, the Juárez cartel.[10]

I wish life was still like that, my uncle Tommy says
But everything's gone straight to hell since Sinatra played Juarez
You could get a cheap divorce, get your Pontiac tuck and rolled
You could take your dolly to the dog track in her fake chinchilla stole.

The Fiesta Club, the Chinese Palace, the Old Kentucky bar
The matadors and baseball heroes and great big movie stars
Those were truly golden years my uncle Tommy says
'Cause everything's gone straight to hell since Sinatra played Juarez

. . . Now Uncle Tommy Gabriel he still plays Fats Domino
He speaks that border Spanglish well, he owns a carpet store
He lives out on his pecan farm, "I don't cross the bridge," he says,
'Cause everything's gone straight to hell since Sinatra played Juarez

It's a song by Tom Russell, who arrived in El Paso in 1997 from Brooklyn in a U-Haul truck. Before that, he had taught criminology in Nigeria, worked in Canadian lumber camps, took time out in Norway and elsewhere besides. But now Russell is the deep-voiced bard of the border, "one of the people who still thinks songs should tell stories," as he says of himself, and of El Paso: "Hell, the town has been semidead for pretty much half a century. If you turn off toward downtown, you'll hit the central plaza with its fountain of fiberglass sculptures of leaping alligators. Up until the 1960s, there were real gators in there, but the drunks fell in and lost their arms and legs." Russell likes to recall Johnny Cash's song "Mean as Hell," in which the devil is looking for Hades on earth, and God gives him a plot of land near the Rio Grande that sounds like El Paso. Notwithstanding which, Russell bought an adobe on three acres "not to find my identity so much as to lose it," he says. Up the hillside was Cormac McCarthy, who "lived in a rattletrap, trying to do the same thing. To be left alone to write. Unfortunately, fame and fans hunted Cormac down and chased him to Santa Fe. I'm still here." El Paso, he says, "is an abandoned midway of cultural impoverishment. When big corporations and big business came calling, decades ago, the city council and powers that be delivered an ultimatum, which went something like this: We'll allow you to move in here, but what are you going to do for us? Big Money squirmed with distaste and walked away." As a result, Russell adds, "the city fathers left in charge bought up water rights by paying off the city council and turned El Paso into one big freeway, the agricultural land both east and west chewed up to build strip mall sprawl and substandard housing." For all that, however, "El Paso is my own Patagonia. Outside and over the edge. Lyrical in its essence, tragic in its fate, comic in its existence. But it's a peaceful place. You find that amusing? The war has not spilled across the Río Bravo. Life is cheap and simple. I like the people."

We are having dinner at a restaurant squeezed between the suburb of Sunland Park, just over the New Mexico state line, and the border, the other side of which is Anapra, the poorest colonia in Juárez. Another train rumbles by, the railway line backlit by the glow of the city Russell sings about in another song, called "Hills of Old Juárez"—a smuggling ballad. It is the city his fictional "Uncle Tommy" loved until "everything went straight to hell," and that Russell used to love to visit for bullfights and the Kentucky Club, the city where Steve McQueen died. But Russell, like Uncle Tommy, thinks twice about crossing the bridge since everything went to hell; moreover, he says, "I wouldn't sing some of those songs now, like 'Hills of Old Juárez.' Any idea that drug smuggling was in some way daredevil or romantic, bandits under the mesquite trees, just ain't admissible anymore. But that ain't to say I don't miss old Juárez and the way it was." Russell has a new song now, about drugs coming north, guns going south, and the ghost of Benito Juárez watching on and shedding a tear.

Like Tom Russell's, my memories of Juárez are of a city that explodes at night. On a Saturday, the Esfinge—Sphinx—disco, shaped like an Egyptian pyramid behind what was the Holiday Inn, was pullulating with a multitude of drinkers and dancers, mostly girls spending their maquiladora wages like there was no tomorrow. For this is a strange economy: wages are pitiful by U.S. standards but not by those of the Mexican interior, and if you want to go out dancing with your friends on a weekend, there might be the change with which to do so. Life on the border is all about inspection: you are forever clocking in and clocking out at the maquila, your productivity is overseen, your lunch break and even your toilet break are monitored, papers are scrutinized by the police, the army, and at U.S. border checkpoints if you are able to cross the bridge. You even get checked by the doorman and security guards here. But once inside, Esfinge is a different kind of inspection: that of a factory girl's body by every male in this ruffian ballroom tripping the light fantastic. And it is an inspection she passes with flying colors, whether she is here to court the boys in earnest, flirt a little, or just shake her bones with the other girls with whom she makes harnesses for car distributors by day, and then head home. I remember them dancing and strutting, all flutter and flicker, simultaneously humiliating and bedazzling their drop-jawed, wide-eyed audience, nine times out of ten refusing the offers of drink or whatever. Factory girl by day in cap and apron, danseuse by night, dressed to kill. But not all the men in their spiffed-up shirts and tight slacks will be content to admire from a distance, nor will their attentions be necessarily amorous. The horror of extreme violence against women came to curse (but also to define) this city and predict the present way of violence in narco warfare.

In here, though, aphrodisia and the music were all that mattered. Like the concupiscence of Nero's Rome, that of Ciudad Juárez was connected in some perverse way to the impending collapse out there: the superabundance, the flowing drinks, the mellifluous arc of a perfect arm and a toss of the hair are a devil-may-care defiance of death in the streets and hard factory grind. Kisses blown and conjoined, acceptance and rejection, tease and tussle, the chessboard diplomacy of the dance floor as it is anywhere else in the world, only in Ciudad Juárez it was lascivious like nowhere else—both despite what was happening outside and because of it. The girls who saved up to go to these glitzier places were called *fresas*, strawberries, back in the day—the nineties and early "noughties." Those who preferred to economize or could not afford an $8 entry fee could go instead to the less lavish bawdyhouse called El Patio and listen to a band singing narcocorridos rather than the thumping techno at Esfinge. But El Patio was voluptuous enough, the debauchees in skin-tight jeans and boots of blue, red, and green crocodile clinging to the girls' fingertips as they spun them around with elastic arms but a firm grip, watching the skirts flying and breaking smoke rings in the thick, damp air. On the border, by the way, a corrido (masculine) becomes a corrida (feminine) when it is being danced to.[11] In El Patio, a visiting foreigner was a space alien, unworthy even of a threat, in fact so absurd that the bravos would buy me a drink—just one. At Esfinge, though, an outsider who was not American got drawn in. It was all "Welcome to Juárez!" and clinking glasses of *paloma*, which normally means a dove but in this dive is tequila and grapefruit. It was written in the fake luminous stars on the ceiling: one was, irrevocably, part of the strawberry game in this place where no one really belongs, apart from those counting the laundered money.

Back in Juárez seven years later, in 2008, Esfinge was subdued. Amexica's great city of the night, over decades of naughty-but-nice, was ill at ease after sundown. Back again in 2009, Esfinge has shut. The nine-story hotel I check into is empty apart from a boxing team from Chihuahua City on its way to fight in Finland. In 2008, Cardona and I had gone for a beer at another dive, Bar Amsterdam. There, one of the barmaids wearing the uniform red microdress, Giselle by name, joined us for a drink. She told the quintessential Amexican life story about making it across the border when she was fourteen, getting as far as Denver and a decent job, only to be stopped ten years later because of a faulty taillight on her car, caught without papers, and deported. Back home, Giselle took the job at Amsterdam, where she could be leered at for a living. She seethed with palpable frustration at it all. She wished the men who came to do whatever they thought they were doing here to cream their jeans would please just play more Creedence Clearwater Revival on the jukebox instead of that endless fucking norteño. Sometime afterward, in July 2009, Cardona sent a story from *El Diario* that read: "Five men were assassinated in a spray of gunfire last night, while meeting in a bar called 'Amsterdam.' First reports said that two of the victims were beside the bar, and three were in the toilets . . . Word reached the first agents on the crime scene that one of the victims had been terminated with a so-called tiro de gracia."[12] Giselle, according to the susurro, had apparently found herself a narco she liked and gone to work in another place, Dallas, which had been closed after its owner was kidnapped and shot dead. Cardona and I return to Amsterdam in October 2009, after the killing. As we walk in, all six barmaids come and sit in a row opposite us, like a chorus line. We are the only customers. We drink a beer and quickly leave through the dark, deserted, and menacing streets. "The narcos," says Cardona, "decided to take over the nightlife, and in doing so, they killed it."

Anyway, all this hanky-panky caper in no country for old men is all very well until you get close to the other old men. On my last night in the empty hotel, the boxing team and I were joined by an American whom it was my dubious privilege to meet in the elevator. He was sweating profusely through layers of fat and the polyfibers of his San Antonio Spurs sportswear at the prospect of an evening with the teen lovely accompanying him to the floor beneath mine. The kind of sleazebag who needs to forget that she is the same age as his daughter, he slapped together two packs of lingerie like a baseball into a glove. *"¡Duerme bien!"* I offered cheerfully—sleep well—to which he replied, "You too," with a look that said he wanted to punch my teeth down my throat, while the young belle smiled with a mixture of defiance and humiliation. I retired instead to watch Telemundo's unrivaled broadcast of global highlights from every major soccer match that day across the Americas, Britain, and Europe, which the Mexican channel does with cosmopolitan panache and an excitable love of the game, wherever it is played, that puts the parochial myopia of American and British sports coverage to shame.

Even in changed Juárez, there are still attempts at public life. In the parking lot of Plaza Renacimiento, there's an impromptu night rally of customized cars—not vintage classics like El Paso's, but roaring, grinding, screeching Toyota Camrys and Volkswagen Golfs, genetically modified with overdeveloped hubcaps and souped-up engines, and low-slung to make sparks against the tarmac. The young drivers race a little, but mainly they just take turns wheeling around the lot making as much noise, smoke, and smell of burning rubber as possible, for the benefit of onlookers. It's edgily hysterical, certainly, but "the best fun in Juárez," says Antonio González González, proud owner of a white Ford Focus with what look like wings over the rear wheels and a chassis millimeters from the road. "During the day, in the maquila, it feels like everyone is driving the machines apart from me, but when I'm in my car, I'm driving," he says. At the other end of the spectrum, October 2, 2009, was a big night when—as if Juárez hadn't suffered enough—Sarah Brightman came to sing and close the fifth Chihuahua international cultural festival. There she was, onstage in the Benito Juárez Stadium in the most dangerous city in the world, wearing a dress that seemed to come from the costume-drama wardrobe, flanked by crooning tenors and a bevy of dapper musicians. La Brightman's saccharine voice wafted across the air, heavy with sulfur fumes from the chemical works and this evening's news of seven more murders. The song lyrics were inescapably bizarre in such a place: "And I think to myself what a wonderful world." The finale, "Deliver Me," rose to a crescendo of fake packaged hope for Juárez, making way for the second elaborate and extended fireworks display in a fortnight (the Grito of independence was just two weeks beforehand). "Deliver me, loving and caring . . . Deliver me, the cross that I'm bearing," she sang sweetly, into the murderous night.

And credit to Ms. Brightman: many, influenced by the headlines, would have shied away from the appearance; she was right to keep it. For Juárez surprises those who come here on business or to take a peep. Journalists who arrive expecting to find a besieged Sarajevo or Grozny are disappointed (or relieved); BBC news presenters in bulletproof vests talking to cameras look downright silly. By day, not much has visibly changed in the little streets behind the cathedral and the plenteous Cerrajeros marketplace, especially on Saturday, when the shroud of work is lifted and Juárez's face is hearty and sanguine. This landscape of flotsam and jetsam for sale could exist only in a border town, and only on a border with America. Everything that is not quite à la mode north of the frontier lines the streets in overload quantities: sixties furniture, soda fountains, hair curlers, Kelvinator cookers and Osterizer blenders, as though the sets of hundreds of postwar movies had been ransacked and put up for sale along Mexican sidewalks. There's a "Venta de Boilers Eléctricos y de Gas Termostatos," a block of sixties sofas and armchairs, another block of sixties cookers, and another lined with predigital electronics: reel-to-reel tape recorders and mono record players, even some early stereo. What a bloated modern city nowadays calls "retro," Ciudad Juárez calls the Saturday market. The centerpiece, though—the masterpiece—is the car mart.

Here is Amexican border economics at its most eccentrically creative, supplying Mexico with refurbished, formerly discarded or crashed (and written off) American cars between five and twenty years old. While the periphery of Juárez is an infinity of yonke auto-repair yards, the arteries running from the marketplace are lined with miles and miles of refurbished models. The man selling one stretch of them, Enrique, explains the system: "We go all together in the back of a van, to the auctions, all over the United States, then drive or tow back the cars that have been discarded. Some have been in car crashes and we rescue them from wrecking yards because we know we can do things with them the Americans won't. Others are just old, or damaged in some way, and the gringos offer such low prices that it's worth our while fitting them up. Sometimes, they're in a really bad state, and we need to do some work on the other side, in our relatives' workshops. That's why we usually go to the sales in North Carolina, Texas, or Chicago." One by one, the cars are fixed up to the point of being able to get them back, via a bribe to Mexican customs. In Juárez, they are made roadworthy again, driven back to the United States, relicensed, returned to Mexico, and either registered with a Mexican plate or driven as a coveted American car. The export "duty" paid to Mexican customs for this second, more delicate, crossing is usually an informal settlement with a specific officer or shift, explains Enrique. The system works: "People come from all over Mexico to buy these cars," he says.

This matey discourse carefully skirts any connection between this trade and that in drugs. As everyone knows, part of the yonkes' work is to fit up the ingeniously secret compartments for hiding drug shipments across the border. Fitting out the cars is an expert business, with container spaces hidden in batteries, tires, door panels, .and elsewhere, often treated with mustard, engine grease, hot chili pepper, or perfume in order to foil the dogs. But even without the more lucrative kitting up of vehicles for smuggling, the economy of the resale market is all the more baffling when we learn how cheap these cars retail for. I asked Enrique's understudy Emilio how much a beautifully done-up Chevrolet Impala costs. "About a kilo," he says, by way of a telling Freudian slip, with a completely straight face, meaning $1,000. Most of this business is probably semilegal, with customs officers working out private import duties, says Emilio, and creates badly needed jobs in a city busy training mechanics. But, given Emilio's ambiguous word for a grand, the term the Mexicans use for a car loaded with drugs for smuggling is *clavo*, literally, a nail. And there is a bar just up the road—the local, indeed, to which the mechanics and salesmen retire for a beer and snack—with a great nail rising from its roof, called, of course, El Clavo.

To say that little has changed in the marketplace is not strictly true. There are army Humvees patrolling the crowds and refrigerators, soldiers in pale desert camouflage, weapons at the ready, safety catches off. And similar trucks driven by the federal police, in dark blue ninja uniforms, eyes peering from behind their ski masks. And nobody quite sure what exactly the Mexican army—an enigmatic but highly potent power throughout the country's history—is up to.

One of the striking things about the spiraling violence in Juárez is that it escalated dramatically during 2009 despite wave upon wave of military reinforcements. The Mexican government's insistence that an increased military presence is the only way to confront the drug violence makes Juárez the litmus-test city of its policy. It is a test spectacularly failed. In January 2009, there were some five thousand soldiers in Ciudad Juárez. On the first day of March, an additional thirty-two hundred troops were deployed in the city with a massive show of force alongside seven hundred federal police officers, all under the banner of what the military now called Joint Operation Chihuahua. The new troops had new uniforms, which could not be duplicated, said the operation's spokesman, Enrique Torres, after accusing narco death squads of dressing up as soldiers to carry out their executions.[13] There was a respite in the slaughter, but only a brief one, and as soon as April 26, Mexico City sent five thousand more soldiers to Ciudad Juárez, bringing the total to more than thirteen thousand. His efforts at police reform in ruins, Mayor Reyes Ferriz announced that the military would take over police functions and other arms of civilian authority, would man checkpoints, conduct house searches, challenge extortion rackets, and guard crime scenes.[14] By April 21, Jorge Alberto Berecochea, who had taken over the Sixth Police District, took journalists from *The Washington Post* on a tour of the Casas Grandes colonia, to demonstrate what the paper reported to be the "sudden, surprising calm" in Juárez.[15] "The cartels are basically wiped out here now," Berecochea said, making a point barbed with half-truth. "They're not operating, at least not in Juárez." He explained the "cockroach effect" the army had, scattering drug traffickers, and proclaimed, "Ciudad Juárez: right now I'd say it's the safest city in Mexico."[16]

It was an extraordinary claim, and a bizarre report. Two months later, the plot thickened: the army said it had captured twenty-five cartel gunmen who went about their murderous business dressed as soldiers. They were never named, and if they were ever charged, the case disappeared like almost all the others. By early June, the escalation and pattern of killing continued, often targeting teenagers. Three adolescents were among five people executed on June 13, according to *Proceso*. Three more the following day; next day, another five.[17] By midsummer, Howard Campbell at UT El Paso estimated that 90 percent of those killed were street-level drug dealers, not smugglers of drugs into the United States.[18] And so it continued through 2009, by the end of which 2,657 deaths had been recorded in Ciudad Juárez alone.[19] From these statistics, and the nature of the executions, a second heresy arises among the attempts to explain the inexplicable in Juárez: that the violence has intensified not despite the army's increased presence, but because of it.

One especially savage massacre was meted out in August 2008, off Avenida de los Aztecas, at a drug rehabilitation center called CIAD No. 8. A car pulled up on the dirt track, the sicarios alighting and shooting to death nine recovering addicts while they were at prayer. The incident lasted fifteen minutes, and accounts from eyewitnesses reported in the local press suggested that military jeeps had blocked off any impediment to the executioners' progress, guarding their way, while others said the killers were dressed in military uniforms (something, claims the army, that cartel killers do). Certainly, the rehabilitation center is only a few blocks from the impressive Camp Militar 5-C, on the main road. Gangland graffiti painted on the stricken building and in the alleyway give some clue as to why, perhaps, the authorities had a stake in this carnage: LOCOS 23, EL SIGNO, and SIGNO RIP read the paint-sprayed tributes. El Signo was a member of a street gang, apparently now penitent or at least "clean," whom rivals wanted rubbed out, possibly with army approval. Or maybe the army wanted him and his fellow patients killed—no one knows, for the systematic massacre of the city's most wretched outcasts is Juárez's cruelest mystery. "The army," says Ignacio Alvarado, one of the original heretics in the Juárez media, with Cardona, "is like Spider-Man. It has a double. There is the real Spider-Man, and there is his dark doppelgänger." No emergency services arrived to help the wounded from the rehabilitation center massacre—they were taken to the hospital by trucks driven by staff and neighbors. Hours passed before the police arrived. No one has been arrested. It was after this attack that the Red Cross in Juárez said it would stop treating gunshot wounds in rehab centers and would not respond to emergency calls after 10:00 p.m., after death threats were made over their internal radio network.[20]

There are three interpretations of the why, who, and wherefore of mass killing in rehab centers. One is that of Pastor José Antonio Galván, who runs a rehab clinic and asylum on the outskirts of town called Visión en Acción: the cartels—el Chapo Guzmán's Sinaloa and La Línea heirs to the Juárez cartel—are picking out former sicarios and other operatives who once worked for their rivals. A twist to this is added by a former patient and now an assistant at another rehab clinic who wishes to remain anonymous: the cartels have an interest in eliminating their own, the logic being that if they are trying to clean up, rehabilitate, and fix themselves a new life, they would become dangerous, no longer bonded to the organization and knowing too much. And there is a third possibility, the heresy, advanced by Cardona and Alvarado: the Mexican army is using the crisis to either facilitate by default, or even engage in a campaign of what they call *limpieza social*, literally social cleansing of society's unwanted outcasts: the undesirables, drug addicts, street urchins, and petty or more-than-petty criminals. The army hardly dispelled this notion when the general in charge of the Eleventh Military District, of which Juárez forms part, described each death on his watch as that of "*un delincuente menos*"—one less criminal. The occasion was a press conference on April 1, 2008, at the State Palace in Chihuahua City, when General Jorge Juárez Loera told the assembled journalists and photographers, "The media are very important to us. Tell the truth, say what you have to say, but say it with courage. And I know that the media are sometimes afraid of us, but they should not be afraid. I hope they will trust us, and I would like to see the reporters change their articles and where they say 'one more murdered person,' instead say, 'one less criminal.' "[21] Sandra Rodriguez of *El Diario* was herself subject to a terrifying slander by the army in 2008 after she began investigating human rights abuses by the military in Ciudad Juárez. When she raised a question about the violations at a press conference, a Mexican army general singled her out and said: "You look suspicious to me." "They were suggesting that I work for a criminal group," says Rodriguez. "They had even been talking about it with the delegate of the federal prosecution service in Juárez, suggesting that I was compromised." Such an affiliation—an outrageous allegation in Ms. Rodriguez's case—is a death sentence in the Mexican media: a number of journalists have been killed not because they were crusaders for truth but because they were placements by one cartel or another, taken out by a rival. Requests were made for access to the army for this book, to ride with its patrols, discuss general strategy as well as these allegations in Juárez—including a request at the highest level with President Calderón's adviser, Ms. de Soto, in Mexico City—but were not granted.

The most compelling public official to emerge from Juárez's war believes that all the above explanations of the killing in rehab clinics and of the poorest on the streets can be concurrently true, including the heresy of limpieza social by the army. Gustavo de la Rosa Hickerson is a fascinating man. Born to a middle-class family in rural Chihuahua, he came to Ciudad Juárez as a boy to do two things: live rough and train as a lawyer. De la Rosa explains all this over an Italian dinner after his second day in exile in the United States—in flight from death threats by the Mexican army. During the 1990s, he was appointed governor of the Juárez jail, a formidable task and dangerous position for anyone. He brokered a truce between street gangs that organized and confronted each other within the prison walls, and so presided over a period of peace, shattered only after he left, when, in March 2009, a riot between gangs led to twenty-one deaths.[22]

In April 2008, de la Rosa was appointed legal director of the Chihuahua branch of the National Human Rights Commission, a rare instance of self-policing by the Mexican government. Established in 1989 by the Interior Ministry, the commission has independent judicial power and can refer instances of human rights abuse to the appropriate prosecuting authority, and this was de la Rosa's role in Chihuahua—in theory. Soon after the arrival of the military in Ciudad Juárez, during early 2008, de la Rosa began to open files on what he believed to be abuses by the military. From January of that year, he collected 154 complaints against the army, including "allegations of house searches without warrants, arbitrary detentions, torture, abuse, and even killings during the detention of victims."

De la Rosa was on his way home from work on September 4, 2009, he says, when he stopped at a traffic light. A driver pulled up alongside him, rolled down his window, and imitated a pistol with his hand—"like this," says de la Rosa, making as though to fire through a barrel of two outstretched fingers, with recoil. The motorist said, "Quiet down, or we'll kill you." When de la Rosa asked his own commission for physical protection, he was refused; indeed, his superiors in the state human rights commission headquarters at Chihuahua City ordered him to stop taking statements from alleged victims of army abuse. Soon afterward, one of de la Rosa's bodyguards was shot dead. On September 22, 2009, de la Rosa walked across the bridge into El Paso and exile. He stayed with his brother, resident in the United States, and two days later had lunch with his son and daughter in the restaurant of the century-old Camino Real hotel downtown. After eating, he kissed his children, wished them safe passage across the bridge into Juárez and return home before dark, and sat down to talk.

He has an imposing stature, a wild mop of white hair, and white beard—everyone, including him, says he looks like Father Christmas. But there is severity too, and in this circumstance even a certain vulnerability. De la Rosa talks about the notion of limpieza social going back a long way in Juárez, to the 1950s when, he said, undesirables and criminals "would be taken up in aircraft and simply thrown out into the desert." De la Rosa does not believe that limpieza social can account for all or even most of the deaths in the Ciudad Juárez war. But, he says, "I believe the police know who the expert executioners are, who the people are fighting the cartel war at street level. I believe they know who is in the Azteca gangs and who is in their assassination squads. When I was at the jail, the administration, CERESO, had a map in the office showing which colonia gangs affiliate with which cartel, and quite a lot on specific individuals, which means that when they affiliate with a cartel, they know exactly who the rivals are. The information we have is that when the killings involve known members of Los Aztecas, they are carried out by Guzmán's people, and vice versa. And as we know, elements of the police will themselves be at the disposal of one or the other."

But, de la Rosa continues, ordering a fourth coffee, "another group of killings, about four hundred to five hundred this year, are of *malandros*— common delinquents, junkies, nothings—such as those in the rehabilitation centers, crack dens, and abandoned houses, taking drugs. They are always people expelled from society: lowlifes, addicts, dressed shabbily, often homeless. They play no part in this war, beyond the fact that they are drug addicts, have no affiliations, and their deaths have no logical explanation. And they are killed in a different way from the drug dealers or informers. They are not ritually murdered or mutilated, and I don't think these killings are the work of sicarios for the simple reasons that I don't think anyone would want to pay the money the cartel sicarios charge in order to kill malandros, and the style of killing is entirely different. You would not need a sicario affiliated with Guzmán or La Línea to kill malandros who had gathered to try and clean out in a rehabilitation center. Cartel sicarios use either a few bullets, or fire sixty bullets accurately through a small area, like a car window. The malandros are also killed by experts in killing—but differently, in ways characteristic of soldiers or the police, in a hail of bullets, sprayed all over the place, mechanically but without regard to the amount of ammunition spent, as is characteristic of military commandos or death squads. The victims are nothing, but their murders are systematic and cruel. I don't have any hard evidence of this beyond ten homicides and fourteen disappearances, but they are all humble people, poor people, not narco traffickers, and I observe that this kind of mechanical killing of the malandros suggests training in the army or federal police. They're always after poor people in the poor colonias, breaking down doors, taking the young men away, and if there's no young man, they take the father, and hardly ever a drug dealer or serious criminal—always malandros, lowlife.

"I would say," he observes, less forensically, "that the army has come to defend the politicians, not the people. I said publicly that a culture of delinquency is growing in the army. My mistake, or my offense, was that

I got involved in military matters. Let me say, though, I don't think the soldiers are necessarily directly responsible for many of the killings, but I am convinced that the assassination units are operating with their knowledge, or trained by them, and often you can see the killers working on one side of an army checkpoint, then on another. I notice this when killers go into the rehabilitation centers on some occasions, and more often into houses to kill maybe four or five people, day after day. They often do this within three hundred yards of an army checkpoint."

But "I am not able to pursue these cases," continues de la Rosa, "or any other that I have investigated." The procedure is that he sends his findings to the state commission, which passes them on to the Eleventh District's military command, which should pass them on to the army's internal investigations division in Mazatlán, Sinaloa. "I do not know which papers reached which destination," says de la Rosa. "All I know is that no proceedings have been brought on any of them." After we have finished our seventh coffee and a glass of wine in El Paso, de la Rosa's main anxiety is to get to Las Cruces, New Mexico, to meet with Molly Molloy of New Mexico State University, who has been monitoring the threats against him—as part of her coverage of violence in Juárez—and rallying support for him in his flight. It gets later; we put off the journey until the following morning. On the interstate, de la Rosa makes a dark joke, saying that when in El Paso, he keeps being recognized by what he describes as the "middle management" of the Juárez cartel, living on the U.S. side of the border in flight from the violence. "They ask me to come and eat in their restaurants." He laughs. "In just two days I've seen seven or eight of them—their capos are still in Mexico, but they're all over here!" De la Rosa has spoken to his office and been told that if he does not return to work by October 6, two weeks hence, he will lose the job he is being prevented from doing anyway. We reach Las Cruces, find Molloy in the Milagro coffee bar near campus, and de la Rosa orders muffins and coffee, showering the waitress with compliments. When I catch up with them later for dinner, de la Rosa is sporting a beige Milagro Café T-shirt.

As we drive back late to El Paso, de la Rosa asks where I am staying.

La Quinta off Geronimo Drive, as always, I reply, nowhere fancy, but it's good and clean, with a fantastic view of Juárez. "I'll come there too," says de la Rosa, without so much as a toothbrush. "The family and I will only get in each other's way; I need to be alone to think." He checks in, half recognized by the girl on night duty who comes from Ciudad Juárez, goes to his room on an upper floor, and makes a phone call sitting on the bed. The news is not encouraging: an intermediary through whom de la Rosa communicates with General Loera urges him to stay away from the city. "I must try and get hold of the general, then my wife, in that order, so I know what to say to her," he says, shifting from the bed to the desk. This tower of a man seems suddenly vulnerable in his courage, still dressed in the Milagro T-shirt. These are clearly private calls, so the best thing to do seems to be to get him a beer from the fridge in my room, number 262 on the other side of the motel. "Negra Modelo or Bud Light?" I ask. "Bud," he answers quickly, "with lime." De la Rosa's room faces directly onto Interstate 10, trucks roaring by a short distance from where his head will be, with luck, sleeping. Mine, as always, is at the back, tranquil, overlooking the border and a panorama of Juárez by night, twinkling lights and belching smoke beneath my favorite balcony in America. I offer to get de la Rosa's room changed to the rear, in the interests of slumber and the view. "No, it's fine." He smiles as another truck grinds by his doorway. "I prefer to look at El Paso."

5

THE HUMAN JUNKYARD

The procession of the possessed sets out soon after the quickening of the eastern sky, while the sun is still low, and meanders its way along the littered bank of dying grass beside Route 45, as the road departs the raggedy outskirts of Ciudad Juárez heading toward Nuevo Casas Grandes. There are 113 of them, walking like marionettes, some mumbling to themselves, some shrieking out loud, others laughing awkwardly or else silently lost in fretted, crazy thought. They are patients of Visión en Acción, a rehabilitation center and mental asylum on the chewed-up edges of the city, for people enduring the hallucinogenic horror of withdrawal from crack cocaine, crystal meth, heroin, methamphetamine, "blue water" glue, and the rest. Some are just schizophrenics to whom no other place would open a door, who have found themselves in the company of the recovering addicts.

They all love this walk; they do it three times a week for exercise, and the outings are high points. And no wonder: the patients spend most of the rest of their lives within the concrete walls and behind the iron doors of the rehab compound where the desert strewn with old tires and garbage meets the gangrened urban outskirts, just past an army checkpoint and one last Oxxo convenience store before the open road. Some of them even live behind bars—in cages, padlocked, for the safety of others and themselves. Some are former killers, some are former nurses, some are former drug traffickers, some are former strippers—but almost all were drug addicts, now "clean" but journeying through an inner landscape of nightmare and cold turkey. Indeed, it had been quite a night, punctuated by cries, screeching, and lament piercing the still of the desert, and the rattling of metal bars against the chains and locks that bound them.

But night has passed now, its phantoms dispelled with the dew on the creosote bushes and discarded tires, and as the caravan of the mad makes its way along the roadside, the walkers gesticulate wildly at passing cars, at each other, at thin air, or at whatever monstrosity or delight they see in their mind's wayward eye. Some motorists look aghast at this surreal parade and swerve away from it, across the road, lest something untoward happen at close range through the car window. Others, though, are regulars along the route and are acquainted with the procession and even some of the individuals. The driver of a white tanker carrying drinking water hoots and waves, and those walkers who notice the greeting wave back and call out strange acknowledgments in return. Alejandro, wearing leather headgear and goggles for vintage automobile driving, bursts into a jog in pursuit of the truck, then stops suddenly, distracted by something in the distance that has caught his eye, or at least his imagination. He used to deal drugs, he says, "all over the world—in China, Japan, and of course France." There is Manuel, striding along, scary Manuel, who keeps trying to kill his mother, on advice from a rapper called Mr. Bone, who visits his visions escorted by "four little witches." And there is Becky, "Crazy Baby," as she calls herself, one of the team leaders and in high spirits this morning, singing, "*¡Escucha la canción de la alegría!*"—listen to the song of happiness. A man called Antonio needs to wear a diaper, only it has come loose and flaps around his thighs as he walks, barelegged, in a motion of semicircles in alternate directions, leaving a trail rather like that of a snake but occasionally barking like a dog. Twenty-one-year-old Olivia arrived only this morning, and now tries to make what she can of her new circumstances, clutching at a doll. Crazy Baby Becky takes it upon herself to keep the newcomer company and make sure she feels welcome. Up on the road itself, at the edge of the tarmac, is Josué Rosales, the man who keeps Visión en Acción ticking, day to day. A former heroin dealer and street-gang fighter in Los Angeles, he now sees to the running of the refuge, and this morning must act as sheepdog, to ensure no one wanders onto Route 45 and under a truck. Like the one carrying groceries, a big one, which now passes by with a hooting salute to the parade that sounds like a great mechanical fart, and the more cognizant walkers call back, knowing this driver well, *"¡Señor Oxxo! ¡Hola, Oxxo!"*—the name of the store chain emblazoned on the vehicle's side. But Marisela, once a topless dancer, prostitute, and crack addict, lags behind in silence; she has had a hard time so far today, troubled by *"muchas memorias"* and had been tearfully worried that the pastor who runs this remarkable institution might be late and the walk not happen.

But she worried needlessly, for there he is, up front, leading the way, José Antonio Galván, who established and directs Visión en Acción. He wears a full head of silver hair 1950s-style, his trousers are tucked into his boots, and he carries a long wooden staff to steady his long stride, adding a biblical feel to this exodus to nowhere in particular along the road, two miles and back again. He too, from time to time, breaks into a jog, then walks to talk awhile. "This is the human junkyard," says the pastor, with a sweep of the arm toward his flock. He was one of them once, a streetwise kid from Juárez who lived illegally in Los Angeles and El Paso, got deported, became a drug addict on the streets back home, and "hit rock bottom, man, the very bottom, before I was saved by the Lord.

"We are the people no one wanted," he says with a kind of pride, "cast out. This is where they send the trash that no one else wants. I run a recycling center for human trash. I take the scrap people off the street and treat them like human beings. When they come to us, they're not junkies or working women anymore, they're not orphans, they're as much God's children as anyone. So just you think about this, brother: back there in the city, the sicarios are killing children, people are kidnapping and raping and killing young girls, people are torturing other people to death, and people are cutting each other's heads off. In here, we're not doing any of that; here we are still alive, helping each other, not killing each other. Here you can shout out loud, walk around naked with your diaper falling off, and no one will judge you or bother you. In fact, we'll hug you. We're crazy here, but we have love, and we have been saved."

All things being relative, the pastor has a point: in the human junkyard of Ciudad Juárez, the procession of the possessed is, in its peculiar way, a procession of the saved.

To drive southwest out of Juárez toward Visión en Acción is to journey through contaminated desert dust along boulevards of shopping malls, nightclubs, and rooms by the hour with names like San Judas Quick Motel, past more compounds of prefabs built to house labor fodder for the maquiladoras, sprawling colonias built from scrap, and wastelands controlled by gangs. In the dust of early morning, Boulevard Óscar Flores passes the so-called green spaces that a civic forum of more enlightened businesspeople called Plan Juárez wants to "reclaim," on which soccer is sometimes played but that are more often becoming dompes for trash. DI NO A LAS DROGAS reads a large billboard—say no to drugs. Another displays the emergency number, 066, which few citizens care to call, because the people manning the hotline are universally believed to be working for the cartels or the security personnel under their control. People joke that calling 066 is the best way to talk to the kidnappers in the event of the abduction of a relative. The road skirts a hillside into which a giant white horse is carved in imitation of that in Wiltshire, England. It was done by order of Armando Carrillo Fuentes, the Lord of the Skies. Through the outlying military checkpoint, one arrives at a half-built cinder-block structure in the middle of nothing and nowhere declaring itself in careful paintwork to be ALBERGUE PARA DISCAPACITADOS MENTALES, a home for the mentally disabled—invariably for those fallen prey to drugs. On the wall beside the iron doorway are painted the logo of Visión en Acción, a sword breaking, and a passage from St. Paul's Epistle to the Ephesians: "Put on the whole armor of God, that ye may be able to stand against the wiles of the devil. For we wrestle not against flesh and blood, but against principalities, against powers, against the rulers of the darkness of this world, against spiritual wickedness in high places."

As the rust-colored iron door is pulled aside by those who welcome us, it reveals what seems at first to be a courtyard of narco bedlam.

People in various states of derangement and decay either cower and jabber to themselves, dancing around like puppets on strings or, rooted to the ground, just stare incredulously at the very air in front of them. Some come forward, as though propelled by electric shocks, to greet us. First is toothless Rebecca, in a red beret. "I'm Becky! Crazy Baby!" Then comes a man, diaper flying about his exposed not-so-private parts, with skin pitted by warts and scars. Then another, in a dirty tracksuit top and shorts, starts to talk, but whatever his story, which he tells in fits and starts, my Spanish is nowhere near understanding a word of it. But neither is anyone else's for whom Spanish is a native tongue. All around is the stench of tribulation, excreta, sweat, grime, and a sense of miracle against all odds.

Pastor Galván, who founded Visión en Acción, has yet to arrive. But the keeper of the lodge, Josué Rosales, starts to explain how these people came here. He has an inexplicable inner calm behind the intensity with which he speaks, in faultless American English, punctuated by Crazy Baby's contributions. "Most of them have been addicted to drugs for years," he says, "crack cocaine, crystal meth, heroin, and some take stuff that can blow your fuse with just one hit. All of it made here in Mexico, intended for the United States, but it only gets as far as the streets of Juárez. See that woman sitting over there, with white hair? She don't say much. She was a strip dancer in a club, got raped, got into crack, went to jail—but she's getting along better now." Sometimes these people just roll up at the gates, some voice inside telling them they're desperately in need of help, "which is why I live here," says Josué, "'cause they could come any time, to welcome them. Sometimes we find them on the street, talk 'em through it, and bring 'em in, to get 'em off whatever they're on, get them some food, attention, and get 'em off drugs. The hospitals, they don't want to know, and someone has to. I ain't got no medical training, but I need to know what to do with them, what kind of medicine to give 'em, how to book 'em in and calm them down if they're freaking out or having bad visions, before the doctor and psychiatrist come to check 'em out. Recently, we've had the Mexican consulate bring 'em in after they get deported, the police too—just bring 'em here, like junk, er . . . well, garbage, I guess I should say"—and Josué allows himself a smile—"'cause I'm a recovered heroin addict myself!"

So first comes Josué's own story, which he takes time out to tell, first on a rickety bench outside his little cinder-block "office" and sleeping quarters on the outside of the heavy iron gates, a story he tells during four visits I make over a year. The pastor keeps a video of Josué arriving at the home on a stretcher, unable to move, bearded and skeletal, his skin like dry parchment folded over his bones. "Sometimes," Josué begins, "you can be on both sides. You can think you're fine, then go back over to the other side. You flip, or take drugs just once, and you're back in the dark. Me, I'm fine now. I think. I do my best. I do my very, very best, and I'm still here, on this side of them gates." He gestures toward the door though which he arrived as a patient three years ago, his veins swimming with heroin and flesh punctured by needles, his bones broken after a car crash. He was in death's waiting room.

"When Josué came," Pastor Galván would recall later, "he couldn't walk, he could barely move. I had to amputate his finger myself. I kept it for a while, to show him, but eventually threw it away." "I arrived on St. Valentine's Day, I later learned," says Josué, "February 14, three years ago next year [2010]. I've seen the video; I was dying. I was in a coma. I was one of *them*," and he gestures across the yard, as afternoon deepens, and a woman who has just eaten asks where the line for food is. "I'd had a car accident and I couldn't walk, couldn't move. I lay here for a year on a mattress in a corner with the door open, watching all these crazy people jumping around the patio, just like I'd been jumping around downtown. And a voice said to me, 'Kill this person inside you who is destroying you.' And the Lord told me not to go back to being one of them again. All I wanted to do was walk, and get my life back."

Born in Ciudad Juárez, Josué went to the San Gabriel Valley in California to live and work. "But I grew up with heroin," he says. "Heroin is always the same thing, wherever you take it—Juárez, LA, it's always heroin. I used to do heroin in California, and deal it too. I did cocaine, angel dust, and all the other stuff too, but got stuck with heroin. And when you get stuck with heroin, you're hanging out with heavy fellas.

Some of them junkies have big houses and nice cars, but some again they sleep in the trash and empty houses. For a while, I had a job in an auto body shop, and I used to lift weights. I had a '62 convertible and a 1946 customized truck. In 1982, I got first place in a low-rider show. But I was doing heroin, I got busted, I went to jail, and that's where I blew my mind. I remember thinking, 'I'm too young for this,' 'cause jail is all about gangs. I was given a knife, and I was fighting. Jail is where I went crazy. When I came out, I knew every gang in East LA and the San Gabriel Valley, and after a while out, I knew every barrio. Serious shit, shit, shit." And Josué lifts his shirt and sleeves to show the scars from bullet wounds. "That one happened in San Dimas, there was a battle in the middle of the night. A gang from La Susa, shooting at us, but I got to take off, running right up the side of the highway, like that"—and he shoots a flat hand through the air, cutting.

Josué's recollection of his past keeps getting interrupted by reminders of his illness, patients interrupting. "There are a lot of feelings in this place for me. I'm only the person I am now because I've been there and I know their feelings." The narrative continues: "I had to come back from LA because my mother was sick, but I kept taking the drugs, man. I was part looking after my mother and part not looking after myself. By the time I got hit by the car, I was spending two hundred fifty pesos a day on heroin, that's almost a gram a day, five or six shots. I was in that scene; some of them got AIDS, some got gangrene, like me. There's always heroin around for fifty or sixty pesos a shot, and you got people needing a fix, seeing other people carrying a load of money around and they're thinking, 'Hey, what's going on here? Hey, hey, hey—I can have some of that money if I shoot what I need and sell on the rest.' That's what happens when you're totally hooked, totally fucked up. If you found some work and got fifty dollars, you'd spend it all on getting a fix. It was just, 'I've got to get fifty dollars so I can get fixed up.'"

Even though this conversation happens in stages, months apart, Josué's narrative is punctuated by feral sounds from within the yard and dormitories looking onto it, sounds from some zone between a scream of pain and a peal of laughter. He continues: "When a car hit my back three years ago next February, something else hit me too. I told myself that if I hadn't been using drugs, that car would never have hit me. I realized there was no one to blame, no one said, 'Hey, try this,' no one pushed me. I'd done this all to myself. They brought me here and I just wanted to go to sleep forever. But I didn't sleep for months. I just watched and listened to the people who were like I'd been, for days, nights, weeks, and months—feeling the pain and watching. Then really I woke up, something exploded, gracias to the Lord. I'm fifty years old now, and I feel better than I've ever felt. When I go downtown, I always see four or five of 'em. People I used to shoot up with. And they call me 'Güero,' blondie, just 'cause I lived in the U.S. Then someone'll say, 'You looking good, man! Wish I could look like you. Wish I could stop taking all these cocktails, shooting all this junk.' That's when my life gets weird, man, very weird. So I get glad I went through that pain, so I can help the others."

From Josué now comes the street-level explanation of what is happening in Juárez. "The market now for drugs in Juárez, it's very tough competition 'cause the drugs are getting so much stronger. You go around the houses: 'Hey, mine's better!' they say, 'mine's stronger,' and people have so many options. And especially in Juárez. If you're somewhere else, you'll come all the way to Juárez to get the good stuff. That's what a lot of these people were doing. Most of these people were addicts, selling drugs to feed their own habit. But they never see the big fellas. They buy it off people one step up the line, and here you don't need to sell pure like the stuff that crosses the border. They buy it cut with rat poison, fertilizer, or whatever; take some then cut the rest again to sell on. Cut it ten times, you get ten times the money; sell it in the wrong place, you get shot. The big guys are nothing to do with this level, I know that. They don't even know what Juárez looks like. They just make the $250,000 a day, the next guy down $10,000 a day, and so on, down to $10 a day. You know who you buy from, and who you deal to, but you never know beyond that, or who is moving all that coke or meth into the U.S. Only other folks know that, way above the street.

"Do you want to see where I lived on the floor for a year?" Josué asks. And we walk through the iron gates again, into the world that was his, and from which he is now separated by the thin veils of his conversion, his responsibilities, and a wall. To say that the stench is unbearable is no insult; it is just to admit that there is nothing like the suffocating stink of misery. A man speaks: Manuel, a former but now part-time crack and heroin addict on a high wire between saving himself and the abyss. When he hears the voice of a rapper called "Mr. Bone," he explains, coherently, "Mr. Bone tells me to kill my mother. 'Kill your mother!' he says. 'Kill your mother!' He comes into my room, and tears fall from my eyes. And when I get with my friends and we smoke some, the four little witches arrive, and Mr. Bone too, and they order me to fight with guns." For four years, Manuel has been here trying to exorcise Mr. Bone and the little witches, and exchange the drugs for religion, or at least survival. "He's getting there," says Josué, "but he ain't there just yet."

A man wearing a soccer jersey joins us, Luis Noreto. "He was a problem for a while," says Josué. "Tried to kill someone three or four times, and tried to kill his mother." (It seems to be a rite of narco passage, this matricide.) "Yes," recalls Luis, "I hit some bad luck, my mother was praying for me with a candle, but I thought it was a sword, so I tried to kill her, and she brought me here." Luis was on crystal meth, "rock" (crack), and sniffing paint thinner. "But now," he says, "I listen to Josué and have found Jesus Christ, and when my mother comes to visit me, I see my mother. I want to stay here forever, and help people like I was, to be like Josué."

So just as Josué modeled himself on the pastor, so Luis models himself on Josué. And now, the pastor himself arrives. There is a term in African-American preaching, the "charismatic" style, and the pastor is its Hispanic mutation. Galván has little (earthly) backing for what he is doing here, hardly any money, but "with love in our hearts, smiles and hugs, and holding them close to our chest, we do what we do in here," he says by way of introducing himself. The patients call out, "Papi!"— Daddy—with excitement, run to him, and he clasps them to his breast, kissing them, heedless of their weeping sores, stroking their matted hair. He looks a bit like a movie star acting the role of a former streetwise kid from the barrios. Which is exactly what Galván is—the former barrio kid. He has a tattoo of an Indian squaw on one arm. "I was born in Ciudad Juárez, it's my city and I love it. But I was fourteen years over there, from 1972. I was an illegal in Los Angeles and El Paso. Yeah, the wild years! Man, I was making money, operating a crane, hanging out, whatever; there were drugs and babes to spend it on and that's what I spent it on." He was jailed for a period—he implies it was for drugs—and deported. "And after I got deported and I was back home in Juárez," he says, echoing Josué and gesturing toward his patients. "I was one of *them*, completely lost."

Galván's conversion happened on the streets upon which he was dying, found by street missionaries just as he now finds others for Visión en Acción. "'The Lord wants you,'" they told me. 'Wants *me*?' *Wants* me? I used to tell those Bible people to get the hell away from me, 'Get the fuck off my back!' I'd cuss 'em, but they treated me in a different way to how I'd ever been treated, so I started treating myself differently. Found a whole lot of needs I didn't have before." There were several spiritual and physical adventures, culminating in an experience that led to the founding of Visión en Acción, an echo of the Good Samaritan. "I was driving through the cold one night and saw people sleeping by the wayside wrapped in blankets of snow. That was when the Lord gave me this mission." The shivering roadside outcasts were Pastor Galván's calling to establish Visión en Acción, which he believes to be his destiny. "The task," says Galván, "is to dignify the lives of these people and to return those lives to them. Sixty percent of them have completely lost their identity. They don't know their own name, age, who they are, where they came from, or why they're here. They don't know what they were doing before they came here, but many get very aggressive when they arrive. That guy there, the big guy, he was brought by eight cops, handcuffed by the hands and feet—he'd tried to kill a guy in the U.S. That one there had a problem with heroin, his arms were all pitted with holes and all them holes infected. And when we go inside their heads, we find that no one ever loved them or hugged them, their mothers didn't care and their stepfathers hated them, they never went to school—they sold Chiclets and newspapers on street corners or worked in clubs if they were girls.

They started out on glue and paint thinner, then different drugs, more expensive and dangerous drugs, then they're hooked.

"But we show 'em the path, the way out, because we've been there too, we know where they are and how to find the path. I was there; I was living on the streets, trying to work out where the next hit was coming from, and the next meal, looking for food in trash cans. Josué too—the director of the hospital brought him saying, 'I'm giving you this man to die.' No, I thought, he's already dead but we can bring him back to life. Now he's my right arm here, and my greatest fear is he'll slide back and start taking drugs again. He says he won't, he won't even use tranquilizers, but we're all on the edge here."

The pastor finds it "weird that there are also people here who know me from my old life." He says this with a strange expression of disdain, whether for them or himself or both is unclear. "They've seen me on the street and lying in a bed, and some of them try to take advantage of me. At first I had trouble with a couple of guys and a woman—I could see into their thinking: 'We used to change this guy's diapers and spoon-feed him and now he's a boss?' But mostly now they see me as a boss, they have to learn that's what I am. There's a hierarchy here, there has to be for it to function."

There is a man called Alejandro Valencia García, with electric blue eyes, who obsessively washes all the cars parked outside the center— wiping them down, polishing them, the visiting relatives' cars, our car, and especially the pastor's. He's the man wearing vintage driver's headgear, a leather cap with earflaps, and tells the pastor, "You fool everybody." "Why?" retorts the pastor. "Because I'm the only one who knows that you're even crazier than the rest of us," Alejandro replies and walks away laughing. "He was a big drug dealer," says Pastor Galván. So it was true, what Alejandro had said, out along the highway, though maybe not about China, Japan, and France.

One Sunday, they await the pastor again. The iron gate is open, it being the Sabbath, and the patients mill around in the shade of trees they have planted, surrounded by benches made of rocks they have set and painted white. And when the pastor's car pulls into the driveway, they surround it, clapping. Others stream through the doorway from the courtyard calling, "Papi! Papi!" Others, on the edges of the throng, wander and wonder, staring with a flicker of recognition, whispering confidences for themselves alone to hear. Because it is Sunday, the pastor is wearing a zoot-style blazer in a paisley design and black suede shoes. He looks as though he is about to sing "Rock Around the Clock," but instead—once the multitude is settled—gets out his acoustic guitar, sits down on the painted concrete bench in the shade of a mesquite tree, and begins to sing. "Who is your friend when you need Him? . . ." A woman sits at his feet, unties his shoelaces, and ties them up again—a deranged but poignant echo of Mary Magdalene at the feet of Christ. *"Cristo sí, Cristo sí, Cristo sí, sí, sí . . ."* The sing-along is extraordinary—uplifting and disturbing. Some sing beautifully, and in tune; others wail like coyotes in a fit of lunar-induced ecstasy. Crazy Baby Becky bashes a tambourine hopelessly out of time but with feeling, singing louder than anyone else, while a lady with a black shawl and cropped hair and a smock stares into mid-distance, smiles, drops the smile, and weeps. Becky puts down the tambourine, takes her head, and lays it in her lap.

Pastor Galván sits down to talk about things that have happened in the ten months since my last visit. "The big thing now," he says, surveying the bedlam around him, slightly stilled by Sunday hymns, "is synthetic labs, synthetic drugs. We're seeing people's brains getting fried by crystal meth and ice. It's easy to transport, easy to hide, but it's causing a lot of dead people, lots of orphans and widows, and a lot more people like you see here. There's been an invasion of addiction in the city— they're everywhere, like human cockroaches crawling around looking for synthetic drugs. Juárez, it's sinking under a flood tide, a tsunami of addicts, all crazy. They've been given video games if they're lucky, so they know how to kill virtually, and when they're out of their heads and need another hit, they'll take the money to go out and kill for real jus' like they learned in the games."

I ask about Manuel, Mr. Bone, and his little witches. "He suddenly recovers his mind and suddenly loses it," replies the pastor. "When he's doing well, he knows who he is. Then he hears the voices, telling him to go and kill his mother, and starts masturbating all the time, in front of people. He's been doing it since he was seventeen years old and started on crack, and now he's twenty-five." One time, says Pastor Galván, "I took him to the store to get cigarettes, and on the way back we stopped at the checkpoint, and as we descended he was at the soldiers trying to get their weapons so he could kill the people in his head, and when I told them I was a pastor, they said, 'What are you doing with this guy, motherfucker?' and they never want to see me with him at the checkpoint again—yeah, a lot of problems, Manuel."

Manuel is a heavyset man who sometimes contorts his face as he speaks, and at other times smiles as though concealing a secret. It has been some ten months since he explained about Mr. Bone and the four little witches, and now he talks quite lucidly, though the content follows his own logic. "I don't have so many problems now, but I do want to go back and party and I still have a big problem with my mother about witchcraft. She also says I beat her, which I do, I like to beat her. My brother was attacking me with witchcraft, but I don't have the papers to escape to the U.S. My wife is in Texas, living with my sister." Rubbish, says the pastor. Mr. Bone, says Manuel, continues to "use spells and magic against me. And he's very tall, as tall as I am. My new mission is Thai boxing," Manuel says, veering into a new theme. I ask, "Can you box against Mr. Bone?" "Hmm. If I recognized him and he made me angry, I could fight him. I'm dangerous when I'm angry." Manuel stops screwing up his face and smiles that secretive smile. "They gave me the weapons to do it, but I never intended to spray people with bullets." We have to let that go. Manuel presses his nose against his face, squashing it, then pulls and stretches it, kneading it between his fingers as he talks. "And then come the four little witches again, telling me I should go home, to have money and women." Would he ever try to fight the four little witches? "I want to fuck the four little witches," replies Manuel. "They look so sexy, they're gringa witches, blond ones, Americans."

We walk back, with the pastor, into the yard, the human junkyard, the concrete quadrangle where the mad and the scared people roam. In a room off to the right, a man rattles the bars of his padlocked cage, growling in short bursts, then suddenly conversing in a winning way, feigning lucidity, asking for help to be let out to return home to his family. "Don't get involved," counsels the pastor. "He knows how to manipulate, even though his brain's gone. He tried to stab someone, so we call him Cholo, the gangbanger. He can get very violent," the pastor continues relaxedly, inches away from the cage. "And Josué's problem is that he's not that strong yet, and if he tried to intervene between Cholo or Manuel and one of the other patients, he could get killed. When Cholo's in a crisis, it's ugly, hard to stop him, so we keep him locked up."

Bounding across the yard comes Becky, Crazy Baby, who, says the pastor, is usually "more than half in command of herself" and is thus a supervisor of the thirty-six women patients. You can see her taking to her role—that girl crying during the singing this morning, whom Becky rested upon her lap. "Ah yes, Lety," says the pastor. "Lety and Elia, they're sisters. They were found chained up in an abandoned house. They'd been chained up all their lives, like dogs, ever since they were babies. Their parents were addicts and finally left them, abandoned."

We pass the line for food served by big Óscar, now a prefect for the men's wards, and we enter one of those for the women. The rows of mattresses and bodies stink noticeably less than the men's quarters, but the insects are just as populous and, as with the men, there is little distinction between being clothed and unclothed, although Becky's regime tries to keep things decent. On one mattress, Lety and Elia cling to each other. Both have shaved heads and wear long frocks. They speak—or rather, make squeaking noises—in fits and starts, staring hard and quizzically. They are like two little children, although they are in their early thirties. "They're afraid of everyone," says Pastor Galván. Apart from, it seems, Becky, who approaches them and strokes their cropped hair. "I take care of them," says Becky, who is about the same age as they are. "They are my little babies." In this world, it matters not where affection comes from, only that it exists at all.

Becky has a deputy in her task as prefect, Marisol, who wears a woolly hat despite the September heat, and closes her eyelids when spoken to with a shy, childlike sweetness—and sadness. "She was a waitress at a strip joint," the pastor informs. "A dancer, doing cocaine and smoking crack, and prostitution to feed the habit." Now she sweeps the yard and cleans surfaces with a dirty rag, in silence. Marisol seems to know where and who she is, but she keeps it all to herself. "I'm jealous of Marisol," says Becky. Oh, yes? "Yes, I am, because she has a little baby, who they bring to visit her. I fell in love with him when he was three years old." (Marisol's child is a girl.) Marisol also plays an important role here, adds Pastor Galván, organizing the women's wards, their food, dressing, and washing. "But she's schizophrenic, terrible depressions, fits, loses herself completely. She had to be locked up for a year, she was so violent." It seems unbelievable, this placid, timid, apparently crushed but gentle soul, but there is no such thing as a surprise in this place—only the threat of the worst surprise of all:

"Now we're in the firing line," says the pastor. "Yes, us—mental hospitals, rehab centers. You had ten killed at the Anexo the day after the Grito; and seventeen were lined up and shot in August at the Aliviane— just little addicts, like we have. They're going around to the rehab centers taking out people who had any business with the other cartels, and anyone else they take with 'em." There have already been some "funny phone calls," says the pastor, at dinner in El Paso, where he lives for safety. "They called up and said they were the police," but that can mean anything in Juárez. "Now we're in danger, we who run help for the addicts and crazy people, we're on the front line, just by being here and doing what we're doing. They could come for us any night now."

Night falls over Visión en Acción, and the pastor has left. Josué— delegating some tasks to Óscar, Becky, and Marisol—administers medication and shuts things down before retiring to his quarters, which he now occupies alone. The darkness that falls is a deep one, out of which the pastor's fears of what has happened to so many other rehab centers loom larger than they do in daylight. The room, or rather the little cubicle of cinder blocks, in which I am graciously hosted to sleep, is, as Cardona points out as he leaves, "right next to the entrance, the first they'd get to if they come tonight." But the iron bed is already made up, and there's nothing for it but to settle in with Josué and chat away the evening by flashlight. We talk about Led Zeppelin and the Who—"Man, they come from England? I never knew that. I used to love that stuff, but we don't get it in here." He talks about his family, while we eat cold burritos, and about his cousin's husband, a U.S. marine, who had "fought in Afghanistan and against that other guy, Saddam Hussein—he kicked his ass too." Josué makes as though to fire a machine gun. "I heard from him all about those countries, it sounds like fun." But Josué had recently attended his cousin's funeral. He died not in warfare but "in Pinkie's bar, having fun, you know [Josué shakes his hips, as though to jive], and in they came, looking for someone. Sprayed the place with bullets." And Josué talks about his work and some of the people in his care. "Look, what I do here is part of my testimony. A lot of people come through here, and we stare at each other in the eyes, and we can see the drugs, we know, yes we know we've been there. In that stare, I say it with my eyes that I've been even worse'n you are now. I say to 'em—staring hard with my eyes, 'cause they wouldn't understand if I spoke it—I say, 'You've come through fire and water and so have I, so I know what you are doing here.' And even though they're crazy, and can't hear a word, I think they kinda understand." He lets on that the benign ones are not always what they seem. "Becky can be real dangerous. Usually she's fine, but when she flips, she flips real bad, she's a violent one. When she gets angry with me she's threatening to kill me and all sorts. Óscar, he's desperate to make it. He really wants to succeed. But man, when he explodes, he explodes. He needs putting down real hard, real difficult to deal with."

Josué wants to watch a movie. He goes to his cubicle, next to mine, rummages around for his DVD player, and sifts through his collection. "I got some titty ones, but hey, how about this? It's about the crucifixion of Jesus, man, this one's gonna blow your mind. I saw it but not really properly." It is Mel Gibson's *The Passion of the Christ*, and into the player it goes. The bloodier the sufferings of Our Savior get, the more Josué's devotion deepens. The flagellation is an especially savage and prolonged episode, Jesus lacerated to the bone. Josué is transfixed. The fiendish elders of Jewry and weakness of Pontius Pilate stir his wrath—

"Motherfuckers!"—and a pitiless depiction of Calvary makes Josué
sweat with empathetic rage, so that by the time of Jesus's convulsions of
pain on Golgotha, Josué's eyes are popping out of his head. Only with the
storm clouds, and winds that rent the temple shroud apart, does Josué
relax again and prepare for bed. There is one last tour of the courtyard,
under the stars. However haunted their slumber may be, those tortured
in the mind rather than by nails to the hands and feet are mostly asleep.
The occasional groan of anguish drifts from the dormitories, on the desert breeze, sometimes ascending into a whine. Josué shines his flashlight
through the bars of Cholo's cage—he is motionless under a heap of blankets. All told, it feels as though some untamed animal is at rest, its af-
flictions abated a moment, by the quiescence of unconsciousness. There
is quiet, but the smell lingers, though even that is tempered by the chill
hanging from the desert night. Josué makes his way back through the
kitchens to our adjacent sleeping quarters, and we exchange good wishes
for the night, so dark in these windowless quarters, with nothing but
desert out there, that even with eyes wide open one is as blind as a mole.

The occasional truck rumbles by toward Nuevo Casas Grandes or
back into Juárez, but otherwise there is silence. Josué has been both
disturbed and excited by the sufferings of his Savior, and the dark feels
darker just for the fact of being on the edges of the murder capital of the
world with 113 recovering maniacs for company, and only Josué and a
wall between us. But it is not the maniacs that constitute the unquiet in
the night, what with the events at Anexo and Aliviane a few days beforehand, and the trick is not to think too hard about those bloody boot
prints all over the courtyard back there, the sticky crimson pools in the
infirmary, or the pastor's fears about this place. So long as the door remains shut, one will survive the night. Sleep comes (with a little chemical assistance), but for the laments that pierce the black from within the
dormitories—the wailing, yowling, winnowing sounds of visions disturbing the sleep of the mad.

Josué's shuffling heralds the day. Through a crack in the door, now
ajar as he begins his duties, a first hint of silver blue across the eastern
horizon makes its entry into my cubicle. The hills to the west, into which

the Lord of the Skies' white horse is etched, respond with a pink hue, and twilight arrives. And into the morning, as the sun rises, the residents emerge into the courtyard to begin another day, mumbling, grunting, or singing but mostly silent as they depart the land of sleep. The first task is to deal with the excreta the night has generated, the stench of which is best removed before it is intensified by sunrise. This involves teams organized by Josué, big Óscar, and others, swilling buckets of water across the dormitories and floors. Part of the same operation is to change the diapers of those who use them, mostly men. The afflicted are lined up in a row outside their sleeping places while those with an awareness of where to direct the body's rejected matter wipe them down and apply new diapers. Then, with the sun bolder, come the showers. There are two of them, attached to the courtyard walls, and all 113 people line up to wash, men under one waterfall, women under the other—that line twice as long on the male side. They leave their clothes in a pile on the concrete slabs, stand under the cold water, and may or may not be scrubbed down by the team of prefects, Óscar and his male assistants for the men, Becky and Marisol for the women. Some, of course, have to be unlocked from their cages for washing down, and this is supervised by Josué himself, working in overdrive. Some of them rattle the bars and scream to be let out; others, like Cholo, just wait in sullen silence to be called and temporarily released for cleansing.

When the bathers are finished, they clutch their own shriveled, crinkly bodies against the cold, dry off with their clothes or a towel if they can get one, go back around to their underwear and pile of rags, and put them back on. It all works estimably well and smoothly; there is order in the mayhem. All the while, the patients acclimatize themselves to morning, test their walk, stop, reflect, walk a little more, stop again, look around them and work it out, whatever it is. They may smile or they may cry at the conclusion they draw. A man called Julio has been completely blinded by the cocktails of drugs he has taken and complains of cold and the noise the others are making. Josué, working like there's no tomorrow, now appears with a collection of brooms, which he distributes. Becky commandeers one and sweeps every corner of the courtyard she can reach. Others follow her; some just stand there, holding their brooms. Alejandro, the former drug dealer, has already donned his open-top driving headgear and started cleaning cars again—the only one parked here and others abandoned in the desert. "See that radio over there?" He points to a car stereo lying in the dirt. "I got that from the truck with a broken window. I'll tell you something," and Alejandro draws near, his breath heavy with something smelly. "It's not a car, it's a plane. It flies."

The sun is risen, it is time for the walk along the highway, and the pastor is late. They gather outside the gates, sit under the trees, and wait. *"¡El camino! ¡El camino!"* they shout excitedly. Marisol stands alone clutching a broom and weeping. "If Papi doesn't come, we can't walk," she sobs. Then she crawls back into her cave of silence. What's troubling you? "Many things." Memories? "Many memories." Bad ones? "Very bad." But the pastor will be here soon, and we can all walk! "I just want to walk. It's so beautiful, the walk. My baby came to see me. But she's gone now. All I want is to have a nice walk, but Papi is gone too." She cries again. "It happens suddenly," says Josué. "You don't know what or why, just hurtin' inside." But not for long, for a maroon car pulls into the driveway and here he is, pulling his staff off the backseat, and off we go.

"We need money," Pastor Galván cuts to the quick. "People like you come and say they care, but we need money. What about you? Can you give us some of what you got?" We stride out to the highway, and Alejandro stays behind to wash the pastor's car. "Let's go all the way to Argentina!" suggests Josué from the roadside as the procession of the possessed winds its way to nowhere in particular, Pastor Galván to the fore, trousers tucked into his boots and pounding his staff into the ground. Out on the road, they talk, even Lety, who amazes. "When we were chained in the house, we were like birds in a cage. When we walk we are alive," she warbles.

And by the time we return, two miles down the road and two back to the center, big Óscar has supervised the creation of a plentiful breakfast. There are vegetables, fruits, beans, and rice. There is water and there is singing, led mainly by Becky, who has not stopped her "Canción de la Alegría," song of happiness, since halfway down the road. The sun is high, the air is warm at last, and another day of heterotopia in the human junkyard begins.

We agree that whatever one believes or does not believe, the bedrock of Christianity is a progression from Crucifixion, via descent into hell, to Resurrection—essentially Good Friday, Easter Saturday, and Easter Sunday. And that whatever is happening here is hopefully some stage between Saturday and Sunday morning. But by the time we get to this conversation, impending night covers the land, the gloaming begins to fall, the witching time arrives, darkness is visible to the east.

We say our farewells and make to go, until the next time. "You call this a mental institution, but when you get back to the city, you're in the real madhouse," says the pastor, "back in the real human junkyard." But he is interrupted by a figure who has clambered out of the yard and is now lurking on the roof, leaning over the eaves and silhouetted against the deep golden flare of last light on the desert horizon. *"¡Yo soy Rebecca!"* comes a voice between a croak and laughter. "Crazy Baby!"

THE WIND OF KNIVES

In Aztec lore, life was a brief passage through a world of pain and malice, prelude to reunion with the ancestors after death. Beyond the boundaries of the world was a universe made from death, whence the winds blew from the four directions. Death had three realms: The House of the Sun, in the sky; a paradise on earth called Tlalocan, and Hell, named Michtlan. Most people—apart from those killed in battle or women at childbirth; those struck by lightning or lepers—began their journey in death through the underworld, in and out of Michtlan. The journey of the dead out of hell was a long and arduous one, across rivers and mountains, encountering devils demanding tribute. But it began with a voyage along a road guarded by a green lizard called Xochitonal, Sign of the Flower, and proceeded across eight icy deserts, through a wind so cold that the deceased needed to burn all his or her possessions—weapons, gifts of passage and the remains and clothing of any captives they had captured in war. The name of the wind was Izchecaya, the Wind of Knives.

—*Bernardino de Sahagún*, A History of Ancient Mexico

When the authorities finally gave Paula González back the medallion of the Virgin of Guadalupe that her daughter María Sagrario had worn around her neck, it was terrible proof of what Paula had been denying for five weeks, refusing to believe that Sagrario was dead. Paula held the medallion in her hands and implored the Madonna, "Where were *you* when they did that to my little girl?"

Paula and her husband, Jesús, had last seen their seventeen-year-old daughter when she rose for work shortly before 4:00 a.m. on April 16, 1998, at their gimcrack home in Lomas de Poleo, a shanty of dwellings sprawled across high desert. Sagrario worked, like hundreds of thousands of other local girls, at one of the American-owned maquiladoras. Normally, Sagrario would leave for the afternoon shift with her father and elder sister, Guillermina, but the Capcom company had changed her routine. Instead, Sagrario now took the lonely mile-long walk down unlit dirt tracks to the main route through another shanty, Anapra, where she would wait for the company-chartered bus to take her and her fellow factory girls to work. After Sagrario failed to return that afternoon, Paula went to the police. "Did she like to stay out late?" they asked. "Did she wear miniskirts and go dancing?" Paula, disgusted, made two thousand flyers: "Missing Teenager. Please Help." Eventually, she learned not from the authorities but a newspaper article that Sagrario's corpse had been dumped near her maquila on the other side of town.

There is a new word in the Spanish language as spoken in Juárez: *feminicidio*, femicide, the mass slaughter of women. There is no other word to describe the iniquity of a singular and savage phenomenon that appeared at first unique to this city at the heart of Amexica—mystifying and vile: some 340 young women found murdered between 1992 and 2001, when I first went to report on these events. Killed in different circumstances and varying degrees of sadistic savagery, with a further 180 or so missing. "They have been dumped in public places, not even like animals; more like trash," says Marisela Ortiz, from one of the groups campaigning to bring the killers to justice. The victims, she says, fit a pattern: "They are poor, young, working class." And when they are found, she says, some "have been tortured, mutilated, bruised, fractured, or strangled and violated." "The killers," adds Marisela's colleague Rosario Acosta, "take no trouble to cover up evidence. With these, the evidence is brazen, right there, every time. Whoever is doing this knows they are immune from the law." "When our search teams fail to find a body, one will appear the next day," says Marisela Ortiz. "There's some code or language: 'Just letting you know we are here.'" One body discovered in 2002, that of Erika Pérez, was found with her pursestrings tied around her neck and underwear around her knees. The authorities say she died "from an overdose" but would not confirm results of toxicology analysis. Another, unidentified, was found wearing clothes belonging to a different teenager whose body was found along with seven others in 2001. Another, Esmeralda Juárez Alarcón, shut down the little market stall where she worked in January 2003 in order to attend her computer class. It was dusk, plenty of people to intervene, police officers to be seen around, including a special downtown patrol. But Esmeralda vanished. Gabriel Alonzo, her boyfriend, still works at the stall opposite hers: "I watched her as she left that day to walk to the school."

And that same month, I stumbled into further horror, and a more sinister implication of apparent official complicity: more bodies found, and either outright denials or silence from the authorities over their existence—as if there were something to hide, something worse than ineptitude. On a visit to Lomas de Poleo, only to say good-byes and pay respects to Paula González and present flowers before leaving Juárez one time, there is news. It comes from E.P. (whose name must be protected), one of the People's Watch vigilantes patrolling the area in absence of any police interest. E.P. had found three more bodies in the hinterland behind the town a few days ago. Strange, because the official number of bodies recovered for that month was zero. E.P. puts on a cap reading JE-SUCRISTO TE AMA—Jesus Loves You—and heads out to demonstrate the location of his latest, grievous find. We set out, accompanied by Sagrario González's remarkable sister, Guillermina, who has returned from work and is seeing to her mother, but for whom E.P.'s narrative is a recurrent nightmare and was once her work too. In rage and grief at her sister's murder, Guillermina had, she explained, established an organization called Voces Sin Eco—Voices Without Echo—to mobilize search parties in the deserts above Lomas de Poleo and pressure the authorities. But, explained Guillermina as we left the shacks behind and drove up into the desert, "We disbanded it as a formal group. We were being used by the media, by the NGOs, people were profiting from us, pretending to help, raising money that never arrived."

We pass through a gate reading PRIVATE PROPERTY in Spanish and out onto land known to have connections with the Juárez cartel and to contain an airstrip, says Guillermina, for light planes carrying cocaine heading north, as well as roads used by no one except the traficantes. In this desert expanse, Voces Sin Eco would comb the land day in and day out, and E.P.'s tireless group still keeps watch for circling buzzards above a possible cadaver. He guides us to a bush to which plastic police ribbon has been attached and demonstrates how he works, and worked last week, he says, pawing the fine sand. "Suddenly there was a hand, then a severed arm." The bodies were arrayed on their backs in a row, each in the shape of a cross, naked and recently killed, with two maquiladora uniforms strewn nearby. "Their arms were chopped and stomachs ripped out," says E.P. "You get used to finding them," he adds. "I've done this so many times." E.P. radioed the police and fellow vigilantes, with some thirteen witnesses to his call, and the authorities duly arrived to take the bodies into official custody. "When they came," says E.P., "they told us, 'That's your work done. You guys can go now.' If we hadn't found them," he insists, "nothing would have been done." As we leave the accursed terrain, a motorcycle rider who has left a plume of sand as he headed to cross our path waits at the gate to ensure our departure. He wears a balaclava mask, says nothing—nor do we. Just get out.

Marisela Ortiz, who founded the campaigning group Nuestras Hijas de Regreso a Casa—May Our Daughters Return Home—had asked the authorities about rumors of bodies found that January. "They denied it, outright," she reports. Marisela Ortega, a journalist from the paper *El Norte de Monterrey*, was told the same, also Diana Washington Valdez from the *El Paso Times*, across the border. "We will provide any pertinent information to the public . . . except for whatever is considered confidential," Valdez was told. To me, despite instant cooperation from the prosecutor's office on other questions, and offers to respond any time, not a word—until later, when E.P.'s discovery was admitted to—on this latest

discovery. Only one thing emerged as certain from this rueful development: the authorities of Ciudad Juárez were, for whatever reason, covering up the discovery of bodies of murdered women. And so another word
in the Spanish tongue came to be oft spoken in Ciudad Juárez during
these days: *el encubrimiento*—the cover-up.

The feminicidio became a badge of Juárez: doctoral theses were published across university departments in the United States; films were
made, including *Bordertown*, starring Jennifer Lopez; many books were
written, and the cause of the women and bereaved mothers in Juárez
resisting the violence, trying to seek the truth against a wall of official
resistance and suffering continual menace, became a rallying cause for
the women's movement in America and worldwide. In the recent explosion of violence in the city—and implosion of the city—the feminicidio
continues; it never went away. Only now it is everywhere across Mexico,
directed against women of all ages, subsumed into the hurricane of violence and yet a distinct strand within it. An investigation by *Proceso*
magazine in December 2009 showed that as narco-related violence spi-
rals, so too does the intensity and cruelty in the killing of women.[1] They
are related: deeply and terrifyingly so, argues one of the leading Mexican Americans currently writing on these matters, Cecilia Ballí. "The
murders of the women in Juárez revealed a certain *style of killing*," she
says. "The fact that many of the killings were sexualized in some ways
related to the broader wave of violence we're seeing now against both
men and women. It has to do with an expression of power, and a particular form of masculine power." Ms. Ballí is descended from two of the
formerly great ranching families of the Rio Grande Valley (as will feature in chapter 9). She has garnered recognition for her brand of narrative journalism and teaches in the anthropology department of the
University of Texas at Austin. "Some of the media coverage of the wom-
en's killings," she argues, "made me cringe. It perpetuated this idea of
Mexico as an exotically violent place, the idea that only Mexican men
are capable of these terrible things. The truth is that people in Mexico

are struggling as much as anyone to understand this chilling type of violence. I'm trying as an anthropologist to understand what is happening, what it means, where it's coming from. Not that violence always means something, but specific types of violence exerted on the body can serve as a form of communication. I think the message has more to do with the killers than with the victims, which is why I think the feminicidios ultimately signal a crisis of masculinity in Juárez, not a crisis with women.

"For me," she continues, "the killing of the women in Juárez is about power more than it is about sexual pleasure. The style of the violence demonstrates a specific kind of male performance and a complete domination of the other person." "Style" is not a word Ballí deploys lightly, and she will use it later to define the "social performance" of the new generation of narco bosses and foot soldiers. "Before, the violence in Juárez was merely functional, but now it's also meant to publicly display a specific kind of masculinity and to reassert that male power at a time when the traditional forms of masculinity along the border are under threat. You see a similar thing happening between men; the way men are tortured by the military and police and by people in the drug world is often highly sexualized. So I personally see a relationship there between the two. Of course, since men's and women's bodies and social status are different, the violence takes different forms and is experienced differently. But all of it is focused on violating the body and on displaying this kind of masculinity that is not simply what we usually think of as machismo."

As we have seen, it was the legitimate global economy that wrought fundamental change in Juárez and provided raw material for the feminicidio: the arrival of the maquiladoras brought to town a workforce that was at the outset almost 80 percent female. According to a stereotype, women's hands are more dextrous, and women can be paid less than men and are more easily exploited. Maquiladora work is relentless, concentrated, and hard on the eye: tiny adjustments to microchip boards, under a searing artificial light. "We cannot really talk because then you would slip behind," says Cinthia Rodríguez, who works at the same maquila as did

María Sagrario González. Two visits to the bathroom a day, no independent unions, and production lines demanding punishing quotas that are slowed down when inspectors visit from American parent companies. "But it's good work," Cinthia concludes. The arrival of so many young women workers plays hard with the chauvinist foundations of Mexican society. For within the enslavement of the maquilas was a liberation of sorts. Esther Chávez Cano established Casa Amiga, the city's first and only center dealing with sexual and domestic abuse. She explained, "Men found themselves no longer the breadwinners. Women exchanged subordination at home for subordination to the factory boss, but this offered a certain independence; they could buy clothes, leave their abusive boyfriends, wear miniskirts, go out alone. And, with middle-aged men unemployable in Juárez, this created frustration, a backlash against women exhibiting independence for the first time. Being financially independent and wearing a miniskirt, however, is not an invitation to one's death."

"The maquilas provided meat for the killers," says Dr. Arminé Arjona, trying to gather evidence of the slaying. "They bring girls from all over, and they're easy to get hold of, for whatever purpose." "From the maquilas," says Marisela Ortiz, "comes the culture of dispensability that underwrites the murders. The maquilas see women who work much as they see our city, as something expendable. So what if a woman is murdered, or ten, or a hundred? There are always plenty more." "If you want to beat, rape, or kill a woman, there is no better place than Juárez," said Esther Chávez. "There are thousands to choose from, plenty of opportunities, and you can get away with it. The lives of women, especially poor women, have no value. They are faceless."

The wind, cold as a wind of knives, whips up sand on the main road through the desperately poor colonia of Anapra, which lies beneath Lomas de Poleo, and to the edge of which the dirt road leading to the city arrives. When daylight comes, this road will be heaving with buses and trucks, kicking up the dust, but in the hours before dawn, through the side streets move shadowy, huddled figures of young women, emerging from makeshift homes, to await the special buses that transport them en masse to work. It was down such a road that María Sagrario González walked after saying her last good night to her family. Along these dark pathways, many a young woman disappeared, to be found, weeks later, violated and lifeless, in the scrub beneath the mountain. At first light, three women from Veracruz explain that they are not even going to work; rather, they get up every morning and go to the maquilas in hope of doing so, having been laid off by a company that went to China, where labor is even cheaper and more compliant. Another, Rosa López Contreras, balks when approached by two males, then explains that she never waits for the bus alone, preferring to stick with friends or else her dog, trained to raise the alarm. These women have forgotten the names of most of their murdered workmates, but María Sagrario González rings a bell. "I remember her," says Rosa. "Everybody knows her mother."

Paula González has a singular, disarming way of talking about her daughter's murder. She moves her eyes across mid-distance and a strange, aloof smile crosses her face when reaching the most heartsick passages of her narrative. The González family arrived from Durango in 1995. Jesús had worked in a sawmill, but "we wanted to come to Juárez to make our lives," says Paula, "although of course the reality is different. After all, the boss of a maquila is like a government official, not a normal human being, because he has everything he needs. All he cares about is that you arrive on time and work. That's all. This area is famous," Paula proclaims. "People say, 'Oh, that's where all the murdered girls come from!'" It is a place of hutches on borrowed land. There are spirited little *abarroterías*—basic stores—here and there; Paula has managed to open one of her own. After her daughter was killed, she says, she retreated even from the neighborhood she had made home. "My first reaction was to close off completely, thinking only about Sagrario. Her father was in a terrible state, awful physical problems. But then some mothers from the neighborhood asked me to be their representative, and to act. And I did."

From somewhere, somewhere remarkable, Paula drew insistent

strength. The resultant Committee of Neighbors meets every Sunday. Rather than dwell on the murders, it seeks to find "ways to protect the living." It has forced the authorities to install a few electrical lines, some water pumps, and even a kindergarten. Not that the authorities had much to do with the latter, exactly: they merely gave Paula a registration license number. It was she who found a teacher, and men of the neighborhood built the little hut to which children are brought at 9:00 a.m.

"When I deal with the police about my daughter," says Paula, "I never know whether I am dealing with a criminal or a cop—probably both. But I feel they have the obligation to tell me what is going on. It's hard to go there every day and see how bored and hostile they are. We don't expect help from the authorities anymore. All we can do is awaken the citizenry." Along the main Ruta Anapra are painted black crosses on a pink background—"less to commemorate the dead," says Paula, "than to warn young women that they are in danger. I do everything for Sagrario," she reflects. "Sagrario was in the chorus at church and taught catechism class. She gave the children sweets, therefore, so do I. From Sagrario . . . ," who is staring out from the photograph overhead, with serious, dark eyes. Paula wrings her hands. "There is little point in asking for the big things, so we fight for the normal things in life.

"Only one thing," laments Paula. "I would love to have taken Sagrario back to Durango so she could have seen her roots. It is so beautiful there, and she was only fifteen when she left. But now it is impossible even for me to go alone." Why? "Because of Sagrario I cannot go. We're a tight family, and they always insisted that if I went back to Durango, I would take Sagrario with me. So that if I returned alone, she would have left them."

"Everything still astonishes me," said Esther Chávez at the domestic abuse crisis center, "even though I have been fighting this for ten years." Chávez, who died in December 2009, seven years after this interview, had returned from Mexico City to her native Juárez to look after her sick mother, intending to leave again, but her mother lived until the age of

YO LAZARO FLORES
APOYO A MI PATRON
EL MONTA PERROS.
ATENCIÓN GARDUÑO
HNOS. FIERRO, DE LA O
Y LOS PUTOS MAYITOS

ATTE. LA LINEA.

TOP: Amexica: The corpse of an executed man hangs, decapitated and handcuffed, from the Puente Rotario, known as the Bridge of Dreams, in Ciudad Juárez, accompanied by a banner of warning—September 2008. (© Alex Tellez / Periodico PM); BELOW LEFT: La plaza: Joaquín Guzmán Loera, leader of the Sinaloa cartel, known as "el Chapo" or "Shorty"—wanted and at liberty (Photograph sourced from a Mexican police handout); BELOW RIGHT: Osiel Cárdenas Guillén, leader of the Gulf cartel / Los Zetas—captured, extradited, convicted, and jailed in Texas (© Getty Images)

The Devil's Highway: Migrants prepare to cross the perilous and deadly desert frontier, illegally, into the United States, northward from the Sonoran town of Altar, after a briefing with the Mexican army. (© David Rochkind)

Urban Frankenstein: Children forage in the blood-strewn aftermath of the massacre of ten patients at the Anexo de Vida—annex of life—drug rehabilitation clinic in Ciudad Juárez, September 2009, one of many such massacres in rehabilitation centers. (© 2010 by Julian Cardona.

Here begins the homeland: Federal police and a helicopter arrive at the scene of another murder in Tijuana—the war in what was once a tourist destination rages between Guzmán and the local Tijuana cartel. (© Shaul Schwarz / Getty Images)

Urban Frankenstein: The corpse of another victim of the slaughter in Juárez, hung by handcuffs to a chain-link fence. Drug-related murders in Juárez make it the most dangerous city in the world.

The human junkyard: Pastor José Antonio Galván, with patients at his Visión en Acción center for recovering addicts and the insane, on the outskirts of Ciudad Juárez

Wind of knives: Women protest for peace in Ciudad Juárez. Since 1997, hundreds of women have been singled out for especially brutal murders in the city— a series of killings that has come to be known as the *feminicidio*.

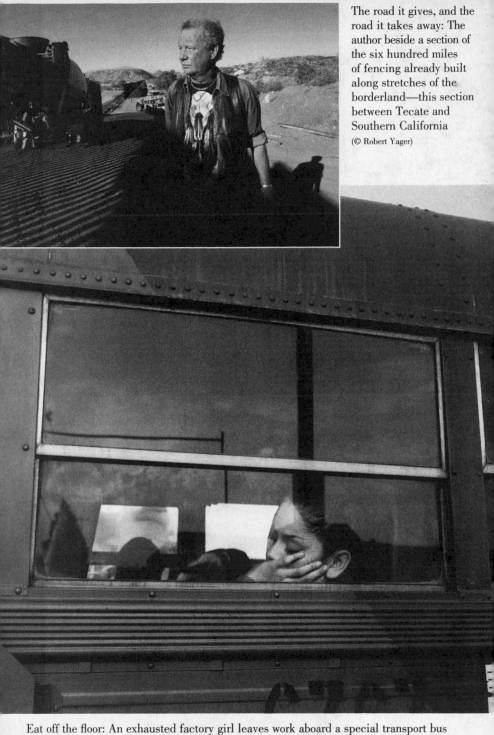

The road it gives, and the road it takes away: The author beside a section of the six hundred miles of fencing already built along stretches of the borderland—this section between Tecate and Southern California (© Robert Yager)

Eat off the floor: An exhausted factory girl leaves work aboard a special transport bus after a shift in one of the thousands of *maquiladoras*—sweatshop factories built along the border to assemble goods for duty-free export to the United States. (© Antonio Olmos Zazvueta)

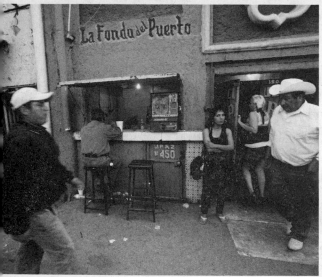

ABOVE: Gateway to the Americas: Migrants prepare to jump and ride a train from Nueyo Laredo across the border into Texas. Trains and trucks carry $367.4 billion worth of trade through this crossing annually. The cargoes are often contaminated with drugs. (© Gary Coronado / Palm Beach Post / ZUMA Press)

LEFT: Amexica: In downtown Ciudad Juárez—the most dangerous city in the world—life goes on, the bars stay open, and cowboy hats and baseball caps remain in style. But soon after dark, the streets will be deserted. (© Robert King / Polaris / eyevine)

ABOVE: Gateway to the Americas: The daily line to cross the border on foot. About a million people walk or drive between the United States and Mexico every day, commuting to work or school, to shop or visit relatives.
(© New York Times / Redux / eyevine)

BELOW: Iron river: A gun store near the border in Texas—this one, like most, denies selling weapons to the cartels, who buy the vast majority of their hardware from gun stores and fairs in the United States. There are three gun dealers per mile within a short distance of the twenty-one-hundred-mile border. (© Getty Images)

Tell them who you are: Santa Muerte, most holy death, is the spiritual icon of the narco war, here kept company by an M1 carbine. (© Redux / eyevine)

Tell them who you are: The Virgin of Guadalupe, Empress of the Americas, wearing the serpent of her Aztec alter ego, the mother goddess Coatlicue, deity of fertility and destruction (© Josh Lord, East Side Ink, New York; photograph © Arnel Hecimovic)

102. Chávez established herself in Juárez, worked as an accountant, wrote a column in *El Diario*, and opened a dress shop. As she heard about the lives of women in the city, she set up Casa Amiga. When the feminicidio began, she tried to push the authorities for answers. The official response was to advise women not to dress provocatively, avoid walking the streets, and "if you are sexually attacked, pretend to vomit. That will be repulsive to the attacker, and he will probably flee." The unofficial answers came in a more distinctive tone. For a girl to go out alone is "like a little treat" said the former prosecutor Arturo González Rascón. "Like putting a candy at the entrance to a school." The former deputy state attorney general Jorge López remarked, "When a young woman goes missing, more often than not, the parents will tell you that she was practically a saint! But then we start making inquiries and find out that she was out dancing every night." The mother of one girl murdered last year was appalled to find her daughter's clothes tossed, some morning later, over the backyard fence. When a police officer came to collect them, he remarked, *"La chavala andaba da cabrona"*—roughly, that slut was asking for it. "You must remember," Chávez had counseled in 2002, "that this is a state in which wife beating was not a criminal offense until a year ago. Not unless the wounds were 'visible for longer than fifteen days.' And even since then, we have failed to get one conviction, because the cases are always said to be too 'complicated.'"

The tragic farce of the authorities' professed attempts to find the killers began in October 1995. Abdel Latif Sharif, an Egyptian and former maquila engineer, was arrested and accused of seven murders. Despite a record of sexual violence, he pleaded innocent. The case hit problems: one of the women he was accused of murdering, Elizabeth Ontiveros, turned up alive. The police forensic expert on the case, Irma Rodríguez, said that the bite marks on his alleged victims did not match Sharif's teeth. Police then arrested a group of nightclub workers belonging to a gang called Los Rebeldes, the Rebels, charging that Sharif paid them to kill seventeen women while he was in jail. They were accused of seven murders, including that of María Sagrario González, while Sharif's conviction for a single murder was overturned in 2000. The case against

Los Rebeldes also collapsed, but the authorities claimed another break in February 1999, when a peasant opened his door one night to fourteen-year-old Nancy Illaba González, blood streaming from a wound above her eye. A bus driver had violated her, tried to strangle her, and left her for dead. The abuser, Jesús Manuel Guardado, and other members of his gang, Los Toltecas, were arrested and accused of fifteen murders, to which they admitted but later withdrew their confessions—extracted, they said, under duress and torture. Subsequently, the bus driver Guardado was convicted and jailed in January 2005 for his part in the murder of 113 women in Ciudad Juárez, along with nine other members of Los Toltecas; two others were also bus drivers.

Events then twisted along a strange course. On May 13, 1999, Sharif's lawyer, Irene Blanco, received a telephone call saying there had been a shoot-out between narco gangs and a victim, Eduardo "Blancas" (an error in the name). She went to the hospital to find her son, severely wounded from three gunshots. He had been driving when the would-be assassins opened fire. Injured, he stepped on the gas, making it to the emergency ward. While he was being operated on, agents from the state police came around to ask the doctors whether he was dead or alive. A month after the attempted murder, a newspaper in Mexico City, *Reforma*, published the account of a whistleblower from the Juárez police, Víctor Valenzuela. Valenzuela had gone to his superiors saying that he knew who was behind the murder of scores of women in the most horrific and sadistic circumstances: people close to and members of the Juárez cartel. The group was, moreover, protected by the police and government officials, including two police officers on Sharif's case. The feminicidio in Juárez appeared to include a statistically small but, in Cecilia Ballí's terms, "stylistically important" number among the three-hundred-plus murdered women killed with a sadistic and sexualized brutality, and allegedly with official sanction.

They stand silent and spectral in the light of dusk: a rose-colored hue in the sky reflecting the color with which eight upright crosses are painted.

They were placed in what was once a cotton field, now a dumping ground for old tires, chemical drums, and stinking flotsam and jetsam. On the crosses, by contrast, sweet, fresh flowers are attached. Names are painted in careful script: Claudia Yvette, Brenda, Bárbara, *Desconocida* (unidentified), Laura Bernice, Lupita, Esmeralda, Verónica. They are the names of eight women whose mutilated bodies were found here on November 21, 2001. The land is exposed, at a busy road junction; rows of windows on the upper stories of houses in a walled community overlook the site. No one wanted to see, or tell about, whoever left these cadavers.

Yellow police tape is still strung out along the ditch behind the crosses, and there's another cadaver, that of a dog. The stench of rotting rubbish fills the air along with the evensong of birds and hum of traffic. But whatever message those who dumped the bodies wanted to deliver, there is one from those who erected these crosses: they do not only mark and mourn, they stare, hush as death itself, in accusation, straight across the scrappy land, to the cylindrical offices of the Asociación de Maquiladoras—the factories' employers' federation. In the evening, the pink paint becomes luminous, reflecting the light of the building and that of the twilight sky. During another dusk, on Mexico's Day of the Dead in November 2002, women from the movement for justice gathered here in tribute "not just to the eight, but to all the dead women," as Marisela Ortiz said. Two torches were lit and planted in the ground. A cross made in stones was carved into the dirt and surrounded by candles. Flowers were strewn and the Requiem Mass said by two priests: "Lamb of God who takest away the sins of the world, grant us thy peace . . ." "It is," says Marisela, "a funeral rite, a dignified burial for all of them."

After years of little headway, the prosecutor, Arturo González, held a sudden press conference, declaring that he had cracked the case. Within five days of the "cotton field" discovery, two bus drivers were arrested, Víctor Javier García Uribe and Gustavo González Meza, and charged with all eight murders. Confessions to rape, killing, and dumping the bodies were quickly secured, videotaped, and shown to the press, with a suspense-movie-style sound track. The drivers said they had been tortured; the authorities retorted that the wounds were "self-inflicted." The drivers retained counsel, Sergio Dante Almaraz and Mario Escobedo, ready to prove the procurement of invalid confessions under duress. On the night of February 5, 2002, Escobedo found his car being tailed by the police. He was on the cell phone to his father as the shooting started; the old man heard his son being murdered by a burst of automatic fire. The police insisted that Escobedo had been mistaken for a dangerous fugitive and had shot first at the officers' car. There were bullet holes in the police car to prove it. Cocounsel Dante Almaraz says he was advised, meanwhile, "If you do not drop the case, we'll kill you the same way we did Escobedo."

"It was an execution," says the man at the heart of the case, Óscar Máynez Grijalva, former forensic chief for the Chihuahua state assistant attorney general, who handled the case of the two drivers. Máynez, having resigned in disgust at the end of January 2002, holds one of the few keys to this serpentine story. He is a young, curiously puckish man who, for all his passionate involvement, talks with the professional's air of detachment when we meet in the lobby of what was then the Holiday Inn. As tutor of police cadets and later chief forensic scientist, Máynez was the first to alert his own masters about the likelihood of a powerful consortium of killers behind the slaughter; he connected fifty-six murders between 1993 and 1999.

Máynez says the "self-inflicted cigarette burns" to the bus drivers' bodies and genitals were twin-pointed injuries made by two-pronged electrodes used by the police. As regards the Escobedo shooting, Máynez noted that bullet holes in the door of the police car supposed to have been fired by Escobedo were on the *other side* (the driver's side) from that which was supposedly attacked and on the other side from the wreckage of the lawyer's car. For Escobedo to have made them would defy the laws of physics. And anyway, adds Máynez, "whoever shot those holes in the police car, they were not there immediately after the incident. Pictures, even those in the paper, clearly show no holes."

Máynez points to no specific culprit, but he is lucid on that about which he is certain, even as far back as 2002. One, "The authorities and business interests in Juárez have been thoroughly 'narcoticized.' Big drug cartels are a force you need to deal with if you go into government. You can't fight that, and—more important—you are able to make a lot of money out of that." Two, "I think behind many of the murders lies an organized group with resources. There are big, powerful forces behind this. The only certain thing is that fact, and that they will continue killing."

The eight bodies in the cotton field were a last straw for Máynez, even before the torture of the bus drivers. When he checked their DNA, in only one case did forensic evidence give a positive identification (the others either were misidentified or the samples contaminated). Five of the bodies, moreover, were covered in "big pieces of concrete rubble. I thought inevitably of possible connections to the construction industry, heavily 'narcoticized,' with concrete easily traced. But those leads were never followed up. After two days, 'case closed.'"

With Óscar Máynez gone, the forensic burden fell upon Irma Rodrí- guez Galarza, who examined body after body and even roamed the streets under cover. But on July 25, 2001, two years after she had foren- sically discarded the case against Sharif, Dr. Rodríguez was preparing a lecture in Mexico City when someone asked her if she had seen the news: "They shot up the family of some forensic scientist in Juárez." Ir- ma's daughter, Paloma Villa Rodríguez, and her husband, Sotero Alejan- dre Ledesma, had been gunned down on the porch of the family home in a brazen execution by men firing AK-47 rifles from two vehicles. The authorities expressed regret that the pair were caught in the crossfire of a drug-related shootout. No suspects were identified or interviewed.

One case particularly disturbed Óscar Máynez, as it did his opposite numbers at the FBI in El Paso: the killing of seventeen-year-old Lilia Alejandra García Andrade, abducted on St. Valentine's Day 2000 out- side a television shop, her body found a week later. The murder, says Máynez, bears the same signatures as those of the women in the cotton field. An FBI report on Andrade's killing was leaked to Mexico City's *Reforma* based on testimony of three witnesses who, failing to gain a satisfactory audience in Juárez, crossed the river. Lilia was abducted on

her way back from the Promex plastics maquila by hit men working for
the Juárez cartel, said the report. The television store was known to be
used as a conduit for cocaine dealing, and among the attackers was a
certain "Raúl," known to the authorities. After the girl was bundled into
a white Thunderbird, sounds of a struggle were heard, and a lookout
disappeared into the shop. Taxi drivers parked on the other side of the
street looked on, said the witnesses, doing nothing. "Someone must have
seen something," says Norma Andrade, Lilia's mother, "and the only
people who could possibly get away with this is someone who had some
connection to the police." The FBI document was dismissed by Juárez
authorities as "erroneous." But across the river, the *El Paso Times* reported that people in Juárez, falsely claiming to be FBI agents, were
knocking on doors in search of the witnesses.[2] Lilia's body was dumped
three hundred yards from the Promex factory. She had been held alive
for an estimated five days, raped, tortured, and strangled. Forensic reports suggested she had been bound by police handcuffs.

Norma Andrade is a wounded but formidable woman, in stature, gesture, and courage. "What kills me," she says, "is that the people who did
this are out there somewhere, maybe doing it again to some other girl.
But I am sticking with my determination that whoever did this be pun-
ished. I am fighting impunity, that the authorities are allowing this to
happen." Over the years there have been endless suspicions as to who is
behind the malefaction of Ciudad Juárez. There are theories about narco
cartel "juniors," male heirs to big landowning and maquila management
families, about police cadres, common domestic violence, snuff videos,
and occult connections. There is even a constituency of academics in
the United States that argues that the deaths have been the subject of
undue attention, since more men were being killed than women, meanwhile. But, "only one thing is certain," insists Norma Andrade. "Whoever is killing is killing for pleasure."

A primary school teacher, Norma lives on the southern edge of Juárez
in a house nearly joyful, filled with playing children, children of neighbors, nieces, nephews, and Lilia's own two children, Jade, now three,
and Kaleb, aged two. They call their grandmother "Mamá," while their

real mother's portrait sits on a shelf, inquisitive, gentle, bespectacled. "The authorities never bothered to call," recalls Norma of the day they found her daughter's corpse. "I heard from someone out of the blue and went down to the morgue. Even now, they never call me. I feel they have lied to me about my daughter's case. They said she had been tied with shoelaces, but I believe it was police handcuffs. They said there were no marks of strangulation, but I know there were. It's up to me to go down there and pester them. If I didn't, I'd never hear from them again." Lilia's murder has been categorized as a "crime of passion." Her (separated) husband was accordingly interviewed and struck off any suspect list— but the crime was not recategorized. "He wouldn't have the trousers to do it anyway," sneers Norma, allowing herself a hollow laugh. "It's hard to think too much about it," she says, exhaling a deep breath. "The facts speak for themselves. She had been dead thirty hours when they found her but had been missing a week. My life has totally changed," she reflects. "You know, I was so happy, I enjoyed everything. But I saw the world through rose-tinted spectacles. Now I trust no one. I could count them on one hand. Only two, actually, Martha Cabrera at the school where I teach, and Marisela Ortiz."

After Lilia was murdered, Norma went to her daughter's former high school teacher, Marisela Ortiz, to urge her to become involved. An elegant woman who hides rage beneath a bushel of civility, Marisela founded Nuestras Hijas in the belief that "it's time to challenge the entire order here, and meanwhile try to take care of the mothers and the children who are orphaned. Many of those are now growing up to be drug addicts or gang members." Marisela has herself become the target of harassment. One night recently, she was driving home, trailed by an SUV. It followed her bumper to bumper, until she gave it the slip. "I was terrified," she says. "I . . . well, it was a clear signal." But it is not threats, says Marisela, that deter her. Nor even the response of the authorities, whom Marisela believes to be complicit anyway. Rather, it is the response of the maquiladoras that "takes away our hope."

Three thirty in the afternoon: shift change at the maquilas. The buses line up outside each factory, waiting to take their load downtown or back up to the colonias. The girls emerge from the fluorescent-lit world within. Some linger to chat, one young woman simply boards the bus, sits down, rests her head against the bus window, closes her eyes, and sinks into sleep. Half an hour later, up the Ruta Anapra, the buses grind in convoy, kicking up great clouds of dust, old American school buses, marked TRANSPORTE DE PERSONAL and familiar companies: Philips, TDK, Delphi, Lear. Occasionally they pull over, fart a puff of exhaust, and drop off workers who then weave their onerous way home between the shacks climbing the hillside.

The silence of the maquila companies over the slaughter of their employees was perhaps loudest in the case of seventeen-year-old Claudia Ivette González, one of the eight found in the cotton field. She had worked for Lear but was sent away one morning for being three minutes late, having missed the work bus. That was the day Claudia, turned away alone, disappeared. The company's official response to her subsequent death was that "González's murder did not happen on Lear property." In response to the attempted murder of the fourteen-year-old bus rape survivor Nancy Illaba González, her employer said only, "It is not our policy to hire anyone under sixteen." The company even filed legal papers against the family for helping Nancy to forge false identification.

Outside the Juárez offices of the Chihuahua state authorities, a forest of little crosses was planted in a scrap of lawn, no longer there. Each cross, beginning in 1993, bore a name, starting with Ivonne Estrada Salas, one for each recovered corpse, and toward 2003 they bunched for lack of space. Many were unidentified because, explained Rosario Acosta of Nuestras Hijas, "so many girls came alone from the South and have no one here that knows them." Inside, there are frosty handshakes with the head of the special office for sexual homicides, young Ángela Talavera, in a smart suit. She is happy, she says, to answer questions. "Many were seduced by men who . . . took advantage of the situation. Most were seduced, but others taken by force. There is no fixed pattern." Ms. Talavera gets little opportunity to speak, as most questions are answered in perfect American English by a bullish, discomforting man, former head of the unit, now an aide in charge of "liaison." The aide details the categories of sexual homicide and statistics involved. There have been 229 during the period under discussion, of which, he insists, 163 have been solved, leaving 66 ongoing investigations. Of these 229, 70 were sexual homicides, of which 24 have been solved, with 46 pending. The other categories include "argument related," "accidental death," and, the largest, "crimes of passion."

I ask about the case of Lilia Andrade, categorized as a "crime of passion." "When we talk about this particular subject," he says with contempt, "her mother always misinterprets what we are saying." On the recent "overdose" case of the girl with panties pulled down and handbag strings around her neck, Ms. Talavera pitches in: "It is true her pants were slightly above the knee, and her handbag on her arm close to the neck. The medical examiner did the autopsy on the body. She did not have any type of sexual assault on her." Óscar Máynez finds the argument laughable: "I have seen no end of overdoses; they do not have panties halfway down their legs and pursestrings around their necks." The question of possible connections to weighty families or the authorities is quickly dismissed. "When I was in charge of this unit," the aide butts in again, "we did have information about a specific powerful person. It didn't lead anywhere. It was one of these powerful people, but that didn't stop us then, and it wouldn't stop us now." And the murdered lawyer, Escobedo? "He wasn't the attorney," snaps the aide. "The attorney was his father. I don't know how it transpired, but unfortunately the younger lawyer was killed. However, it had nothing to do with the bus drivers." "Mario Escobedo *Junior*," affirms Óscar Máynez, "was the registered attorney for one of the bus drivers. That is in the records." The meeting concludes with an assurance from the aide that only three of all the bodies recovered between 1993 and 2003 were mutilated. The FBI, he says, is welcome in Juárez— "for training," but not to help with investigations. Meanwhile, the movement outside is preparing to go above the heads of the prosecution team.

.   .   .

A year later, Rosario Acosta came to Washington, D.C., for the first hearing at the headquarters of the Organization of American States, as Nuestras Hijas endeavored to consider legal action through the OAS Inter-American Court of Human Rights, sitting in Costa Rica and established by a Holocaust survivor, the formidable Thomas Buerghental, now the presiding judge representing the United States at the International Court of Justice in The Hague. Rosario's journey turned out to be a first step down a long road, but when we met for lunch in Starbucks among the glass and steel of Washington, the pellucid light in Rosario's eyes was already fading. "It is a desolate landscape now," she said. "There's no one to turn to in Mexico anymore. While this game goes on, more women die. No, that road has ended now. We need to play a bigger game, or nothing. This can only be solved if we challenge the mechanism whereby the law is enforced. What drives me," she goes on, "is not activism anymore, it is rage and sorrow. Sometimes I feel the organization is full of women working together, sometimes that we are just a few, and sometimes that I am totally alone." Rosario talked not only about the crimes but also their impact after ten years on Ciudad Juárez—and this in 2003, four years before the outbreak of the present narco war. "This is a decomposing society. We are witnessing its destruction—women in pain who cannot turn to society, suffering cancer through stress, children to take care of, and domestic violence against women rampant." The battering of women in Juárez is through the roof, she said: even those rare instances reported to the police increased by 300 percent during the month after the eight bodies in the cotton field. "It's logical," says Rosario, "if they can kill women and get away with it, then why shouldn't they beat them close to death? It's common now for men to taunt their wives, 'If you tell on me, I'll dump you in Lote Bravo,'" a colonia where a number of bodies were found.

"This message of complete impunity is having terrible effects in all directions," said Esther Chávez at the crisis center around the same time. "It is now so bad that women come to me who cannot do anything about beating because their husbands threaten to kill them. What can I say if a woman says, 'I can't come again, because he says he'll dump my body in the cotton field'? If the police would only intervene in these cases, we might start to break that cycle of impunity."

Back again at Norma's lovely but poignant home, she—as Shakespeare said—"bears it out even to the edge of doom." "I'm proceeding with my own investigation," she insists with foursquare resolve, "looking into that narco television shop." Down at the police station, "their attitude gets worse and worse, but I won't let this go, whatever that means for me." She slams the palms of her hands onto her knees and turns her attention to Lilia's children, sticking pieces of yellow paper onto a stencil drawing. "My husband doesn't like what I am doing," continues Norma. "'Think of the children,' he says. But that's the whole point. I do it for the children. So long as they look at me and call me 'Mamá,' I have Lilia with me and a reason to get up each day and fight on."

In December 2009, the Inter-American Court of Human Rights ruled against the Mexican government in three test cases involving murders of young women in Ciudad Juárez. The court found that Mexican authorities failed to adequately investigate the murders of Claudia Ivette González, seventeen, Esmeralda Herrera Monreal, fifteen, and Laura Berenice Ramos, twenty—all killed in the cotton field. The report, running to 167 pages, also said Mexico failed to protect the victims and that the government must publicly acknowledge its responsibility, publish the sentence in official government records, and build a monument in memory of the victims. Authorities must investigate the murders and bring those responsible for the slayings to justice. The case was without precedent, the first time the court had ruled against Mexico on a human-rights complaint and the first ruling to recognize murder according to gender— whereby women are killed only because they are women.[3] The mother of Laura Ramos, Benita Monárrez, had petitioned the United States for asylum, such were the threats from police officers and government officials menacing her to drop her case. The ruling came just as mothers of some of the victims and their supporters set out on a march from Ciudad Juárez all the way to Mexico City. Two months previously, however, in mid-September, President Calderón had undertaken a cabinet reshuffle and appointed Arturo Chávez Chávez as attorney general of the republic to replace the outgoing Eduardo Medina Mora. Chávez was formerly the lead prosecutor in Chihuahua, a post he held during the 1990s, when investigations into the murders of young women went nowhere. "It is like sending a wolf to protect the lambs," said an opposition parliamentarian. In testimony before a Senate committee, Chávez had acknowledged failings by his former agency but said he did his utmost as state prosecutor to investigate and prosecute the slayings.[4]

"This year, however," Marisela Ortiz reflects, two weeks before the ruling in Costa Rica, "the number of murders of women is higher than in the previous year, and that was an increase on 2007. We have had more than two hundred this year now. The violations and killings are of a different kind, many kinds—in the home, on the street, on the way back from work, and some directly connected to narco trafficking. But one thing is consistent: there is always a reason for not investigating. The police will always find a reason to wash their hands of the crime." We meet in Sanborns, as we almost always did over nine years, only this branch is in an outlying shopping mall, not downtown, because it is evening. "I can't get safely to the one we went to before," she explains. "I had to move out here because of all the threats." Marisela is dressed elegantly and exudes resolve and charm, but she looks exhausted. "The state has found a way to be a little less offensive about the killing," she continues. "There are not the same insults about the girls inviting the kidnaps and tortures with their dress." But "we are still having to investigate all the cases ourselves, and they're different from before, more varied. Some are university students taken off the street, some are even of school age. Most are taken when they go downtown looking for work, especially since the recession, because that's where all the buses go, and they have to change buses after dark. They're not always raped, sometimes killed in the style of Mafia executions because they have something to do with narco traffic. Others are abducted and killed while selling sexual services to the federal police; they get into difficult situations if they accept very high fees for gang sex. But to be honest, it's not important to me how a woman is killed. What is important is *why*, and the fact is that these men kill women because they are women, and because they can." And she echoes Cecilia Ballí's point: "The killing of the women here was an indication of how things would go. That men would think this was a way to exert their power, to overwhelm women and other people with such violence, until such point as that kind of violence spreads like cancer and becomes a part of the culture. So you end up with this madhouse. There was an execution in September across the street from where I teach, and the sicario came to pick up his child so it could watch the execution."

Marisela's own life continues to be threatened. "My car was shot at twice, from a black vehicle with tinted windows, but I wasn't hurt," she says, switching from coffee to a modest liqueur. "I had to move house and live apart from my daughters to keep them safe. And I have a couple of escorts, but they work indirectly for Arturo Chávez, so that since he was ratified as attorney general my enemy is protecting me! Maybe that should make me doubly afraid. But I can't stop. The day I stop means that I have accepted that this is the right way."

I revisit Paula González near Christmastide, and she has a model nativity scene laid out on the floor. A center for children in Anapra that was merely a gleam in her eye and a piece of cleared desert scrubland in 2002 has been completed, thanks to private donations, and named after Sagrario. A sign of restored faith? "Maybe," replies Paula pensively. "At the beginning, I prayed a lot, and I still do. Not in church, but here at home, to the Virgin of Guadalupe. I have always been a very religious woman and believed in the Resurrection and in the miracle of Guadalupe. But I never really recovered my faith after that moment, when Sagrario's Virgin came back to me, the one she wore around her neck. Maybe with time, I will get it back." Her deep, comfortless eyes move across the photographs of her dead daughter and back to mid-distance. "Because justice is what I crave. Justice against her killer, and against all of the killers. There is no justice in Juárez, so I have given up on that. I have my work to do here, meanwhile, and wait for the justice of God."

INTERMISSION: THE ROAD IT GIVES, AND THE ROAD IT TAKES AWAY

What do the coyotes mean when they yodel at the moon?
         —*Edward Abbey,* Desert Solitaire

I had always wondered about those people who sit next to motel pools that are only a couple of hundred yards from a highway. But I did just that, after a long stay in Juárez, for a whole four hours, applying SPF 15 and listening to the clamor of trucks thundering down Interstate 10 at very close range. The more exhausting Juárez gets, the more wonderful it is to sit by La Quinta's pool inhaling aromatherapeutic emissions from the chemical smokestack just over the border, embarrassed by hardworking cleaners, and soaking up ultraviolet, it feels like—near wild heaven. This was the last day in El Paso for a while, and before an evening with the singer Tom Russell, whose music I played after toweling down, on my way to Cowtown Boots and the Lucchese factory outlet, and continued to play during the next several thousand miles, in various loop-de-loops across the Texas borderland on one side, Chihuahua, Coahuila, and Tamaulipas on the other. One song made me especially sad and another made me especially happy. The first goes:

> *Then he finally got married and he had two little girls*
> *But he didn't see 'em much cause he had to see the world*
> *And the lie that he told 'em is I'm like most men*
> *It's always down the road that the dream begins*

And the girls grew up to be pretty and wise
They said, "You could've seen the dream by looking in our eyes."

And the second:

But we'll sing "Hallelujah!"—we'll sing it in the morning
And thank the Lord for giving one more day
For ones who passed on through, we'll sing this one for you
For the road it gives, and the road it takes away.

Next morning I left El Paso an hour before sunrise, right in my face along Interstate 10, heading into the eternity of Texas, which accounts for the entire eastern half of the U.S. side of the border, the Rio Grande's left bank, all the way to the sea. From El Paso to the mouth of the river and the border's end is 645 miles as the crow flies, but as the Rio Grande flows it is 1,254 miles, and five times that by automobile, especially if one is zigzagging to and from the hinterland on either side. Driving alone in America, the car radio is one's companion, channels changing of their own accord as one proceeds from one signal range to another. So that without touching the dial, one is serially accompanied by classic rock, apocalyptic Christian soothsaying, country music, pulsating norteño, and windbag talk radio. Every now and then there's a public broadcasting station, discussing health care or playing Sibelius (why it's usually Sibelius, I don't know). Channel changing is achieved not by flicking the dial but by one of the main themes on any journey through Amexica: boundless distance. The kind of distances film directors can measure only with receding telegraph poles by day; the kind of distances to which private cars surrender after dark, their drivers tucked up in motels, so that one shares the night highway almost exclusively with trucks and the colored lights with which each Teamster makes his sixteen-wheeled monster distinctive. Distances across which the endlessly long, thrilling freight trains rattle and surge so that sometimes in the desert night I would pull over just to wonder at their thunderous

passing—a highly erotic, industrial excitement that never wears off—
"Nine hundred thousand tons of steel," as the Grateful Dead song goes,
of which an iron horse of the Santa Fe, Kansas City Southern, or Union
Pacific is made, virile, all-conquering, plowing and hooting through the
desert night.

For the Aztecs, Tezcatlipoca was the supreme god of the sky. He was
a "Smoking Mirror," and no wonder, for the Aztecs made their mirrors of
gossamer-thin obsidian, and obsidian is black. It is at night, heralded by
the sumptuous colors of sundown and twilight, that the sky comes alive
above the desert. In the skies over Amexica, one can attempt to learn the
ancient Native American art of stargazing. I remember seeing Indians
sitting alone in South Dakota, staring skyward for hours—and envying
them. So I bought a metal chair from Walgreens for $11 to try it myself.
I parked, walked, and kept walking—although no landmark butte or
rock seemed to get any closer, such is desert distance—until the dark
blue band that is the earth's shadow opposite sunset rises and fades into
the mauve light above it, which is that of the sun illuminating the atmo-
sphere.

After dark, there are three fundamental rules: (1) wait at least fifteen
minutes until you really start looking into the depth of the constellations
of so many stars like God is throwing sugar at you from the deep; (2)
never forget that it is all moving (or rather, as Galileo realized and for
which he was excommunicated, you are moving) and that you can watch
this happen by keeping your eyes on the horizon; and (3) always take
your empty beer bottles with you back to the car. There is nothing more
depressing than finally finding what one thinks is a spot of mystical iso-
lation only to find that frat brats and cholos have already turned the
place into a venue for Miller Lite drinking contests and/or a landfill for
the disposal of condoms and Burger King packaging.

Somewhere near Coyanosa, Texas, I recalled my father telling me as
a child that many of these stars were extinguished millions of years ago,
yet the light they emitted continues to reach us, and there are only 350
million years to go before we in the Milky Way collide with our next-
door-neighbor galaxy, Andromeda. It all seems to make sense in the

desert, as though the universe were almost as big as Texas itself. The endlessness of Texas: where there is nothing quite like the feeling that one is entirely alone—until suddenly, behind the constellations, fulminate the sounds of the creations of man: the roar of fighter planes and sometimes even a sonic boom. Or, after hours of nothing but signs by the roadside warning, with a gratifying existentialist twist, DUST STORMS MAY EXIST, frantic lights flash ahead, where the Border Patrol has pulled someone over and has him pinned, spreadeagled at gunpoint, against his vehicle.

Above all, after nightfall, there is the coyote, the prairie wolf whose name derives from the Nahuatl word *coylotlinaut*, an Aztec deity whose followers wore the animal's fur—and is the jester and "God-dog" of a thousand Native American stories, and according to the Navajo, creator of the Milky Way. The trickster whose resilience has defied all erosion by modern man of its habits and habitats, by outwitting him at every turn, even increasing the number of pups in a litter when under threat. The jackal of America that hunts in groups of closely related couples and unleashes its flesh-creeping range of haunting sounds across the desert night: howling, yipping, yapping, sometimes almost laughing. Their chorus, whether it is sung for territory or for fun—no one except the coyotes knows—seems to bring the night to a standstill, unless there are domestic dogs around, which can be sure to go into a frenzy, knowing something deep down about these distant wild cousins with whom they have so much—though so little—in common. But keep going until daybreak, for the loneliness can be sublime when a lilac light of dawn fades the constellations in the vast sky, by way of fanfare for the golden desert sunrise, like firelight across the land.

Turning off I-10 at Van Horn, via the truckers' travel center, the railroad and Highway 90 run hand in hand back toward the border through scrub and grassland. An incongruous roadside shrine, at the entrance to a ranch containing and advertising Prada shoes, gives some idea of the upcoming arty settlement of Marfa, south of which the landscape changes dramatically, suddenly huge and isolating again, with horizon after horizon, layer upon layer, of mountain ridges ahead, turning green to blue to gray into the distance, as the frontier comes back into view. After miles of savannah and scrub, the first ocotillos since Arizona appear again, and buttes rise against the skyline.

If only TV teenage soaps hadn't kidnapped the word "awesome"—for that is what these mountains are, such is the dread, southward along Highway 67. Only the awe emanates not only from nature; it has also to do with the arrival of dusk in the most remote of the twin towns along the border, clinging together and surrounded by an expanse of mountainous wilderness and what feels like infinite nothing: Presidio on the Texas side and Ojinaga over the river. Although they live as one, clinging together in the emptiness, Presidio's clocks are an hour ahead of Ojinaga's, which often leads to confusion. Here, the Rio Grande ceases to be the trickle that divides El Paso from Juárez, its waters back there plundered by the farmers of New Mexico, for it is now joined by the Conchos River and a lusty current. In fact, what is from now on called the Rio Grande or Río Bravo is almost all water from the Conchos. Presidio by night is a place of mobile trailer homes to which cling canisters of butane gas, a place lit by isolated fluorescent lights against the glow from over the river of the larger Mexican town, behind which rises a steep, impassable escarpment.

It was that mountain slope on which the joint U.S. and Mexican operation against the drug baron Pablo Acosta was banking, for it gave him no way out. What the SWAT teams on the American side did not know was that the operation over the river was in part arranged and paid for by Acosta's trusty lieutenant, Lord of the Skies Carrillo Fuentes, who needed to be rid of his mentor in order to reform the Juárez cartel under his authority. The history hangs heavy in the deep valley, into which a mist rises from the river after sunrise.

Perhaps surprisingly, behind the corrugated-iron Subway sandwich store in Presidio is a small villa with a diplomatic plaque above the portico and cloister within, up the walls of which bright flowers climb, with a fountain in the middle of it. This is the Mexican consulate, where Héctor Acosta Flores presides, supported by his tireless aide, Elsa Villa, who busies herself with "a massive workload, mostly protection of Mexican nationals, their documentation, what they need to present themselves to the U.S. authorities, birth certificates, ID, labor rights, family rights—the everyday machinery of Mexican life on the border." The office handles three hundred cases a day and covers eighteen prisons, to which it organizes visits for the Mexican families of inmates. "We had to get involved in riots recently," says Acosta, "in Pecos jail—most of those involved were Mexican. The rise in numbers detained for deportation, or with cases pending, adds to convicted criminals—it's a lot of work. But we did manage to have nine independence Grito ceremonies in nine jails this year—that was quite something!" In Presidio and Ojinaga, it is Health Awareness Week, which Acosta is helping to organize on both sides of the river. Today's business opens with a seminar in Ojinaga on health and migration, for which we of course arrive an hour early because of the time difference we both forgot, allowing for a breakfast of sickly sweet cakes. There follows an interesting and edgy exchange in which the director of the Ojinaga hospital (also called Acosta) and some of his paramedics quiz a man from Mexican customs called Porfidio about delays in getting the migrants home once they have been deported, leaving them stranded in Ojinaga. "If they don't have any money, how are they going to get home?" asks the director. Apparently there is a plan afoot to help, but "I know of no such plan," grunts the customs man. "How many millions of dollars do these people send back to Mexico?" protests a paramedic called Clara, lambasting the "functionaries," while Consul Acosta looks a little shamefaced, adding, "I am arguing that the government do all it can to help." There's a Woody Guthrie song called "Deportees" about the nameless people made to "ride the big airplane," but the truth is that they don't get their names back when they reach the borderland of their own country either.

Apart from the migrants who roam the streets looking to earn a fare home, Ojinaga is one of those places that appears entirely normal and probably is—"unless you're here on bad business," says a man called Raúl in Kick Ass Pizza. The bar and pizzeria—one of many here, pizza clearly a favorite in the middle of nowhere—is quiet and friendly, with curiosity getting the better of suspicion. Raúl is keen to talk about melons and onions, for which the surrounding area is famous, and the annual onion festival held in town, rather than any illegal form of commerce. A random compliment along the lines that because of Pablo Acosta, famous Ojinaga is where it all started is greeted by silence and, oddly, a peal of laughter from a man at a table in a corner by the pretty lace curtains who then buys me a shot of tequila, insisting to the barman that it be a good one, and leaves.

As we had returned over the bridge to Presidio earlier, Mr. Acosta from the consulate explained that his is an "itinerant consulate," meaning that its constituency includes two towns away from the border but very much part of Amexica: Midland and Odessa—the names rang a bell for me, having covered the Bush administration for several years, for these towns were the New England dynasty's western colony, cradle for its recent money and the place where its most recent political sons, Jeb and George W., were raised. Odessa and Midland require a detour north, through a landscape of desert mountains that cast a blue shadow over the heat, then becomes a barren scrub across which dust devils fly and trains rumble like iron snakes. I took a walk toward a railroad line, just to watch them forge a way through the now crepuscular light, their own lights visible and the sound of their hooting audible at least ten minutes before reaching a deafening crescendo as they thunder by. I stayed until way past dark, then on into the country of apparently humble origins in which the Bush dynasty entwined with the oil barons of Texas.

America likes to think of the Bush era as the distant past, whether with regret or relief, but until recently, a member of the Bush family had for half a century occupied the White House, a Senate seat, or a governor's mansion, and the family continues to fascinate here around its fortress in this corner of the Lone Star State's wild west, nowadays very much part of Amexica. It was here that a young pilot back from World War II called George Herbert Walker Bush was sent by his father, Senator Prescott Bush, to a trainee job with the International Derrick and Equipment Company. Derrick was a subsidiary of Dresser Industries, controlled by the Bush family and selling more oil rigs than anyone in

the world, later absorbed by Halliburton, of which Vice President Dick
Cheney became chairman, keeping things in the family, so to speak. The
Bush family settled in Midland, although the workshop of the area was
scrappy Odessa, where the white working class live on one side of the
tracks, blacks and Hispanics on the other.

The world did not hear much about Odessa until one fateful day in
December 1998 when George W. Bush was governor of Texas and the sky
turned black after an "upset" at the Huntsman chemical plant, which was
literally on the wrong side of the railroad tracks, where the Mexicans live.
(An "upset" is an unplanned accident releasing pollution, not part of the
plant's normal running procedure, and does not count in its regulatory
tally.) Lucía Llánez, whose family came from Tabasco and thereafter the
border, lives in this tightly knit community of bungalows squeezed between the chemical plant and railroad, and she will never forget that day:
"It was dark all over, cars on the interstate slowing down and putting their
lights on because they couldn't see, though it was day. There was a rum-
bling like trains that rattled the windows, and people were going to the
hospital for watering eyes, allergies, and problems breathing. The cloud
stayed two weeks." In Odessa, where Mexico came to live on the Bushes'
doorstep, I ate some of the best fajitas I had eaten along the entire road,
found a motel with a room looking straight across the parking lot at a
railroad line, and—by now a hopelessly addicted trainspotter—sat
propped against the wall drinking beers and watching them crash by, dividing Mexican Odessa from white Odessa, until turning in and allowing
the rattle and hum of Union Pacific to hammer me to sleep.

The next day, I hear the story of how Huntsman goes back to the
days of George H. W. Bush's arrival, when Odessa was a town of what
the retired fireman Don Dangerfield calls wildcatters. In the forties, the
air force bombed deep holes in the giant Permian oil basin in a search
for oil, which then attracted a stampede of speculators who would, recalls Dangerfield, "spend the nights in a hotel, the End of the Golden
West, and gamble their lots in rooms so thick with cigar smoke you
could hardly see." Among them was a man he remembers well: John

Ben Shepperd, a former attorney general of Texas and member of the White Citizens Council, came to seek his fortune out west by setting up the El Paso Products Company, later Huntsman.

George H. W. Bush landed in this mayhem but quickly decamped twenty miles northeast to Midland, where new millionaires like him established a country club and Harvard and Yale clubs, met at the Petroleum Club, and played golf on irrigated lawns. Midland was, at the time, one of only two towns in America (the other was Los Angeles) with their own Rolls-Royce dealership and more millionaires per capita than any other town, out here in the dusty desert. This was where Bush Senior built his oil fortune, launched a political career on its shoulders, and raised his sons Jeb and George W. in the art and language of power, which the latter feigned to speak from the White House over two terms. Decades during which the Mexicans arrived to work the chemical pipelines in Odessa and water the lawns and golf courses of Midland, so that now more people speak Spanish than English in Odessa and Midland. Driving back to Presidio and the border, I parked at that same spot from which I had walked to watch trains roll through the twilight two nights ago, only to find that I was walking against the tracks of my own still perfectly indented footprints, coming at me in the opposite direction, as though walking backward against time. It was the strangest feeling out there in forever, Texas, and not out of place, for in this desert, time and space curve into their own endlessness.

Southeast from Presidio, Highway 170 leads to one of the most famous and famously spectacular natural monuments in America, Big Bend National Park, but there are lovelier and less crowded wonders to behold on the way, past Redford in the less celebrated Big Bend Ranch State Park, and a stretch of border at once baffling and gratifying. Past Palo Amarillo Ranch, the winding road, deep in a valley, runs right alongside the bubbling brook that the Rio Grande has become. Here, you could play a game of catch between the United States and Mexico, and no one would see or interrupt you. There is no fence, no Border Patrol, no sign of any sensors—but that could be a trick. If a child kicked a ball across, you could kick it back, or you could bring as much cocaine or as many Salvadorans as you wanted. Of course, the roads north are no breeze, but you would be inside the United States. At the Coronado River access point, the Rio Grande flows by like a pleasant pastoral brook in which you could wash your face (try doing that in El Paso). The only fence is a wooden one put up by the state parks service, and the only signpost is that instructing DO NOT BLOCK THE BOAT RAMP. PETS PROHIBITED. BY ORDER. On the far bank, twenty feet away, rocks rise to a small hill, and that is Mexico. The road passes redheaded buttes at the foot of which redheaded vultures pick at the carcass of a desert fox by the road. It climbs and overlooks the great ravine that is Madre Canyon, where a picnic area looks across the running water at Mexico on the other bank, with toy tepees instead of parasols for shade and tables set for a riverside snack.

Then, to stay on course (for this is no tourist trail to the Big Bend), my route swings north toward Alpine, Texas, and into a moonscape, a flat horizon punched by Kokernot Mesa and the five-thousand-foot peak of Hen Egg Mountain. Along these long, liberating stretches of road, not only is there no phone signal, but the digital "radioset" channel-surfing function just whizzes through the numbers that it thinks locate a radio station, finding nothing. Heading east between Marathon and Sanderson, even the railway track is like an oxbow lake left behind by a river: cut off, going nowhere, home to an abandoned, idle row of boxcars painted with graffiti in the rust.

The destination is not a butte or mountain; it is one of the very few people to whom one can talk and who can say they met Pablo Acosta and the Lord of the Skies himself, Amado Carrillo Fuentes. Don Henry Ford farms a ranch at Belmont, near the agricultural center of Seguin, Texas, once the high, arid plains have become grassland through which runs the Guadalupe River. Ford was a dope smuggler from near Fort Stockton, a way north from Hen Egg Mountain. It was a trade he chose, for which he was jailed, escaped, and was jailed again, and about which he wrote a book called *Contrabando*. His meetings with the drug lords over the river were remarkable. That with Carrillo Fuentes, during his years of apprenticeship to Pablo Acosta in Ojinaga, was part of an attempt by

Ford's smuggling partner, Óscar, to get into the big time. They meet in a motel room for negotiations over mountains of cocaine, during which Ford has the temerity to say he prefers not to get into any business that involves killing people. He and another smuggler are left, but then returned for, taken out into a parking lot stark naked, interrogated, and then into another room, where Óscar is in the process of being beaten senseless by Carrillo Fuentes's men. "I had no idea then how powerful Carrillo would become," says Ford. The meeting with Acosta comes later, while Ford is on the run from prison and guarding a stash of marijuana, spotted and taken by Acosta's men, then recognizes the man himself. "Don't look into my face," snaps the drug lord. Ford is interrogated, held, and in an extraordinary exchange asked by Acosta whether (and why not) he had ever killed a man. The dialogue is knife-edge tense, Ford pleading only for his life—which he is granted, Acosta also insisting that he take his load of marijuana "as a gift from me," even though Ford has said he would rather leave without it. "Yes, sir," agrees Ford, when Acosta presses the offer.[1]

The gateway to Ford's ranch is open, flanked by the lone star flag of Texas. The access road winds through the green, deepened by a day of steady rain, past a lake to the house Ford and his wife have only recently completed. There is no one there at first, just a noisy greeting by a pack of dogs and countless cats and kittens. Eventually, Ford arrives in his old pickup, the gentleman cowboy farmer, with a difference. Quite a few differences, actually. It is afternoon, and a gray one, and there is a quick glance around the immediate vicinity, with a full tour of the property promised for tomorrow. Ford also breeds, and loves, racehorses at a stable near Seguin, from which a horse he feeds in a field here has retired. "He can't race anymore, this old sack of shit," says Ford. "But he's a good horse, gentle soul, so the kids love to ride him."

If there is one thing Ford does not want to talk about over the three days and two nights he graciously hosts me at his ranch, it is his book and his life as a narco trafficker. But we have barely finished our first cup of tea at the table in his great kitchen before he begins to talk about the CIA, cocaine, and Iran-contra, and about his own second book, *Ru-*

minations from the Garden. He writes, "I have had a hard time convincing people that I dislike revisiting my past. I did write a book about it, I'm not looking for pity. I chose my path then and now." In conversation, Ford does, however, reflect on the old trade, as darkness falls and we eat spicy stuffed jalapeño peppers to die for. Leah Ford and I drink beer, Don is teetotal and prefers tea. "The area I was living in, that was southeast of Ojinaga, you kill someone and it makes you somebody. But the thing was, I never ran cocaine. I refused to run cocaine. It's a fucker, and I wouldn't do it. I put that in my deposition, my plea, but they edited it out of the tape. The cops were trying to turn me into this coke dealer, and I said no, I'm against hard drugs. But they didn't want the judge to see that. No mitigation . . . Yeah," Ford reflects, without much relish or even interest, "I still meet some of those people. I met someone recently and I said, 'Who do you work for?' and he said, 'I don't work for no one.' He was just like the Mexicans you meet in my yard. He said he'd love to go back but couldn't take the risk, back into the middle of it all now. They can kill you just because you were once a name they knew."

"Look," says Ford, leaning across his kitchen table. "I know the business I was involved in. You hear about all these people backpacking across country with the dope, but that's all shit. That stuff is going right through customs, I know it is. Taxi drivers going back and forth, the same cars getting waved through every day by people on the U.S. side who know. And as for the trucks—Jeezus Christ! All you have to do is get paid to do what you'd do anyway, wave ten percent of the trucks right on through. I've heard that if you have the money and you know Los Zetas, you can get anything you want into the United States—you can get it waved through, and they might even ship it on up for you in a nice fucking Border Patrol vehicle." From the old days, Ford remembers, "In my day, a place like Ciudad Acuña was run by Chapo Guzmán, but now it's all Zetas. And it's not just drug dealing. You got taxis sit there all day, and have to show one hundred percent occupancy even though they haven't taken a single fare. The taxi firm works for Los Zetas, Los Zetas launder their money, and the driver registers busy all day without driving anywhere."

This being a dairy ranch, Leah churns butter in a big porcelain jar as we talk. It is turning slowly, and Ford takes the bowl, as he delivers a point about the cash crossing back into Mexico. An investigation by the Associated Press in December 2009 found that only a fraction of the river of cash flowing through the border was being intercepted.[2] During 2008, the Customs and Border Patrol in El Paso alone confiscated $2.8 million in cash, but most of it was in a single, massive $1.9 million load heading to Ciudad Juárez from Kansas City, Missouri.

"I read that two hundred million's crossing the bridges," says Ford. "That's two hundred kilos of cash if it's in hundreds, 'cause a bill weighs a gram. If it's in twenties, that's a thousand kilos. How are you gonna spend that in Mexico? You can't get rid of that kind of money! They say there's five hundred billion a year in this business. Dammit, there's only eight hundred billion of currency circulating in cash at any time, so am I gonna believe that five-eighths of that is drug money? Of course not. So how does all that money get back into circulation? It does through legal funds, don't it—how else? Or am I just dumb? You can't bank all that cash. You can't roll into a bank and say, 'I gotta deposit a truckload of dollars, quick.' You got to find someone who's gonna launder that money and take a cut, you got to find someone whose going to reintroduce it into legal channels. If you've got a semiarticulated truck full of cash, you go to Mexico City and you find the representative of a big-assed American bank to do you a favor for a big-assed cut. And the money's gonna go via that representative to some even bigger smart-ass on fucking Wall Street. How else is it gonna work? You gonna find guys driving round Mexico spending cash out of a semi truck? I don't think so. It's Bob Dylan, ain't it: 'Steal a little and they put you in jail / Steal a lot and they make you a king.'"

But what compels Ford now, and the real subject of his book, is self-sufficiency. Like many Americans electing to live and farm in reclusion, in enviable quarantine, from the hullabaloo. "When I came out of prison, after five years surrounded by the constant noise, stress, and confusion of a federal joint, I found the idea of living alone in a forest kind of appealing," says Ford. But he is watching hard, watching the oil run out, what he believes to be the guzzling of a finite resource by the planet generally, even by his own peers "turning too much diesel into too much of the wrong kinda food, with bigger and bigger machines. Well, if all this breaks down, I'm gonna be prepared. I'm gonna be able to feed myself, my family, my children, and even a few of my favorite people. We receive an inheritance, and God willing, we get to leave a legacy."

Morning starts especially early for Ford as a farmer, and he begins the day with darkness outside and a scour of his overnight e-mail before we go out through the misty chill smelling of moist, fresh earth, Jack Frost underfoot, and milk the cows, which Ford does by hand, into a bucket, squeezing. After breakfast—a warming bowl of rice, egg, and the freshest, creamiest milk I've ever tasted—we prepare to go to Gonzales, the nearest town.

There is word again of Texan secession from the union, as is the formerly Confederate Lone Star State's constitutional right. It never happens, but it's much discussed in these parts, on a cyclical pattern depending on who is in the White House and especially since the election of Barack Obama. Before that, the secessionists had quieted, not least because one of the guiding characteristics of the Bush presidency was the fact that George W.'s team was led by his father's Texan men of steel, Karl Rove and Dick Cheney, the heavy hand of Texas big oil and many who had served Bush's governorship—the idea being that if Texas has to be part of the union, then one might as well forge the union into being Texas. But it's not like that anymore. Obama is not only black and a Democrat, he's a Yankee. And so the language and threat of secession now reenters Republican politics, and the battle for the party's nomination in gubernatorial elections. As the lexicon of secession that accompanied the Clinton years resurfaces, Ford's neighborhood becomes the secessionist heartland. This is logical: Gonzales is where, in 1835, the first battle of the Texan revolution against Mexico was fought. The Mexican army asked that a cannon it had loaned the Texans to fight off Apache raids be returned, to which the Texans retorted with what became a legendary taunt: "Come and take it." When the Mexicans tried to do just that, in Ford's words, "They got the shit shot out of them." So as

Ford and I drive to Gonzales to pick up cattle feed and deal with the bank, we pass a flag flying from a ranch gate with a lone star, a cannon, and the slogan written on it: COME AND TAKE IT. "The government can say whatever it fucking wants," spits Ford. "We're all disaffected, we're too far from Washington, D.C., we feel left out of the equation and over-taxed by too much federal government." Still, Ford is wary of the "red-neck secessionists—I sure ain't one of them," he says. "I don't go to things like the secessionist Tea Parties they have—they got over five thousand to that." In American political parlance, to be left-wing tends to entail a sympathy for federal government, while right entails libertari-anism. Ford, though, produces an ingenious four-way "political com-pass" quiz whereby one answers questions about various issues and is then placed on a grid between left and right on a vertical scale, and "libertarian" and "authoritarian" on a horizontal one. He comes out in the bottom left-hand corner, a left-wing libertarian, and while that stakes out a vertical difference between him and his antigovernment neighbors, it binds him to them on the horizontal scale.

Ford's other distinction is his fluent Spanish and deep love for Mex-ico; Ford is a horseman, and man of the borderland. He is not unlike the principal character in Cormac McCarthy's *All the Pretty Horses*. "Over on the other side, you got people who are as far away from Mexico City as we are from Washington, and that man is our neighbor. What I see is that we end up with a bunch of countercultural rebels on both sides of the border with more in common with each other than we have with the capital cities." Ford wants to hear some of that countercultural rebel stuff, so we head off to see a young singer-songwriter whom Ford has taken under his wing somewhat, scheduled to play a gig in New Braunfels, over the other side of Seguin, Ryan Bingham. Bingham's songs have been the sound track to the whole stay, two discs Ford and Leah play over and over again. "Found him on the circuit here, playing to just a bunch of people, and wrote him up in a cowboy music magazine I con-tribute to. He's the real thing. Parents ran a roadhouse in southeast New Mexico. He grew up sleeping in the same beds where prostitutes worked. His uncle was a rodeo rider and he was riding competitive rodeo in

Mexico by the age of five but got thrown by a horse, messed his hands up. Now Ryan writes songs, sounds a bit like Dylan and making a name for himself."

It's a drive, the night is cold, the opening acts endless, the crowd small when the boy comes on, in a Dylan Rolling Thunder white hat, a Dylan voice, and Dylan looks. The songs, sung in a small yard under an avenue of pecan trees, are poignant, deep felt, and of the frontier ground they come from: "Tell my mother I miss her so," sings Bingham. Ford leans over and whispers: "His mother died just recently." Bingham swigs from a can of Shiner beer, fairy lights wink from the branches of the pecan trees, the frat-brat audience is barely listening, but he sings on: "'Cause hard times they come and they go / Most of the time they're in the middle of your road."

One can feel Ford's tough love for this boy, immersed, it appears, not only in the young singer's music, life, and words but also his own youth, after a fashion. There is more than a faint echo of the dope-smuggling cowboy in this son of a roadhouse on stage, assailing his acoustic guitar and straining his larynx, even for these jocks with their beers and bimbo blond girlfriends. These jugheads should get work as speed bumps on the road: they have no idea what they are listening to, giving an authentic cowboy rocker like Bingham the pronghorn metal rock salute with one hand and raised Bud can with the other as he sings a heartbroken but gritty song called "For What It's Worth." And as we leave, which has to be early if the cows are going to get milked in the morning, the young man begins to sing "The Times They Are A-Changin'," written by his muse in 1963 when his father was probably younger than Ryan is now. "I can't say I don't worry about Ryan," muses Ford. "There's a side of him that stays detached, then there's a side of him that's like Jim Morrison, autodestruct. Be interesting to see how he handles success. Funny thing, capitalism: takes a protest song by a poor boy and turns it into big business. Bit like the church, I guess, taking something as revolutionary as Christianity and turning it into a religion." And he thinks back instinctively to his own past. "Drugs are a symptom, not a cause. Ask the addicts, they'll tell you. What the hell happened, and why? What's the root cause of that stuff I was smuggling?" He leaves his question hanging from the night as we drive through the gates of the ranch.

The sun beats down next afternoon, through bigger, older pecan trees than those around Ryan Bingham's stage, with venerable trunks. There's been a bumpy ride around the luminous meadows and woodland, refreshed by rain. Now the sun is out, and down by the lazy-rolling Guadalupe River, Ford's foreman on the ranch, Manuel García Guajito, and his assistant, Abraham, are cutting dead branches. They take a break as Ford applies the brakes and alights to chat. Manuel has what might appear to some as strange conversation, which turns from wood clearance to Los Zetas, about whom Manuel has things to say. "I don't think Los Zetas are bad people," he asserts. Why? "Well, they're not. They're good. My brother was driving a bus in Tamaulipas once, which broke down. And Los Zetas helped him, they got help, and helped him fix the bus." After this eccentric account of Los Zetas as an emergency roadside service, there's also unusual word from the underworld of migration, a steady current through these parts as reliable as that of the Guadalupe River. "In the old days," says Manuel, "when the coyotes brought people over, there was always trouble. They got robbed by the polleros, the women were violated, everything was trouble. Now Los Zetas have taken over, and it's all under control. Everyone coming through says the same. They take more money, *claro*"—certainly, of course—"but it's much safer. You keep your things, and the women keep their honor." But the surface of things is of little interest to Manuel García, who has worked with Ford many years and whom Ford respects greatly: "good a land manager as you'll ever find." What interests Manuel are the happenings and phenomena in the extraordinary world he inhabits while he runs this ranch, seeing not the beauty of the pasture and wildwood, the shafts of sunlight that shine through and illuminate the leaves of oak and pecan trees, nor hearing the mellifluous singing of birds. Manuel has his visions.

"I saw gold and silver mosquitoes," he relates, "and others of fluorescent colors, biting people and taking out their DNA. Taking our DNA elsewhere, a bit like Noah's Ark. But there was no ark, they were taking each of us, and every animal, to another time, or another place." Some might nod politely and leave Manuel to his chopping, but on a long after-noon, Ford and I stay rooted to the spot and wait for more. Ford is a man with a short bullshit-endurance fuse, and he not only wants to talk more to his foreman, but says this: "He said he'd seen a tornado of eagles, going 'round and 'round, upward. And the funny thing was that two years later, there was one. Most far-out goddamn thing I ever saw: like a cyclone of eagles, swirling in a circle toward the sky, just like Manuel said." Now Manuel continues: "I've seen a lot of people walking down the highway there. Their clothes are all torn, and they're hungry, and we offered them some food, but they didn't know what to do with it. They were walking like zombies, right along the road." He sweeps his arm toward Highway 80 and the distant border. "Thing is, I'm not afraid of dying. What I'm afraid of is being alive and not being able to help these people out on that road."

7

"EAT OFF THE FLOOR"

In May 2000, shareholders of the giant Alcoa aluminium company assembled in Pittsburgh, Pennsylvania, to hear their chief executive, Paul O'Neill, for the last time. O'Neill had served the company well, and those who had invested would be sad to see him go. On the other hand, there was a great honor awaiting him: President George W. Bush would soon announce O'Neill's appointment for the post of treasury secretary in what the business community regarded as a powerhouse administration, at the commanding apex of the new president's economic and financial agenda. Alcoa and its subsidiaries had plants all over the world, including a number of maquiladoras, mostly automotive assembly plants and joint ventures just inside Mexico. One of those was in the city of Ciudad Acuña, opposite Del Rio, Texas, and made electrical distribution systems for light and heavy vehicles—"electrical octopuses," as the workers call them.

The twin cities of Ciudad Acuña and Del Rio are the first in what now becomes the eastern third of the borderland, after the deserts and mountains descend in altitude toward rolling Texas ranch land and the vast Mexican state of Coahuila. The land becomes greener, semitropical, and, on the U.S. side, more densely scattered with towns and small industrial settlements from here to the sea. On the Mexican side, the cities of Acuña and, a little farther downriver, Piedras Negras have been utterly transformed by the arrival of scores of maquiladoras, an industrial revolution in what was horse-and-cattle hacienda country, now assembling the contents of America's supermarket shelves and auto dealerships. Ciudad Acuña was, until the recession of 2009, the fastest-growing city in the country.

Reports of protest against poor conditions and wages had emanated from Alcoa's plant in Acuña since two chemical exposures in 1994, one of which had caused a three-day shutdown with 179 workers sent to the hospital for evaluation. Despite a reputation for concern with workers' safety, O'Neill had reportedly brushed these whispers aside at another shareholders' meeting in 1996, saying that conditions at Alcoa's plants were so good the workers could "eat off the floor."[1] But at that meeting in 1996, also in Pittsburgh, a shareholder rose to speak. He was no ordinary shareholder: his name was Juan Tovar Santos and he was himself a worker for Alcoa in Ciudad Acuña. Tovar Santos addressed the assembly with a bulletin from the shop floor of the maquiladora. He spoke about intoxication of the air by materials used in the factory. He spoke of relentless working hours and pittance pay. He described punishing production quotas and the iron regulation of breaks—to rest the eyes and fingers, to eat, even to use the lavatory—which no worker was allowed to do beyond two timed visits of one minute each per day, using only three sheets of toilet paper per visit. He spoke about discrimination against pregnant women and workers having to leave after industrial injuries without compensation. Matters had become so bad, said Tovar, that riot police had had to be called in to quell a demonstration in the factory yard with tear gas.

The intervention had been carefully and long planned. The clutch of shares enabling Tovar Santos to speak had been bought by a support network for workers in the maquilas led by the Quaker American Friends Service Committee and a group of Benedictine nuns in San Antonio led by the extraordinary sister Susan Mika. Both teams worked in concert with one of the most impressive and cogent organizations along the border, the only one of its kind, the Comité Fronterizo de Obreras, Frontier Committee of Women Workers or CFO, based downriver from Acuña at Piedras Negras. The committee had come to represent men too, and Tovar had been one of the driving forces behind it. The CFO is not a union but a pressure group and cadre of people working in, or sacked from, the maquilas and devoted to harassing, educating, agitating, inciting, motivating, fomenting, prompting, and blandishing. In Mexico, trade unions are traditionally affiliated with the central Confederación de Trabajo México, the confederation of labor or CTM, a vast bureaucracy. The CTM-affiliated unions are known by democratic currents and militants as *charros*, for which there is sadly no translation other than the literal "horsemen"—"union hacks," perhaps, or even "scabs."

Such institutionalized organization of labor is a legacy of the seven decades of power invested in the PRI, which proclaimed a veneer of sympathy with organized labor, not unlike that of the Peronist system in Argentina, with unions ceding a measure of control to the corporatist state. President Salinas Gortari talked about "the indestructible historic pact between the Revolutionary government and the working class," sealing it with the union leader Fidel Velázquez in 1988.[2] When the maquilas were brought to Mexico by the PRI, there was little changing the notion that a union is not there to rock the boat. Quite the reverse, it was now there to keep the PRI's industrial peace, even with the new wave of investors from north of the border. In Ciudad Acuña, however, even this is luxury: the city boasts itself to potential investors in North America as being the only one along the border in which the maquilas are entirely "union free," which is music to the ears of boardrooms across the United States but is a red rag to the bull of the CFO. In the postmodern, globalized marketplace, just as in the postmodern drug war, there is little place for the old lexicon. In the world of globalized production, the idea of structures to negotiate pay and conditions sits uneasily within a doctrine of profit free from restraint, which carries a big stick whereby if the Mexicans get too difficult, an employer can simply move to China or some other place where the wages are even lower and the workers docile. Only it takes longer, and costs more, to cross the Yangtze into Texas than to cross the Rio Grande, and for this reason maquilas are spreading south within Mexico, into the interior, where the decrease in wages payable on terrain of abject poverty more than offsets increased costs of transport.

In his excellent book on maquilas, Alejandro Lugar found that "the life of working-class people at the U.S.-Mexico border is so fragmented, and yet so systematically inspected, that a culture of rebellion, or of class mobilization, was not found . . . The ruthless working conditions, the cutthroat competitive performances among workers, and the struggle over decadent tools of production often led to the unmaking of class." His conclusion, based on years of work on and in the factories, no doubt describes the landscape accurately and in justified despair.[3] But strangely, the arrival of a new workforce on the border worked in two directions. On the one hand, the generally rural agricultural population that came north to work in the factories had no experience of unions or organized labor when they confronted their new transnational employers. On the other hand, the new workforce "undermined old spaces of union control while opening up a space for non-PRI militant unionism," wrote Altha Cravey in a study of maquila labor.[4] Into that new space, the CFO emerged to try to ensure the basics of decency and fairness at work, that the endangered species enshrined in its slogan "Dignity, Justice, Solidarity" were not banished entirely, as the employers avowed, from the globalized industrial landscape in borderland Mexico.

Juan Tovar Santos has now left the border and settled in Torreón, at the southern tip of Coahuila, of which Acuña is the far north. But I caught up with him two years after a second visit to Pittsburgh in 2000, tending to the engine of a car propped up on blocks of wood and concrete outside his home in Colonia 28 de Junio on the edge of Ciudad Acuña. "I'm a mechanic now, and have been since they sacked me," he said, with both wariness and a hint of humor. "I was never an activist before, I just came here from Zacatecas to work in the maquila eleven years ago, and was hired the following day—the wages were 150 pesos a week in 1991, about $15; they were 700 when I left, about $50, but worth much less in the shops.

"We'd all come from the same farms in the south of the state; we knew each other and had had enough shit from landowners during the privatization. There were nine of us in a local factory committee, and we started trying to get direct meetings with the managers." The things he remembered best about the Alcoa plant were the poisonings and untreated industrial injuries, the sacking of workers after being injured, the lowest wages in Ciudad Acuña, and "having to apply for toilet paper, being allowed one piece per go, only being allowed to go to the toilet twice a day and not being allowed to spend more than a minute about one's business in there. It was particularly hard on the women." There were only one thirty-minute break for lunch and two five-minute breaks in the nine-hour workday. Tovar and his committee "tried to talk to managers in the factory, but no one wanted to listen. Then we had an idea that we would try and get the board itself, in the United States, to listen. The CFO got involved. They said that if we wanted that, they could make it happen, with their contacts." The CFO, he says, had been contacting workers inside the plant since 1994; the shares were duly bought by the AFSC and San Antonio nuns and the plan laid to attend Mr. O'Neill's shareholders' meeting in 1996. "A number of people were invited to go to Pittsburgh," says Tovar, "but they were too afraid to do it, so I said okay, I'll tell the boss what's wrong in this company. So with Sister Mika and the Quakers we wrote down a list of complaints, they brought translators, and off we went, to an old hotel downtown, I don't remember its name. We went to the new company headquarters and had a great time—our problems were back here, not there. Only when I stood to speak, there was an argument between O'Neill and the chairman of the meeting, and the chairman said the people should hear what the workers have to say."

Once Tovar Santos had spoken, Alcoa's response was immediate. The following week, O'Neill fired the chief executive of his Acuña plant for failing to inform headquarters about the intoxications in 1994 and made sure that toilet paper and soap were available across all eleven of his Mexican borderland factories. "The week after we got back," says Tovar, "the Alcoa human resources people showed up. They offered us a choice to work in all different places, any shift we wanted. They asked how much we wanted just to leave all this alone. I said that didn't interest me. A man called José Juan Ortiz offered me a hundred thousand pesos just to quit, and I said no."

O'Neill was eventually replaced by a tough new CEO, Alain Belda, but negotiations through the religious shareholders continued. Alcoa promised, says Tovar, that "nothing would happen to those of us who had campaigned for better conditions." However, he says, "those conversations occurred just a few weeks before the attacks on September 11, so that no one was really looking when the company turned against us. I was accused of sabotage," Tovar says, and "almost immediately afterward they sacked the ringleaders involved. The plant was locked down tight so that the CFO could hardly get a foot inside." Tovar has a brother in Dallas, "and I'd like to go across. I tried to get a visa, but there's not much chance of that now! My brother says to try and cross as a wetback and I'm thinking about it, but there's an issue with my mother and father. So I earn my living this way now, fixing cars. I'm quite good at it, actually. I don't have anyone to boss me around like in the maquila, and if I work hard I can operate my own bonus scheme. If I fix up a car for myself I have a travel subsidy, the days off are more generous, and I can wipe my ass as often as I want."

On New Year's Day 1994, the same day as the Zapatista revolt at the other end of Mexico, the North American Free Trade Agreement came into effect, evaporating duty barriers and tariffs between Canada, the United States, and Mexico. As the great historian of Mexico Enrique Krauze writes, "Even coming up with the idea of the North American Free Trade Agreement was a violation of the Eleventh Commandment of official Mexican mythology: Thou Shalt Not Trust Americans."[5] Barack Obama is the first president since 1994 to show any sign of wanting to "upgrade" NAFTA, in other words tighten the flow in favor of some measures aimed at protecting American jobs and manufacturing. His mention of the possibility proved to be a sticking point during a meeting with President Calderón the week before Obama's inauguration.[6] NAFTA was a boon to business and free trade, a blow to jobs in America, and transformed the economies of Mexico and the border. For the narco cartels, NAFTA was a gift, the perfect cover for their traffic, which multiplied overnight while the bureaucracy required to ship it diminished. But it had all started with the maquiladoras three decades before. Although they are now the emblem of the NAFTA treaty, the maquilas, which defined the border's new economy by bringing the millions north (and now define it in reverse, as recession and competition from Asia cause depopulation), were NAFTA's pilot scheme and a symbol of Mexico's subjugated but dependent relationship to the U.S. economy.

In 1961, after thousands of former migrants returned across the border after the United States ended the Bracero Program, President Adolfo López Mateos, followed by Salinas Gortari, drew up the PRONAF, or Programa Nacional Fronterizo, seeking to lure American corporations to northern Mexico. It offered loans, tax concessions, and free-zone status for the import of goods into the United States. The United States was hardly going to spurn the occasion to enjoy bargain basement third-world wages and industrial costs on its doorstep, and the U.S. Border Industrial Program was duly drawn up on the American side and put into effect in 1965. Mexican fortunes could also be made, leasing to the North Americans, and jobs created in a "developing" country. As in Juárez, the necklace of maquilas was accordingly built along the border, where cities burgeoned with those come to seek employment, but little or no attempt was made to create infrastructure capable of sustaining the new labor force—not water, roads, electricity, schools, or adequate housing. As profits soared, the wage gap and that in family budgets between workers on either side of the border widened, thus antagonizing relations across the frontier in Amexica. The early maquilas thus became a scale model not only for NAFTA but also for the global economy, staring the first world in the face across the Rio Grande. While the maquilas paid wages close to slave labor by U.S. standards, people in the impoverished villages of the South and interior—Oaxaca, Zacatecas, Chiapas, and Durango—viewed them as money indeed. Whole communities in the Mexican interior became ghost towns as their populations headed north, not to try to cross the border but to work on the Mexican side, creating not only an explosion of trade but also the busiest border on earth and work that is both comparable to factory labor around the world but also unique in its way. The collective edifice of the maquilas is calculatedly impregnable. The factories are architecturally ugly and soulless, homogeneous and monolithic, reflecting the toil undertaken within them and the human condition required to perform it. They are invariably surrounded by fencing, barbed wire, and security lodges or gates manned by guards, not so much to protect as to control. They are collated into "parks," the ambience of which could not contrast more strikingly with the cluttered streets from which most workers commute: sterile, colorless, angular, and clean. The parks throttle the towns to which they have moved, built around their edges in locations that bring fabulous wealth to those who own the land and strangulation to everyone else.

The only spoke in this wheel of production—wheel of life, indeed, as envisaged by the transformation of the borderland by the maquiladoras—is that the human race, and especially the Mexicans among it, has not quite yet been reduced to the automaton this cybernated model demands. Even in the maquiladoras of Amexica, these feeder plants of globalization, little irritants are at work, such as unofficial lotteries, under-the-counter cosmetics sales, jokes about line managers, or flirtation during stolen breaks. Dangerous in different ways to the new corporate uniformity is the questioning of this bludgeoned order by the CFO, and the indefatigability of a woman called Julia Quiñones.

Of all the big cities on the Mexican side of the border, Piedras Negras, forty miles downriver from Ciudad Acuña, is to date the easiest to be in and the safest. One can stay at the Autel Río with families in transit and walk out at night to eat or relax in bars where staff are fully clothed. Tourist shops are open, and a few Americans still browse the bric-a-brac. The name of the city means Black Rocks, but, says Julia Quiñones, who runs the CFO from its office some twenty benign blocks from Bridge 1 over the Rio Grande, "though we are Piedras Negras, we are also called the Frontera Blanca, the white frontier. For some reason, touch wood, the narco war has not greatly affected us. No doubt they are here, but not in our everyday lives."

Julia Quiñones is effervescent, with a ready laugh, boundless energy, and mischievous fun-poking, but also resilient and indurate when dealing with abuse of the rights of labor, and pretty tough too when dealing with her own people. After nearly a decade of visiting Piedras Negras, it is always wonderful to find her again, not a volt of her energy gone, nor a jalapeño sting from her severity—though she has developed a sparkly smile that was missing in the earlier days of struggle. From its humble office, and with its stretched resources, the CFO has had an influence against all odds and entirely against the zeitgeist. For instance, says Quiñones, at one point in 2004 during the dialogue with Alcoa, the company said it needed to cut wages, extend working hours, and trim benefits. Such measures, it claimed, were necessary to avoid moving the plant to Honduras. The CFO organized a ballot, asking workers which option they preferred: to accept the changed conditions, or to refuse them and challenge the company to leave. "We called their bluff," says Quiñones. "Of those who voted, eighty-nine percent told them to go to Honduras. Part of the company did go to Honduras, but it came back again."

In Mexico, "it had always been the men who worked," says Quiñones, yet from the outset "the maquilas employed mostly women. This caused social disruption and resentments—men unused to looking after kids were staying at home cooking while their wives were out at work, often harassed at work by male supervisors." The proportion of female workers was at its highest during the 1970s, she says, when the first generation of maquilas were built as assembly plants. A next generation would produce more complex products, such as electronics and electrical auto parts, and a third, latest round would involve "new technologies and computer chips." The CFO, she explains, was originally formed in 1979, in the state of Tamaulipas, backed by supporters in Edinburg, Texas, knocking door-to-door in the sprawling new colonias, collecting information and offering advice on conditions, hours, pay, and domestic disruption. Although CFO was not a union as such, union branches affiliated with the CTM found themselves unable to accept wage cuts and quota increases because of pressure by the CFO.

In 1980, age fifteen, Quiñones took her first job in the Piedras Negras maquila operated by Johnson & Johnson, sewing hems on medical fabrics and bandages. "We had a union," she recalls, "affiliated with the PRI and functioning in the interests of the company." She was paid by productivity, and after five years "I was exhausted and fed up with always having my finger punctured by the needle on the machine and pulling it back so the needle tore even more." Julia was seventeen when the CFO organized its first assembly workers in her plant, suggesting that they vote on whether to accept a wage cut. "I thought, 'Why don't we always do this?'"

In 1986, Quiñones joined the new CFO regional committee covering the states of Tamaulipas and Coahuila, and the following year established a local CFO organization for the two cities of Piedras Negras and Ciudad Acuña—made up "mostly of women," she says. "Our first aim was to give the workers a voice of their own, not through a union that was beholden. Our second aim was to make workers aware of the law and their rights, and the third was to work in the colonias to support people and stop their lives being like a parade of ants to and from work. The maquila depends on us being machines, and the CFO was formed here to tell the workers they were human beings, and the first thing that makes you a human being is knowing what your rights are. At first, there was no hope, complete apathy. But we started by talking about sexual harassment by the managers and taking up cases. Then we took the logic of that into the colonia: if it's not okay for the supervisor to yell at you and abuse you, it's not okay for your husband to do that either. So we became a force in the colonias, and the more that happened, the more we became a force in the maquilas, talking about wages, health and safety, pregnancy, and conditions."

With time, the CFO moved its headquarters to Piedras Negras, and Quiñones became its primary, later full-time, mover and shaker. Guided by the CFO, an unprecedented series of thirty face-to-face dialogues began between employee representatives and Alcoa, after Juan Tovar Santos's intervention. They were deftly handled by the man who had always led the initiative for the Quaker American Friends Service Committee, Ricardo Hernández, and more enlightened managers at Alcoa proved willing to venture to the Mexican side of the border for seventeen meetings—seven in Acuña and ten in Piedras Negras—to discuss hours and conditions, on which some important agreements were reached over renewal of protective clothing, sexual harassment, vacations, and injury benefits. "The workers were speaking directly to the company," says

Hernández, "prompted by the CFO, though the CFO organizers weren't allowed themselves to come to the meetings. The workers were there, I was there, Sister Mika was there, but the CFO did all the work."

Colonia Luis Donaldo Colosio in Piedras Negras is a shantytown made up of one long street, a continuous strip of wooden shacks built with planks and tarpaulin roofs tumbling into one another and sharing each other's backyards. The colonia is sandwiched between the Airport Industrial Park and the main railway line, along which freight trains roll through from Mexico City and Monterrey so that, Julia Quiñones says, "children quite often get run over and killed." The housing development location suffers from regular flooding whenever there is heavy rain, turning the dirt that makes up the street and most people's flooring into mud. In addition to houses tucked behind the slat-wood fence that runs parallel to the railway line, there are corrugated iron bodegas selling household basics.

A roll call of the industrial park and its neighbor, the Parque Industrial Piedras Negras, reveals a backyard production line making the icons that adorn the temple of America: the Mex-Star factory makes wrapping for straws for McDonald's. Another factory, Southwest Manufacturing de México, makes wiring for Harley-Davidson motorcycles. Dimmit Industries, which closed in 2001, made jeans for Levi's. And there's a factory called FAMX, formerly the Fujikura half of Alcoa's interest, that makes the electrical circuits that keep America switching on the ignition.

Three thirty in the afternoon, and it's shift change again, in another town. Rows of school buses past their sell-by date north of the border line up outside each factory, waiting to take their load downtown or back up to the colonias. The workers emerge from their windowless, fluorescent-lit world, down a flight of steps, and into the forecourt, blinking in the sunlight. There is a crush waiting to get through the chicane of an exit, everyone dressed in either a blue or green tunic, patient but eager to get past the security fence that is supposedly to keep people out—but that's unconvincing—and the guards. Some girls pick out a waiting face and blow a kiss at a boyfriend through the chain-link before taking a walk, arm in arm. Others chatter among themselves as they board the buses; others again stare, hypnotized with fatigue.

It is here in Colonia Colosio between the factory and the railway that Leticia Ramírez lives, and here that Leticia works. She takes some finding—four visits before she is finally home. She works hard, all the overtime she can get. Her house is a four-generational revolving door of two visiting sisters, their children, her daughter, her daughter's children, other relatives come to visit, and her mother from Zacatecas trying to have a holiday with the brood—plus dogs chilling out in the dirt. She has a striking appearance: flame-red hair, a skin condition that has affected her face, the figure of a sixteen-year-old even though she is forty and a grandmother, a lambent smile and vise-grip handshake. Leticia has the aura of Semtex or some compressed plastic explosive. She was with Alcoa for eight years until 2003 and now works at the Elektrokontakt factory from which she has just returned, the rear wall of which is visible from the yard where her teenage nephews are sitting around barefoot, countless girls tend countless babies, and old Abuela takes in the evening sun in a rickety chair wanting dinner, so we cannot be too long and we're lucky to have caught Lety at all.

"I was involved in the CFO right from the start," she affirms. "I was like Julia, asking questions, challenging them: 'Why should you take away a day's wages if I'm five minutes late?' 'How can you reduce my bonus just for talking?' I was always asking the CFO for advice, and soon people were coming up to me for tips on how to get around this problem or that. What we did was learn our rights and educate the others, house to house, in the colonias mostly. There was knowledge to learn from books, and there was the question of confidence at work. The managers have these two big problems: they think they're smart and they've convinced themselves you can't resist their masculine charms. Both are nonsense, so if you have your wits about you, you can run rings around them, or at least put up a fight, even if they win in the end. They started talking to us, granting better benefits, but I was blacklisted and left. Things started to slip back after we, the CFO crowd, had left the factory. We need to be on the inside *and* the outside. Right now, we're campaigning on Mex-Star over there"—she waves at another stark wall enclosing another factory within view. "The McDonald's place, it's dangerous," she claims, something they use in a glue to make the plastic that wraps the straws.

Now, says Leticia, finally at work again after five years on the blacklist, "I get better pay, but only because I work longer hours." Her ten-hour shift is 7:00 a.m. to 5:00 p.m., which brings home 600 pesos, about $50, for a five-day week. But "I work as late as they will let me every evening [as we know; she had never been home when we called previously] and at weekends if possible. I have to, to feed everyone. I'm a mother, a grandmother, and a daughter—families to feed here, parents to feed in Zacatecas." The colonia, she says, "is quite a place to live. We're all on top of each other, as you can see, and there's not much sleep with the trains six feet away—they're on their way from Mexico City to Kansas, and even Canada." Two little boys idle on the rail tracks, torturing a frog. "You!" shouts Lety. "Get off the line! Idiots, they're always getting killed."

There was one creepy maquiladora, says Julia Quiñones, "which gave me the spooks when I visited it. They made body bags for the American military. The ones they use to bring the dead soldiers back from Iraq and Afghanistan. There was a problem, they closed it. It was the strictest of all: no chewing gum, no music. No wonder, the boss was an evangelical Christian."

By 2008 and 2009, the maquiladora landscape has changed in Piedras Negras since my early visits here a decade previously. Although gains had been made at Alcoa, the company responding to the CFO's initiatives, a new arrival in Piedras Negras, the Lear Corporation, has brought with it new problems, says Quiñones: "paying wages under a new 'flexible architecture' management model, of forty-six dollars for a fifty-hour week. Among the lowest of all, in terrible conditions. We are having to work with victims of serious industrial accidents and injuries with no recourse to compensation."

And there is further turbulence for those employed, or formerly employed, by Alcoa in both Acuña and Piedras Negras. Alcoa's interests had been in part a joint venture with the Japanese Fujikura company. But in 2009, Alcoa, wanting to divest and focus on aluminum production, sold its share of operations in Ciudad Acuña, Piedras Negras, and other borderland cities to a California-based company called Platinum Equity. One immediate problem on the ground in Piedras Negras and Acuña is that the AFSC and Benedictine nuns in San Antonio were, as Hernández says, "owners of stock in Alcoa, using those shares to speak to the company and bring the workers to the table. Now, there's a whole new board of directors, of an equity company without stakeholders, so we no longer have a formal platform for discussion."

Piedras Negras's appealing architecture after crossing from Eagle Pass dissipates as one progresses into the miles of drably uniform Infonavit housing, built and mortgaged by the government to maquila workers, designed either deliberately or by happenstance to be without character. In one such forlorn terrace of cuboid habitations, Dora Luz Córdoba lives in a relative's house, rain lashing the leaking roof. She has a pink streak in her hair. It's a gesture of defiance, in its way, and she needs to be defiant, unable to work after suffering an industrial injury at the new Lear factory and laid off without compensation, she claims. "I only got to work there two years," she complains, though it wasn't much fun. She operated a machine punching nails into a metal plate, only one day last year the nail punched into her hand. You only get gloves, she says, "so as not to contaminate the circuits," and she didn't qualify for a pair. "I suppose I have myself to blame, but I'm angry that no one trained us, just put us in front of that machine; it was never explained how to use it. And I'm angry that they didn't give me any protection for my hands, especially after a man near me lost his finger." The accident happened at 2:00 a.m., and Dora was bundled off to an emergency doctor chosen by her employer, though she was made liable for the taxi fare. She claims she was told she was fine and could carry on working, though she had lost the use of a thumb, so she labored on with one hand. It was her personal doctor who insisted on an appointment with social security, but Lear declined to accept that Dora's injury was an industrial accident, as she claimed, and no benefit was forthcoming. "So now I do what I can.

I clean, mostly, people's houses, front yards, or I mind kids, anything." Often while doing the rounds in Piedras Negras, one will come across Dora, in one neighborhood or another, sweeping, scrubbing, wiping, polishing, or dusting like an outdoor scullery maid with a shock of pink hair in a town where everyone works for someone else.

Dora came from Monclova in the south of Coahuila to work in the maquilas. She is only in her early thirties, but she looks wearier. She recalls the main meal breaks, described in most maquiladora contracts as something to be "enjoyed"—*disfrutar*, it says in the workplace rulebook—as especially stressful. "If the workers exceed the thirty-minute limit, they will receive disciplinary action," reads the rulebook.[7] "It's supposed to be half an hour," says Dora, "but okay: you have to line up to clock your card out, then you line up to use the bathroom if you want to wash your hands before eating, then you line up for the food, and then line up to clock back in again. That leaves about five minutes to bolt your food. Everything has to be done to the second, even your meal break. If you're late back from lunch three times at Lear, you lose a day's wages. The managers are always on your back, inspecting you, checking you, throwing their weight around, and of course trying to make a pass. All we could do to get rid of the stress was dance. Every Friday I'd go out with the special people I bonded with at work, the ones I had friendships with, jokes, and sometimes romance. And I used to lose myself in the music and a drink, and in a dance club you could take it out on the ones who were sneaks, sucking up to the bosses. I'd work all evening, come off a shift at 2:00 a.m., dance all night, and sleep all next day. It was heaven."

If there's one thing worse than Dora's maquila working life, it is being thrown out of it. For how different is the life of young Sara González Noriega, in a similarly tiny but well-kept house on Calle Mar Muerto, Dead Sea Street, making racks that enable car seats to recline. The shift from 5:00 p.m. to 2:00 a.m. pays her 700 pesos (about $55) a week, plus the $6 bonus she keeps to spend strictly on herself, for treats or outings with friends. "I don't like the job, but I like going to work," says Sara, "because I get bored at home now that my son is in school, and I like the jokes we make about the *jefes de línea* [line managers]. They're mostly vulgar, but not always. There's one who really fancies himself, always flirting and bossing us around, but he's so short and we call him 'Dobico,' after a dwarf on TV. We do it every time he passes and collapse laughing." The managers are mad, she says, "really insane. They have to regiment everything, enforce a strict dress code—no bracelets or anything. They might let us chew gum, but if they make us stop, we squash it into the machines! If you miss a single day, they dock twenty dollars' pay, nearly half the week. I have to start at five, but there can be problems leaving my son, and if I am five minutes late, they dock a whole day's wages. You have to sign this form accepting whatever discipline they give you." "Article 107 of the Labor Law," interjects Carmen Luria Vidal, a CFO organizer who accompanies us, "prohibits arbitrary fines for workers, whatever the reason. Did you know that?" "I do now," replies Sara, flashing a smile. "Only sometimes people are scared to talk about things like that, in case they get sacked. When they find out that a worker is studying their rights, they ask, 'How do you know? Where did you learn that?'"

Men were at first a minority of 25 percent of the maquila workforce along the border, which is now about evenly balanced. Reynaldo Bueno Sifuentes is part of that equation, after thirteen years with Alcoa and now at AEES, the factory now owned by Platinum Equity, with his baseball cap on backward, buzz cut, and red T-shirt, and piles of cinder blocks propping up a car on which he is working in the front yard. He earns "the same pay as when I started," about 940 pesos ($75) a week including overtime, if there is any, and is happy to be driving a forklift truck stacking crates rather than working on the production line. But even that is insufficient for a young family—who soon join us, his wife and two children—and so Reynaldo joins the procession over the bridge each weekend to Eagle Pass to sell plasma and raise extra cash. "I go twice, for sixty dollars," says Reynaldo, "two-thirds what I earn all week at Alcoa. It pays for small things and extras, details, fixing up the bathroom and car, toys for the kids. But you have to be careful selling plasma. I've seen people who don't eat right or sell too much, and they're dizzy all the way home. I've seen them falling over on the bridge coming back."

Reynaldo's dream, he says, "is to be a mechanic. In the maquila, though it's much more dangerous than driving, and eventually for myself, just fixing up cars back there." I think of Juan Tovar Santos, the original troublemaker, fixing cars and wiping his ass whenever he wants.

Reynaldo was part of the CFO dialogues with Alcoa executives and one of the plant delegates nominated by the charro union leaders. As such, he was supposed to attend what Ricardo Hernández calls the parallel "pantomime negotiations" supposedly to prepare the workers' positions and brief the union leaders who would themselves negotiate. In reality, these meetings were held so that workers could be briefed on what the leadership had decided, and, says Reynaldo, "when the time came for the contract negotiations at the Alcoa plant in Piedras Negras, which is unionized, no one would tell me when the negotiations were happening, because I'm with the CFO and I know the book of labor law. So how was I supposed to brief my shift if I can't go to the negotiations? So I'm walking a high wire now—there are threats, but only verbal ones so far. The snitches'll say, 'Let's kick this guy' right in front of the manager, to please him. So we'll see, but I ain't backing down."

Behind Julia Quiñones's offices there is a maquiladora run by the CFO with a modest workforce of eight. With a difference, as one might expect: the Maquiladora Dignidad y Justicia employs women sacked or retired from the jungle of maquilas out there, working to timetables that fit their lives, making goods for sale on the Internet, made of organic, "fair-trade" materials. "Once," says Julia, "we got an offer to make holsters for guns, from a company called Maverick Arms. We turned it down because it was part of the arms industry. Shame, we'd have made them much better holsters."

Two ladies have come to work at the CFO's own maquila this morning, Sonia, who made Levi's for eleven years at the Dimmit factory, and Herlinda, who worked as a seamstress for Barry Industries in Ciudad Acuña making slippers for America's favorite family mall megastores. Where will America be without them? Who knows, but both ladies have meanwhile been retrained by a third woman, Ofelia, suggested by Julia Quiñones. Sonia and Herlinda remember the days of the twelve-hour maquiladora shift, which has now been reduced to nine by most employers. Twelve hours from 6:00 a.m. to 6:00 p.m., that is, punctuated by a ten-minute break at 9:00 a.m., thirty minutes at midday, and another ten at 3:00 p.m. Sonia was eventually promoted to quality control, "inspecting miles and miles of fabric, having made it myself for many years. They got more and more strict, 'Do it quicker, do it quicker,' so there's a chain of pressure, which I had to pass on. There was one we called Jalapeño, because he was always stinging us. The twelve hours got you five hundred pesos [$40] a week; you had to work weekends to get the extra two hundred. Eventually, I had to leave because I lost my eyesight from concentrating all day—before, I could see like an eagle, now I'm blind as a bat—and because the bones in my ankle got all messed up from standing for eleven years. I'm not a small lady," she says with a laugh, "and I started having trouble walking."

Herlinda spent twenty-two years making slippers, seven days a week. "Sometimes we had to increase production because there was an emergency, like when the buyer first started ordering them by the thousands, and if we didn't complete the order in time, the buyer might go somewhere else." Interestingly, to wrap a straw for McDonald's is a much slower process than stitching a slipper. Herlinda would sew a base figure of 84 slippers a minute. In a day of 720 minutes minus 50 minutes for breaks, that is 56,280 slippers per day and 393,960 slippers in a seven-day week. This level of productivity paid a basic wage of 600 pesos a week—0.0015 peso (0.00011 cent) per slipper. "But we could earn an extra three hundred pesos a week if we increased our productivity by an extra thirty slippers a minute, which I learned to do," says Herlinda—114 slippers per minute, totalling 76,380 slippers a day, or 534,660 in a seven-day week. Herlinda almost certainly didn't do this, but if she had worked at the higher rate for all her twenty-two years, and not accounting for any days off she must have taken, she'd have amassed a career total of 613,331,400—well over half a billion—slippers, over a career average of 27,878,700 (nearly 28 million) slippers a year. But that was not enough, not fast enough, not cheap enough. Suddenly, says Herlinda, "the factory closed. It went to China, and after twenty-two years I lost my job. But everyone kept talking about this Julia, who had helped the workers and was retraining specialists who had lost their jobs, so here I am." She beams through her spectacles, a woman now in her forties, with the fingers of an eighty-year-old but nimble as a child's as she serves herself from the aluminum trays containing a hearty lunch of fajitas that Julia has brought in from a taquería around the corner.

Of course, this workshop could not begin to try to compete in the service of America's appetite for slippers. But it is a growing concern, it has its catalog and its business: T-shirts, tote bags, handbags, sweaters, blouses, and shirts. "My dream is to grow this workshop into an export business," says Ofelia, who was herself a seamstress but self-employed in her house "because I had six sons," making school uniforms and habits for monks and priests and, once, even the bishop's robe. The CFO maquila now has important partners, like the Minnesota-based North Country Fair Trade, and a high point came when the Mexican fashion designer Juan Pablo López asked the women in Piedras Negras to realize his designs for various haute couture shows in Paris. The ladies catch their breath with pride at the very thought. "We made a summer and winter collection," purrs Ofelia, "all fair-trade materials, all organic: blouses and dresses for the women, and some shirts for the men. And there they were on the DVD, on a catwalk in Paris, paraded by models!" López's design drawings are on the wall, garments named after and reflecting the planets and their qualities. "Earth is men's stuff, as you can see," enthuses Ofelia. "Mercury is a pretty blouse and Mars this sexy minidress. Jupiter's lovely, a blouse with big baggy sleeves, but look at Pluto, a frock with a high waist, hem above the knee, and designs from Chiapas."

A hard few days in Piedras Negras end with a get-together in a dimly lit room at the back of a house in another shantytown, Colonia 28 de Junio, of buildings made of wood and this one, belonging to the Ozilia family, of concrete. The walls are covered by the Virgin of Guadalupe, Club América, and children's drawings, and it is hard to tell which of the people dangling their legs from both stories of bunk beds and sitting across the floor are Ozilias and which are family, friends, or workmates. This is a social occasion, not another collective gripe, though the two tend to overlap. Arturo and Luis, two of the old guard, sing the praises of lotteries that operate in most maquilas. Arturo says that tickets for the official state-run lottery sell for less in the maquilas than they do on the street, but with the same prize money, because the salesman's commission is lower. To be caught selling tickets, though, "gets at least a four-day suspension and usually the sack." Marginally less risky are the sweepstakes held, and odds offered, on horse racing and football. "I won fifty pesos on a nag running in Torreón last year," says Adrián, "for a stake of only five, though I've probably spent another one hundred since." Gabriela and the girls are dependent on thriving cosmetics markets that operate unofficially in the maquilas. "The older ladies who can cross to Eagle Pass buy them in bulk and bring them back to sell in the toilets. The only snag is going into the bathroom two at a time to check out what they've got without being seen. Usually, the sales and raffles are on pay-day, but it's getting easier now to pick up your winnings or perfume after work." "Better to go to Eagle Pass to buy cosmetics," says Julia Quiñones dryly, "than to sell your blood."

The old baseball stadium in Ciudad Acuña is rickety but precious, the kind of ground that would melt the heart of an aging American aficionado of the game who feels out of step with electronic scoreboards and a thumping disco beat through the seventh-inning stretch. The Acuña stadium didn't make it into Ken Burns's series on the history of baseball but it reminds one that this is still a pastoral game, though invented in the city. There are little windows in the brickwork through which to buy tickets, scuffed concrete steps into the stands off which the paintwork has been worn by decades of boot heels. The crowd is arranged on wooden bench seats without numbers, "Krakejak" is on sale from an ad hoc stall for 10 cents and Tecate with lime and salt in a bottle for 35 cents instead of the $7 that Americans pay for a Bud Light in plastic. This afternoon's game is a Coahuila state cup knockout fixture between Acuña's Atléticos and Saltillo, and the crowd is full of piss and vinegar with Acuña winning 8–1, sitting pretty with bases loaded at the bottom of the eighth. A third strike collapses the chance to go 12–1, but the standard is high, the signaling and second-guessing sophisticated, and at the close range afforded by this stadium, you get to savor those moments of sudden acceleration and deceleration, after the tension of carefully calculated nothing.

Across the scrap of land outside, a market is in full swing selling *ropa usada*—secondhand clothes brought from Del Rio across the border and hung for sale—knockoff CDs, and very unofficial soccer kits: those in Acuña who are not fans of baseball tend to be devoted to the Santos de Torreón soccer team. Boys accordingly play soccer in the dust wearing either local green or Club América yellow, and a crowd of tambourine-bashing evangelicals sing on a corner, Los Aleluyas as they are jokingly called. Jehovah's Witnesses, Testigos de Jehová, are more commonly known as "Testículos de Jehová" (which shouldn't need translating), jokes Óscar González, our companion.

In June 2009, after the sale by Alcoa to Platinum Equity, the workers in Ciudad Acuña, supported by the CFO, uncertain about the future of their forum for dialogue with company executives, made a decision: they would seek recognition by a trade union—that of Mexico's coalminers—which would be a fly in the ointment of the city's selling point north of the border: union-free Ciudad Acuña. This is not a shift away from the CFO, which is not a union and cannot legally organize a workplace. Quite the reverse: the CFO is as usual part of the plan. The CFO's office in Ciudad Acuña is located at the end of a dusty stretch of road along which a *pulga* (literally, flea) market sprawls, blaring music by our narcocorrido friends Los Tigres del Norte. And inside the CFO office, on two consecutive September afternoons in 2009, groups of mischief makers meet to discuss the progress of the idea to organize the first union in the city's maquilas, before moving on to work their shifts. These were all members of the dialogue forum, the legacy and tribe of Juan Tovar Santos and his day out in Pittsburgh. A man called Juan Carlos Palomino remembers the riot back in 1994 in the parking lot: "They came in with guns, attacked us by force." He feels his blood rush even now. "People were fainting from the tear gas, women too, they didn't give a damn about the women." And "after they sacked two hundred forty people, they thought the problem had gone away—ha ha! All they'd done was steel our nerve and spread two hundred forty people to fight in other maquilas!"

The group on the second afternoon included Sergio from Veracruz, who works in Plant 2 of AEES, with a red T-shirt and ruddy face, and Javier from Tabasco, with a ponytail pulling back the hair from his handsome face and a baseball cap on back to front, leaning forward, elbows on knees throughout the discussion. "There've been numerous advances as a result of our meetings with the executives," says Sergio, citing a few: deals over pregnant women and protective shoes, time out for medical emergencies, and recognition of grades and differentials. "But there's been a change since the company was sold by Alcoa, noticeably by supervisors and managers going back to the old ways." The men use the word *prepotencia*—prepotency, throwing their weight around. "We're worried about the recession, but especially the way they respond. Laying people off, increasing the quotas, constantly repeating the threats to leave for Honduras or Asia, whether that comes from the top or not." The uncertainty takes a social toll on Acuña as it did on Riberas del Bravo in Juárez, Javier talking about "people returning to Veracruz or the south of Coahuila, nine out of ten of the empty homes left being invaded by gangs and addicts. It all helps organized crime sink roots into the colonias. Kids don't go to school, and things disintegrate socially. It's not Ciudad Juárez, but we're on the road to Ciudad Juárez." The fact that things are quieter here, and the CFO's mind's on other things, does not mean Los Zetas are any less active. Joe Morales, a former security coordinator for U.S. and transnational companies investing in maquilas across Piedras Negras and Ciudad Acuña, said that the narco traffickers were "in complete control of the streets and get very little resistance from those they extort. It's every citizen for himself if they are confronted by the drug lords. If the drug dealers need to kill someone, they take them outside Acuña so they don't attract attention of the Mexican federal officers or the military."[8] In 2007, Los Zetas organized a street party for Children's Day, with food, cakes, and drinks. A banner was posted: HAPPY DAY TO ALL, FROM OSIEL CÁRDENAS.

"Because of who we are," says Javier, "we think the solution to all the problems has to start where the problem starts: in the workplace. We need to improve the quality of life, and that starts at work. It all begins with that." Hence the aim to create a union local, but why the miners' union? "Because it's a strong union," says a man called Nicolás Rojas Romero. "It's less charro than the others, doesn't kiss the boss's ass, and has a history in Coahuila—the coal mines in the south of the state were always well organized." Ciudad Acuña's promise north of the border was that such a thing would never be tolerated. But contact has already been made with the miners in Mexico City, who are now ready to recognize a local across the AEES plants belonging to Platinum Equity, in union-free Ciudad Acuña. How Platinum Equity will react is anybody's guess. "It feels like back to Pittsburgh!" laughs Juan Carlos Palomino, like an old trooper called back to the front after too long in the rear echelon.

Once past the usual ring of PEMEX stations and Oxxo convenience stores that flank any Mexican border town, and Colonia 28 de Junio, where Juan Tovar Santos lived, the road out of Acuña and back to Piedras Negras crosses flat land reaching across toward the border, through groves of mesquite trees and nopal cactus, wholesome and delicious with beans, and the pretty little town of La Purísima—the most pure. But before reaching the most pure, there is a sudden jolt. A white-painted chapel stands on the south side of the road, alone. Julia Quiñones presumed it to be just another Virgin of Guadalupe and paid it no heed, puzzled by my demands to pull over.

The skeleton within is shrouded in a cloak of colors, the spectrum of the rainbow. In her bony right hand, she holds a globe—the earth, the whole world, the sphere of continuum and eternity. In the left, a bunch of white flowers someone has placed there, roses and lilies, the flower of purity presented by the archangel Gabriel to the Mother of Christ. At her feet, candles burn in glass holders bearing her image, only in the pictures the cloak is hooded and black and she carries a scythe. Also on the ground, in homage, offerings of oranges, Tecate beer, ashtrays full of cigarette ends, and scratch cards. An iron grille across the face of the chapel is locked. To partake in this homage, in this petition for protection and blessing, one needs access to a key, one must be initiated. On the side of the chapel is painted an oration:

> *You who await the exact moment*
> *To extend your hands to me*
> *To enter the time ordained*
> *Protect me from evil and all memory*

The skull of Santisíma Muerte is unadorned. This is rare. She is usually crowned, at least with flowers, if not a miter. She stares north with her hollow eyes. And the black light of her gaze stares through those eye sockets of bone toward the river, the Río Bravo, Rio Grande, call it what you may; under this gaze it matters not a fig. The river: the flowing border, its waters now moving into a new chapter in this war, a new terrain— that controlled by the Gulf cartel and Los Zetas, where all the rules change, the landscape changes, and the air itself is heavy with the cartel's power, deadly and intact. The skeleton's eyes stare toward the river as it winds now toward a bridge called the Gateway to the Americas, where the war began.

GATEWAY TO THE AMERICAS/PAX MAFIOSA

The headlights aimed along Highway 85 coming in from Monterrey throw bedazzling beams through the dust kicked up around truck stop Veintiséis, 26, so that the encampment of drivers, roadside cafés, and police officers at their checkpoint is coated in a thick, illuminated mist of powdery, pulverized dirt. Although the trucks are parked up like a military column, many of their drivers have kept the engines running, so the granulated dust is also heavy with noise and fumes, chugging Volvo and belched PEMEX diesel. There is no day or night in the trucker's world, only light and darkness; there is no clock apart from that which measures pickup and delivery times, delays. North of the border, the commandment is set in stone and monitored by tachometer, an accord between the Teamsters and haulage companies: after ten hours driving, you rest ten hours. But on this side, in Mexico, things are more flexible. Or maybe not so flexible, there's just a different kind of rule: you drive all the hours God gives, pep yourself up with chemical cocktails to do so, and make as much money—that is, drive as many miles—as you are physically capable of, devil take the consequences. But even a Mexican trucker must eat, sleep a little, and do other things while off the road.

Veintiséis is the name given to the truckers' republic that has sprung up around the customs post and police checkpoint fifteen miles south of Nuevo Laredo, the city that with its twin on the U.S. side, Laredo, makes up the gateway to the last, industrial leg of the border journey. The bridge between the two downtown areas of each city is called the Gateway to the Americas, because this is the border's commercial fulcrum, at which you arrive either by freeway up from Monterrey in the South, or down Interstate 35 from Dallas to the north. Or, of course, as I did: along the flat border road from Eagle Pass, Texas. The railway bridge and three other road bridges between these cities form the umbilical cord of trade connecting Mexican and Latin American freight, and Chinese exports, with North America. Forty percent of all trade between the United States and Mexico—equivalent to $367.4 billion worth—crosses the Rio Grande here every day, loaded onto thousands of railcars and eight thousand trucks crossing in both directions, converging from all over the United States and Mexico to transfer their payloads to drayage shuttle trucks at vast freight-forwarding yards on either side of the border. More than a million barrels of crude oil a day cross the line here, along with 432 tons of jalapeño peppers, 11,000 ATMs, 16,000 television sets—all this and more through a town that on the Mexican side didn't light the streets until recently and on the U.S. side was a sleepy cowboy town famous for the song "The Streets of Laredo." Now, neither side can mix concrete fast enough. Los Dos Laredos form a commercial DMZ full of freight containers as far as the eye can see. There is charisma and excitement in the whole thing—trucking—in both these twin cities.

Laredo, Texas, is the fourth-biggest port—and the biggest landlocked port—in the United States, after New York, Los Angeles, and Detroit. Some five thousand trucks a day cross north, and four thousand south, over the busiest bridges in the world. But here's the rub: although 97 percent of the transport is legal, an estimated 3 percent is contraband—invariably drugs northbound, guns and cash southbound—making this the principal crossing point for narco cartel exports and these drivers their witting or unwitting transporters. The cartels' war—which began here in earnest in 2005—was for the prize corridor, the most important plaza of all. The U.S. authorities' war is against a simple logic: the more trade that comes through Veintiséis and across the border, the more drugs come with it.

Behind the rays of the headlamps at Veintiséis are other lights, the pale yellow or bright fluorescent lanterns of the *comedores*, places to eat, each marked with a hand-crafted sign. Approaching night, the place is all bustle and hustle. Exhausts farting, brakes screeching, reverse gears grinding, and the drivers checking out the deals in the comedores. In the middle of this arcade is a little chapel, lit from within by flickering candles burning on its floor and in alcoves in the walls. On the back wall are painted the images of the Virgin of Guadalupe and San Judas Tadeo, beneath whom is written an oration: Dame la mano firme y la mirada vigilante / Para que llegue a mi destino / Sin accidentarme ni dañar a los demás / Líbrame de los conductores brigandos y agresores. Grant me a firm, vigilant hand to lead me to my destination, without hurt to myself or others—and deliver me from "bandit and aggressive drivers"—for thine is the eternal ribbon of asphalt, for ever and ever, Amen.

In Comedor Johanna, two drivers sit on red plastic chairs at a red plastic table eating fajitas. They are Juan Gabriel Morales from Tabasco, driving a load from the Pacific port of Lázaro Cárdenas, and Alfredo Cornelio from the gulf port of Veracruz, hauling a container from a depot outside Mexico City. Juan Gabriel has two front teeth missing from the upper tier, a chest thick with hair, and a ring with a crown of thorns on it. Alfredo wears a Chivas T-shirt and shorts despite the damp drizzle. Neither is told what his load is nowadays, they complain. Both men are exhausted and glad to have made it. "The road gets harder," says Juan Gabriel, the older man, "more checkpoints, more delays, more *mordida*," bribes to pay along the way. "It's crazy," says Alfredo. "There's more work than ever, but more hassle on the route—because of the problems." Their friend Jorge emerges from the gloom of the desert and backyard behind Comedor Topo Chico next door, zips up his fly, and reclasps his belt buckle with a hand of four aces on it. It's too late to eat, he says; he'll have breakfast in the morning and a beer for now. Jorge looks the part: black ponytail, Durango boots with a harness and buckle, tight jeans.

Beyond the banter, no driver wants to get into an involved discussion about anything until morning, that is to say, in five hours' time, at 5:00 a.m., same place. There are things to talk about, says Juan Gabriel, but for now we'll just exchange team news between Chivas and Liverpool, and talk about Barcelona. Barça's following in Mexico and among Mexican Americans is ubiquitously passionate, not least because the Mexican national captain, Rafa Márquez, played at left back for the Catalans. But the issue now is to find somewhere to sleep, not having available the cabin of a truck personalized with religious articles and pictures of women wearing only cowboy hats and boots. The first hotel on the northbound road was the Campo Real, but the din and squealing from the adjacent Bar Jaguar, from which one presumably adjourns in company to bed, made us U-turn back to the five-mile line and the Motel California, with courtyard walls painted yellow ocher with a touch of pastel green to give the chipped cement that southwest adobe feel. The man at reception gave us the keys to rooms 5 and 7 in exchange for 200 pesos each and asked how long we wanted them for. "For the night," I replied, and his reaction said it all: part shrug, part compliment at the prowess entailed by a rental longer than an hour.

The world over, truckers sleep in the cabins of their juggernauts to save money (though Europe and the United States have different facilities that offer a driver a bed). In Mexico, where every peso counts, there is only one reason a trucker would spend good money on an iron bed and clammy sheets. Come to think of it, Comedor Económico La Sirena back at Veintiséis had been exactly as it proclaimed itself, some of the yellow tables occupied by *conductores* tucking in, others by groups of sultry ladies chain-smoking and crossing their legs in skirts so short, for all the chill of night, there was little left to the imagination. And before long, that one reason starts assembling in reception and sure enough there's a knock at the door. I feign sleep. Knock, knock again. Towel around my waist, I answer the door to say *"Disculpe, pero . . ."* "You like my hair?" which was beautifully permed for sure but not the first thing you'd notice. "Twenny dollar, thirty for my fren' join us," the visitor continues, all this in passable English. "Thank you but no, I just need to sleep." It seems rude, so I say it again in Spanish, out of some weird sense of etiquette: "no offense, er . . . thank you, no." It was enlightening to learn what kind of real woman a Mexican trucker prefers to spend his hard-earned wages cuddling up to, for all the size-zero, snake-waisted pinups wriggling around the walls of their cabins. Some of these buxom behemoths patrolling Veintiséis and the Motel California would weigh in at a tonnage above some of the sixteen-wheelers themselves.

By 5:00 a.m., Comedor Johanna is in full swing as ebullient Veintiséis gears up for another day of NAFTA. Of last night's company, only Jorge from Puebla, looking chipper in a clean Wrangler shirt with embroidered horseshoes, has kept the 5:00 a.m. rendezvous. "So you stayed at the Motel Californicada!" he growls with laughter, raising a thick eyebrow as though to ask, "and how was she?" Jorge calls hookers not the usual *putas* but *arañas*, which means spiders, and calls the ones at Veintiséis *garrapatas*, literally ticks, whereby they are particularly pushy. "Not my type," I offered, trying to sound more macho than prudish. "You should've stayed in my truck and put me in the motel," retorts Jorge, who says he's fed up with the food at Johanna's so we take a stroll across the pitted roadside tarmac through a battleship gray dawn to the first eatery inside the line drawn across the highway by police inspection booths.

Jorge started driving after losing his job as a mechanic in Córdoba, south of Puebla. "The Mexican driver," says Jorge, "is the best in the world because he has to be. It's not like the USA—there's no job protection, no guaranteed rest, no limit on the time you can drive. The company will never pay for a second driver, so it's all down to you. The pressure comes from both the company and the other drivers. The crazier they are, the crazier I have to be. We set our own pace, always driving farther to make more money, always stretching it, pushing it." Jorge has been driving trucks the length of Mexico for eleven years and "I know every mile between here and Monterrey, Monterrey and Mexico City, and down from my town to Guatemala. I know every trick—ha, and I know every *cachimba*." That's a new one. It means literally fireplace or hearth, but Jorge means the kind of roadhouse where you can get fed, drunk, and laid—and score drugs—all in one. "In Zacatecas and the South, you get everything money can buy whenever you want," assures Jorge. One hardly needs to ask how Jorge and his comrades perform these miracles of itinerant sleeplessness over weeks, months, years, for they are not miracles. "How much do you get paid for this?" I ask. Jorge looks around him, checks that the cook is stirring eggs, and pulls out a plastic bag full of pills and a little packet of silver foil. "This much." He smiles with a grimace.

At that moment, Juan Gabriel comes in and orders coffee. Juan Gabriel being a family man, Jorge explains that we're just talking about driving, a lot of driving. Juan Gabriel has seen the highways change, he says, especially of late, since the drug war began, in 2005, here in Nuevo Laredo. "The timing is stressful. You have your load, your deadline, and delivery date. If you fuck it up, you don't get paid. After five years, I think I know every trick, and suddenly new checkpoints, new hassle. And it gets scary," Juan Gabriel admits, though he seems ashamed, for Mexican truckers are supposed to be unacquainted with fear. "You're coming out of San Luis Potosí toward Saltillo and there's a checkpoint that wasn't there before. You've no idea who it is. If it's the army, you can usually talk your way out of it, even if you have to pay. But what if it's the police? Or the police working for the bad guys from here who are big in that area?" (No one utters the word "Zetas"; we shall see why.) "You just have to get the papers out and give them what they want—you can try, but the company won't pay it back."

What both Juan Gabriel and Jorge want to talk about more than anything else is the moment that, as it happens, first brought me to Laredo in 2001. In a narrow window of time between his election and the attacks of September 11, George W. Bush, as former governor of Texas and devotee of free trade, had made the first overtures of his presidency to Mexico. Vicente Fox was the first foreign head of state with whom he met, and President Bush proposed the unthinkable: he wanted to admit Mexican trucks into and throughout the United States. Instead of a drayage system of forwarding yards and shuttling loads across the border, the long-haul trucks containing goods from the South, and from China via Lázaro Cárdenas, would simply line up for inspection and roll over the bridges. The proposal drew flurries of reaction from all sides and in all directions. U.S. haulage firms accelerated their already substantial financial stakes in transporters based in Mexico. The Teamsters union was outraged: jobs regulated by decades of negotiation were threatened by drivers working to timetables that were recklessly nonexistent. Ironically, the left and right swapped sides: the isolationists and the right wanting to tear down the border, while environmental groups joined the fray with dire warnings about Mexicans, the trucks they drove, and the way they drove them. In the event, the proposal was scotched by 9/11, but it had begged all kinds of questions about not only NAFTA and the vagaries of free trade but the border itself. It sent particles of interest flying about like those in a nuclear reactor, smashing into one another from all directions.

At every truck stop in Mexico, the passing moment fueled a conversation that will never end. "Let me drive to Chicago!" enthuses Jorge, eating breakfast like a bear. "We could beat those gringo truckers' asses off their cabin seats!" Juan Gabriel says, with more deduction, "If they let us cross the border, that would change everything. We'd make more money than the gringos even though their wages are higher, just because we'd drive so hard. We'd drive them out of a job with equal competition. That's why it'll never happen. But I respect them. They're doing what we would do—I wish we had the Teamsters instead of a charro union. They're drivers, we're drivers, we're the same people. If I was a Teamster, I wouldn't want crazy Mexicans driving everywhere, popping pills."

We walk out to the parking area, past the police checkpoint, behind a very different eating joint that amalgamates Church's Chicken, Subway, and Daily Roast. Along the way, an entire village has been built up around Veintiséis, with houses where comedor owners, cooks, dishwashers, waiters and waitresses, used clothing dealers, prostitutes, engine repair mechanics, and their children live, and yards where rangy dogs, cats, cows, goats, pigs, and rats cohabit with them. Comedor La Güera also operates a full-service market with detergents, shaving gear, batteries, penknives, and knockoff audio and video entertainment, while Restaurante Jalisiense is attached to a yonke, La Maroma, fixing up cars and exhausted engines. And all along the way, the ground is littered with discarded little aluminum packages that once contained pills, the overnight dosage of downers to sleep and amphetamines to get you going again. There are hundreds of them strewn across the dust, but they are only the slightest microshaving off the great block of narcotics pulling up at Veintiséis and moving on through. The drugs are aboard the trucks, in bulk, heading straight into the United States of America. There is no reason why, if 40 percent of cross-border trade moves through here, 40 percent of the drugs shouldn't either, if not more. That is why the drug war began in Nuevo Laredo, and that is why the Gulf cartel and Los Zetas made sure to win it.

The battle for Nuevo Laredo was the beginning of the current phase of Mexico's agony. It announced a new level and kind of violence: some two thousand were killed in 2005 across the country. The Sinaloa cartel sent a lieutenant called Édgar Valdez Villarreal (La Barbie) to lead its siege of the Laredo trade route. He used the Internet to show videos of four Gulf cartel killers being beaten, ending with one being shot in the head. Valdez had been raised in Laredo, Texas, and been given his nickname— because of his pale complexion and blue eyes—in high school, where he was a football star. El Barbie was the only American citizen to reach these heights of a Mexican cartel, until he was killed in 2010.[1] After one firefight late in 2006, the dead in Nuevo Laredo "lay in pools of blood flowing into the Rio Grande," after which men with assault rifles "picked up the bodies of the victims, threw them in the back of pickup trucks and headed out of downtown."[2] In June 2005, President Vicente Fox sent in a token military force, but as a commander of the police department, Enrique Sánchez, said when asked by journalists where the soldiers were during the fighting, "That's a good question. Where are they?" It was a barbed remark, with federal officials at the time briefing that Nuevo Laredo's police department was at the disposal of the jailed Osiel Cárdenas Guillén, leader of the Gulf cartel and creator of Los Zetas. At the same time, Alejandro Domínguez Coello, a former federal law enforcement official and president of the chamber of commerce, became chief of police in Nuevo Laredo. He was honest, and assassinated seven hours after taking office.[3] Within days of his murder, the U.S. government closed its consulate, comparing Nuevo Laredo to Baghdad, a city of "bazookas, grenades, and machine guns," said a businessman after watching a twenty-minute battle.[4] Throughout, the cartel hung their narcomantas, one reading, WHAT ELSE COULD YOU WANT? THE STATE OF TAMAULIPAS, MEXICO, THE UNITED STATES, THE WHOLE WORLD—TERRITORY OF THE GULF CARTEL. Another promised that Los Zetas served BETTER FOOD THAN NOODLE SOUP, the standard fare for serving soldiers.[5]

But the war has in 2009 abated. Nuevo Laredo is uneasily calm, or has the appearance of a calm that could blow at any moment. When the human rights campaigner Raymundo Ramos Vásquez shows off a narco villa in the exclusive Madero neighborhood whose owner switched loyalty to the Sinaloa cartel five years ago—attacked with bazookas, incinerated, and still empty—he does so as though it were both a cautionary tale and tourist attraction. But Nuevo Laredo lives the peace of the tomb, or a Pax Mafiosa. "There has been a truce," says Ramos. "I don't know the details, and I don't want to know, but the Gulf cartel has won, the Sinaloa cartel has lost, and they have reached an accord. I can only guess that Guzmán pays some kind of tax to use the corridor, if he uses it at all. The Gulf cartel controls the corridor again, and the federal army patrols every block of the city, twenty-four hours a day, three hundred sixty-five days a year." During 2010, the Pax Mafiosa ruptured as fighting broke out between the Gulf cartel old guard and elements loyal to los Zetas.

But this nevertheless remains a monolithic society in which no one dare speak the word "Zeta." In every town under their control, Los Zetas have another name in everyday parlance, a code word used as a vain insurance policy by the few who dare speak of this subject; here it seems to be "El Pirámide," or just the generic "bad guys," as everywhere else. It is an absurd charade—anyone who talks about Los Zetas is at risk whatever he calls them—but the shying away from the word is fundamentally important. It shows that the faux mystique of Los Zetas works and intimidates, that their name has become an evil talisman, and to avoid uttering it is a primal act of superstition. To speak it, on the other hand, feels like self-condemnation. Ramos talks about the Gulf cartel but never uses the Z-word. There are, though, exceptions of insane courage.

Driving back with Raymundo Ramos into town one day, there was an extraordinary coincidence, speaking of brave people. I asked after a mutual friend of ours, Elisabeth, and Raymundo said he hadn't seen her for nearly a year, since the three of us were last together, in fact. At that very moment, in a little street behind the church of the Holy Infant downtown, there she was. Elisabeth was once a leading attorney in town, fighting domestic violence as a public defender for five years and taking on cases of wrongful conviction in jails for four years. She was the first woman from Nuevo Laredo ever to volunteer for national military service. But in this city, her curriculum vitae makes Elisabeth unemployable, a transgressor of the values that sustain this society (which she is). No curia, tribunal, or court will touch her, though she still carries her résumé around every forum in town.

In her hurt and rage, Elisabeth is another rare soul who testifies to what is happening, but unlike Raymundo she does so with a devil-may-care fury heedless of consequence. After the joy at the serendipity of the meeting, we adjourn to a friend's house in an alleyway behind the church for coffee and incautiousness. "I watch them control everything, different people but always the same interests. First the police, then Los Zetas—let's call them by their name [she is the only person who does]—beating the city into silence. They control everything in this town, everything that moves, every particle of our lives." Shouldn't you be careful, saying all this, Elisabeth? "It's driven me mad being careful. If I am so dangerous, let them kill me. If they do, at least I'll die with a clean conscience." People know Elisabeth. As we walk around and toward the church, they greet her from underneath the parasols that shade their taco stands but make sure not to tarry too long talking, lest someone see or hear.

On the back of a truck, there is a sticker of Santa Muerte and the words DIOS ME GUÍA, ELLA ME PROTEGE, God guides me, she protects me. "Just look," spits Elisabeth, "there's a cult of death across this town. It is sick, dying from within." We enter the church and breathe the musky air with relief. Elisabeth caresses the feet of the saints with fervent exhalations. "Here, I am safe," she says beneath the figure of the Virgen del Carmen, and the words EN LA VIDA PROTEJO / EN LA

MUERTE AYUDO / Y DESPUÉS DE LA MUERTE SALVO—In life I protect, in death I help, and after death, I save.

Nuevo Laredo's peace is a hideous, browbeaten calm, but it serves as a model that the Mexican government, or any future Mexican government, keeps as an option, especially if the PRI were to return to power by beating President Felipe Calderón's PAN out of popular exhaustion with his war. In the extreme: Mexico's choice may one day be between the implosion in Juárez, where the war grinds on, or the Pax Mafiosa of Tamaulipas. The only problem is that a national Pax Mafiosa would be entrusted to Guzmán for safekeeping, so what deal to cut with the Gulf cartel and/or Los Zetas? (These latter two were synonymous—until 2010, when an as yet unresolved internecine power struggle exploded here and downriver.)

When I return to see Raymundo Ramos a year later, in 2009, the "peace" is one year older, the town almost buzzing, such is the façade of the Pax Mafiosa and the determination of these people to live as best they can. Raymundo and I convene in the front room of the house of a friend of his. He is an intriguing man—secretive about his life but boldly forthright in his utterances and analysis. He runs the beleaguered Nuevo Laredo Committee for Human Rights, working as a rapporteur to the United Nations Commission on Human Rights, but his casework mainly involves complaints against the army—he stays well clear of problems caused by Los Zetas. "The difference between here and Juárez," he begins, "is that there, the plaza is still contested—a battle between gangs, cartels, and the army. Here we don't have that problem. The plaza is tranquil, it's peaceful now compared to three years ago. Here there's one cartel and the army. But the volume of traffic going through Nuevo Laredo doesn't change. All it means is that the accord between narcos at the highest level must be holding, between the Gulf cartel, Guzmán, and La Familia. Laredo is the main crossing point for trafficking throughout all the USA, we're right in the middle of the distribution network here, and no one wants to give it up entirely," he warns ominously. "The Gulf cartel and Los Zetas hold the terrain, and anyone else must pay a tax. The army is here, but that doesn't affect the traffic either: you notice that President Calderón is fighting a war against the narco traffickers, but not the narco traffic!" And he echoes Ignacio Alvarado in Juárez: "It's a strategy to control the traffic, not to eradicate it. Calderón's war is a political flag, a battle against the impunity of the narco traffickers. He's lowered their status in society, but it has done nothing to interfere with the economy the narco generates, the transportation and delivery networks that come through here—a structure that remains intact—and the infrastructure that has been established to launder money. All that is untouched. So the drugs cross over, and then what? The supply chain is in Mexico, and the distribution and demand chain is in the U.S., where the infrastructures are also intact. The U.S. wants to try to stop the drugs coming over, but like Calderón, they don't go after the money or the infrastructure. Laredo–San Antonio–Houston: it's a seamless supply chain and a seamless financial system." And here in Los Dos Laredos, the essential link in the equally seamless transportation chain, "this is closely tied to NAFTA. We supply the U.S. with goods, and we supply the U.S. with drugs, through the same corridor, aboard the same trucks." The more goods, the more drugs; the percentage is consistent. "The U.S. has friends, and it has interests," says Raymundo. "In the cases of both goods and drugs, Mexico is not a friend, we are an interest. Depending on who you are in the USA, Mexico produces the goods and delivers the drugs.

"But things have changed," he says. "Before the war, and during the PRI time, the narco was granted impunity, so he thought he was the boss, but actually the politicians and the police were the boss of the narco. Now, after the war and with PAN, the cartel in Tamaulipas has become a parallel structure; they are not subject to the political parties, they are a parallel government. Before, the policeman and politician were the bosses of the narco. Now the narco is the boss of the policeman and politician, and does what he wants."

The sudden rupture of the Pax Mafiosa and fighting between the Gulf cartel and Zetas from February 2010 came as a surprise in the apparent vice grip of the supposed alliance between the two over Nuevo Laredo. One possible explanation for the rift, advanced by U.S. and

Mexican intelligence, is that the Zetas had become almost victim of their own success—too ambitious and greedy for the other cartels to tolerate further. Elements within the Gulf cartel's old guard were also being cut out of the loop, seduced into joining their old enemies from Sinaloa in a front against the Zetas, whose exact role had become unclear once the Pax Mafiosa had been enforced, and who had become a cartel in their own right.

Ramos was once a journalist for the local paper with a reputation for fearless reporting on the narcos, *El Mañana*. But, he says, "I just couldn't carry on. It became too dangerous to be a reporter here. What would be the point risking it? The papers can't publish the news—it's too dangerous for them to do so." In imploding Juárez, people bandied around the words "Línea" and "Guzmán" with relative ease in public, for all the raging violence. Here, barely anyone speaks, and in the local press, nothing. As any visiting reporter trying to cover Nuevo Laredo—and all Zeta or Gulf cartel territory—knows, this terrain is harder and more frightening than Juárez. Juárez has a functioning, albeit assaulted, mass media; a visiting journalist has reason to be there. In Juárez, there are press conferences, interviews, and articles about the violence. The tabloid arm of *El Diario* newspaper, *PM*, makes a point of getting to the latest atrocity first, for a gory front-page photo. In Nuevo Laredo, the opposite prevails—the press has been bludgeoned by Los Zetas into silence.

Nuevo Laredo is one of those towns in which the local paper is a local institution, as is the family that owns it, one of the most prominent and respected in the state: the Cantú family, the head of which is Heriberto Ramón Cantú, with his wife, Ninfa Deánder, as its matriarch. The executive editor of the paper, and others the family owns, is their son Ramón Cantú, an impressive man, something of a good-living rake, charming, clever, forceful, and unreliable in his appointments. But the doors of his newspaper are protected by a bulletproof, bombproof screen, atop which is an understated memorial plaque commemorating an attack on the paper by Los Zetas with grenades and guns in February 2006, targeting and injuring a veteran journalist investigating narco smuggling and conditions in the maquiladoras, Jaime Óscar Tey. Two years previously, in March 2004, the editor, Roberto Javier Mora García, was stabbed to death in his SUV, outside his apartment. The case developed a gruesome momentum of its own, after the arrest of a homosexual couple living in the apartment above Mora's, one of them a U.S. citizen, Mario Medina. Both were convicted of the murder, and Medina was stabbed to death in a hallway in Nuevo Laredo's state prison. He had accused the Tamaulipas police of torturing him, but said in an interview the day before his death with *El Mañana* that he was confident of being proved innocent.[6] And it was not only in Nuevo Laredo that journalists were being attacked and killed. In January 2010, Mexico's National Human Rights Commission published a tally of fifty-six reporters killed over the previous nine years, with eight missing and seven newspaper offices attacked.[7] In most cases, the assailants were narco-trafficking cartels hitting reporters investigating drug traffic, corruption, or crime, said the report. But the susurro in Mexican journalistic circles is that in a few cases, reporters put themselves at the disposal of one cartel, or had been threatened into doing so, thereby targeted by another. The Committee to Protect Journalists has assiduously traced the attacks and in its report for 2008 came up with a lower casualty figure and damning indictment of the Mexican authorities. "Powerful drug cartels and escalating violence made journalists in Mexico more vulnerable to attack than ever before," read the report. "Most crimes against the press remained unsolved as Mexican law enforcement agencies, awash in corruption, did not aggressively investigate attacks. With no guarantee of safety, reporters increasingly turned to self-censorship to protect themselves."[8]

But Ramón Cantú defends his ground with estimable tenacity, though he takes care to do so on the U.S. side of the border, on the public occasion of a "War on Drugs" conference in El Paso. In private, he confides, "I'm sick of the whole thing. I want to talk about something else, about the future of this place, trucks, and trade." But at the conference podium he bites the bullet: it was made clear, he says, "that we should not use the word 'Zetas.' And I took the view that the lives of our staff are more important. This war is not going to be won by a newspaper or magazine. We have to be aware of our safety as well as benefit the community. We spend a lot of time looking out for our own safety so as to avoid more complicated situations . . . We're censoring the newspaper, because we have to get our children to school. If we get some anonymous tip or call, we have to decide what's correct and what's incorrect. These people," he reminds his audience in case it urges him to brandish the sword of truth at all costs, as many do, "they just kill you. They don't make up a slander that you're having an affair, or taking money from the Mafia. If they don't like you, they kill you. We have to be very calm. Yes, I've received complaints: 'Why don't you publish this or that?' And I try to explain that I felt bad that we're not doing our job, and then a lady calls, and we must report something. Next day, *they* call and tell me that two of my reporters have been kidnapped and advise me to keep silent. I'd like to say I had a bit of courage, but these are innocent reporters covering social affairs— what am I going to do?"

Other journalists in Nuevo Laredo do speak what they cannot write— off the record. One editor says of the crossings into the United States, "The Mexican government can put all the money it wants into the customs and inspections posts; it's all useless. A customs officer is as afraid of organized crime as anyone else. What are they to do when a convoy of fifteen Suburban SUVs pulls up at the forwarding yard or even at the bridge? And men get out wearing paramilitary uniform and ski masks, carrying AK-47s. If it's a forwarding yard, they're told to open the truck. If it's on the bridge, they're told just to let a truck through across the river. They're not asked, they're told. What do they do? They move to one side. They open the door. They let the truck cross, they don't ask or say anything. They just look the other way—who wouldn't? This is a military unit; they wear hand grenades in their vests. They don't need to ask people to cooperate. This is what happens here, this is how it's done." He hypothesizes: "How can you deal with a military formation? You can militarize customs instead of having civilian law enforcement, and have regular shoot-outs on the border bridge, but I can't see that—you'd be having battles all day. You can check every truck, but what happens to NAFTA if you check four thousand trucks a day? The line would go all the way to Chiapas!" We are talking late. There's an edition due. None of this can be broadcast locally. "When the truck reaches the U.S. side," he continues, an impeccable source, "they have their corrupt officers among the honest ones. They are approached, offered money, and threatened. You play and get paid or you pay with your life; they're bought the old-fashioned way."

At the end of a street running through Colonia Victoria and down to the reeds along the riverbank and the border is a migrant shelter called the House of Nazareth run along similar lines to the CCAMYN in Altar, catering mostly to desperate Central Americans waiting to cross, or else deported back. Over the road is a blue-colored wall tagged with graffiti, not of gang names but those who have died. EL VERACRUZ RIP—the implication being that this was a migrant from the state or city of that name who perished in the desert. Wrong.

A posse of lads is shallying around the wall, apparently nonchalant but watching over the stretch of land between the end of the street and the border. Presuming them to have something to do with the migrant shelter, and the priest in charge not available, I saunter over for a chat. "No," says a rapscallion youth in a gray zip hoodie and jeans. "They died here in accidents, in this colonia." "That's my brother," says another, in perfect English, pointing at a name on the wall. So you're not migrants, then? "No, we're from here." These boys need to be spoken to, but carefully. "Antonio" lived in Houston awhile. "Came back after a few years—got deported." So these people were killed? "Yeah." So Colonia Victoria was bad during the war, and when I ask where's a place to eat, Antonio talks about a restaurant called the Esquina, now a shell, which "closed during the killing and never reopened because the owner was shot." A slim boy is standing on the corner wearing nothing but a pair of dirty shorts, a red baseball cap on backward, and expensive new sneakers. He has said nothing so far, but suddenly a walkie-talkie in the pocket of his shorts crackles to life. He takes it out and walks away around the corner to talk. There's a feeling that I'm not supposed to be here while this communication takes place, so we shake hands and I leave, saying I'd come back to see the padre.

I returned a week later, to find Antonio speaking to a friend at the Fox motorcycle service station near the memorial wall, to which we walked back together talking about Houston and his deportation, past houses made out of wooden slats. I was alone—probably not a good idea, but being a clueless gringo can be a form of protection, as was the proximity of the House of Nazareth, where I feigned an appointment for which I had been stood up again, and was therefore obliged to wait around. I thought it might help to be European, which apparently makes me a *gabacho* rather than a gringo, and wore a Barcelona shirt with MÁRQUEZ and a number 4 on the back, the Mexican captain's shirt. The fact that it was official merchandise was worth twenty minutes of valuable conversation, which rolled along sufficiently as to have me slouch up to Abarrotería el Brego for some beer so that we could pour down a couple of cold ones as the sunlight sweetens and deepens, and I take a risk. I ask the boy wearing the hoodie if they might be able to sell me something *de la buena*, some *trueno verde*, green thunder. There's a frisson. Antonio looks at the boy with the walkie-talkie. My move: It's your work, no? Silence. "Maybe, yeah," says Antonio, "but we don't do weed." *¿Coca? "Chiva,"* heroin, he replies immediately in Spanish, "but not us, other people. We watch." And in English again: "For export only," and he laughs. The boys address each other as *carnal*, a form of "bro," but apparently thicker since it implies common blood. If these are not smugglers, they are *halcones*— falcons, lookouts. Well, I say, respects and God bless your brothers, and cross myself, looking over at the names on the wall. "It was heavy," says Antonio. In 2005? "Yeah." Guzmán's people? Silence.

Next day, the shelter is shut so I tell the boys I have to wait. They don't believe me, nor do they want to talk about Barcelona. Okay, I ask, but getting nervous: Tell me just one thing, and I'll go. Do you work for yourselves, or are you part of the pyramid? Antonio screws up his face as though he has just eaten a jalapeño too fast. Then he stares back. "Kind of connected," he says in English. "Everyone is." The walkie-talkie crackles in the young boy's pocket again, and I leave for the last time.

On the outskirts of another city, he balances his weight in the shade of a walnut tree, through which dappled sunshine falls. "Oliver" is a big man, with a belly and a second one beneath it. He moves slowly and wears a yellow T-shirt and gray tracksuit trousers. One would like to be able to say that he has the keen, darting eyes of an executioner, but he hasn't. Like him, they are slow but not languid; they are considered. They do, however, have a certain extinguishment in them. He was, so his employer had said, a member of a gang affiliated with the Gulf cartel, and a sicario—an executioner, though Oliver doesn't like that word. He prefers *asesino*.

For all its importance and size, Nuevo Laredo lies in a far northwest corner of the state of Tamaulipas, Los Zetas' home territory, but it is not their bastion—that lies farther downriver. And it was in Nuevo Laredo that the war showed how little sense of brotherhood there really is within the cartels, happy to kill out of factional greed within the same organization. Guzmán's attack on Nuevo Laredo in 2005 was an opportunistic push after the arrest and extradition of Osiel Cárdenas Guillén two years earlier, but the arrest led also to an internal struggle within the Gulf cartel, as the seizure of a capo often does. Cárdenas's power base was Matamoros, and his soldiers were Los Zetas from that town, with Nuevo Laredo far away and run by an old guard in the Gulf cartel, some of them loyal to Chava Gómez, whom Cárdenas killed to assume supremacy. They had their own deals with the local police and, crucially, with the haulage industry, and needed subjugation by Los Zetas from down in the valley. Oliver's gang served a network that Los Zetas from Matamoros needed to bring to heel, but his faction fought its ground. The fault line across which Oliver was fighting was more or less that which broke open again in spring 2010, his Gulf cartel faction being what appears to have been seduced by former rivals among the old Sinaloa foe to pitch once again against "the people from Matamoros"—the Zetas.

Oliver won't say for whom he worked, only that he was one of Los Tejas (which he sometimes calls Tejanos—Texas and Texans). It was, he says, "a gang"—*pandilla*, he calls it—on Calle Leona Vicario in Colonia Victoria.

"We carried out tasks for the organizations in this area of Tamaulipas, in Nuevo Laredo. It also has connections over the river." Oliver had been a truck driver in the United States, and a drug addict—he is now a born-again Christian. "I looked up the Tejas guys there in San Antonio while I was trucking over there," he says. "I was taking some heavy stuff and suffered mental problems. I got deported." Back in his hometown of Nuevo Laredo, in need of work, Oliver hooked up with the gang again, by now formally affiliated with the Gulf cartel. The "truck driving," it seems, had involved distribution of drugs. "We were in the colonia; we were safe in the colonia, but only in the colonia. Outside of that, you don't know who you're dealing with. You don't know who's armed and who isn't. So you work for the organization and they work for you. First, they get you dealing. Then they get you dealing a little more. But if you're good, the real money is in killing." How much? Silence. Oliver stares back, waiting for another question. He could get up and go, but he doesn't; he just sits and waits. There are other people around; his boss isn't far away. It's not easy to talk—Oliver is on probation for promotion at work, back to a post he held but lost. He wants it back a lot more than he wants to talk to me.

How did it start? "It started with fights against the gangs from other colonias. They were creating problems. We got told they were shaving the product, or going over to the guys from Matamoros who were coming in [Los Zetas]. I killed one guy in a parking lot, between Victoria and the Puente Dos. I shot him." And? (There's no point in asking those daft "how did it feel?" questions. Oliver would probably knock my head off with a flick of his finger.) "And he died."

Until 1994, says Oliver, "the organization was straightforward. I wasn't involved in smuggling. Most of the drugs were going through the POEs, and they were taking care of that, but some of the gang would organize for distribution with people we knew on the other side, in San Antonio. What they needed to make things run smooth was enforcement." What's enforcement? "Enforcement is getting problems off the cartel's back." There's another silence, which Oliver finally fills of his own accord, heaving his huge frame from one side to the other and rolling his eyes. "I killed a guy on orders—he was *drogado*." Here the slang kicks in: in border street talk, "drogado" can mean in debt as well as drugged. "He hadn't paid, he was moving stuff and he wouldn't pay back what he'd sold. He died." Where? "In his house." Why? "For the money he owed the cartel." That is all.

The reason I am at this place, a medical institution, is to talk not to Oliver but to his employer and manager about the wonderful work he does with drug addicts, of which Oliver was one. Oliver was doing well and about to become one of the manager's top assistants, but he backslid into the gang and into drugs. Then he returned, like the prodigal son, desperate to get back to where he was, said the employer. "But it had to be on my terms. 'I'll take you back,' I told him, 'but you'll have to start at the beginning.'" "It's hard," says Oliver, softening, almost confiding, "always that temptation."

After 2003 and Osiel Cárdenas Guillén's arrest, "there was more to do," says Oliver, "just more to do. Now I know it was because the people from Matamoros didn't like my people, and my people didn't want the people from Matamoros moving in. I never tortured anyone. I beat the shit out of people. But I never tortured anyone, like they do now."

Oliver speaks in short phrases; his breaths do not accord with the beginning or the end of a sentence. As he speaks, he rolls his heavy head back and adjusts himself and his weight on the metal seat around the tree trunk. "I ran a guy down with my truck," he says. "I made a big mess." There is no point fishing for details. "This'll only stop when people stop taking drugs," says Oliver. The body language is a strange mixture of sloth and strength, like a drowsy animal that can become dangerous in the blink of an eye. "I was never part of the people who were cartel and police," says Oliver, at last exhibiting some pride in himself. "We were on the street, in the colonia. The cops didn't trust us. I was in it for the *territorialità*"—defense of the turf—"that's why we're trying to stop the guys from Matamoros. I'd seen my friends die. I was doing it for the Calle Leona and for my carnales in the gang, and because it paid."

Oliver says he played no part in the war between Los Zetas and Guzmán between 2005 and 2007; he had begun his road to recovery from drugs and endeavored to live his new life by then. But memories are long and the danger remains, says his employer. "He's a threat to us all. He was a sicario; he was one of the gang affiliated with the Nuevo Laredo Gulf cartel faction, and Los Zetas could come for him anytime. Which is very dangerous for all of us." "I was not a sicario," insists Oliver. "I was an asesino. I didn't kill enough for a sicario, and I didn't get the money a sicario gets. I did other things. I was an asesino"—an assassin, then, but not an executioner.

One of the things the editors and reporters on *El Mañana* are eager to talk about is the 97 percent of merchandise crossing the river that is legal. Not just because it changes the subject, but also because "trade is the only viable solution to the problems," says Ramón Cantú, "good jobs and a strong economy for the city."

The four road bridges that make this the Gateway to the Americas are the Colombia Bridge to the northwest over the Nuevo León state line; the World Trade Bridge toward Laredo, which carries the bulk of traffic; the Gateway to the Americas itself (also known as Bridge 1), which connects the two main streets downtown and has a pedestrian pathway; and Bridge 2, a short way east. A fifth is planned. The railway bridge, or Puente Negro, between the Gateway and World Trade bridges, is owned by Union Pacific, which charges the other principal user, Kansas City Southern, for its use. But with Kansas emerging as the new rail hub of the United States, the muscular KCS line, which had bought into Mexico's network during privatization, is masterminding plans for a second rail bridge, its own, connecting Lázaro Cárdenas to Laredo.

"It's been a flag of this paper as the voice of the city: get the new rail bridge," says *El Mañana*'s editorial director, Antonio Martínez Santoyo. "It will complete the infrastructure we need to cope with future traffic. It's now more than just trade between Mexico and the U.S., it's China too— some of the goods not even destined for the United States. A route has expanded over the past five years bringing goods from China, through

Lázaro Cárdenas, up through Laredo, and out through Galveston or New Orleans to Europe, by sea and train. It's quicker than coming through the Middle East, and the new 'post-Panamax' generation of ships are too big to get through the Panama Canal and sail the Atlantic. So it all has to dock in Mexico and proceed by rail. For now, trucking is the bedrock of this town, and Laredo over the river. Every one of those truckers and workers in the yards has a relative who works in freight over on the other side. However, there'll come a time when the fuel situation will change, making sea and rail the future, and we can be part of that. The whole thing is a lesson of history. For centuries, Valparaiso in Chile was the stepping-stone between Asia and Europe, then the Panama Canal, and now it can be Los Dos Laredos."

It can. But for the problem: in Nuevo Laredo, almost every business is shaken down by extortion rackets run not by the local cholos, as in Juárez, but by Los Zetas or the Gulf cartel. Bigger business needs protection by a bigger stick, but Los Zetas' attention to detail is thorough.

In the maze of alleyways behind the border parking lot downtown, a group of ladies engage busily in one of the most established businesses throughout the borderland, *ropa usada*, used clothing. They are called *chiveras*, and they work in every city on the Mexican side, going over to the United States to pick up secondhand clothes to bring back for sale— which is, unbelievably, against a Mexican law forbidding the import of used clothes for retail.[9] Nevertheless, in every Mexican border town, garden fences and roadside railings are lined with jeans, shirts, blouses, baby wear, skirts, and frocks for sale.

In Laredo, on the U.S. side, in a low gray building with a brick-red sloping roof, a team of women and girls overseen by an Anglo manager sort mountains of ropa usada. The warehouse is one of many along Santa Isabel Avenue beside the Union Pacific railway sidings and inspection yards. It is hot, hard work, which the women undertake with genial high spirits: piles and piles of clothing, tied together in bundles, are sorted according to type, thrown into canvas containers marked with labels like MUJERES LEISURE, WESTERN, or TEEN. There is even an Amexican word for this process, the verb *clasear*.[10] The ladies are helped by their daughters after school's out. Rick, the supervisor, is wary of any conversation that gets too detailed, but the money is fair, and the labor's done with gusto. Then the problems begin.

Over the bridge in Nuevo Laredo, a woman cooks chicken and corn for her daughter and friends in a little house near the bridge car park. All these ladies know and visit the warehouses and sorting depots along Santa Isabel Avenue, from which they collect ropa usada and bring it over the Gateway to the Americas bridge, in big zip-top bags. Some of the women sell their loads to people who retail it from their fences to boost the punishing family income. Others sell directly themselves, but none escapes the tap on the shoulder. Unbelievably, the Zetas and Gulf cartel—an international criminal syndicate dealing drugs worth billions of dollars into the United States and to Europe—has the ropa usada ladies firmly in its sights. Of the women in the whitewashed room, none pays less than one peso in ten as a tariff on the sale value of what she brings across the bridge from Laredo, most pay two pesos, and one pays three, probably because she sells direct. This is not a street-corner crew of teenage thugs, this is El Pirámide, Los Zetas, though of course not even the boldest-speaking of these women in their head scarves would consider using the word. "The customs is right there in the parking lot," she says with a dry laugh. "And if they're not on duty, they come to the place where we distribute. That's how it is. What's the point of arguing? I need the work to get the money that's left to eat and send my daughter to school."

But these are just the small fry. Raymundo Ramos and I are driving through the horizons of forwarding yards and containers when the strangest thing happens: a sudden storm of little moths fills the air as far as the eye can see and they fly into the windshield like hailstones. They almost eclipse the pale, hazy sun and make the panorama of haulage and rungs of yellow cabins in the chicken wire, dust, and dirt even more surreal. Still, we keep passing the yards, at a slower pace: ALA, Cargo Consolidada, Transportes Mineros de Coahuila, Fletes México, FEMA, Aeromexpress. Ramos always chooses his words carefully, alternating on and off the record with meticulous attention to what he is saying. He has been talking about "the cartel" levying *cuotas* and mordidas from local businesses. "Do these freight companies pay the cuota—extortion money—as well?" I ask. "Everyone," replies Raymundo. To whom, the police or the cartel? "The cartel." Is that on or off the record? "On the record." Are you sure? "Yes." Is that normal? "It's totally normal. It's the system. Those who get killed in Nuevo Laredo now," he says, "are not part of any turf war; they're usually businessmen who have problems with the cartel. But none of this has had any impact on the drug traffic or the cuota that everyone must pay."

On another occasion, the line of drayage, or shuttle, trucks waiting to cross the busiest bridge in the world, World Trade Bridge, a couple of weeks later stretches back for miles, the truckers expecting at least a five-hour wait today and alighting for coffee and breakfast tacos at the roadside stands. A group snacking at a little stall called Takos Kora has just been hauling plasma TV sets and domestic white goods from Korea and China. They complain that enhanced security makes two runs a day more strenuous to complete. They object to the amount of tracking devices and checking the drayage companies are now obliged to carry out to make sure the shuttle goes straight from the forwarding yards to the bridge, not via some other place where the load may be tampered with and a little extra put on board. "If there are drugs in the container," says a driver called Luis, "they'll have been there all the way, and you'll know nothing." And anyway, says another man, these new seals they put on the containers are all very well, "but the bad guys know how to break the seal, do what they want, and put everything back looking like nothing had happened." The conversation, already a bit awkward, winds down. Then a driver wearing a brown bomber jacket and smoking silently until now says, "Sometimes, the bad guys just come into the yard in a troca, and just say, 'Open the container.' There's nothing you can do but turn away, wait, get in the cabin, and drive."

Thirteen miles north of the border, Bill Sanderson shoots a dart of spittle through his front teeth onto the tarmac and points his cowboy boots toward the entrance to the Pilot Travel Center. A Teamster of twenty-three years, Sanderson was born in southern Missouri, raised in Little Rock, Arkansas, "but now I live in Carlisle, Pennsylvania, 'cause it's the crossroads of trucking and it makes life easier. I get to see more of my wife and kids that way, if I'm living right on the depot." Crossroads it certainly is; Carlisle should be twinned with Laredo. There, in a diner at 3:30 a.m., I once interviewed Jimmy Hoffa, Jr., president of the International Brotherhood of Teamsters made famous by his father, who is believed to be entombed within the concrete of a bridge over the New Jersey Turnpike. "I love it," says Sanderson without hesitation, "doing this job. Right amount of freedom, right amount of home. I can say I know every mile between here and Dallas, Dallas and Little Rock, where my parents are, Little Rock and Nashville and Louisville, and between Louisville and Pennsylvania, pretty much every inch. I know just where to stop when the hours are up and the clock's gonna catch me out. But it's always different: different weather, different time of day. And there's always an adventure, up to Montana, always someplace you don't know yet." Sanderson wears a great T-shirt: BORN FREE. TAXED TO DEATH.

This is Port Laredo, the truckers' lair, equivalent of Veintiséis on the U.S. side, on Interstate 35, the spinal freeway that connects the freight yards with San Antonio, Houston, Dallas, and all stations north. And it could not be more different. You can choose between McDonald's and Subway to eat right here, or any number of other chain favorites within a couple of miles down the I-35 business loop. If you don't care to eat in, your meal can be ordered and your number called by loudspeaker into the forwarding yards. You can buy special phone cards called Truckerbucks. You can buy a T-shirt reading CHRIST IS THE **ROCK ON** WHICH I STAND. A voice comes over the PA: "Shower customer number one fourteen, your shower is ready. Please proceed to shower ten." There are slot machines and a bewildering range of scratch cards. PUMPKIN SPICE CAPPUCCINO IS BACK, says a sign, as though it ever went away. Sanderson acknowledges a man wearing a fluorescent orange jacket and combat fatigues. He is traveling with his wife and child, in defiance of the lonesome trucker stereotype, but Sanderson leaves him to his itinerant family Sunday lunch. "There's places I'd rather be than Laredo," says Bill, who is down collecting a mixed load for Yellow Freight. "But it's an interesting-enough town, on-the-edge kind of thing, seen a few problems but that don't affect me. People is kind, that's for sure, though I can't say I like the food. Some of the boys like it and used to visit over in Mexico too. But you never caught me going across there, oh no, not even when it was quiet. I'm a family man, got responsibilities. Far as I'm concerned, you kiss good-bye all your rights as a human being soon as you cross that border."

In the old days, says a driver called Mitch from Springfield, Illinois, a taxi would take you in a group of four for $25 each over the border to what is called the Zona de Tolerancia in Nuevo Laredo. "He'd wait for everyone to finish their business and bring you back. Only twenty-five bucks, and you didn't spend much more'n two times that over there," says Mitch. But that caper has ended since the war started. Maybe it is coincidence, maybe not, that since I was last here, a new building has risen over the road from the Pilot Travel Center: the multistory City Limits Adult XXX complex. This is an air-conditioned hypermarket for sex aids, sex toys, naughty nurse uniforms, S&M appliances, blue DVDs, the lot—open twenty-four hours with dark reflective glass to prevent any distinction between night and day, and an ATM by the double door. On a sweaty Saturday afternoon it is fairly well patronized; on a Saturday night, it's teeming. "They hang out in the motels around the Howard Johnson's down there," Mitch had said. "You'll see a bunch of guys parked up at the six ten truck stop on Santa María next to the movie theater and that's them. The pussy's all Mexican."

The Dos Laredos freight system works like this: once past Ventiséis, Mexican long-haul truckers take their loads toward the border and fan out along the two great *anillos periféricos*, ring roads that circumvent the south of the city. From these yards operates the system of drayage (the Mexicans have adapted the word to *drayaje*)—shuttle companies. Some are locally and independently owned; others belong to the big long haulers. The latter operate smaller, usually older cabins to which the containers are affixed and that take the merchandise over the river, via a long wait, skirting the edges of a city to which ten thousand men have come to live as shuttle truckers in the freight yards that extend the length of Airport Boulevard and the giant ring roads: mile after mile of stack upon stack of containers waiting to go; row after row of little cabins returned, having just handed over their load north of the border or else waiting to go. And row upon row of bigger, newer cabins also parked, ready to head back through Veintiséis to the south or Lázaro Cárdenas, pick up another container, bring it back, and do it all again. At any time, there are thirty thousand containers in Nuevo Laredo awaiting transport and easily tampered with, loaded with freight that does not appear on the ledgers. Once through customs and on the U.S. side, the drayage drivers take the load over the flyovers and overpasses connected to the international bridges and deposit them at any one of the miles and miles of forwarding yards, flanking Mines Road, officially known as FM1472, to the west, and Port Laredo to the east of the freeway. Even the streets on which the yards are located have ambitious names: Interamerica Boulevard, Pan American Boulevard, and Trade Center Boulevard. Many of these are U.S. owned, with names like Swift Transportation, but an increasing number are Mexican, like Despachos del Norte.

Aldo Fernández has the rare distinction of being a trucker who actually lives in Laredo, among these yards where Pan American Boulevard meets Mines Road and, "right in the middle of them," he says, "you'd never know there was residential housing in here." He does so not only because he comes from Nuevo Laredo, so this is home, but for reasons similar to Sanderson's. "If you live near the depot, you get more time at home." Employed by Tri-Nat of St. Louis, Missouri, Aldo is a committed Volvo man. "This is 2009," he says, beaming, "best truck I ever drove." His usual route is to Oklahoma City, but last night he came back from Detroit, and tomorrow he's going to Canada, "where they open the border at eight a.m., so you have more waiting around than here, but less paperwork. I see the whole of America, but I know how it works here." There is "total camaraderie between truckers," says Aldo. "I'm Hispanic and I speak Spanish on the CB. Someone else may be black, someone else may be white, but if you're a trucker, you're just a trucker. When you get into trouble, the nearest guy helps you out." However, there is "no camaraderie between the long-distance gringos and the drayage drivers who bring their loads over from Mexico. The Americans never speak to them when they switch the loads 'cause they're just in little four-wheelers. It's more like, 'Hey, motherfucker, out the way!' when they're backing up." But they need to be careful, watch their language. "If you come to Laredo and talk shit about Mexicans on the CB, that's not a good idea," says Aldo. "There was some guy a couple of years back talking all that wetback stuff and hairy Mexican women. He was doing it on the CB radio and parked up. Only his truck didn't move from the truck stop, and six days later they had a look inside and found him stabbed to death in the cabin."

In Laredo too there is no avoiding frequent offers to transport smuggled drugs from cartel contacts in the forwarding yards, says Aldo. "You get offered money according to how far you'd go. So much to take a load to San Antonio, more to New York. It's a dumb game to get into—a couple of my friends are in jail for that. They get the offer, think it's easy cash, get caught." Are the drugs loaded up in the Mexican forwarding yards, or do they come all the way? "Usually they've come all the way," replies Aldo, preferring to change the subject, since this is a social dinner with a friend from Nuevo Laredo over for the evening. He takes us down by the river to show us a trick the drayage drivers play. Beneath the Gateway to the Americas bridge connecting downtown Laredo with its Mexican neighbor, they have parked their cabins overnight. "They walk back across the bridge, get drunk, sleep in Mexico, and walk back across to start from this side and avoid the morning rush-hour line on the bridge."

The Czech composer Antonín Dvořák wrote his greatest string quartet, No. 12 in F major, op. 96, "The American," in a little town called Spillville, Iowa. He had gone there by way of a retreat from New York, where he was not always happy, knowing that he would find in these rolling hills, not unlike his native Bohemia, a community of fellow Czechs. It was a blissful summer in '78: Dvořák would take a bucket of ale down to the banks of the Turkey River at five each morning and compose, so that moments in the quartet's molto vivace third movement replicate in music the exact notes of the birdsong to which he listened. No piece of music ever written evokes the scale and lyrical serenity of America's open spaces more than the quartet's mellifluent lento second movement.

The arrival in Laredo of the internationally acclaimed Bellas Artes Quartet of Mexico City to perform Dvořák's masterpiece one evening in October 2009 was hailed in a series of speeches as a cultural high-water mark in the city's long history. "A wish come true," said the host, the provost of Texas A&M University. The freight business elite of the Gateway to the Americas made sure to be there for the occasion, resplendently dressed. Many spoke Spanish, and continued to do so through the music, although the woman next to me who asked out loud, as we approached an especially lovely moment in the allegro, "Why is everyone being so *quiet*?" did so in broad Texan.

Sitting in the front row was Laredo's first citizen, who looks like an FBI agent with his quarterback frame, spivvy suit, and shaved head—probably because he was an FBI agent. Raul Salinas's position keeps him so busy that he is obliged to look at his computer screen and tap away throughout most of our interview, but this is a man who can chew gum and walk at the same time, for he makes a salient point about "the high wire we're on, between needing to keep goods coming through, and stopping that illegal percentage. We've had problems on the border, sure. We have crime statistics that tag us." When Salinas qualifies this by insisting that "bad news sells, and that's been our problem" and that "the drug and violence situation has been exaggerated," he sounds like a bad salesman. But when he insists that he "won't accept a compromise in the fact that we and our Mexican neighbors need to support each other as cities and keep the bridges open," he sounds like a mayor. "We can't slap our neighbor then ask for his help—that's a mistake we constantly make with Mexico. We're the number one inland port in America, and we don't need a damned wall between us and the number one inland port in Mexico." He says that "it's more difficult being mayor than an FBI agent. As an agent, you investigate crimes and send people to jail. As the mayor, you gotta run Laredo."

In Mayor Salinas's city hall, an estimable diplomatic system operates: an office is occupied by a consul from Nuevo Laredo, a Mexican ambassador from the twin city, Gerardo Lozano. Born in Laredo, Texas, raised in Nuevo Laredo, and educated in San Antonio, he would appear perfect for the job. He also talks straight, less convinced about what Mayor Salinas called the "exaggeration" of drug trafficking. Lozano puts it the other way around: "Amazingly, the narco war hasn't affected trade. More traffic is arriving in Nuevo Laredo than we have the infrastructure to deal with, and that's our great challenge—to build and provide it. But it hasn't affected drug smuggling either. Let's say that only three percent of the merchandise is illegal; that's probably about it, despite all the technical devices. But three percent is three percent of whatever's coming through. Imagine, if eight thousand trucks a day cross the border, and three percent of what they bring is contraband, that's a hell of a lot of contraband." But Lozano's crusade now is to ensure for Nuevo Laredo the fifth road bridge, the implications of which are being weighed by Miguel Conchas, director of Laredo's all-important chamber of commerce.

Conchas keeps the figures, and they are staggering—for 2008, truck crossings: 3.2 million; rail car crossings: 335,000; percentage of all U.S.-Mexican trade: Laredo, 40.9 percent, all other ports, 59.1 percent; U.S.-Mexican total trade: exports, $151.5 billion, imports, $215.9 billion; total trade: $367.4 billion. Conchas ponders: "The problem is always one of logistics—how to ship it all, and ship it fast enough. That will be Laredo's task as long as the Mexican long haulers are prohibited from coming over. The recession has affected us slightly, but the amount of cargo will grow now that Kansas City Southern has bought the railway line from Lázaro Cárdenas to Nuevo Laredo and we're getting the new bridge; that'll mean a big increase. It's part of talk we're hearing about a supercorridor—bringing less in through the U.S. ports like Long Beach and New Orleans, deepening the Mexican Pacific ports, and bringing it all straight up through here to Dallas and Chicago, cheaper and faster. We're on the brink of that." This supercorridor is much discussed, with its potentially cataclysmic impact on the U.S. docklands and other jobs in the support industries that support them. "But just as all this is happening," says Conchas, "business is confronted by the major problem of the drug trade. Legitimate business knows that you can't always guarantee what your drivers are bringing across."

If the Rio Grande, which unites and divides Amexica, has a living human son, his name is Keith Bowden. Bowden navigated the watery borderline by kayak, from El Paso to the sea, as war raged through Zeta country in 2005. He was trying to experience the beauty and power of the river in the wake of the loss of his young wife to slow and painful cancer. Bowden kept and published a record of his voyage, which he called *The Tecate Journals*. There is an intensity, an existential solitude, about Bowden that draws one in rather than orders one away. He is strikingly good-looking and physically trim—a sports coach as well as teacher of English at Laredo Community College. On the wall of his windowless office is a photograph Bowden took of a moment in the river's flow as it rounds a colossus of red rock along the Big Bend, on which one inevitably comments. He takes it down and says, "Have it." Although Bowden is more afraid of rapids than of Nuevo Laredo, he speaks as someone who knows the narco foot soldiers well, as a baseball coach in Ciudad Acuña and in Nuevo Laredo, where he could hardly avoid the young men's other interests and activities. "In one year," he remembers, "I lost fourteen ex-students or players. Kids I'd coached or taught."

Among the young baseball players he coached was a boy named Ricardo who "made a swift descent into the Nuevo Laredo drug-trade underworld, and his transformation from innocent adolescent to cold-blooded killer was total." Ricardo's uncle was a standing member of the FBI's Ten Most Wanted list, and Ricardo bragged to Coach Bowden one day that he used the baseball team as cover to smuggle "a hell of a lot of loads. The last time I saw him," writes Bowden, was "a chance encounter at the same Nuevo Laredo baseball fields where we were once team-mates—he boasted that he was killing fifteen people a month 'as part of business.' I assailed his barbarism as 'chicken shit' and demanded he explain the logic . . . 'People with babies and mothers and little sisters. That's what you do. You kill people and you brag about it. I can't accept that.' Ricardo buried his head in his hands and wept like a child." Bowden never saw Ricardo again. "A rumor surfaced that he had been hacked into five hundred pieces." The body of another student, Alicia, was found beneath a construction site, to which police were led by yet another boy who studied with Bowden. He likewise vanished; "his specific instructions leading to the discovery of her corpse were among the last words he ever uttered."[11]

Between this world and his, the river, says Bowden, "there's a kind of oblivion, even hostility, toward the natural elements. Nature's a hard sell to people on both sides of the river. By the time people are five years old, they dislike the river, distrust it, they're afraid of it—they're told it's filthy and polluted, it's something migrants cross, it's where bodies wash up . . . Only when you're out on the river for days do you get a sense of it, both as nature and as the border." So one gets a strange view of a war from a kayak. "When I came through here, it was during the crazy time," he says of his river passage between Los Dos Laredos, "the middle of the war, wondering whether I'd see bodies floating on the river. But what really worried me were things like currents, things I had to have a sense of and could do something about. My fear did not come from people; it tends not to when you're trying to kayak through Big Bend or facing down a charging mountain lion. The person who could do me the most damage was myself, by making one tiny mistake."

In days not long ago when the *Houston Chronicle* was one of the great newspapers in the world, it carried weighty, definitive supplements on burning issues of the day in western America, one of which, in October 1993, was about the Rio Grande. The supplement followed the river from its source to the sea at Brownsville: A CLEAN START IN COLORADO, A FILTHY FINISH IN THE GULF ran the headline. But there was beauty and poetry too, as the Rio Grande, "like any river . . . it keeps trying to shed itself of the filth dumped into it. Given enough time, enough water, enough air, any river can remedy many pollution problems."[12] But if one talks now about a river full of metal as the Rio Grande flows into its final, tropical stretch of borderland, people will not think you are talking about pollution. A river of iron, in these parts, means something else.

IRON RIVER/TELL THEM WHO YOU ARE

Metalwork and metalware strewn across every table, stretching all the way to the back of the hall—weaponry of matte gunmetal gray. The guns are expertly made, all of them—although it is much easier to feel affection and admiration for the venerable collectors' items with worn wooden butts, or the latest hunter's shotguns, than the wholly inorganic steely weapons that make sense only in combat. Quite apart from what an AR-15 is designed to do so effectively, its steely, glaucous gray emanates a somber foreboding all its own. Apart from the fact that a Czech vz.58 Military Folder-Polymer is said to be among the best-value variations of a Kalashnikov, its leaden slatiness commands menace in itself. Apart from the full-time rimfire boasted by the new Colt M4, its griseous coldness is itself intimidating, just to look at—even before it is picked up, sized up, deftly handled, and wiped down by a hefty man demonstrating his sure touch of familiarity with the heavy weapon's ways and whimsies. But one must not apply European squeamishness to a gun show in Texas. It is a citizen's right to bear arms in America, and the Sunday afternoon crowd here in the Convention Center at Pharr, on Highway 281, is for the most part made up of families and couples come to browse, farmers protecting their livestock and duck hunters come to stock up on ammo, collectors hunting for bargains, and kids who just want to shoot rabbits, blast away in a quarry, or punch holes in the back of road signs or in the BP symbol at the company's gas stations, as they do after the Gulf oil disaster. That's America, whether you like it or not. Matter of fact, this gun show at Pharr in October 2009 is far less brazenly militaristic than another three times the size held a few weeks back at the Pima County fairgrounds outside Tucson, Arizona. There, the former Blackwater USA—some of whose guards were acquitted in December 2009 of murder in Iraq, where they opened fire on a crowd—had a stall abundantly stocked with tactical combat gear, night-vision equipment, body armor, and a lot of other stuff you need for all-out warfare more than you do for duck hunting. There, it wasn't just a matter of the AR-15 semiautomatics being lined up for sale as here in Pharr. There was a banner hanging from the ceiling beckoning buyers to a wide range of the deadliest weapons available on the open market, at reduced prices.

But there are nevertheless a couple of twists to holding a gun show in Pharr during October 2009. The hall is about six miles from the Mexican border and eight miles from Reynosa, Mexico, fortress city for Los Zetas and scene of ferocious internecine fighting a few months later, in spring 2010. Back in January 2009, three off-duty police officers were enjoying a celebration drink at El Booty Lounge in Pharr when a man lobbed a grenade into the bar. The explosive was traced to Monterrey, an hour across the border.[1] In March 2009, seven months before this gun show, the first coup in President Obama's week-old offensive against gunrunning, Project Gunrunner, was a haul of semiautomatic barrels, firearms accessories, and gunpowder crossing from Pharr into Reynosa aboard a tractor trailer.

A seller at the Pharr gun show called Billy—a courteous and friendly man with a ponytail—is extolling the virtues of the body armor he has for sale, the intensity of the fusillades it can withstand, the specific kinds and caliber of ammunition. He has an especially rare weapon on his stand: a Heckler & Koch M3 Super 90, but made under license by Benelli in Italy. "There's not so many of them out there," assures Billy. "I got it off a guy was ex-military. Just shows how badly the armed forces need these weapons—must've been Heckler & Koch were running to max capacity, so they got 'em made under license by Benelli." Billy talks me through the advantages: he likes this thing called an "annular knurled ring," which would enable me to "switch to the semiautomatic recoil system," thereby moving from a manually operated pump-action mode "to

being able to fire full-power combat loads in rapid semiautomatic mode."
There's an "underbarrel magazine," which can hold "eight rounds for police or military versions. That's a rare piece"—a snip at $1,300. Another
man takes me through the benefits of an AR-15: "the ultimate urban
rifle," adaptable to thirty-round Magpul magazines as used by "our troops
in the Middle East." A new model he has on the table has a forearm
design enabling the shooter to "fit rails at all twelve clock positions," he
says. I tell him I'm not a U.S. citizen, so there's a problem. He gives
me his card and says to call so we can "work something out." Just as one
must not be Euro-sanctimonious about guns in Texas, one must not engage in racial profiling. But what do those Mexican lads over there with
shaved heads and tattoos on their scalps want with an SHF R50 magazine-
fed bolt-action .50 BMG rifle with a twenty-two-inch barrel? How many
farmers and antelope hunters really need, from the same stall, an ASA-
M4A3 16-inch .223-caliber carbine machine gun, a Santa Muerte wallet,
and an ammunition pouch with ARRIBA TAMAULIPAS—Go Tamaulipas—a favorite Zeta slogan on YouTube?

At the back of the hall, up a small flight of steps, is a bookstall.
Among the many perfectly innocent catalogs and trade volumes are U.S.
army manuals on counterinsurgency warfare, with tips on bomb making,
how to blow up bridges, and other useful things to know while out hunting deer. For $25, there's a *Militia Combat Manual*, with a second chap-
ter on "Combat Operations." "An ambush is an active form of a defensive
position," it counsels. There are sections on "Bounding Overwatch,"
"Immediate Assault," and "Urban Assault": "when entering an enemy
building, always throw a fragmentation grenade first." In the section on
"Acquisition of Military Equipment," the manual says, "In this section
we are talking about the theft of military equipment from military bases.
Sounds hard? Well, it isn't." There is of course a section on explosives
and how to blow up buildings, and diagrams showing "Electrical blast-
ing cap attached to car battery."[2] It is hard not to flash back a moment,
to the night of April 19, 1995, the year *before* this manual was published, when I landed in Oklahoma City. The killers of 169 people, including 19 children, in the Alfred P. Murrah Federal Building came

from this constituency of militia manual readers and they were not lone wolves; they were part of a fomenting culture—Americans killing Americans in the name of America. Now here's a variation on that theme: Americans selling guns that arm the cartels that kill each other so as to peddle the drugs that kill Americans. The cartels' guns of choice are the AR-15 and AK-47, the automatic versions, of course, the sale of which is illegal in the United States.

But what are these manuals, selling for $15 a pop, six miles from the Mexican border in Pharr, expertly written and cheap at the price? One white-covered volume is one of the Full Auto series, telling you how to "modify" your AR-15. "The purpose of this small book is to clarify and explain the procedure and parts needed to convert a semi-automatic AR-15 assault rifle to be a selectable, fully automatic weapon." Figure 11 reads, "an auto sear is being inserted into the pocket of the lower receiver where the take-down pin engages the lug of the upper receiver. Figure 12 shows the auto sear fully installed."[3] Also for $15, with a blue cover, is the conversion manual for the all-time favorite cuerno de chivo, the AK-47. Step six is "Re-assembly" of your fully automatic Kalashnikov: "You are now ready to check the timing of the bolt with the movement to auto sear, which should release the hammer."[4] But there are waivers. In the AR-15 manual, the publisher affirms that he "produces this book for informational and entertainment purposes and under no circumstances advises, encourages or approves of use of this material in any manner." The AK-47 booklet advises that "all conversions must be done by a licensed Class II manufacturer." Zetas: Do Not Try This at Home.

Since the election of Barack Obama, discussion of the flow of weapons from the United States to the cartels has found a place on the U.S. political agenda, become a recurrent theme for the Mexican government, and is almost de rigueur in media coverage of the border crisis. But all this is recent, part of President Obama and Secretary of State Hillary Clinton's final acceptance of some "coresponsibility" for that crisis, as Clinton put it on a visit to Mexico City soon after taking office in 2009. Until very recently, however, such a suggestion was almost taboo. Certainly, gunrunning to Mexico and "coresponsibility" for the drug war had played no part in Bill Clinton's agenda when he was president between 1992 and 2000. President Obama is pressing the Senate to ratify the Inter-American Arms Treaty, which was, to be fair, signed by President Clinton in 1998 but stalled on Capitol Hill, and seeks to crack down on illicit firearms with regulation of the import and export of weaponry across the hemisphere, and to increase cooperation among law enforcement agencies. To gun lobby hard-liners, even the discussion is seen as yet another attempt at creeping gun control, while others who support the Second Amendment's guarantee of the right to bear arms nonetheless recognize that gunrunning to Mexico is a separate and justified discourse.

President Obama has made no effort, though, to reinstate the domestic ban on semiautomatic weapons imposed by Bill Clinton in 1994 but which expired in 2004, just as the war began in Nuevo Laredo. As recently as 2008, Raymundo Ramos was a near lone voice making the point that while five thousand truckloads a day were crossing from Nuevo Laredo to Laredo, five thousand also came back, and that this countercurrent of goods exported from the United States into Mexico involved smuggling in the other, southerly, direction: not of drugs, but guns. The counterflux that those few U.S. law enforcement agencies taking the threat seriously called "the Iron River."

"It's obvious," Ramos said on that occasion, "that without the drugs, there would be no war. We all know that. But without the guns, there would be nothing to fight the war with." It is indeed obvious, but apart from the U.S. Bureau of Alcohol, Tobacco, Firearms and Explosives (ATF) and a report by Lora Lumpe, well ahead of its time in *Covert Action Quarterly* in 1997, few people north of the border considered it an issue. Lumpe's work demonstrated that the Arellano Félix brothers' weapon that killed Cardinal Posadas Ocampo in Guadalajara had been smuggled from the United States.[5] Not too many in Mexico made much noise either, though the Iron River did gain some diplomatic traction after the appointment of a forthright ambassador to Washington, Arturo Sarukhán, in 2006. But Ramos was able to say as late as 2008, "I've been campaigning for five years now for tougher action against smuggling guns. I raise the matter every time I meet with the authorities on either side of the border. The Americans don't see it as a major problem, and the Mexicans? Every time they find an arsenal, they act all surprised! For the Americans, it's a billion-dollar business, and the Mexicans do not have the political will to get serious with gunrunning."

It is of no disadvantage to the narco cartels that the four states bordering Mexico—Texas, New Mexico, Arizona, and California—cherish the lore of firearms as part of their heritage and identity. It is of no disadvantage that they are among the states in which it is easiest to buy weapons. Speaking to a conference in El Paso in August 2008, Michael Sullivan, then acting director of the ATF, said the U.S. and Mexican governments were cooperating in an effort to trace weapons seized in Mexico's narco war, finding—to no one's great surprise—that between 90 and 95 percent of them originate in the United States, "mostly from the four Southwestern states. Two-thirds of them were traced back to Texas." That year, 90 percent of 20,455 weapons seized by Mexican authorities for which traces were requested showed a purchase in the United States, with Texas, Arizona, and California accounting for most of them. The irony and tragedy was that they had also already been used. The gun smugglers were described by the prosecutor in one case involving a gun dealer in Arizona shipping hundreds of Kalashnikovs as operating "like a parade of ants."

Ironically too, the ideological right that stands so firm on people—and, of course, drugs—crossing the border northward also opposes restrictions over marketing the hardware the narcos need to shift southward, and the frequency with which they can buy weapons. Although the Justice Department brands the narco cartels as a "security threat" to the United States, there are more than sixty-seven hundred arms dealers within half a day's drive of the border—three dealers per mile of frontier. One of them, called X-Caliber, a distance away in Phoenix, was shut down in spring 2008 for allegedly dispatching hundreds of AK-47s and other weaponry to Mexico. The dealer, George Iknadosian, won a reprieve, however, when in March 2009 a judge threw out the case against him, finding no evidence of fraud or illicit dealing, even though some of the seven hundred weapons he was accused of selling to smugglers were identified in a shoot-out in Sinaloa in 2007 in which eight police officers were killed. The state of Arizona was appealing the decision at the time of writing.

Known as straw buyers, agents for the narco cartels and gangs cruise gun stores and fairs to buy the weapons. Court records from innumerable trials tell the story of the iceberg of which they are but a minuscule tip: Adán Rodríguez, age thirty-five, was struggling as a carpet layer in Dallas when he was tapped by two men called Kati and César from the Gulf cartel. They came up with the idea, with $12,000 cash up front, that if he went around telling gun dealers he was a private security employee and showing them his ID, he might need the 112 assault rifles, Beretta handguns, and other weaponry he managed to procure for them. All he had to do was take the hardware to a safe house in Dallas and pick up a commission of between $30 and $40 per gun, in cash, with marijuana stored between the bills. At the time of his arrest, Rodríguez's contacts were hoping to upscale their order to include hand grenades and rocket launchers. "The temptation got over me," Rodríguez told the judge in Dallas who sentenced him to five years in jail in 2006. The ATF's special agent in charge in Arizona, Tom Mangan, had said candidly, "Gun shows have become particularly troublesome. You see the Sinaloan cowboys come in; you see them with their ammunition belts and their ammunition boots. You can see the dollies being rolled outside to their cars. Why do they need high-powered guns? Because the Mexican military is armed too, and they need to pierce that armor."[6]

In June 2009, the U.S. Government Accountability Office published a report that left no rational room for doubt: "many of the firearms fueling Mexican drug violence originated in the United States, including a growing number of increasingly lethal weapons." The agencies responsible for combating gunrunning "do not effectively coordinate their efforts," said the GAO, "in part because the agencies lack clear roles and responsibilities." Moreover, "agencies generally have not systematically gathered, analyzed, and reported data that could be useful to help plan and assess results of their efforts to address arms trafficking to Mexico."

The GAO notes that for the very first time, the National Southwest Border Counternarcotics Strategy only recently includes a chapter on combating arms trafficking and that "while U.S. law enforcement agencies have developed initiatives to address arms trafficking to Mexico, none have been guided by a comprehensive, governmentwide strategy." While the violence in Mexico "has raised concern, there has not been a coordinated U.S. government effort to combat the illicit arms trafficking to Mexico that U.S. and Mexican government officials agree is fueling much of the drug-related violence."[7]

From Laredo southward, into deep Zeta country, the border becomes tropical and urban, palm trees and concrete. The road on the Texas side of the river winds its way through the town of Zapata, where, appropriately, the local auto repair shop is called Guevara's Garage but many humble Mexican-American residents suddenly found themselves rich, after oil was found on their patches of land. The next town is Roma, where, the Vatican will be pleased to hear, the church of the Holy Family is full to bursting on a Sunday morning—only next door there is a raid by five flashing police cars on a branch of Mr. Pollo fast-food chicken. Next comes Rio Grande City, where the popular, mustachioed Starr County sheriff, Reymundo Guerra, was taken out of his office in handcuffs and pleaded guilty in May 2009 for using his position as a law enforcement officer to help the Gulf cartel. Guerra was friendly with an operative for Los Zetas called José Carlos Hinojosa and took money in exchange for giving Hinojosa tips on the movements and tactics of his colleagues, information on upcoming raids on stash houses, and closing a case against one of Hinojosa's associates.[8]

On the Mexican side, the same Highway 2 that left Tijuana for Tecate, away back west, now finds a way through tropical flatland beneath a huge sky to a daunting town called Miguel Alemán, where every pair of eyes seems to follow a stranger. Now the borderland reaches its most easterly and most southerly terrain, the tapered southernmost tip of the United States from which Mexico City is only 470 miles. The Rio Grande

Valley on the Texas side and tropical Tamaulipas on the Mexican right bank combine to weave the border's richest historical narrative and most complex social tapestry. It is a land apart and a special place, fiercely proud of its heritage and identity astride the border, past and present. An identity born of heritage, indeed—unlike anywhere else along the borderline—which this chapter explores by looking back toward family and religion drawn from the past, into a present when the themes of place, God, and heritage are felt even by the cartels themselves.

On the Mexican side of the valley, the road heads toward Reynosa, which has become a bustling industrial center, and Matamoros, which despite industrialization has held true to its roots in estate ranching and commerce. The Texas side is also dominated by a pair of cities, McAllen opposite Reynosa, and facing Matamoros, Brownsville. They could hardly be more different: both are poor, but McAllen has sprung from almost nothing in no time, a sudden player threatening to rival Laredo with a proposed second trade corridor from Reynosa into the heart of Texas, along a new Interstate 69. Brownsville, on the contrary, is seeped in epic history and for all the strip sprawl along the highways is at heart sedate and unarguably the most charming city along the border, enchanted by laden, lush palm trees and ubiquitous oxbow lakes known as *resacas*, left behind by the slow-winding river as it strolls and slouches its way out to sea. McAllen is new money, Brownsville is old, and each rather resents the other for it.

The observances, remembrances, and rites begin early on the Day of the Dead in Reynosa, in the church of Our Lady of Guadalupe and in the main plaza into which its steps descend. Last night in McAllen, Mexican-American children had celebrated Halloween like any other American children, dressed in their ghoulish best, and out for a treat at Taco Palenque dressed as Count Dracula, his brides, and his victims. The Day of the Dead in Reynosa, however, is unchanged, uncolored by orange and black bunting, even on the border. Inside the church portal is a special exhibition of "Los Más Famosos Santos Incorruptos Mexicanos," the most famous incorruptible saints—but not all saints, only the Mexican ones. The stories of their lives and martyrdom are told along with the guarantee that "Death is not an entity / It is a simple transition from the elemental life to the celestial homeland." But in Mexico, the dead are never far from the living, especially after the night when the veil is drawn back. In Reynosa of late, the Reaper has been given a helping hand by years of violence. Today belongs, however—though the menace is never entirely dispelled—to everybody's departed ones. The sky is deep blue, the special bread of the dead is baked, and it tastes good.

Outside in the square, altars are being built and decorated, the first thing being to lay thousands of petals in patterns on the flagstones, of flowers called *cempasúchil* ("flower of a hundred petals"), representing the rays of the sun illuminating the path to a celestial home, and *garra de león*—lion's paw—so that the sidewalk is ablaze with white representing the sky, golden yellow representing the earth, and resonant purple, the color of mourning. Around the bases of the altars are abundant offerings and ritual matter: incense, sticks of cinnamon, bowls of rice and of carefully chosen minerals, semiprecious stones and common pebbles. The food is "to nourish the soul of the dead," explains Patricia Espinoza, age fifteen, and water to "quench their thirst." The cross symbolizes not the Crucifixion but "the four directions." On the ground, salt is scattered so that the bodies of the dead will not rot, and candles are arranged to light the way of their souls. Twigs and sticks are included so that the dead can bat away malicious spirits.

An especially splendid altar has been made by students at Antonio Repizo high school, steps made of cardboard flanked by tables like wings decorated with papier-mâché skulls. The steps are covered in offerings—dolls, bottles of tequila, dancing skeletons, books—and a New York Yankees shirt—atop which is a framed photograph of Guillermo López Treviño, who lived from January 10, 1907, until July 18, 1983. "He was my great-grandfather," says Lorenzo Martínez Rendez, age fifteen, in his pidgin English, "a cowboy, farmer, and very worker. He is my hero; he is always with me." "It's important to all of us," says his school friend Mario López Villarreal. "It's a celebration of those who bore us, to thank them and heed their advice. We've made the shrine to Lorenzo's great-grandfather, but he represents all of our ancestors, so we feel part of a chain." "This is not superstition," says their teacher, Ana Teresa Luebbert, helping to arrange bowls of spices on the tarmac. "The eyes of the dead are always upon us. They watch everything we do. If the young can reach them, they will be guided, though I sometimes wonder what the ancestors must be thinking now, with all that's going on."

By now, it is midmorning, and buses out to the cemeteries on the edge of town are filling with families, couples, and ladies carrying flowers, mementos, picnic chairs, and children's toys as offerings to those who died in infancy. Everybody carries a bunch of little mauve-colored flowers special to this day, called *jesusitas*—literally, little female Jesuses. There is piped music aboard the retired American school bus, not the local, lilting ranchera dance music one might have hoped for, but grinding soca from the West Indies. "It's specially for the Día de los Muertos," says my companion Mario Treviño, a man with many strings to his bow, on both the city's dark and bright sides, working for a human rights office dealing mainly with deportees, and on cultural events in Reynosa, such as poetry readings here in Zeta country. The bus pulls up on a stretch of land between the baseball stadium and Reynosa's largest complex of cemeteries, on which a multitude is assembled, a great throng in the dusty heat, making its way to the headstones past stalls selling floral arrangements of every kind, and *pan de muerto* to eat.

In Reynosa, like everywhere else, you live by status and wealth—and you are buried that way too. Our souls may arrive as equals to be either admitted through or turned away from that last pearly border checkpoint in the sky, but the corporeal remains are interred according to the ducats you left behind with them. First comes the resting place for those at the bottom of the pile—blessed are they, for they shall be buried here in the potter's field. Around the modest headstones of the Panteón Sagrado Corazón, cemetery of the sacred heart, families hold something between a dirge, wake, party, and grave cleaning. Bands of musicians hawk their services, playing mariachi music, local ranchero, and traditional ballads of the departed, depending on the mood. The Hernández family sits in silence and the girls cry as musicians sing "Amor Eterno," usually reserved for a departed mother. Another group over in the corner is whooping it up—the ladies tapping their feet to the music while sitting on deck chairs beside the graves, the men and boys standing with their beers and every so often pouring a few drops into the earth under which Manuel Ramos López is buried, that he may wet his lifeless lips as he used to. The Morales family is serving a meal for eleven people around the memorial stone to its matriarch, Lucía, which is draped in a pair of dungarees. "She used to sell ropa usada," explains a daughter, "so each year we bring some to put on the grave." The girls are studying a flyer for the special Día de los Muertos celebration at Frida's disco club later on.

Those leaving behind a slightly bigger stash of mint leaves are laid to rest in God's mid-ranking acre. Here families hold picnics too: some pen--sive and restrained, others exuberant and vivacious. Two musicians accompany one family sitting in silence, and sing a lachrymose but soothing ballad of remembrance by a famous Argentinian singer, Alberto Cortez, called "Mi Querido Viejo," my dear old man. And finally, we reach the Pantéon Español, the Spanish cemetery, "where the business families are buried," says Treviño. Here is respite from the clamor. Inside the gate, one is greeted by girls emerging from a gazebo. They're dressed in smart air-hostess-like uniforms, only with a higher hemline and appropriately black neck scarves, shoes, and stockings of mourning, and they ask if one would like to participate in a raffle to win a voucher toward the funeral of a relative. Elegantly dressed people walk with decorum through the Jardín Juan Pablo II, wherein perfectly pruned roses climb wire latticework. The lawns of the Jardín Padre Nuestro and Jardín Navidad—Christmas garden—into which the cemetery is tastefully divided, are impeccably manicured. No one wants a raucous ranchero band here; instead there are silent uniformed ushers and "sanitary officers."

At the rear are mausoleums and family vaults as would line a big Italian cemetery containing centuries of the deceased, in mock monumental classical design. But this is not the executive class of dear departed. There is yet another cemetery, says Treviño, "for the very rich." It is out of town, beyond reach of the soca-rocking bus. "There, the people we don't want to meet come to mourn, and who don't want us there today. It's where the top bad guys go, and the police, to be buried and settle their accounts." We have no car, but I express a foolish interest in going, somehow. "If you go, you're going alone," says Mario, suddenly firm. "Not me. They'll spot you right away; they'll ask: 'What are you doing here, gringo?'" I'll tell them I'm reporting on the Day of the Dead. "And they'll tell you no you're not, you're DEA, and find a place for you to stay in the cemetery." Mario is a much braver man than I, and this is his town, not mine; this is also a moment to defer to local knowledge rather than arrive at the pearly checkpoint ahead of schedule, on November 1, of all days. Instead, we eat delicious chiles rellenos from a stall manned by a friend of Mario's, find a bus stop, and head back to town. Mario also buys a bunch of jesusitas, and on the bus back a lady explains in detail how he must put them in a vase and let them dry until June 24 next year, the day of St. John the Baptist, then bury them—and they will grow again in time for next year's Day of the Dead.

In the covered market downtown, the Dark Side store stands out from the others selling food, magazines, and tourist bric-a-brac (though there are no tourists, not even today). It is a Goth shop, at first sight of the kind you would find in New York's East Village or a city in Lancashire. The owner, Zombie Raúl, wears long, jet-black hair, mascara, and a black leather coat. His wife dresses in black lace and violet chiffon, and wears black nail polish. Apparently even their child wears Goth baby clothes. All of which takes mettle and feistiness in a place like Reynosa. So we talk about the local Goth scene, for which Día de los Muertos is a key-note day in the calendar. It being Sunday, Raúl's shop is the only one in the arcade that is open, lest anyone be caught short, on this important festival, of a Metallica T-shirt or fingerless gloves with luminous bones. I ask about the cultural ancestry. "No," he says, "not so much Iron Maiden, more Sisters of Mercy, Mozart, and Beethoven." Well, so be it, and we have a terrific time talking about how Wagner's Niebelungs hammering on their anvils really was the first great heavy metal riff, and as for that big double punch in Siegfried's funeral music, say no more. Raúl was not a music student, he studied the visual arts, "but when I heard that stuff,

I knew it was part of what I believe in." Which is not strictly Goth, he hastens to add, it's Dark Side. "It's a way of life, being aware of the beauty of things, and that all things are transient and must die, so obviously we're engaged in the Day of the Dead, but in our own way." The Dark Side people in town are, he says unsurprisingly, "the educated people who can think for themselves. We like to think beyond this culture in Mexico; we're open to new ideas, horror movies, and different kinds of music." This is an extremely refreshing young man to meet on the Day of the Dead, but how does all that go down in Reynosa? "It means we have to live in our own world, but that's okay—because the fact that we refuse to participate in the compartmentalization sets us apart from all that shit." All we need to do is exchange a glance to know what "that shit" is. There is one point over which that shit intrudes, however: Santa Muerte. "They took our iconography. The hooded skeleton, the scythe—that's ours; that was metal and Goth long before it got to be anything to do with that shit."

Mario Treviño's tour of the marketplace, arts center, and historical museum inevitably leads to some discussion of what his Goth friend Raúl called "that shit." We adjourn for food and coffee, over which he speaks courageously while carefully looking over his shoulder and stopping whenever anyone comes within earshot. "What you see on the bridge is a circus," he says. "The soldiers standing there—it's a farce. Everyone knows the drugs go north and the guns come south across the bridge all day. People who earn hardly any money can get a hundred dollars cash for bringing a gun over for Los Zetas. The region is a hub for guns all over Mexico. They're supposed to be illegal in Mexico, unlike the U.S., but everyone here has a gun; some people have six guns. They get them from the army too—the soldiers are poor, and for ten thousand dollars they let the bad guys in, and they take what they want." A man selling pan de muerto for the Drogadictos Anónimos counseling service on Day of the Dead had said, "But the army's good, we can trust them. The police, they're just the troops of Los Zetas. They tell them where the soldiers are going. You see them on the corner, waiting, watching the troops go by, then radio the movements through to Los Zetas, so if they ever had a chance of catching anyone, it's too late. The only way they ever get them is with an inside tip-off."

That is what Los Zetas presumed to have happened in November 2008 when federal army troops arrested the founder and one of the founding commanders of Los Zetas, Jaime González Durán, aka "el Hummer" (as per his preferred SUV), after a fifteen-minute shoot-out in Reynosa. The paramilitary unit that took el Hummer also hauled 428 guns of every kind and capability (including 288 assault weapons and automatic or semiautomatic machine guns), antiaircraft missiles, 287 grenades and bombs, and half a million rounds of ammunition. With the betrayal said to have come from within, Los Zetas went on a rampage of violence.

Within weeks, the bodies of a longtime Mexican army general and two of his associates were found executed beside a road into Cancún. General Mauro Enrique Tello was the highest-ranking military scalp to be claimed by any assassination thus far; he had been methodically tortured, driven to the jungle, and shot in the head. A week previously, he had been appointed by "Greg" Sánchez, the mayor of Cancún, a Caribbean vacation playground, to face down the penetration of the tourist economy and transport routes by Los Zetas, which threatened the ability of Mexico's number one beach destination to attract visitors.[9] The general had led the initial military crackdown in December 2006 against La Familia, and now Mayor Sánchez wanted him to organize a hundred-strong armed unit to confront Los Zetas. Anyone who feared the worst in Cancún was on the right track. Within a week of the general's murder, federal agents had arrested Cancún's chief of police, Francisco Velasco, known as "the Viking," and six other officers, and flown them to Mexico City for interrogation about their alleged roles in the general's murder. Federal prosecutors compiling the case, still pending, against Velasco estimated that as many as seventeen hundred of his officers in Cancún's police force were working for Los Zetas.[10] He was known locally for driving around in his black Nissan Armada SUV playing narcocorridos glorifying Los Zetas; his favorites were said to be "Z Dynasty" and "Pact of Honor." Although painted with police logos, the vehicle had been reported stolen in Mexico City in 2006. A week after the murder of the general, police arrested a cell of seven Zetas from Tamaulipas who had set up a stall in Cancún.[11] Los Zetas accelerated their operations against the Sinaloa cartel's cocaine routes in central and southern Mexico, arriving suddenly and horribly in places like the small, lazy agricultural town of Ixtlahuacán del Río near Guadalajara, where five decapitated heads were found in beer coolers with messages such as "I'm coming for you, Goyo."[12] Los Zetas' offensive had meanwhile hit neighboring Zacatecas, with the most audacious prison break since that by el Chapo Guzmán in 2001. A convoy of seventeen vehicles backed up by a helicopter approached Cieneguillas prison. Thirty men alighted, some dressed in police uniforms, and marched into the jail, where they rounded up and freed some forty prisoners affiliated with the Gulf cartel.[13] Los Zetas escalated their war in Central America too, killing ten Guatemalan agents in an attempted police ambush on a Zetas drug consignment in April 2009. When the killers finally fled, they left behind a truck containing seven hundred pounds of white powder and—perhaps more significant—an arsenal of eleven M-60 machine guns, a stash of claymore mines, a Chinese-made antitank rocket, and more than five hundred grenades, as well as uniforms, bulletproof vests, commando uniforms, and thousands of rounds of ammunition.[14]

The Central American front is crucial to Los Zetas for many reasons: it secures control of a land route for cocaine from the producing countries, it provides a strategic outlet for smuggling to Europe and Africa, and it is the source of another Iron River, weaponry of a different, heavier, caliber. Although the Iron River's deepest flow is from the United States into Mexico, an investigation by the *Los Angeles Times* showed what amounted to an arms race between cartels in military-grade weapons from Central America. The attack by Los Zetas on the Independence Day celebrations in Morelia used fragmentation grenades—weapons of war. In Mexico itself, industrial explosives plants are robbed of material that can be used to make car bombs and roadside ambush devices. Grenades used in three attacks in Monterrey were linked to a single warehouse in the city, reportedly belonging to the Gulf cartel and raided in October 2008. Much of the cache seized on that occasion was made in South Korea, including fragmentation grenades.[15]

As with Raymundo Ramos upriver, it is abuse by the army and the concerns of migrants and deportees that most preoccupy the organization for which Mario Treviño works, the Centro de Estudios Fronterizos y Promoción de los Derechos Humanos—center for border studies and promotion of human rights—run by Rebeca Rodríguez. Ms. Rodríguez directs her rage not at Los Zetas specifically but at the circumstances that have turned the town into "a combat zone, in which the human rights situation is critical, a war between the military and the criminals, in which the civilian population has no stake but is held to ransom. The first human right to be trampled in Reynosa is the right to feel safe when you take a bus ride or walk the street. Look at my hands: we don't wear jewelry, we don't wear expensive clothes. If you do, you could be kidnapped. In other countries, when a crime is committed, you go to the police, but we daren't do that, because we have no idea who we're talking to.

"In February [2009], we had a shoot-out in an elementary school, between the soldiers and organized crime, innocent children caught in the crossfire. We live in fear of organized crime and equal fear of the military." The battle in the Felipe Carrillo Puerto elementary school happened on February 20 after men driving an SUV opened fire on federal police attempting to stop their vehicle. Soldiers took positions on the school patio and inside its low-walled compound for a shoot-out lasting two hours, with grenades exploding in the street and teachers ordering pupils to lie on the floor while they stacked desks against the windows to trap stray bullets. "The bad guys feel they are lords of the streets," the sixty-one-year-old principal, Martha Aguirre, had said.[16] The battle was but one of many spasms of fighting between the army and Los Zetas. That same month there were running gun battles at six points across Reynosa, Los Zetas commandeering vehicles to block roads and create a stockade.

One battle lasted an hour, with the Mexican government claiming six dead among the narco gunmen.[17]

The violence in 2010 between the Gulf cartel old guard and Zetas that for a moment blew open Nuevo Laredo hit Reynosa and the surrounding area much harder. During the fighting in February that year, eight reporters were kidnapped around Reynosa, of whom two vanished and one was tortured to death. From the city, Mario Treviño sent a message reading: "Reynosa is in mourning. . . . For the moment the city is a no man's land, the caravans of death rolling through the streets." Armored cars cruised around town staking out territory, respectively marked CDG for the Gulf cartel or xx for Los Zetas—fighting pitched battles against each other and the army. Later, in November 2010 after the assassination of Antonio Ezequiel Cárdenas (Osiel's brother) by the marines, the nearby small town of Ciudad Mier was subject to the first instance of wholesale "cleansing" by the Zetas—all its civilians ordered out of their homes at gunpoint, more than three hundred fleeing en masse to encamp on the border town of Ciudad Aleman opposite Roma, Texas. Across Tamaulipas, other villages and communities had been cut off by gunmen's roadblocks, their gas stations incinerated and shops closed as the scourge of "cleansing" territory by narco paramilitaries became more common. In February 2011, an entire village in Durango was torched.

Ms. Rodríguez echoes the arguments of Gustavo de la Rosa in Ciudad Juárez: "The cartel is growing and expanding, and increasing its weaponry. But you can't fight crime with crime," she says of the army's record of "state torture and murder in Reynosa. They don't protect us. They are around our houses, but they are not around the houses of the narcos. If you say that out loud, you're the fifth column—they call me the fifth column. But the worse the army, the more the criminals will organize the people against them." There have been large demonstrations against the army here and in Matamoros, downstream, which the cartel has been suspected of organizing—blockades by taxi drivers, for example, known to be under their control. In February 2009, demonstrations against the army blocked nine bridges connecting Ciudad Juárez and various towns in Tamaulipas to the United States, with federal authorities accusing the

Juárez and Gulf cartels of paying the demonstrators in order to mobilize them. In the same month, antiarmy demonstrations mobilized by Los Zetas extended to the state capital of Nuevo León, Monterrey, blocking the center of the richest and second-biggest city in Mexico.[18]

Although Monterrey is seen as too cleanly built of glass and steel, too much an embodiment of the new Mexico, too peppered with sushi restaurants to be a proper Zeta fortress, an investigation—the only one of its kind—into the city's undergrowth by Tracy Wilkinson of the *Los Angeles Times* found Los Zetas to have sunk deep roots in its poorer barrios such as Independencia. The barrio's long history of small-time drug dealing has allowed it to be penetrated by the Gulf cartel, which paid residents to stage huge demonstrations blocking the roads.[19] The *tapados*, as they were called, were paid small amounts of cash (about $13), or with cell phones and even school knapsacks filled with domestic supplies, to turn out against the army. Meanwhile, back in Tamaulipas, came a warning from the U.S. and Mexican authorities: Los Zetas were said to have procured forty bulletproof vests emblazoned with the letters FBI and DEA.[20]

Monterrey, though, is the center for what one might call the underground of artists that exists in cautious defiance of the narcos. There, a group of artists of remarkable bravery and innovation works. One is Francisco Benitez, who collects (or takes) photographs of the narcomantas hung in public places, also making his own, in protest. He is fascinated by the new, perverse literacy of the narcomantas, of which he says, "They are, in their own way, messages. Some of them are directed to the civic population in order to spread fear, showing a certain bluff of power over the official authorities. It is a means of telling everyone that they own these territories, that there is nothing to do against them." He collects his photographs into a book/installation that has become an archive of the strange, vile, macabre humor, menace, perverse literacy, and obscenity of the narcomantas.

Except that Franciso also makes his own, by way of pastiche and comment. "My 'narcomantas' are a reflection of the situation that exists in Mexico," he says. "Some of them are black—black thread embroidery on black material—because they are related to the black flag of anar-chy." One of the embroided messages reads, "Soldados de Plomo y Poli-cias de Paja"—tin soldiers and straw cops. "It used to be a common line on the narcomantas' messages as a derogatory way to indicate the au-thorities," says Benitez. "And in a certain way it happens to be true. Any kind of crime committed by criminals goes unpunished. The authorities do nothing but cooperate with the criminals. More than a message for peace, this work is a critique of the whole situation."

Benitez adds: "Personally, I think the narcomantas reflect several social situations that have to do not just with narco cartels, but with is-sues of basic education, employment, and social indifference," espe-cially among, he says, quarters of the artistic community. Though sometimes, the real thing can blow horribly close, as happened to one of Benitez's students. "I teach at several institutions and workshops," says Benitez, "and one day I took a call on my cell phone. It was one of my students asking how to spell a word correctly. I told him, and he asked me for some other word. No word in particular. So I was curious and asked him what he was doing, and after an odd attempt to explain, he told me that someone knew he was studying art, and asked him to make a narcomanta, for good money. The student already knew this person, and tried to avoid problems, because this was an offer he couldn't refuse. Fortunately, he heard no more from this guy."

Benitez works alongside a friend, Tomas Hernández, who carves re-liefs in wood in a constructivist style. One especially graphic piece shows two pipelines, one dripping black oil, the other red blood. "It's hard to find artists or artwork that challenges these issues," he says. "Sadly, the artistic community avoids them, or the references are shy and lateral." Not Tomas, however, who collects his "discarded pieces of wood and cardboard from squatter ghettoes. My materials were part of improvised houses abandoned by their inhabitants, and by this means I try to give the materials a second chance." Of his pipelines relief, called *Hole in the Ground*, explains Tomas, "A machine-gun canon targets the viewer, and in the background we can see stylized veins, one of them drips oil, and the other drips blood, and in the meantime, everything is consumed in flames. It is about economic interests, and neoliberal politics combining together to perpetrate chaos everywhere." Tomas picks up some of the themes about postindustrialization in Juárez: "What is happening here in Mexico is postpolitical and postindustrial. I choose the constructivist aesthetics for my artwork so as to relate to the idea of an industrial world. Monterrey is a postindustrial city, but the common people are still attached to the values of the nineteenth century. It generates despair when people don't understand why they cannot have work as safe as their grandparents had; and in this awful war, teenagers make up the death squads—the consequence of lack of education, and social failure."

Third in this trio of bold innovations in Monterrey is Jessica Salinas, whose work is starkly, and shockingly, terrifying. It divides into two categories: one shows portraits of beauty queens crowned, ensnared, and killed by narco gangs, their posed bodies fading into decorative wallpaper, which is what they were. The others are assertively grotesque sculptures of machine guns and pistols with erect phalluses for barrels. She works, she says, "with the subject of criminality out of control, and its collateral damage, from a feminine perspective—pieces intended to graphically portray the phenomenon of cartel beauty queens as trophies for the capos, until such point as women take the cartels under their own leadership, flashing firearms all the time. It is a situation I portray by relating the male anatomy to machine guns and firearms." She certainly does, with such sculptures as *Anatomic Plates: Missile Gun and Smith and Wesson*—handle, trigger, then stretched back foreskin and all.

"So we're balancing here," says Ms. Rodríguez back in Reynosa, "which is a difficult task." She discusses the cartel with extreme care: "They're doing what they are doing for the money, for the girls, the lifestyle, and the power of money. But they have become a military formation, not a social formation." The sage Treviño has been listening and says something simple but of importance: "They're doing it for the money, yes, but more than that. They're doing it for kudos. They're doing it to show that they can wear this T-shirt by this designer worth this much money, instead of that one the other guy is wearing. It's like stripes on a military uniform—corporal, sergeant. You walk around and everyone knows what rank you are, because your T-shirt is worth three hundred dollars, or your sneakers. They're doing it for the money, so they can show off the things the money can buy. It's a system of rank: if you have this T-shirt, you get a cute girl to show off; if you have an even more expensive T-shirt, you get an even cuter girl. But you can't be seen in the T-shirt you wore last year, which has gone out of style—that would mean you hadn't climbed the ladder. Same with the cars, same with the haircuts. They're disgusting people, high on amphetamines, but in Reynosa they can wear the uniform of their rank, and they're somebody." It is a simple but perceptive analysis.

Meanwhile, "the economy has become dependent on illegal money," asserts a lawyer working in Reynosa who prefers to remain anonymous. "Drugs, guns, and people smuggling: it's a cycle of illegal money." In contrast to the criminal anarchy in Juárez, "if you work on the domestic drug market, just selling a little on the street, you pay a commission to the narcos. If you are in legal business, you pay a quota to the narcos. They control the police, so the police don't protect you, then the narco comes to you and says, 'The police can't protect you, so we will.'" (Or as a businessman over the river in McAllen puts it, "They say, 'We'll protect you from us, if you pay us to do so.'") "That way," continues the lawyer, "the narco is in total control of the economy. Likewise the political parties: there are elections between the PRI and the PAN, but they are no more than a matter of Calderón and the army supporting PAN, so the narcos back the PRI. You have the army on one side, the narcos and the police on the other, and the middle—the economy, education, political life—collapsing, normal communication broken down." Although the spring of 2010 saw a sudden and ferocious internecine conflict between the old guard of the Gulf cartel and Cárdenas's military wing, Los Zetas, "our problem," says Rodríguez, "is not like elsewhere. In most places, there is a war between different gangs." Despite the tensions, "this has always been the territory of the Gulf cartel. Reynosa is a one-company town."

Not only a one-company town but now an insurgent one-company town, at all-out war with the Mexican state. If it was ever the determination of the Mexican government that the crisis should be solved by the restoration of the PRI's old narco order, under one strong cartel with tacit license from the government to operate, such a strategy has now been overtaken by events. If, as the susurro has it, el Chapo Guzmán was—or may one day be intended to be—that one licensed monopoly cartel, then the plan has failed, thrown off course by collapse in Juárez and the ferocity of Los Zetas. Los Zetas can be bought off—anyone can in this game—but at what price? And if Los Zetas are to preserve the Pax Mafiosa in this territory, what price Guzmán? The mysterious treaty in Nuevo Laredo offers a tantalizing but terrifying answer: an uneasy arrangement among the cartels, with the loser paying a tax to the winner, and the price of peace being the kind of public submission Ms. Rodríguez is describing, of society and the economy to the power of the cartel.

The word "Zetas" is conspicuously absent from this discourse in Ms. Rodríguez's office, although it has gone well beyond what most people in Reynosa dare to speak. Another human rights worker in town who cannot be named says it privately: "We call them the Last Letter of the Alphabet. We don't call them Zetas—it's too dangerous to acknowledge their existence or use their name, which is mad, since they're so proud of who they are and boast it around all the time themselves. It is like this: if someone crosses them, they pay the price, either in cash or with their life."

Around the center of Reynosa is a system of canals built partly for irrigation and partly to channel floodwater from the Rio Grande. Along the canals are banks of grasses, and over them are bridges with yellow railings. To have a city surrounded by a system of moats is warfare's most tried and tested defense—as Los Zetas realize only too well. The activist speaks of displays of strength of which no word has hitherto escaped Reynosa: "It was February thirteenth [2009] when they did it for the first time," she says. "They just sealed off the city center, as a gesture of intimidation, with roadblocks at the bridges. To show they can do what they want, and to show the army they can do a training exercise. They did it again on the seventeenth. This time they hijacked buses across the bridges over the canals, boarded the buses, ordered the drivers to swing

them around and everyone to get off, then took the keys. Usually they do
it for two or three hours at a time, but once the buses stayed there for
fifteen hours, no one dared move them, and the city felt in a state of
siege." Some days later, a woman dared to speak, if only briefly, about
being on one of those buses. "We jerked to a stop. There was banging on
the door and four men jumped on, shouting at the driver. They wore balaclava masks, but we all knew immediately who they were. They ignored
us. It happened quickly: they shouted at us to get off the bus, quietly and
no one would get hurt. One lady insulted them because she was late,
but nothing happened. A few stayed and watched the driver steer the bus
across the road. He got down and was sent away. They just left the bus
there, empty, in the rain."

"One time it happened," said the activist, "a male friend of mine was
getting married, and his bride couldn't get to the church! She was coming
downtown when Los Zetas shut the bridge, and everyone got worried, especially my friend, because his bride arrived so late for the wedding!"
Over the bridge in McAllen, the narrative of Los Zetas and the bridges
becomes even more serious. It is not only those into downtown Reynosa
that the narco militiamen are blocking in their shows of strength; they
have another audience to impress, which involves a more audacious display across other bridges: those into the United States. "It was a bad day
here, about April or May [2009]. They blocked several bridges, the international bridges into the U.S. It's never happened before; they just shut
'em down."

The businessman in McAllen talks on condition of anonymity, as well
he might. But his knowledge and veracity are unimpeachable, and what
he knows has never been leaked. "They called us here at the company,
and they told me that whatever I got to get over, I had to get it over by two
p.m. Just get your stuff across, they said, 'cause we ain't reopening for a
while. They said it would be peaceful; they were just making a point.
And boy were they. What they were really saying was, 'We're running
the show.' These are people who roll up with rocket-propelled grenades
and can stage a four-hour shoot-out with the military. When they roll up
to close a bridge, people do what they say. The only bridge they left open

was the one over from Progreso, because of the tourism that still crosses there." No word of this ominous maneuver was spoken by U.S. authorities at the other side of the bridge, or by the local Texas politicians or press.

McAllen is becoming a city that looks north as well as south, turning in the direction the trucks will one day be going, it hopes, past the signs posted along Highway 281 toward Houston reading FUTURE INTERSTATE 69. Which is also the direction the genealogy of the businessman Sam Vale's family has taken. His ancestors are from Reynosa, but his office now sits atop the only tower in McAllen from which Spanish-language news, soccer, and showbiz feed into almost every household in the Rio Grande Valley. Vale is regional director of the Mexican Telemundo televison network and also owns the ultimate piece of Amexican real estate: a border bridge—that between Camargo, Tamaulipas, and Rio Grande City, Texas, for which each crossing vehicle pays him a toll. Mr. Vale, who typifies the new, muscular McAllen, tells the story with gusto. Originally the bridge was co-owned with another businessman, Vale's father holding a minority 40 percent. Through a series of clever manuevers, threatened lawsuits, and hard-faced verbal dueling, each episode increasing the stake by increments, the Vales secured majority and then sole ownership. All other bridges across the Rio Grande are the property of the federal government, apart from one other, whose owner's name happens to be Sam Sparks, says Vale, "so that to own a bridge, you gotta be Sam, Sam, or Uncle Sam."

Vale's office is decorated with artwork and antiquities from Mexico's recent and distant past: paintings, religious artifacts, and carvings. "They're the result of what I call the Mexican way of doing business," says Vale. "You see something you like, you name a price for what you are selling which you know the guy can't accept, then you ask, 'What else you got?'" Vale's ancestry was Mexican ranching and later commercial aristocracy from another world: "My grandmother used to send her dresses by steamship to be cleaned," says Vale, "in Paris." He is a man of presence, wears a full mustache, an open shirt, and gold jewelry, and talks entertainingly and with ease. He is Tex-Mex, big on the Tex, is generous with his time, and believes passionately in McAllen. Throughout the family's rise in the real estate business, he says, it had been surrounded by "people who wanted south Texas to be California. But hell no, I always said, we are what we are, that was the first principle." The second was that "whatever we do, we do with Mexico, rather than spend billions of dollars building a damned wall like this is Israel and Gaza." Laredo, he says, "always had that integrated mentality and did well out of it." And he looks at the sweep beneath us, out beyond the heavy oak desk in his top-story office. "When I was in high school, all this was fields." It sounded lovely, compared to the vista of concrete sprawl and the strip mall next door shared by Country Omelette, Viva Life Christian Book Shop, the Armory Guns 'n' Ammo, signs on posts advertising AutoZone, and a billboard that reads YOUR WIFE IS HOT. TINT HER WINDOWS. But that is not what Sam Vale means about the fields; he means the opposite: build all over them.

"McAllen lives or dies on the basis of international trade, starting with the fact that forty percent of retail in this town is Mexicans coming over here to buy stuff." But that is not where it ends. "We have people sitting there working out how to make money for this city. What next? What else? This valley is churning big time," says Vale. "The city must be part of the action that Laredo's part of" and establish its own inland port along its own trade corridor. "Laredo has a system it likes, but we can make it cheaper by letting the Mexican long-haul truck come straight across to the point of delivery, cutting out the shuttle." No drayage trucks here: this will be the boys from Veintiséis crossing over as far as the Pilot Travel Center. The mind boggles.

Vale has no illusion that "all the money is lily-white, because it's not. But around here, the cartels only affect you if you're involved in some way, you owe them, or sold them computers. The people who pay the cartels on this side have a part of their business that's illicit, some extension of the system over there, where no one can function without agreement with the Zetas." And, of course, there is the Iron River: "The biggest industry the cartel is involved in this side of the border is the import of guns from the

U.S. You've got a family, you get the Gulf cartel six to ten weapons at fifty dollars per week per gun—that's good money. A lot of people, myself included, have been clamoring for the ATF to be given more resources in this region. The government talks about sending one hundred more—dammit, we need one thousand, we need people working undercover on the other side, we need men on the ground who can root out the people selling the weapons around here and the gangs who are buying the weapons and getting them to the cartels. They're buying up parts and assembling them on the other side of the border. But all this hardware has to be stashed somewhere; it has to be taken to Mexico one gun at a time. There has to be a collection and distribution network, and it's got to be broken."

But Los Zetas' penetration of the legal economy runs deep. One astonishing story, told by an attorney in McAllen with good connections, affords a rare insight into the world of Zeta Inc. It involves them stealing condensate from oil terminals belonging to the Petróleos Mex company and exporting it to the United States. The scam was said to have been personally overseen from jail in Houston by Osiel Cárdenas Guillén himself. "They got the contacts inside the Petróleos Mex company," says the attorney, "and were literally siphoning off the condensate, bringing it from Monterrey to terminals in the U.S., with all the correct paperwork. Coming up through Pharr, up to Houston. How do we know this? Because something happened: a man called Manuel Gómez was found decapitated." The background to the murder, says the attorney, swearing inside knowledge: "Gómez was working with the cartel to provide transportation. He never used his own vehicles, always smaller trucking companies. He was responsible for hauling these tankers to refineries in Houston, for use in jet oil products. He even had a name in their circles: 'Manolo.'" After a while, the cartel operatives on the receiving end in Houston "started to notice a shortage of product arriving at the refineries, a shortfall in the cartel shipment. And what did they find out back in Monterrey? That Gómez was siphoning off his own stash. They figured it out and cut his head off."

According to one assessment of Los Zetas, in a briefing by the DEA in 2009, such is the extent of their criminal empire that only 20 percent of the syndicate's turnover is now generated by drug trafficking. This can be seen as a terrifying corruption of the economy, but Vale insists it can be looked at another way. "If the economy is right, they'll condemn themselves to respectability. They'll realize that the big money is mainstream. As things are, Los Zetas and the cartels are infiltrating the U.S. side—they're in Houston, they're in New York City, they're all over the Indian reservations. But these gangsters are going to have children and these children are going to have to learn legal business. Of course I'm not saying we make agreements with them, but you wait for them to condemn themselves to legality, then instead of fighting about it, you find some way to settle it. At the moment, you have a battle over an illegal product, with the profits going into semilegal business. It's painful, and we have to face that down. But it's a growing pain; they can't fight forever. They're already buying up houses on South Padre Island like the British do in Spain, and when the war is over it'll be like the old waterfront in New York—they'll start doing things in a more licit way, then go legal."

In defining McAllen as the town figuring out how to make money, swashbuckling Sam Vale had said, "Brownsville, by the way, doesn't think like' we do; it's more old-fashioned." Such generalizations always need to surrender to exceptions, but they are not without their grains of truth, and Vale's remark defines the curtain that divides the two cities on the Texan side of the valley, connected by the sprawling concrete overgrowth along Highway 83 or Highway 281, running parallel right along the borderline: the big sky and long story of the Old Military Road. It is one of the great highways in America, not because of the curious border towns it passes through, or the sweeping palms and tobacco fields that line the way, not even for the fact that Mexico and the river are never more than half a mile away, and sometimes a few feet. Indeed, if there is anything that makes the highway surreal, it is the border fence, cutting like a gash across the landscape, and often across the back of people's gardens. What makes the Old Military Road so richly agreeable to travel are the historical markers erected by various institutions at various stages along the way. It was an Indian trail used by Spanish explorers in the sixteenth century, initially established to connect settlements to one another; later a military road connecting the Texan and U.S. forts at Laredo and Brownsville during the Mexican wars; then a stagecoach, mail route, and inland supply line for cotton during the Civil War.

By definition, the narrative followed by an eastward journey along the Old Military Road to Brownsville is not a chronological one. Past a glorious avenue of palm trees to the south, one arrives at the site of Toluca Ranch, founded in 1880 by Florencio Cano on land owned by his Spanish ancestors, once covering ten thousand acres. There is high drama at the next marker, Río Rico. In 1906, says the plaque, the Rio Grande Irrigation Company dug a canal that "altered the natural course of the Rio Grande," abandoning 419 acres to the south of the river, in Mexico. After a treaty of 1884, says the marker, the "popular gambling community of Río Rico, which flowered in the '20s and '30s, became subject to Mexican jurisdiction." Later, in 1970, the United States ceded the communities of Río Rico and El Horcón to Mexico, starting an eight-year legal battle that ended in the granting of U.S. citizenship to two hundred natives of Río Rico born prior to 1970. Nature's border does not always coincide with mankind's, and the river knows best.

As one nears Brownsville, the road is marked by the site of the Rancho de Santa María, commandeered as a military subpost by Fort Brown, and a mile farther is the site of Villa de Reynosa, built by Juan Miguel Longoria (1815–1875), who fathered seventeen children with three wives, the last of whom was Teresa Guerra, one of the great "matriarch ranchers of Texas." Two miles farther along, two markers and a cannon stand together. One plaque marks the route taken by the Spanish general Alonso de León, fighting French incursions in 1685. "The spot where," reads another marker, "American blood was shed on American soil. April 25, 1846. Here Captain Philip Thornton and 62 dragoons were attacked by Mexican troops." The cannon, aimed at the border, was placed there in 1846 by Lieutenant Thomas Barlow Chapter, against the Mexicans. Three miles (and eighteen years) later, "Col. John S. Ford of the Confederate Army defeated the Union forces. June 25, 1864." Now the border fence almost touches the road, passes through Garco's construction yard, then behind a carwash and auto sales outlet in La Paloma, and back right up against the road, which then runs past Dark Side of the Moon Tattoos and into Brownsville.

One marker along the way had located the Battle of La Bolsa, fought in 1859, which ignited a conflict that was named after the man who fought here, Juan Cortina. The Cortina Wars witnessed the only seizure by land of U.S. territory in the nation's history. In 1859 and early 1860, reads the plaque, a "series of raids . . . led by Juan N. Cortina (1824–1894) led to skirmishes with companies of Texas Rangers and U.S. soldiers." Here at La Bolsa, it says, "a battle occurred . . . between Cortina's raiders and Capt. John S. 'Rip' Ford's Texas Rangers." Cortina, a Mexican from north of the border, led a raid on Brownsville in 1859, occupying Fort Brown with two hundred men and hoisting the Mexican flag from its ramparts. He was eventually thwarted by a mobilization of Texas Rangers.[21]

Diles quién eres," says Dr. Antonio Zavaleta, special assistant to the provost at the University of Texas at Brownsville—Tell them who you are. It was the title of a paper he presented at a conference on border identity, and a dicho he heard in childhood—as well it might be, for Dr. Zavaleta's paternal great-great-grandfather was General Juan Cortina. His academic post is therefore all the more apposite because the university campus occupies the site of the old Fort Brown captured by his ancestor.

Dr. Zavaleta's office is a museum to both his ancestry and his imagination. The room is a wonder: if Sam Vale wheeled and dealed his way into a collection of artifacts, Zavaleta has accumulated a treasure trove. He works surrounded by totem poles, icons, painted panels, carvings, and masks representing deities, saints, spirits, sprites, and banshees—presided over, of course, by the Virgin of Guadalupe. Here is a roomful of the syncretism—mumbo jumbo, if you prefer—of multiple and multi-layered faiths that has defined the border's history and the road, and infused the air it breathes even more than the violence. It has done so all the way from the demolished Santa Muerte chapels above Tijuana to this room: a council of the incorporeal at the border's far eastern edge. General Juan Cortina looks down with a commanding and perfectly somatic aspect from a wall by the window—"Diles quién eres," indeed.

Zavaleta is captivated, personally and professionally, by what he calls "folk Catholicism," as believed and practiced by the people of Mexico and the border, rather than the kind issued in papal bulls and edicts. Folk Catholicism retains elements of pre-Columbian faith, which have remained as part of Christian iconography and practice in Mexico, whether it pleases the Vatican or not. Zavaleta is expert in a central part of this overlay of faiths: *curanderismo*—the work of *curandero* faith healers as embodied by the Niño Fidencio, who practiced in and around Espinazo, Nuevo León, during the 1920s. And when I arrive to talk, by coincidence, copies of Zavaleta's new book have just been delivered: a selection of petitions sent by e-mail to the curandero healer Alberto Salinas, an acquaintance of his, almost entirely from Mexican Americans, together with the curandero's responses. They range from requests for advice on schoolwork to that on demonic possession, from injuries to a baby by a lunar eclipse to dancing with death and, inevitably, in pursuit of deliverance from the power of Santa Muerte. Most correspondents, one infers, are young.[22]

"I went through over seven thousand e-mails," says Zavaleta, "and noticed a subliminal pattern that had a lot to do with very traditional curanderismo. They had come to this through word of mouth, at home, in schools, villages, or churches, and what they sought was a subtle mix of spiritual, artistic, and scientific or medical treatment and advice, a holistic process. We could choose only one hundred ninety of them, but they are one hundred ninety lives, very particularly expressed in a way that was modern to the eye, but ancient." He makes the connection by waving an arm around the room. "All this is pervasive in our culture. It's in every being on the border. This stuff," which seems either distant or exotic to the modern eye, "is very real to people, every day," says Zavaleta. "Dancing with the devil, feeling the eyes of the dead upon you, the patron saints of your home or traveling, saints' days, magic numbers and colors, protective talismans—it cuts deep and is always close to the surface. It plays a role in your life and community. These are poor people, but throughout, there's this deep understanding, even in the world we live in, of forms of faith and belief that go way back, from which the healing and magic traditions of all religions in Mexico including Catholicism are drawn." Zavaleta has a professorial air, for sure, but there's something more than that: this is not academe, this is a life's faith as well as a life's work, ever since, he says, "I was raised a Catholic in Brownsville, Texas, but of Mexican ancestry, and educated by a priest from Ireland.[23]

"I know priests who admit that it's not a problem if people don't believe what they're doing, so long as they keep doing it," says Zavaleta. "But we're not like that—folk Catholicism is something primal that never leaves you. It doesn't leave even people who go off to become born-again evangelicals. They sing in chapel, they go to Bible classes, then they come back to their roots in the primal mystery. They'll take in the great work—food stalls in the barrio, soup kitchens, all good—but then they come home. To not wanting to disappoint their patron saint, feeling unlucky at the eye of a certain animal on you—not Bible class, but *this*!"—again, a sweep of the hand across the room, past the dancing skeletons, the plumed serpents, the bright birds, and the mesmerizing figure of the Virgin of Guadalupe, standing atop the new moon. "It's like asking someone on a beautiful warm evening," says Zavaleta, "'What would you like to drink, a cup of coffee or a nice cold beer?'"

Zavaleta's book contains the case of a boy who feels trapped by a pledge he has made to Santa Muerte. He petitions the curandero Salinas "as a matter of life and death," fearing that Santa Muerte will "collect on a broken promise." "He knows there's a payback," says Zavaleta, "and is afraid it will be with his life. He's terrified and reaches out for help in a desperate way, but one that understands the deep history of what he is doing." And at last, here is the conversation I have been waiting to have since that fearsome afternoon above the dam in Tijuana. "Santa Muerte was resurrected in Mexico City twenty-five years ago, in the poor Tepito neighborhood. And was adopted by the narcos—that's what everybody knows," says Zavaleta. "It's a huge cult now; among the young, it's become a way of identifying with power, with easily accessible evil. For the narcos, it's obviously something more sinister and dangerous, but it's they who've mutated Santa Muerte into this image. She's been made into a pop saint by the drug traffickers to sublimate their cult of death.

"If you go back, Santa Muerte was not evil. She was, strictly speaking, the representation of a folk saint to which a woman prayed to get her wayward husband back—of course she means more than that! She represents a holistic relationship between life and death, a cycle and totality. The image of the reaper is inaccurate; that's something new. If you see Santa Muerte as a black-hooded reaper on the back of a car, it's more likely from Tamaulipas than Mexico City. Santa Muerte originally wore not black but the colors of the rainbow. It's important that she represent the universality of the colors. Originally, she held not a scythe—that's another narco creation—but the world, the globe. Her power is that she holds everything in her palm."

The appeal of the cult to young people, says Zavaleta, "reminds me of when, as a fifteen-year-old, I brought home a book by Aleister Crowley and showed it to my mother. And I can see that sentiment everywhere now. The gold standard in folk religions is to see what's selling—it's as true now in the marketplaces as it ever was with the sale of indulgences and relics. Now you'll find shops broken into and the only thing missing the thieves wanted to steal is a statuette of Santa Muerte. There's been a rash of these thefts in the valley. Here in Brownsville, you have little kids in elementary school, third grade, who are doing Santa Muerte. They wear the gold chains, they talk to the statues, and it's obvious that their fathers are drug dealers; if you talk to them, they'll tell you their fathers work for the cartel. This is serious, and dangerous, but our reaction is different from that of the mainstream church." How so? "If you ask someone who practices curanderismo, he will distinguish between this new cult of Santa Muerte and her original meaning. But the church will not. They'll give you a blank look, dismiss it all, and offer you God with the right hand or the devil with the left—that's the way it is. If you ask someone who believes in curandero healing, they'll grapple with it, engage in cognitive discussion, go back to the original meanings of what is really happening, understand them, and find a way out."

Where does "Diles quién eres" come from? I ask. "My grandfather said it to me once, in Spanish. I was about twelve years old. I asked him what it meant, and he looked at me sternly: 'Tell them who you are.' I asked him to tell me the story, of this Juan Cortina I was descended from, and he did. I felt like a newborn child."

Elizabeth Street in Brownsville, running a block north of the border, is a destination point for shoppers from across town, of course, but also the northwest corner of Tamaulipas. Cross-border shopping is a theme—although now menaced by the narco war—that defines the frontier. As in Calexico, as in Laredo and everywhere in between, there is this delicate balance between what is more affordable (or less unaffordable) on the U.S. side and on the Mexican side. It is a matter of careful judgment, on which side of the border the bargain may be hiding, with regard to both domestic essentials, and some little luxury or treat that doesn't appear on the list prepared in advance.

The Signature Store is a cavernous adventure, miles of fluffy bears, zip-up bags for ropa usada, marker pens, Tupperware and cutlery, towels with designs of Sylvester Stallone or Marilyn Monroe to choose from, flashing antennas and model New York taxicabs. El Toro Sporting Goods is stacked with perfumes, soccer jerseys, and bags with Mickey Mouse or the Dallas Cowboys star on the back. And in this marketplace of essentials, little luxuries, and junk, stands the temple, H-E-B. A Texan supermarket chain that strides the frontier, with consulates in every Mexican border town, H-E-B is an institution. The parking lot in Brownsville is a social scene at sundown, a gossip exchange, an opportunity to chat, a place to compare phone applications and bets on horses. About half the license plates are Texan, the other half from Tamaulipas, while over in Matamoros, the ratio is about two to one in favor of the indigenous Mexican shoppers.

Over in Matamoros, the H-E-B is more department store than supermarket: an array of electronic goods more expensive than in the United States, sofas and armchairs at much higher prices, a spectacle of cheap chili and jalapeños without rival. But the pièce de résistance is over in the corner: Pastelitos, the bakery. Here, at apparently reasonable prices, is a fanfaronade of cakes decorated electric pink, yellow, or blue. This is the cake department to end all cake departments: cakes shaped like racing cars, Spider-Man and Catwoman, Mickey and Minnie Mouse, with inscriptions in sugar icing like "Machito," in blue, for little boys, and "Florita," little flower, in pink for girls. A corpulent man in a chef's hat who looks quite like the pastry he is baking heaves a humongous cake covered in sugared Technicolor over the counter, received with difficulty on the other side by two girls—this is Brian César's birthday cake, personalized in turquoise icing.

At the end of the row of shops on Elizabeth Street back across the border, however, is a Pandora's box of a shop. Written above the door is AZTECA: YERBERÍA. GIFTS DOLLS REGALOS MUÑECAS. SE LEEN LAS CARTAS—Herb shop. We read cards. Azteca is an omnium-gatherum of spiritual, religious, and magic accoutrements and a child's dream made real. Hidden among flowers or lined up on shelves are dolls of every kind. There are white plaster statuettes: of Venus, of fine ladies in ball gowns, of the three magi, amorous cherubs and mischievous putti as well as Christ both in manger and on cross. There are shelves of remedies for every ailment of the mind, body, or soul: herbs, oils, and essences of cactus. Four shelves are devoted to devotional candles to every saint, angel, and archangel, including Santa Muerte in all her incarnations. But guiding and presiding over all of this—framed, sculpted, painted onto candles, cast in silver, gold, plaster, and plastic—is the figure who oversees it all and everything along the border, standing on the moon: Queen of Mexico and Empress of the Americas, the Virgin of Guadalupe.

The first of many prayers offered early on Saturday, December 12, 2009, in Brownsville was spoken through a megaphone and chilly, damp fog hanging from the dark sky—unusual for a tropical night in America's poorest neighborhood. But the people of Cameron Park had converged nevertheless, in the parking lot behind the Church of San Felipe de Jesús on the outskirts of town, to prepare for the procession of Our Lady the Virgin of Guadalupe. And they did so, they knew, along with tens of millions of others across Mexico and along the borderline. As the Christian world prepared to commemorate the Nativity, Mexicans—including twenty-eight million Mexican Americans and probably the same number of Mexican citizens living legally or illegally in the United States—celebrated what is for them a more spiritually cogent and enchanted day. "In the name of the Holy Virgin Mary, Mother of God, and Nuestra Reina"—our queen—implored Father Héctor Cruz into the megaphone, "and please keep to the side of the road": three years ago a drunken driver plowed into the parade, injuring three pilgrims. Accordingly, behind a pickup truck leading the way, we set off, just after 3:00 a.m., in pilgrimage to the church of Our Lady of Guadalupe, on Twelfth Street downtown. We walk at a pace, for this is no stroll and there is some way to go. Pounding those three hours through the dark were mostly young people, couples in hoodies holding hands, fathers with little children, women and girls clutching bunches of roses in December (for such was one of the Virgin's miracles when she first appeared), and the striking image of the Queen of Mexico standing on a crescent moon among the rays of the sun. A young man called Luis walked, now having to commute to work as an ironworker "way north in Alabama and Georgia" because there were no jobs left locally, his wife four months pregnant; he had returned especially for this pilgrimage. A young woman called Gabriela Méndez had two weeks ago been laid off by H-E-B, now wondering what next, only glad to be able to concentrate better on basket-making class. Wearing a splendid Mexico 1994 World Cup bomber jacket, Alfonso—a steward keeping the parade in line—had been on all thirteen "Guadalupana" pilgrimages from Cameron Park since their inception, but just lost his job as a chandler in the harbor at nearby Port Isabel. "This," he insists, however, "is the day of *esperanza*"—hope—"for us all, and for all Mexicans."

Cameron Park was until recently a Mexican-American colonia, which means simply neighborhood but on the U.S. side means that it was too poor to be incorporated and granted services such as lighting, running water, or paved roads, because it raised no tax revenue. A movement by civic groups in the 1970s, later spearheaded by the remarkable man who was until recently parish priest at San Felipe de Jesús, Michael Seifert (he has since left the priesthood), registered Cameron Park's residents as voters and won the attention of the city, county, and even the state of Texas, so that the trailer homes gradually grew permanent extensions and the oil lamps became electric lights.[24]

The area remains in many ways a Mexican colonia, as we walk first along pitted byways past little "bodega" kiosks that are windows of private homes, past guard dogs barking at the pilgrims as they wander the empty streets like a spectral procession toward the city. Then out onto the main artery into town, Arroyo Boulevard, past dark stillness on the resacas left by the winding Rio Grande—past deserted Wendy's and unlit golden arches, we are joined by tributaries of other pilgrims. It is strange and welcome to see this city becalmed at night: in motionless abeyance and wrapped in damp darkness, depopulated but for our muffled steps past mute buildings and dwellings. A twenty-four-hour Valero gas station is lit and open, though, selling famously good breakfast tacos, which tempt a few folks in search of nourishment and warmth to tarry. All along the way, the pilgrims sing. In fact, the choir on the back of the truck is not deemed good enough and as we pass Coffee Port Road the hooded, anorak-clad choristers are ejected and stewards appeal to the now several hundred pilgrims, *"¿Quién canta?"*—who can sing?—in search of substitutes. The special hymns duly continue, with greater glow: *"Y eran Mexicanos"*—They were Mexicans—goes the hymn, to whom the Virgin of Guadalupe appeared in 1531. Past Don Quixote Street they walk, then alongside the freeway, and even that is deserted.

After three cold hours, the procession enters a bath of fluorescent light, the church resplendently decorated for Mass, which begins during darkness at 6:00 a.m. There is a justifiable sense of authenticity among those who walked, even if the best seats have been taken by others who drove. The altar is gleaming white, the choir dressed in bright indigenous Mexican colors, and the priest has the image of the Virgin embroidered on his cream-colored robe as he reads, apocalyptically, from the Book of Revelation. Drummers wearing lambent golden Aztec costumes and dancers in headdresses of peacock feathers perform, presided over by the icon of Guadalupe.

Icon of Mexico in the deepest sense, the Virgin of Guadalupe is at once dynamic, mystical, and omnipotent. She appeared to what is commonly referred to as a "poor Indian," a Nahuatl peasant baptized as Juan Diego, over a series of encounters in 1531, during which she tasked Juan Diego to convince a doubtful archbishop to build a sanctuary in her honor. This was achieved through a series of divine signs as proof: first of roses in December, then her image branded on the peasant's cloak. The image was left in the open for a century: while the sanctuary was blackened by charcoal smoke, the image remained colorful and clean. As it still does today—untarnished, unfaded, defying modern scientific logic.

But the Virgin of Guadalupe is much more complicated than that. After Mass, there is a hearty breakfast of *huevos a la mexicana* with Michael Seifert, who has thought, preached, and spoken about the image and the Virgin Queen it portrays in his former parish of Cameron Park. "Cameron Park is in, but not of, Brownsville," he says. "Surrounded on all sides by one of the poorest cities in Texas, Cameron Park is so poor that not even Brownsville wants to have anything to do with the place." It is pertinent, then, that the Virgin of Guadalupe appeared to a peasant in the cotton fields. "She is the cry of the poor and the redemption of the poor. But it is not that straightforward: the poor Indian was from a warrior caste, vanquished and converted by another warrior caste [the Spanish conquistadores] and in this, the Virgin is the child of rape, but pregnant—both queen and outcast, pregnant with the mixed-race mestizos," after a far from immaculate conception. So the Virgin of Guadalupe is both spiritually and ethnically syncretic: a mestiza, icon of both pre-Columbian and Catholic spirituality, and of the indigenous and Spanish people. Indeed, in one of the great works of Mexican literature, the Nauhatl-language *Huei Thamahoicoltica*, or Great Event, she is defined only in terms of pre-Columbian, Mexica lore—an echo of Coatlicue, goddess of the Aztec pantheon, who lived among the moon and stars, and gave birth to the primary god Huitzilopochtli after being impregnated by a "brilliant hummingbird feather carried on the wind," and who, like the Virgin of Guadalupe, had her sanctuary on the mountain of Tepeyac.

"And the Virgin of Guadalupe," says Seifert, "is also a symbol of defiant hope in the dark days of now. She is a social lament and helps us in our resistance. She is what stands between places like Ciudad Juárez and total despair. And unlike any other Madonna, she is standing. If you look at her left knee, she is even dancing." It is an extraordinary proposition. Yes, says Seifert, she is "a young woman, dressed as an Aztec queen. We know this from the colors and the style of dress, from the sun and the moon and the stars. This cosmic princess is standing, while among the people of those days, royalty sat, always and especially in the presence of the lower classes [as do portrayals of the Madonna in European art]. She is of course pregnant, as we can tell from the way her robe stands forth, and from the dark sash, and she has her hair down. But she is in a dance, as well, her knee lifted forward."

Equally unexpected is Seifert's sudden about-turn: "Then I think to myself: Is it all opium? Opium of the people, to keep them servile?" What a thought—heresy on December 12 from a former priest—and what a terrible moment for Seifert to have to leave. His wife, a pediatrician, has arrived, and they must record pictures of a newborn baby to send by Internet to grandparents in Mexico, who cannot get papers to cross the border and visit.

Some weeks later, Seifert sends further thoughts on the Virgin of Guadalupe. Seifert goes back to the Nahuatl equivalent of her name, Coatlaxopeuh, pronounced "quatlasupe," which he constructs as "Mary Who Crushes the Serpent." "At the heart of the Spanish conquest," concludes Seifert, "is rape. I don't mean the figurative rape of the country and the culture, but the rape of Indian women by Spanish soldiers." And the child of that rape, he argues, "would be a bastard, in the harshest technical sense of the word, a child without a past, without a people, for she is not an Indian; she is Other. This child, however, would be the most lasting reminder of the first, violent encounter between Europeans and the Aztec nation. She was Mexican, and she and her brothers and sisters would become yet another nation, another great people, a new people. In the humiliation of rape, a new race was born, a mestizo race, the Mexican race." Diles quién eres: the Virgin of Guadalupe, telling Mexico who it is.

.   .   .

In the sign of peace at the end of Mass after the pilgrimage from Cameron Park, there is flesh-creeping poignancy after a year of violence across and along the border. But a woman in the front row shatters any riptide of thorns with a cry of redemptive defiance: "*¡Viva la Virgen de Guadalupe!*" "*¡Viva!*" roars the congregation, as the sky quickens outside. "*¡Viva San Juan Diego!*" "*¡Viva!*" they respond, as gray dawn breaks. "*¡Viva Cristo Rey!*" "*¡Viva!*" comes the reply. Sitting in a pew on the nave is the writer Cecilia Ballí, who has narrated the trials and triumphs of poverty and resilience in Cameron Park. "You notice," she says, "how today, Jesus Christ comes third, after the Virgin and Juan Diego."

The Rio Grande Valley was ranched and farmed by a small number of great families before the border was drawn across it, two of which were the Ballí and Hinojosa dynasties from whom Cecilia is descended— great ranchers and owners of land. In many ways, both grandiose and bitter, the history of the valley and the border is the history of the Ballí family, which once owned—but was swindled out of—Padre Island and proved so in a lengthy court case, a judge in Brownsville ruling in favor of the extended family in 2000. Ms. Ballí wrote in *Texas Monthly* that the victory "was for all of us to relish. In a way, its story is universal. For it is a story about how some people are washed out of their own histories." Even more important, though, was the "deep sense of pride and rootedness that these families share." Cecilia's father had "died sick on a hospital bed, and other than a little bit of pride and lots of love, he couldn't leave us much. He was a cab driver with cancer. He was forty-one. But he left us a special last name, and there lay the treasure."

Cecilia Ballí and I drive across the land her own immediate family comes from, south of the border, stretching like low polder under an expansive but leaden winter sky toward the sea. We pass a small store— "that belongs to a relative," she says—then a huddle of green houses where her mother was raised, and farther down to the ranch where her father grew up. Along a fence beside the road, a man wearing a straw cowboy hat has hung a particularly upmarket selection of ropa usada for sale, with a fine old Wrangler shirt to buy. "I remember your grandfather," he says to Cecilia. "I drove a tractor on his ranch; I pasteurized and sold milk." Past a gas station and the inevitable Oxxo store on Highway 5, a road leads off to the left. At its entrance are a refreshment stand selling beer called Minisuper Bisby and three parked buses. It is not a road down which one turns, says Cecilia—it leads to the ranch where Osiel Cárdenas Guillén was raised. The ranch along that road itself constitutes a kind of wayside "historical marker" in the narrative of Mexico's narco cartel culture. Ms. Ballí argues that it helps explain a shift in the social composition of the region's drug cartel, which she believes perfected the style of violence now seen in all of Mexico. "Osiel Cárdenas comes from a very poor family that lived just on the fringes of a Mexican border city, literally and metaphorically. His predecessors in the Gulf cartel tended to be businessmen and to come from the middle class, or at least from well-connected families. Osiel didn't initially have the same kind of access to politics and politicians. His way into the business was by becoming a federal cop. He represents the poor urban underclass that the Mexican government has always neglected, whose men basically have two options to genuinely climb out of poverty: go work on the other side of the border, or join the trade."

And what happens to these poor young men coming into the business for the first time? "They finally get to experience power, what it is to be respected, and they're not as invested in the old social networks or political debts, in the old way of doing things. They don't just co-opt, they confront. The first thing Osiel did to become the boss was kill his associate; that's a departure from the past. People talk about him being particularly violent as a person, and once his enforcers, who came to be known as Los Zetas, formed, they began branding a new style of violence, and it's a style that other cartels in Mexico have learned to match." "Style" is not a word Ballí uses lightly (she developed her own point in chapter 6 about the murders of women in Juárez). "People say this is all about money," she notes, developing Treviño's point in Reynosa, "but I think it's about money and something more. It's a social performance, a show of power, a very masculine form of power. They are saying, 'We are somebodies,' in a country where that was not supposed to be possible for men of their class. I think in some ways the willingness of Mexico's rich to ignore the poor is coming back to haunt them. This isn't the poor's revenge on the rich; they are simply finding their own way to wealth and to social recognition. Especially since the old avenues for becoming a man in Mexico—you got married, found a job, and supported your family—are shifting. Some men are now opting to establish their manhood this way, and this is hurting everyone."

And yet even the cartel forms part of this narrative of heritage, place, and identity, argues Ms. Ballí. "The cartel here does still have ties to the community. People here know their names, they know who they are. Maybe they grew up or went to school together, or married distant relatives. And although they've gone national and international, their leadership is still from northeastern Mexico and they're proud of it. They celebrate its music, its language. Regional identity is extremely strong in Mexico, and these guys like to assert the fact that they're from Tamaulipas and from the border, a place the rest of Mexico has always shunned. You see this pride displayed on the Internet, in YouTube clips extolling the Gulf cartel and Los Zetas, and in the way they decorate their trucks. We like to talk about 'imagined communities' in academia, and I think the Mexican cartels have done an impressive job of harnessing those regional and communal identities, so that people almost root for them the way they would root for their soccer teams. And so when we talk about their struggles to retain control of their territories, we're not just talking about drug routes; we're talking about their ability to say, 'This is our place.' I think this is something that distinguishes the Gulf cartel from others. Aside from La Familia in Michoacán, the other cartels are made up of people who have moved around various states in northern and northwestern Mexico, many of them originally from Sinaloa. The guys who took over Tijuana were from Sinaloa, not from Tijuana." Diles quién eres: Los Zetas too are telling who they are.

"People here don't condone drug trafficking," says Ms. Ballí, "but they understand where it comes from. I think we're at an interesting crossroads now, though. The community is more silenced than ever, and everyone understands that something has been lost, something pretty big has been lost. The cross-border life that was so special about this place is changing every day."

There's a joke they tell in Matamoros. First day of term and the schoolteacher welcomes the new children, supervised by the principal. "All children with names beginning A to M sit over here," says the principal, and they do. "All children with names beginning N to Y sit over there," and they do. "What about children with names beginning with Z?" asks the teacher. "Oh, they can sit wherever they want," replies the principal, crossly.

The claw marks of artillery shells that pockmarked the walls of Sarajevo or Grozny do not usually form part of the landscape of the narco war, but in Matamoros they do, at the site of a shoot-out between Los Zetas and the army during September 2009, beside a construction site and Tacos al Vapor stand on Primera Street in a smarter neighborhood of town not far from the river, nor very far from army headquarters hunkered down in a storage depot, with its heavy gate, security lodge, sentries, and visible fleet of parked jeeps. According to eyewitnesses, the shooting lasted two hours after the army tried to stop a car, which then ran the soldiers' roadblock. Los Zetas, apparently already in position to cover the car, reportedly took nine casualties, according to the unconfirmable susurro, the army admitting to none. After the incident, Los Zetas are said to have sealed off the area and—giving tactical purpose to the exercises in Reynosa—boarded buses, ordered passengers off, and taken the keys.

I talked for a while, sitting on a wall, with a man called "Arturo," from Monterrey, now living in Matamoros, one of the few people I met there prepared to discuss Los Zetas. If they call them El Pirámide in Nuevo Laredo and the "last letter of the alphabet" up the road in Reynosa, I asked him, what are they called here? "We just say 'the Letter,'" said Arturo. "Half the town works for the Letter one way or another. The only way to avoid them is do things like make sure that your car insurance is in order, because some day you're either going to get hit, or someone'll make sure you got hit, and there's a fifty percent chance that the owner of the other car will be working for the Letter. You better make sure that any damage gets paid off quick, with full third-party insurance, because you don't want to be owing anything to anyone in Matamoros. Because they won't just come for your car, they'll come wanting your house, everything you have, and *you*." Los Zetas, he confirms, "shake down everyone in town. From big business to the small vendors, the taco stands, the mariachis. They all need to commit to the Letter people; nothing happens in Matamoros without them. So there's no war here, apart from between the army and the cartel, though for a while it was between the cartel and the Letter. Now the Letter people have the police on their side, and I don't think the army can ever really beat them." The internecine fighting between the Zetas and Gulf cartel tore Matamoros apart too, but with the military playing a heavier hand. During February 2010, shoppers in the H-E-B branch in town were subject to a shootout between the army and Zetas across the parking lot. In 2010, while on a rampage against cartel leaders, Mexican marines shot dead Antonio Ezequiel Cárdenas, brother of Osiel, and known as "Tony Tormenta." Strangely, although Ezequiel had succeeded his brother after the Godfather's arrest, he took sides against the Zetas in the internecine war. Following his death, the Zetas hung banners gloating over the traitor's killing.

The PRI mayor of Matamoros, Erick Silva Santos, graciously agrees to see me and a colleague—Dudley Althaus of the *Houston Chronicle*, for whom this is familiar terrain—without an appointment. Mayor Silva insists, "We are not in a war zone. This is a conflict between the government armed forces and a group of narco traffickers," who, he concedes, "have very sophisticated equipment and weapons." But, he says, "I have nothing at all to do with this fight. The law does not permit us in the municipal city hall to intervene. The law does not permit me to mobilize the municipal police to intervene in narco traffic." How very convenient.

After this encounter with a man really grappling with the crisis, Althaus and I adjourn for lunch at a restaurant that is a silent Matamoros landmark. Only Althaus can remember why, from his days as a reporter on *The Brownsville Herald* over the river. The simmering violence in Matamoros was inevitably part of his beat, and Althaus covered the murder of a gangster called Casimiro Espinoza—reportedly on orders from the godfather of the old-time racket in town, Juan N. Guerra. "This was 1984," remembers Althaus. "We heard the news and came right across—it was my first-ever story in Matamoros. 'El Cacho' [the Horn], they used to call Espinoza. He was the only other serious gangster in town who was anything like a threat to Guerra. And Guerra made sure to rub him out. I think that was when we first heard the name Juan García Abrego, who was said to be behind the killing: he was Guerra's nephew and ran the Gulf cartel until ninety-six, after which Osiel took it from there. Looking back, that killing of Espinoza was when they consolidated power. Félix Gallardo was still running the federation down in Guadalajara, but that murder was with hindsight the birth of the Gulf cartel. This is when the old man Guerra used to sit at the back of this restaurant, holding court, and talk horse racing." The restaurant has thus been renamed Don Juan's, and the sign represents his favorite horse, riding crop, and hat. The real hat hangs from the wall inside. We eat well, the service is polite, only the man behind the bar fixes us all the while with dead, unshining eyes, cold as steel and ice.

Back from the sentry posts leading to Osiel Cárdenas Guillén's ranch, Cecilia Ballí and I sit at a beach café on a windswept winter afternoon, the sun throwing spears of light, which children call "ladders to heaven," onto the sea from behind battleship gray clouds, creating ponds of light on the ocean's indigo surface. The rain comes ashore, and clusters of Sunday trippers bring their seafood fries and chowder beneath the shelter that was built to be shade from sunshine. This is Padre Island, proved by the court in Brownsville to be the rightful property of the Ballís, Cecilia's ancestors having been swindled out of their land. "There are special dynamics on the border that you don't find anywhere else," she says. "For instance, there's a different sense of time along this part of the border. These communitles in the valley, especially the ones on the Mexican side of the river, date back to the eighteenth century, which in Europe may not seem old, but in the United States means a lot. We've been here almost as long as the thirteen colonies.

"But ever since Mexico lost this region to the United States, Mexican Americans in Texas have always been made to feel like foreigners, even though this has been their home—our home—for generations. After the border was drawn, we began to psychically experience a gradual process of separation from Mexico, though of course culturally and socially some of the ties remained. Because Mexico is right there all the time, there's always that sense of threat of the Other, and Mexican Americans constantly have to prove that they're American enough. When I was growing up we were made to feel embarrassed that our parents didn't speak English, even though most people in Brownsville were Mexicans. That's changing now with more immigration and the rise of a public Latino identity in the United States, which allows us not to have to hide who we are. The valley itself has changed a lot; now you hear Spanish regardless of where you are. But there's still that double movement happening. There's a cultural and emotional connection with Mexico, but most people live it on this side of the border, with other Mexicans who are here. Those of us who actually cross the border back and forth are statistically a minority. So here in the valley, Mexican Americans are becoming both more Mexican and more American at the same time, if that makes sense. I always wonder: Why are people so surprised when they come to the valley and find that Mexican Americans are really patriotic? That all our kids are signing up for the army? Well, if all your life people have questioned whether you belong, you find yourself having to *prove* that you're an American."

One of the ways for teenage boys to prove their Americanness has been to play the all-American game better than the Anglo-Americans—high school football. The book, film, and television series *Friday Night Lights* was set in Midland and Odessa back in west Texas, but nowhere is Friday night fever for the local team fiercer than in two small, poor towns joined at the hip in the Rio Grande Valley, Elsa and Edcouch.

Sam Vale had said, "The problem with Elsa is it's too far north from the border, too far east of McAllen, and too far west of Brownsville." But he was talking about the town's battered economy, not about the Yellow Jackets football team.

Indeed, Elsa is not on the way from anywhere to anywhere in particular. Most major employers, apart from the school district, have left or gone bankrupt, but the place has a sanguine, resilient feel to it; it is gladsome and vivacious. There is no way a visitor is going to get in and out of the Valero gas station or Stripes store without an affable interrogation, and the boys at the Elsa Body Shop fixing cars that most garages would give up for dead are happy to carry on a companionable chat about the Yellow Jackets, even when they are lying back under the vehicle, wrenches in hand.

In the Gladiators' stadium at Roma, the home stand is sparsely populated, for all their cheerleaders in minitogas and a march past by male pupils dressed as legionnaires and centurions carrying plastic imperial fasces and standards. The away stand, though, is packed, the brass band giving it what for, cheerleaders waving golden pom-poms, crowds whooping, and yellow-and-amber flags with pictures of bees on them waving. Roma is a good ninety-minute drive from Edcouch-Elsa, but it feels like half the population has made the journey even on a Thursday evening. Among the crowd are four generations of the Montalvo Flores family, from seventy-seven-year-old great-grandma Ida to little Deena, age six. "I graduated from Elsa High School in 1950," Ida rasps above the noise, "and hardly missed a game. I watch 'em wherever they go. You got to support the kids. We're such a small town, and we may be poor, but we're rich enough to buy our season tickets." Her eyes glint from behind her spectacles. "I'm sorry about my ugly gringo name," she offers out of the blue, though Ida had sounded just fine to me. "My mother's best friend was the midwife and my mother promised to name her baby after her." An additional excitement is that one of the family, Isaac Prado (it is too complicated to work out how he fits genealogically; there are twenty of them in the party), is playing his last game before graduating. "It's hard to take," says his father, Enrique. "He's wanted and waited to play for years and years, and so have we all, and this is the last time." Isaac's girlfriend is a cheerleader, now sitting with the family.

So this thing between the cheerleaders and team stars isn't just a myth from *Friday Night Lights*, I ask my host for the evening, José Saldívar, who has driven all the way and will drive all the way back. "Oh, no," says José, "it's almost a requirement," hastening to add that he married a librarian. His father, also named José, has come with us, also a fanatic season ticket holder since he moved to Elsa in 1988. "I could count on one hand the games I've missed." Mr. Saldívar fixes up classic and vintage cars for a living; they're mounted on bricks in his front yard. "I'm working on a fifty-five Chevy right now." The Edcouch-Elsa team for which José played in the 1990s is the envy of the valley, "even though our town is not," he says. "Everyone resents us and everyone wants to beat us because we have the best record." Elsa has won six district titles and made the state play-offs sixteen times, a tally unequaled by any other team in the valley and for which the Yellow Jackets became more widely known as La Máquina Amarilla, the Yellow Machine.

Elsa and Edcouch, says José, were agricultural communities dating back to the 1920s; Elsa once boasted the largest fruit-packing shed in the world. In the 1970s and '80s, however, fruit picking and packing, and industries related to them, went into decline. In the period since, "unemployment has been high and opportunities are scarce—the school district is the biggest employer, and they let two hundred people go last January [2009]. We're said to have the highest teenage pregnancy rate in Texas. There's a lot of alcoholism even among the kids, a lot of drug abuse—a couple of my friends are in jail for dealing." (In 2006, a mother in Elsa was targeted and killed in front of her children. In revenge, members of her family went in pursuit of the murderers and killed them. "Zeta business," says José.) "But the more this defines the town, the more passionate it has become about the football," he says. "The 1959 team had been a legend during the good times, but now it's obvious why people are so enthused—football is all there is. *Friday Night Lights* was a story that needed to be told—we here just think it was told in the wrong town!

"It's interesting that it was American football," José continues, at the wheel, Dad in the back, as we pass through Rio Grande City on the way to the game. "The town is poor and Mexican American, and soccer is the Mexican sport, but it never really got a hold in Elsa, and in the valley only as first-generation migrants arrived. The people who were born here grew up with American football and wanted to play American football." In the mid eighties, a man called Hugo de la Cruz began doing commentaries of games on local radio. "He became an institution across the valley," says José, "a must-hear for all football fans, but everyone knew he was Elsa through and through so he got people pissed, and the more he got people pissed, the more they wanted to hear his show—it was a bit like the team."

But beneath this burning sporting ambition cuts a riptide of ethnic identity. "Our town is one hundred percent Mexican American," says José. "Our team was always one hundred percent Mexican American and one hundred percent working class. And I can remember the coaches being pretty up front about it, when we went to play teams that were Anglo and more affluent. We wanted to beat the pants off them, being who we were and where we came from. One coach in particular used to tell us in the dressing room, 'Come on, guys, do it for la raza,' for the race. He'd say it even if there was only a handful of white kids on the other team! And oh, man, we wanted to beat them so bad; there's no doubt it made us play harder.

"In the fifties, playing football was a way to prove that you were an American, to break the segregation barrier. I've heard about Mexican Americans walking into chemistry class and being told to 'get out to your cotton fields where you belong!' and that's where it started, needing to prove yourself on the football field. But it carried on after desegregation. So long as you were Latinos made to feel foreigners in your own country, and playing the Anglos, you were going out there to make a point and beat their ass. It helped, to be honest, that the game is physical—who's the toughest, who can beat up who. It was a way of knocking someone out legally, without getting arrested."[25]

Tonight, La Máquina Amarilla prepares itself for the sack of Roma, another 100 percent Hispanic team, but Roma has never beaten Edcouch-Elsa, and although 2009 has not been a good year for the Yellow Machine, "even in a bad season, it's a big thing to beat Elsa." A scrappy game fails to impress either José or his father: "It ain't the team it used to be," laments José. Final score: Roma 14, Edcouch-Elsa 21. On the radio driving home, Hugo de la Cruz hits the airwaves, reading the scoreboard as on any sports show but diverting for a buildup of fanfares and corridos before announcing that from Roma tonight. A lady named Helen calls in and accuses Hugo of bias in favor of a team that didn't play that well. "We're not supposed to diss the kids," retorted Hugo. "Anyhow, who won?"

José Saldívar now teaches at Harlingen College, midway between McAllen and Brownsville, a town very much in the Rio Grande Valley but at its portal. When you turn your back on Harlingen and drive north, the palm trees thinning and eventually disappearing into the great flatlands of southeast Texas, toward the metropolis of Houston, you leave the border behind you, but not the borderland.

There is a perverse beauty in the landscape below the iron bridge where Highway 610 crosses the Houston Ship Channel: great towers of light and fire as far as the eye can behold; sinewy steel piping, plumes of smoke and flame twinkling into a Texas night wrapped by a shroud of pollution hanging from the sky. It has long been said that, as the author Sam Quinones puts it, "Los Angeles is Mexico's culture factory."[26] And that the gangland style of "pseudo-romantic culture of drug trafficking" are in many ways exports from Los Angeles to Mexico.[27] This is no doubt true. But in the new landscape, according to the new and altered maps since war broke out, first in Nuevo Laredo and then across Mexico in late 2006, the Mexican narco capital of the United States has moved to the citadel of oil: Houston. As the Tijuana cartel collapses, and arteries of the narco transport routes into the heart of America follow those of trade, Houston becomes the gateway, the hub of the wheel. If LA is the old imperial seat of Amexica, Juárez–El Paso its fulcrum, and Los Dos Laredos its spinal cord, the capital metropolis of Amexica is now Houston.

In April 2008, Special Agent Carla Mayfield of the ATF testified to a court in Houston about an investigation into serial purchases of 328 weapons from two branches of a gun dealer called Carter's Country by a circle of twenty-two people, notably one John Philip Hernández. Hernández was an unemployed machinist, arrested a few weeks beforehand, with most of the rest of his ring still at large. According to Special Agent Mayfield, twenty-eight of these firearms—purchased for a total of $352,134.04—had been recovered in Mexico and Guatemala. The case was only the tip of an iceberg, but it was one of the very few that documented and illustrated the flow of the Iron River from Houston to Los Zetas—for once, named in open court. Hernández had used his Texas driver's license number 15436960 to buy twenty-three firearms costing nearly $25,000. One reappeared in Puebla, "during an incident in which a businessman was kidnapped and murdered." Another emerged in Oaxaca, "during an incident in which Los Zetas . . . opened fire on the Mexican army." A weapon Hernández bought on July 12, 2006, read the court papers, "was recovered in Acapulco, Guerro [sic], Mexico. This incident is commonly referred to as the 'Acapulco police massacre,' due to the fact that more than a dozen armed assailants attacked two offices of the state attorney general and executed four police officers and three secretaries."[28] In November 2009, another case came out of the sting at Carter's Country: a windshield repairman called Christian Garza was charged in Houston—and pleaded guilty—with a role in a wider conspiracy to traffic more than three hundred weapons across the border to Los Zetas.[29]

In 2008 alone, two hundred indictments were issued against straw buyers working for twelve arms-trafficking rings along the frontier. Border checks of southbound vehicle crossings have been stepped up by both U.S. and Mexican customs. But there remain elements integral to U.S. national gun law that militate against effective action. A ban on assault weapons passed by the Clinton administration in 1994 expired in 2004, with no attempt by George W. Bush to reimpose it and President Obama shying away from a confrontation with the gun lobby. There is no computerized national gun database or registry in the United States—investigations and convictions depend on a paper trail. Records of gun sales remain with dealers, so that it is up to the ATF to take the initiative if a gun is recovered at a crime scene, or the dealer if he or she suspects a buyer—indeed, the system depends on tips and audits, with most dealers happy to cooperate with the ATF.

"All our investigations show that Houston is the number one source for firearms going from the U.S. into Mexico, number one source in the country," says the man in midstream of the Iron River's flow, Dewey Webb, special agent in charge of the ATF's Houston office, which covers a vast swath of east Texas and the borderland as far as Del Rio, opposite Ciudad Acuña—in effect, the territory controlled by the Gulf cartel and Los Zetas. It is the largest ATF region and the easternmost on the border, neighboring those run from Dallas, Phoenix, and Los Angeles.

Webb is an interesting man, a Native American from Oklahoma City (he wears his ATF ID on a necklace of turquoise). He has devoted his life to the bureau, having joined in the 1970s and worked all over Texas. He is a large man and chooses his words carefully but talks with estimable transparency and honesty about the scale of the problem facing him, and with that mixture of moral contempt and professional respect for his quarry that makes the difference between a good and a great cop. He turns a scheduled one-hour briefing into a three-hour conversation on a wet December afternoon in his unmarked office near Houston's George Bush Intercontinental Airport. In the reception area are plaques honoring the four agents the ATF lost in the siege of Waco up the road in 1993.

Webb opens, against the received wisdom, by saying that smuggling of arms to Mexico is now more commonly achieved by buying from licensed dealers than from gun shows, and that the ports of entry used by everyone else far outstrip consignments across open land. Smuggling guns, he says, is an entirely different kind of operation from smuggling drugs, demanding different expertise, "mainly because a gun just weighs so much, and it's so bulky," needing to be dismantled and taken through the border in parts for reassembly.

When he first joined the service, Webb recalls, the drug gangs were

serviced with "occasional trafficking from the U.S. People would call
relatives to get weapons, and there were arms going down for political
unrest in Mexico." Often, weaponry was trafficked by boat. Recently,
though, "we've seen an upsurge in this war, fighting for territory and
needing the weaponry to fight for territory, and I've seen both a surge in
the volume and a change in the nature of the weaponry. We're now looking at high-caliber rifles, AR-15 rifles and a couple of dozen variations.
They want top-of-the-line, very-high-quality weapons." Some of the guns
are bought here in Houston, he says, but "a lot is carried down here to
Texas from places like Chicago, Minneapolis–St. Paul, and Michigan.
Washington State was always a hot spot. This happened after we put a lot
of effort into this area after it started off in Laredo in 2005. So Houston
is both source and hub city, while in the Rio Grande Valley it's a smaller
fishbowl and easier to see what's going on; the flags get raised quicker."

It is not Webb's job to comment on gun, or gun control, policy, not
least because he relies in part on the cooperation of the vast majority of
honest dealers and to an extent on the industry. Besides, no one knows
guns better than he does. But he asserts clearly, "So long as we in the
United States make it easy for these people to buy weapons, we will be
the easy touch for these criminals. Texas has eight thousand gun dealers, and in the city of Houston, there are fifteen hundred. The pattern
we're seeing is that they'll go to the shows to buy ammo and supplies,
combat gear, and so on, and to the dealers to get their weapons, using
straw buyers for fifty dollars per gun, on up. They come, and they just
keep coming back. It's simple because we make it simple . . . There's no
black market in the U.S.; the guns are not being stolen. It's all legal. You
can make fifty dollars a day going to two or three dealers. But there are
still red flags: when a woman asks for a large rifle or if the dealer just
asks the right questions."

Don't Lie for the Other Guy is a campaign Webb's agency has
launched as it starts to punch into the straw-buying networks like that
run by Hernández, along with the National Shooting Sports Foundation.
Observe: Webb needs to work with gun owners and users, not against
them. Yes, Webb concedes, much of the military-caliber hardware comes

from Central America: "If they need a weapon, and they can't get it in the U.S., they'll get it from somewhere else." But, he insists, "the bottom line is that the United States is the nearest, the cheapest, and the easiest place to buy, for the cartels to get their weapons." But there is at last a wind of change, for the better, says Webb. "For one, the agencies on our side are on the same page." Second, "we're working with the Mexican authorities in a more proactive way; we got more people in Mexico, running more agents." The vetting procedures for Mexican hires have improved, he says, gratefully. And accordingly, "we're getting more results" and understanding the cartels better. "They're very smooth in their operations and the way they do business. They're managed like corporations, until it gets to the violence. Sometimes they want a gun because they want a gun. We're seeing them wanting the best: Mac 10s, Mac 11s, AR-15s, nine-millimeter pistols. They want better weapons than I've seen in thirty-three and a half years. But then sometimes they want a gun because they saw it on TV. Then they get kind of like a wannabe Scarface. Then there's the fact that they all have the same trend: they have to defend their territory. And for that, they are busting each other's heads, and I know for a fact that it's costing them dear." The cartels, says Webb, "are also looking for alternative sources of income: human trafficking, kidnapping for ransom, and I've seen the cartels involved in oil." But in the end, it comes down to the drugs. "If people were not buying the dope, they wouldn't have the money to buy the guns; that's the bottom line."

So far, Webb's efforts against the smuggling from Houston itself have focused on three cells, including Hernández's, and 328 traced weapons taken across the border by them alone. In January 2009, the authorities in Houston also arrested ten members of a gang called Tango Blast Houstone, indicting four more on the run, for distributing marijuana and cocaine for the Gulf cartel from Houston. The arrests highlighted the position at the center of the wheel of Houston's gang culture and gangland in the business of the cartels, using their contacts across the state, and thence the country, to distribute drugs. The arrests followed an investigation by both Webb's agents and those of the FBI, who noticed important differences between this new gang and those to which they had become accustomed over time—markedly the old-guard Texas Syndicate, established across jails in Texas and California during the 1960s. The differences between the two gangs echo the changes between the "classic" and new-wave narcos south of the border. Behind the glass façade of its new headquarters in Houston, agents involved in busting both generations of gangs talk about the varied ways they put themselves at the disposal of the cartels, with very different structures. The FBI agents give their names, even present business cards, but prefer not to be identified. The expert on the Texas Syndicate—I'll call him "James"—is chisel-jawed, terrifyingly fit, with a vise-grip handshake and as courteous as he is direct. The agent who masterminded the bust of Tango Blast is more quietly spoken and considered—I'll call him "Mark." There is also a woman at the briefing, who studies gangland patterns, movement, and psychology, by the name of "Angela."

The Texas Syndicate, says James, "has a leadership structure, its members have ranks—the *sillón*, or chairman for each region, like a lieutenant, and soldiers called carnales. It's blood in, blood out—you kill to join, and you can never leave. You wear the tattoo and the gang is your family even if you get old, leave jail, go into business, or have a family. Many of them live a low profile—family men in regular houses who hold down jobs, don't draw attention to themselves. Some of them are middle-aged now. They'll hold juntas, meetings and assemblies where they take votes or discuss disciplining members." The Texas Syndicate, which grew in response to the power of other criminal gangs in California's jails, fits into the national network of gang affiliations and rivalries that an annual report by the Justice Department monitors for its role as distribution network for the narco cartels. James says that sometimes, "if there is a business opportunity, you'll see the gangs put their differences aside.

"It's historical, formed in California and grown in Texas, and they've been major dope traffickers over the years. Some are very big drug dealers indeed—and they are killers." Tango Blast, however, is a bigger, wider, looser organization. "It's more fluid than the Texas Syndicate, a bit like Facebook," says Mark. "The gang changes according to what you need that day, from who, to do what. There's no blood in, blood out, no initiation rite that we know of, no set rules. One day, you need a guy who can bring in five kilos, so you deal with him and make the contacts you need to get it where you need. Next week, you need to pick up and shift twenty kilos from someone else, and you may use different contacts. That's what makes it the biggest gang in Houston—we estimate about twenty thousand members, a lot of people doing different criminal activities who don't necessarily know each other like in a traditional gang structure. It's part of the time we're in—they're kids, they have no code, no rules."

Sometimes, says Angela, "you'll get kids committing crimes just so they can get sent to jail to find the gang and join. We're seeing a lot of young guys trying to join; it's the cool thing to do, the in thing to be. So in addition to the gang members, you get a lot of wannabe gang members who then become criminals, go to jail, and become gang members. There's a lot of prestige, there's the opportunity to make money, there's an intimate sense of belonging to a brotherhood, knowing that if I would kill for them, they would kill for me."

Ironically, "the tight structure of the Texas Syndicate makes it possible to plan strategies against them, dismantle cells by filling in the spaces," says James. Mark adds, "The fact that Tango Blast doesn't have that kind of structure makes it harder to catch them. Only the thing that makes it a little easier is that they don't know how to hide. Not like [James] said about the Texas Syndicate keeping a low profile. When we bust these guys, they had luxury cars, Bentleys, Maseratis, diamond jewelry." One of the men this team is most eager to find is Raúl Madrigal, who taunts them from file photographs: basking in a bubblebath, posing on a beach, and even sticking up a finger—all from Mexico. Madrigal allegedly made so much money helping the Gulf cartel pump marijuana and cocaine into the United States through Houston that the FBI has sequestered $18 million in assets and nine luxury cars, including a Bentley sedan and two Maseratis, and a three-wheel motorbike with ostrich-skin seats.[30]

Dane Schiller of the *Houston Chronicle* monitors the city's underworld connections to the cartels across the border as both a job and a driven personal fixation. Schiller's work locates the narco hub of Amexica firmly in Houston—not just for distribution of drugs and cash, and the procurement of guns, but also for killing. Killing like that of Santiago "Chago" Salinas, a Gulf cartel operative shot in the head at point-blank range in 2006 at the Baymont Inn and Suites on the Gulf Freeway, three weeks after his brother-in-law was found dead, charred in a barrel of diesel near Monterrey, across the border in Mexico. It was the third attempt on Salinas's life in one year—he had been left for dead after the first, in Mexico, when a bullet intended to kill him went through his jaw. According to Schiller, the person believed responsible for that first shooting was Daniel "Danny Boy" Zamora, who had grown up in Houston and was part of an enforcement crew for the Sinaloa cartel—himself later killed in a shoot-out in Mexico. A second attempt on Salinas's life was made in 2006 at a Mexican seafood restaurant in Houston called Chilo's—also on the Gulf Freeway, only this time the spotters got the wrong man, killing a maintenance worker in front of his family. But the third attempt killed Salinas, as he answered the door of room 142 at the Baymont. This time the killer was believed to be Danny Zamora's younger brother, Jaime, a former employee of the Houston Parks Department, accused of the murder and that of the innocent man in a seafood restaurant parking lot—as well as smuggling drugs. Jaime Zamora has since pleaded guilty to trafficking in cocaine and awaits trial in Houston for capital murder, to which charge he pleads not guilty. In another case, a married couple were found tortured to death in their home on Eastwood Drive in northwest Houston, 220 pounds of cocaine found in the attic, and the nephew of Osiel Cárdenas Guillén himself, Pedro Cárdenas, was left dead in a ditch in nearby Madden County.[31] What intrigues Schiller most, though, are two things: how the profits from all these drugs, the spoils of this war, vanish into the economy of the United States; and the figure of Osiel Cárdenas Guillén himself.

In 1999, Schiller learned, two agents from the FBI and DEA were escorting an informant around Matamoros in a jeep and were surrounded by Zeta troops. Cárdenas himself appeared, and—thinking better of executing all of them—demanded that the informant be handed over. The agents argued, "If you do that, it'll be Kiki Camarena and Félix Gallardo all over again. They'll fight you to the bitter end." Cárdenas let the convoy go.

Every day of Cárdenas's trial, which ended with his conviction in February 2010, Schiller was there, and every day he was asked to leave. "It happens every time: there I am, the only person in the public or press gallery. And every time, the marshal comes and tells me to go and wait outside. So I wait, and then it's over and time to go. It's all being done in secret again, and it's getting kind of interesting that everything is being done in secret," says Schiller of the days before the conviction. "That whatever pleas Osiel Cárdenas is being offered, he must be giving them something pretty good in return. If this man is who they say he is, and what they say he is, then he's in a position to answer quite a few questions in front of the jury box. But it never happens, and it's incredibly frustrating. This man holds the secrets of what is going on, this unlikely Al Capone, and they're making damned sure to keep them from us." Finally, on February 23, 2010, Schiller got to write this story: "Behind armed guards and locked doors—in a secret hearing of judicial privacy not even given to some 9/11 terrorists or East Coast mafia dons—Osiel Cárdenas Guillén, one of the most feared drug lords in history, was sentenced to 25 years in prison Wednesday. In a Houston courtroom sealed to the public, he also was ordered to forfeit $50 million, a small slice of his estimated earnings.[32]

"The famed drug lord has not been seen publicly since he was ushered in shackles into a Houston courtroom in 2007 to be read his rights when he arrived in Texas," Schiller continued. "Despite a protest from the *Houston Chronicle* on Wednesday that the public had a right to be present for the sentencing of one of the most hunted men in recent times—in a case that has cost American taxpayers millions—U.S. District Judge Hilda Tagle kept the hearing closed without explanation."

Which brings Schiller to his other point. "Where does it all go? The cash," he asks rhetorically, over breakfast in a diner next to a Shell gas station west of downtown Houston. "I'm no accountant," says Schiller, over breakfast at the gas station. "But fifty billion dollars profit from dealing drugs into America? It blows my mind. Or am I crazy? What I'm thinking is: If you, the United States, are not lying to us, then where is this money? Where are these people handling the money, who are they? I know that the guys on the ground in law enforcement in this town want to go through that door. They know this is the center of things now, in this war, and that's where the answer lies. But that's a hell of door to go through."

EPILOGUE: EL SOL NEGRO (THE BLACK SUN)

In ancient Mexican lore, there lies behind the sun that shines a black sun that leaves this world to shed light upon another, beneath. The Mexica believed the black sun was carried by the god of the underworld and was the maleficent herald of death, though not death as finality. The Mexica lived in a condition of expectation of calamity and catastrophe, yet their preoccupation with·death was a blend of fear and devotion to the moment of reunion with their ancestors, in the land upon which the black sun shines. And behind the sunlight of the deserts of Amexica—which turns to fire during eventide—there is some maculate, black light that gives nothing back, unshining behind the eternities of space and sky, or the bustle and music in all those labyrinthine streets lined with hot peppers and freshly gathered pistachios tumbling from every open storefront.

And one feels the rays of that dichotomous black sunshine especially after talking to Dr. Hiram Muñoz, of the forensic autopsy team back in Tijuana, where all this began. This is a man who sees the world very clearly, from the slabs on which the saprophytic corpses are laid for inspection. Dr. Muñoz defines his work as "spending my life trying to scientifically interrogate people who cannot talk, who have suffered terrible pain but now feel nothing. They can only communicate silently through the terrible things that have been done to them. I have to look for a cause, not a result. I have to rewind the movie, work out what was done, and why." Why did he choose this job? "Because I love medicine, and I love the law. And because I lost my father when I was eight years old, and in his last words, he told the doctors, 'Whatever you do, do it freely, but with exactitude.'"

Muñoz is a man of courtesy and exceptionally good humor. After discussing the various mutilations and their significance, he says that "the principal message is to the other cartels. They want respect, they want to say, 'This is what we do,' and sometimes they say it in written messages too, perhaps a joke, like the emergency number to call. There's also a message to their own people, of course: toe the line, or we will do this to you. The more brutally we get you to do things, the more brutally they could happen to you."

But there are gradations within these barbarities, and this is what fascinates Dr. Muñoz. "Sometimes they are done by a medical student, sometimes by just a butcher. It is the medical students who have something to say. They are the ones trying to speak to us. I look at a cut-off toe. How was it done? Was it done well? Was it done from the left or the right? If it was done well, exactly between the bones, the person is more dangerous. If the finger was wrapped up tight before it was cut, we know we are dealing with the medical student, employed by the cartel hierarchy. If it's just hacked off, we're dealing with a *mana*, a street thug. You need to cut it properly if you are going to send it to the victim's family, or the police.

"That Alejandra girl," he says, "the model and cheerleader, I really don't think that was the work of someone working for el Teo, as we're told. There was nothing one could do with fingers broken that crudely. When we see women and children mutilated, that is very serious—it's probably not a direct target; they're doing it to show someone else they know how to do it and to drive them mad." Decapitation, "as I told you last time you were here, that is another matter. Again, it is significant how well it was done. If it is done badly, it shows nothing more than savagery. But if it is done well, it's a primal message: not only are we going to kill you, we're going to cut you in pieces. It's a message to all of the kind from which the victim came.

"The difference is this: in what I would call normal times, I kill you and make you disappear. Now they are shouting it, turning it into a kind of grotesque carousel around their territory. In normal conditions, the torture and killing is private; now it is a public execution using extreme violence, and this is significant, I think. We need to say one thing first, however: these people are drama queens. They think what they do makes them powerful, masters of the universe. But they're not. Ultimately, what they do is pathetic. We have to remember that. They keep saying they're poor people—well, they're poor in culture, that's what they are. They have no culture.

"The narcos in the old days had been to school. They knew that to be kingpins, they had to provide light, hospitals, and schools. That way, they could keep a low profile, win respect, and protect themselves. Félix Gallardo was a businessman, using the same commercial acumen as Carlos Slim, the mobile phone man. If you play by the rules, I leave you alone. If you cross the line, I destroy you. These new people just want luxury, power, and more power until they either get arrested or killed. That is why they are doomed, and that is why they say so much about our society. They reflect a society without values. I don't even think they are against our society, I think they're products of it. People without culture or values in a society without culture or values. A society that has gone from Frank Sinatra to that 50 Cent man I see on television. They're both associated with criminals, almost everyone is if they really want to make it—but look at the difference between them! 50 Cent is the new role model for the narco, Sinatra is old school—I know which I'd rather have. The new narcos are like 50 Cent; he says it all, product of a society that's lost its way. Money and power are what counts."

Muñoz sees this point as reason to let out a raucous laugh. He is a big man, demonstrative. Can one be nostalgic for the golden age of corruption? I ask. There had been so much misplaced nostalgia for what Julián Cardona called the "classical" era of narco cartels. Dr. Muñoz retorts with another question: "Do you prefer it like it is now?"

Dr. Muñoz considers what this war means in historical terms, which I had not expected this conversation to comprise. Or maybe I had, when we met briefly and made sure to talk properly, later. "Consider how all the great civilizations fall, the marks of their last days." He cites ancient

Rome and "the terrible nature of public execution in its final phase." Torture and violent public execution had also marked, he says, "the end of the Middle Ages and the Spanish Inquisition, as they gave way to the Renaissance and science. There are these great moments of civilization, of science, but they try to be bigger and better than they are, and when they fall, they resort to grotesque public execution. And I think we are now in a moment of crisis, in the culture of global business."

Muñoz again refers to what he calls those "times of normality," when "the narcotraficante saw himself as a kind of bandit, but also a gentleman, a *patrón*. He would distribute generously, even if it was from prison, make sure the village had electric light, gifts for Mother's Day, presents for children. But this was no different from the manager of the maquiladora who allowed his workers a cigarette break or free coffee machine. It meant nothing sincere, it just kept everyone making the product." Then he reaches for what I have been calling the "postmodern" or "late capitalist" phase. "But what happens when this system reaches a state of crisis?" asks Dr. Muñoz. "Look around you: recession, crisis, factories closing. The narco is in the same position as everyone else, and everyone else is in the same position as the narco. You must keep supremacy, you must keep control. The narcotraficante is the most global of all global businessmen, and now he must make you loyal or afraid. And he must do these public executions involving mutilation as a demonstration of power, as all these cultures do, in their final phases."

I suggest that despite the heinous work he does, Dr. Muñoz strikes one as a swarthy man who appreciates the sight of a pretty girl, a good wine, a good meal. "I spend all day with the dead," he replies, "so I have a duty to love life and live it to the full. When I am with my colleagues, we are always joking about death, and joking *with* death. I live like a man who sits eating a delicious taco on the street there, aware that every moment could be his last. One bullet, and he is dead."

AFTERWORD: BLOOD MONEY

Of the Sin of Usury: To take usury for money lent is unjust in itself,
because this is to sell what does not exist, and this evidently leads
to inequality which is contrary to justice. . . . Money, according to
the Philosopher, was invented chiefly for the purpose of exchange:
and consequently the proper and principal use of money is its con-
sumption or alienation whereby it is sunk in exchange. Hence it is
by its very nature unlawful to take payment for the use of money
lent . . . and just as man is bound to restore ill-gotten goods, so is
he bound to restore the money which he has taken in usury.

—St. Thomas Aquinas, *Summa Theologica*

Just before sunset on April 10, 2006, a DC-9 landed in the port city of Ciudad del Carmen, on the Gulf of Mexico. Soldiers from the Mexican army, waiting to intercept it, found 128 cases packed with 5.7 tons of cocaine, valued at $100 million. But something else—far more important and far-reaching—was discovered in the paper trail behind the purchase of the plane by the Sinaloa narco-trafficking cartel.

During a twenty-two-month investigation by U.S. agents from the Drug Enforcement Administration, the Internal Revenue Service, and others, it emerged that the cocaine smugglers had bought the plane with money they had laundered through one of the biggest banks in the United States: Wachovia, now part of the giant Wells Fargo.

The authorities uncovered billions of dollars in wire transfers, traveler's checks, and bulk cash shipments through Mexican exchanges into

Wachovia accounts. Wachovia was put under investigation for laundering the proceeds of crime. Of special significance was that these activities began in 2004, when the first escalation of violence along the
U.S.-Mexico border ignited the drugs war.

Criminal proceedings were accordingly brought against Wachovia,
though not against any individual, but they never came to court. In
March 2010, Wachovia settled the biggest case brought under the U.S.
Bank Secrecy Act, through the U.S. District Court for the Southern District of Florida. In March 2011, when the year's "deferred prosecution"
expired, the bank was in effect in the clear.[1]

All told, Wachovia paid U.S. authorities $110 million in forfeiture,
for monies proved to be connected to drug smuggling, and a $50 million
fine for failing to monitor the former sum used to ship twenty-two tons of
cocaine.[2]

More shocking, and more important, the bank was sanctioned for failing to apply the proper and necessary anti-laundering strictures to the
transfer of $378.4 billion—a sum equivalent to one-third of Mexico's gross
domestic product—into dollar accounts from so-called *casas de cambio*
(CDCs) in Mexico, currency exchange houses with which the bank did
business.

"Wachovia's blatant disregard for our banking laws gave international cocaine cartels a virtual carte blanche to finance their operations," said Jeffrey Sloman, the federal prosecutor who handled the case.
Yet the total fine was less than 20.5 percent of the bank's $12.3 billion
profit for 2009. On March 24, 2010, Wells Fargo stock traded at
$30.86—up 1 percent on the week of the court settlement.

The conclusion to the case—greeted by a deafening silence across
the U.S. media apart from the estimable Bloomberg financial news
service—was epic.[3] But it was only the tip of an iceberg, demonstrating
the role of the "legal" banking sector in swilling hundreds of billions of
dollars—the blood money that is a result of the murderous farrago of
Mexico and other places in the world—around their global operations,
now bailed out by the taxpayer.

At the height of the 2008 banking crisis, Antonio Maria Costa, then head of the United Nations Office on Drugs and Crime, based in Vienna, said he had evidence that the proceeds from drugs and crime were "the only liquid investment capital" available to banks on the brink of collapse.

"Interbank loans were funded by money that originated from drugs trade," he said. There were "signs that some banks were rescued in that way."

Wachovia was acquired by Wells Fargo during the 2008 crash, just as Wells Fargo became a beneficiary of $25 billion in taxpayers' money. Wachovia's prosecutors were clear, however, that there was no suggestion that Wells Fargo had behaved improperly; it had cooperated fully with the investigation.

Mexico is the United States' third biggest trading partner, after Canada and China, and Wachovia was understandably interested in such a volume of legitimate trade.

But José Luis Marmolejo, who prosecuted those running one of the casas de cambio—called Puebla—at the Mexican end, said, "Wachovia handled all the transfers. They never reported any as suspicious." He added, "I am sure Wachovia knew what was going on. It went on too long and they made too much money not to have known."

While doing research on the Wachovia Mexican case, I obtained documents that had previously been provided to financial regulators. It then emerged that the alarm that was ignored came from, among other places, London, thanks to the diligence and integrity of a man who, with this case, emerges as potentially one of the most important whistle-blowers of our time. A man who, in a series of interviews over several weeks, adds detail to the documents, laying bare the story of how Wachovia exposed itself to one of the world's biggest laundering operations.

Martin Woods, from Liverpool, England, now in his midforties, joined the London office of Wachovia in February 2005, as a senior anti-money-laundering officer. He had previously served with the Metropolitan police drug squad, where he excelled. As a detective, he then joined

the money-laundering investigation team of the National Crime Squad—
Britain's equivalent to the FBI—where he worked on the British end of
the Bank of New York money-laundering scandal in the late 1990s. The
investigation into Lucy Edwards (a former Wachovia executive) and her
husband, Peter Berlin, who were laundering millions of dollars of Russian criminal money, was mounted jointly with the FBI, after the couple
moved from Queens, New York, to London.

Woods is still a cop in the best sense: punctilious, exact, with a ro-
guish humor and passion for the city's (Red) soccer team, but moral to
the core. Thus he was an ideal appointment for any bank eager to operate
a diligent and effective risk-management policy against the lucrative
scourge of high finance: laundering, knowing or otherwise, the vast proceeds of criminality, tax evasion, and dealing in arms—and drugs.

Woods had the eyes and instincts of a police officer, not those of a
banker. This influenced not only his methods but also his mentality.
"Maybe it's just something that comes from having once-Catholic roots
in Merseyside," he says. "I want to be comfortable, but I think that a lot
of things matter more than money—and that marks you out in a culture
that appears to prevail in many of the banks in the world."

Woods was set apart by his modus operandi. His speciality, he explains, was his application of a "know your client," or KYC, policing
strategy to identifying dirty money. "KYC is a fundamental approach to
anti–money laundering, going after tax evasion or counterterrorist financing. Who are your clients? Is the documentation right? Good, responsible banking involves always knowing your customer."

When Woods looked at Wachovia's operations, the first thing he noticed was a deficiency in KYC information. And among his first reports
to his superiors at the bank's headquarters in Charlotte, North Carolina,
were observations on a shortfall in KYC among Wachovia's operation
in London, which he set about correcting. At the same time he imple-
mented what is known as an enhanced transaction monitoring program,
gathering more information on clients whose money came through the
bank's offices in the City, in sterling or euros.

By August 2006, Woods's new monitoring program had identified a number of suspicious transactions "relating to casas de cambio customers located in Mexico." Primarily, these involved deposits of traveler's checks in euros. The checks had sequential numbers and the deposits were larger than any innocent traveler would need, with inadequate or no KYC information on them and what seemed to a trained eye to be dubious signatures. "It was basic work. They didn't answer the obvious questions: 'Is the transaction real, or does it look synthetic?' 'Does the traveler's check meet the protocols?' 'Is it all there, and if not, why not?'"

Woods discussed the matter with Wachovia's global head of anti–money laundering for correspondent banking—a bank receives deposits and makes payments on behalf of a foreign bank—who believed the checks could indicate tax evasion—a criminal offense in most countries. Woods undertook what banks call a "look back" at previous transactions and submitted a series of SARs, or suspicious activity reports, to the authorities in the UK and his superiors in Charlotte, urging the blocking of named parties and large series of sequentially numbered traveler's checks from Mexico. In 2006, Woods issued fifty SARs related to the casas de cambio in Mexico.

To Woods's amazement, the response from Wachovia's Miami office, the center for Latin American business, was, at best, antagonistic. One senior U.S. manager in Miami called the SARs "defensive and undeserved." The documents say that Woods "came under pressure from the business to change to develop a better understanding of Mexico."

"Wachovia," says Woods, "had totally ignored all the factors that signaled they should not have been doing this business in this way in this place. Instead of thinking, 'This is how drug trafficking works,' they would say, 'This is how the textile business works.' 'This is textiles, I am in Mexico' was the message I was getting. 'I know Mexico better than you.' 'I'm in Mexico, you're not.' To which I thought, 'Well, I know money laundering better than you do.' My job was to use my abilities to try and spot money laundering through the bank that was employing me. That's what I was paid to do, and that's what I was doing. But that didn't matter. They were interested only in how to make more money for the bank so that they could make more for themselves. Their reaction could have been, 'You are exactly the kind of person we need to work for this bank,' but instead some held the view, 'You'll never work for this bank again.' It was reverse logic and a continued endorsement of the criminality."

As it turned out, Woods was on the right track. Wachovia's business in Mexico was coming under closer and closer scrutiny by U.S. law enforcement. Wachovia was served with a number of subpoenas for information on its Mexican operation. Woods has subsequently been informed that "Wachovia had six or seven thousand subpoenas, an absurd number. So at what point does someone at the highest level not get the feeling that something is very, very wrong?"

In April and May 2007, Wachovia—as a result of increasing interest and pressure from the U.S. attorney's office—began to end its relationship with some of the casas de cambio. But rather than launch an internal investigation into Woods's alerts over Mexico, Wachovia hung its own money-laundering expert out to dry. According to Woods, the records show that during 2007, "I continued to submit more SARs related to the casas de cambio, and I continued to come under pressure from the bank.'"

In July 2007, Wachovia's remaining ten Mexican casa de cambio clients operating through London suddenly stopped doing so. Woods did not believe this simultaneous action was coincidental; indeed, he was concerned that the abrupt cessation of business was a response to a tip-off as the feds advanced on the bank. Later in 2007, after the investigation of Wachovia was reported in the U.S. financial media, the bank finally ended all remaining relationships with the Mexican casas de cambio globally.

By this time, Woods's personal situation within the bank had become untenable. While the bank acted on one level to protect itself from the federal investigation into its shortcomings, on another it focused on the man who had been among the first to spot them. Woods sought guidance from a London law firm, which, he says, "agreed with my concerns," upon which he filed further SARs relating to the money from Mexico, requesting information from the bank that would assist him with his inquiries. "I was given nothing," he recalls. "Many of my e-mail requests to senior managers went unanswered." On June 16, Woods was told by Wachovia's global head of compliance that his latest SAR need not have been filed, that he had no legal requirement to investigate an overseas case even if the money involved was coming through London, and no right of access to Wachovia documents held overseas.

Woods's life went into free fall. He was hospitalized with a prolapsed disc and notified the office, and he was told by the bank that he had not done so in the appropriate manner as directed by the employees handbook. He was off work for three weeks, returning in August 2007 to find a letter from the bank's compliance managing director, dated August 7, which was unrelenting in its tone and words of warning. The letter addressed itself to what the manager called "specific examples of your failure to perform at an acceptable standard." The "performance failures are more than just repeated instances of your continuing performance problems but are now operating to put the business for which you are the registered Money Laundering Reporting Officer in serious potential regulatory jeopardy. You are also putting the entire London AML (anti-money-laundering) Compliance Program at risk by your failure to perform." The letter even predicted, in a twist of ultimate irony, the upcoming federal case against Wachovia: "I have explained in detail," wrote the manager, "the potential regulatory jeopardy (large fines, regulatory sanctions, reputational damage, etc.) that can result from failures in a regulated firm's AML program."

The managing director added, "Your continued failure to concentrate your work efforts on agreed upon priorities is placing the business for which you [are] the MLRO in [an] unacceptable position." Woods was accused of "failure to review our high risk customer population," of all things. The letter made further—now bitterly ironic—reference to "this serious situation in which we find ourselves" and threatened "the formal setting of a disciplinary hearing" in which to resolve it. The date was set for August 12, but it was postponed. Woods, on the verge of a breakdown, was put on sick leave by his doctor on August 11.

In his written responses, Woods set out his case and related all that had come across his desk from Mexico, only to be told that the hearing would take place on August 26, in Woods's absence if necessary. Woods applied for an extension and was granted one "until such time as I had returned to work." Woods was duly given psychiatric treatment, enrolled in a stress management course, and put on medication. His doctor advised him that returning to work "would have a severe adverse impact upon my health."

Late in 2007, Woods attended a social function at Scotland Yard, where colleagues from the United States were being entertained. There, he sought out a representative of the Drug Enforcement Administration and told him about the casas de cambio, the SARs, and his employer's reaction. The feds and officials of the office of the comptroller of the currency in Washington, DC—the part of the Treasury Department that regulates and supervises all national banks—then "spent a lot of time examining the SARs" that Woods had sent to Charlotte from London.

"Their liaison people in London got back in touch with me a while afterward, and we began to put the pieces of the jigsaw together. The money coming through London, in euros, was a drop in the ocean of Wachovia's business with the Mexican casas de cambio," says Woods, "but it was a small window through which the parent organization could and should have looked at the dollar operation"—which was exactly what the U.S. authorities were now doing. What they found was, according to Antonio Maria Costa, former head of the UN Office on Drugs and Crime, merely the tip of the iceberg of what was happening to drug money in the banking industry, but at least it was visible and it had a name: Wachovia.

Back in June 2005, the DEA, the criminal division of the Internal Revenue Service, and the U.S. attorney's office in Miami began investigating wire transfers from Mexico to the United States. They were traced back to correspondent bank accounts held by casas de cambio at Wachovia. The accounts were supervised and managed by a business unit of Wachovia in the bank's offices in Miami. A CDC, explained the court documents in the case, "is not a bank." It is a "licensed non-bank currency exchange business" that does not hold deposits, maintain accounts or issue lines of credit, but does allow for exchange from, in Mexico, dollars to pesos and vice versa.

"Through CDCs," said the court document, "persons in Mexico can use hard currency . . . and wire transfer the value of that currency to U.S. bank accounts to purchase items in the United States or other countries." The "nature of the CDC business allows money launderers the opportunity to move drug dollars that are in Mexico into CDCs and ultimately into the U.S. banking system."

The document continues, "On numerous occasions, monies were deposited into a CDC by a drug trafficking organization. Using false identities, the CDC then wired that money through its Wachovia correspondent bank accounts for the purchase of airplanes for drug trafficking organizations." The court settlement of 2010 would detail that "nearly $13 million went through correspondent bank accounts at Wachovia for the purchase of aircraft to be used in the illegal narcotics trade. From these aircraft, more than twenty thousand kilograms of cocaine were seized."

All this occurred despite the fact that Wachovia's office was in Miami, designated by the U.S. government as a "high-intensity money laundering and related financial crime area" as well as a "high intensity drug trafficking area." Since the drug cartel war began in 2005, Mexico had been designated a high-risk source of money-laundering activity.

In April 2006, say the court papers, FinCEN—Financial Crimes Enforcement Network, an agency of the Treasury Department responsible for fighting money laundering—"warned the U.S. banking and financial industry of potential misuse of correspondent banking relationships with Mexican CDCs. FinCEN specifically warned of the repatriation of bulk cash, multiple wire transfers initiated by CDCs remitting funds to jurisdictions outside of Mexico that bear no apparent business relationship with the CDC." "As early as 2004," the agreed court settlement would read, "Wachovia understood the risk that was associated with doing business with the Mexican CDCs. Wachovia was aware of the general industry warnings. As early as July 2005, Wachovia was aware that other large U.S. banks were exiting the CDC business based on AML (anti-money-laundering) concerns." But "despite these warnings, Wachovia remained in business."

Not only that, they then took over the business of another bank that was pulling out because of difficulties with dirty money. "In September 2005, Wachovia purchased the right to solicit the international correspondent banking customers of Union Bank of California (UBOC). Wachovia knew that UBOC was exiting the CDC market due to AML problems. Wachovia hired at least one person from UBOC who had a significant role in the CDC business at UBOC. After UBOC exited the CDC business, Wachovia's business volume increased notably."

On March 16, 2010, Douglas Edwards, senior vice president of Wachovia Bank, put his signature to page ten of a twenty-five-page settlement, in which the bank—but no individual—admitted its role as outlined by the prosecutors. On page eleven, he signed again, as senior VP of Wells Fargo. The documents show Wachovia providing three services to twenty-two CDCs in Mexico: wire transfers, a "bulk cash service," and a "pouch deposit service" to accept "deposit items drawn on U.S. banks, e.g., checks and traveler's checks," as spotted by Martin Woods in London.

Between May 1, 2004, and May 31, 2007, Wachovia processed at least $373.6 billion in CDCs and $4.7 billion in bulk cash, a total of more than $378.4 billion—a sum that dwarfs the budgets debated by U.S. state and UK local authorities to provide (or not provide) services to citizens.

The damning settlement document gives a fascinating insight into how the laundering of blood money works. It details how investigators "found readily identifiable evidence of red flags of large-scale money laundering." There were "structured wire transactions" in which "it was commonplace in the CDC accounts for round-number wires to be made on the same day or in close succession, by the same wire senders, for the benefit of the same account."

Over two days, "ten wire transfers by four individuals . . . went though Wachovia for deposit into an aircraft broker's escrow account. All of the transfers were in round numbers. None of the individuals or [the] business that wired money had any connection to the aircraft or the entity that allegedly owned the aircraft. The investigation has further revealed that the identities of the individuals who sent the money were false and that the business was a shell entity. The plane was subsequently seized with approximately 2,000 kilograms of cocaine aboard." And there was more to come: "On another occasion, over a seven-day period, a CDC sent more than $1.3 million in wire transfers through Wachovia for deposit into a plane broker's accounts. These were a total of fifteen wires, and they ranged in amount from $63,000 to $127,500. All of this money was intended for the purchase of an aircraft, but the money was seized by law enforcement before the deal was completed."

According to the document, many of the sequentially numbered traveler's checks, of the kind dealt with by Woods, contained "unusual markings" or "lacked any legible signature." Meanwhile, "Many of the CDCs that used Wachovia's bulk cash service sent significantly more cash to Wachovia than what Wachovia had expected. More specifically, many of the CDCs exceeded their monthly activity by at least 50 percent."

Recognizing these "red flags," the U.S. attorney's office in Miami, the IRS, and the DEA began investigating Wachovia, later joined by FinCEN, while the office of the comptroller of the currency carried out a "parallel investigation." The violations they found were, says the document, "serious and systemic and allowed certain Wachovia customers to launder millions of dollars of proceeds from the sale of illegal narcotics through Wachovia accounts over an extended time period. The investigation has identified at least $110 million in drug proceeds were funneled through the CDC accounts held at Wachovia."

The document cited seven areas: (1) "lack of policies, procedures, or monitoring controls governing the repatriation of nearly $14 billion of United States dollars in bulk cash for high-risk CDCs and other foreign correspondent bulk cash customers"; (2) "failure to conduct monitoring of over $40 billion in monetary instruments flowing through international foreign correspondent accounts in the form of RDC [remote deposit capture] for a two-year period"; (3) "failure to conduct adequate levels of due diligence of high-risk CDC customers"; (4) "failure to adequately monitor . . . to fulfill suspicious activity reporting obligations"; (5) "failure to implement monitoring controls or limits for sequentially numbered traveler's checks"; (6) "failure to detect and report suspicious activity in a timely manner on the $378.4 billion in wire transfers that were processed by Wachovia for the CDCs"; and (7) "failure to implement effective anti-laundering audit coverage." The staggering $378.4 billion was overlooked, according to Wachovia, because its Philadelphia office, which was tasked with monitoring wire transfers, had only a month for its investigation. The anti-money-laundering unit "could not keep up with the volume of wires. The suspicious activity went effectively unmonitored."

With regard to bulk cash: "Wachovia had no formal written policy or procedure for the monitoring of bulk cash to ensure that suspicious activity was reported." Wachovia continued to accept $47 billion in "remote deposits" such as traveler's checks and money orders, although "none of these instruments were subject to examination for 'smurfing' [executing financial transactions in such a way that they do not leave a paper trail], structuring, or other common money-laundering techniques associated with these types of instruments." The authorities found that 64 percent of the checks "contained unusual markings" of the kind that are "readily identifiable patterns of money laundering activity." Wachovia "failed to establish any internal policy or monitoring procedures to implement or enforce" its own rules on standard pouch activity.

The settlement concludes by discussing Wachovia's "considerable cooperation and remedial actions" since the prosecution was initiated, after the bank was bought by Wells Fargo. "In consideration of Wachovia's remedial actions," concludes the prosecutor, "the United States shall recommend to the Court . . . that prosecution of Wachovia on the Information filed . . . be deferred for a period of twelve months."

While the federal prosecution proceeded, Woods had remained out in the cold. On Christmas Eve 2008, Woods's lawyers filed suit against Wachovia for bullying and detrimental treatment of a whistle-blower. The case was settled in May 2009, by which time Woods felt as though he was "the most toxic person in the bank . . . no one would talk to me."

Wachovia agreed to pay an undisclosed amount, in return for which Woods left the bank and agreed not to make public the terms of the settlement.

After years of tribulation, Woods was finally formally vindicated, though not by Wachovia: A letter dated March 19, 2010—three days after the settlement in Miami—arrived from John Dugan, then the comptroller of the currency in Washington. Dugan said he was "writing to personally recognize and express my appreciation for the role that you played in the actions brought against Wachovia Bank for violations of the bank secrecy act. . . . Not only did the information that you provided facilitate our investigation, but you demonstrated great personal courage and integrity by speaking up when you saw problems. Without the efforts of individuals like you, actions such as the one taken against Wachovia would not be possible."

The so-called deferred prosecution detailed in the Miami document is a form of probation whereby if the bank abides by the law for a year, charges are dropped. So in March 2011 the bank was in the clear. The week that the deferred prosecution expired, a spokeswoman for Wells Fargo said the parent bank had no comment to make on the documentation pertaining to Woods's case, or his allegations. She added that there was no comment on prosecutor Sloman's remarks to the court; a provision in the settlement stipulated that Wachovia was not allowed to issue public statements that contradicted it.

But the Wachovia settlement leaves a sour taste in many mouths, in law enforcement and especially in Woods's. The deferred prosecution is part of this "cop-out all round," he says. "The regulatory authorities do not have to spend any more time on it, and they don't have to push it as far as a criminal trial. They just issue criminal proceedings, and settle, so it never has to go to trial. The law enforcement people do what they are supposed to do, but what's the point? All those people taking all that money from drug trafficking and murder, and no one goes to jail? You are not going to stop them that way, because there's no incentive for them to do so. And you are not making my job any easier trying to stop this from happening, nor are you making it any easier for law enforcement."

. . .

One of the foremost figures in the training of anti-money-laundering officers is Robert Mazur, lead infiltrator for U.S. law enforcement of the Colombian Medellín cartel during the epic prosecution and collapse of the Bank of Credit and Commerce International in 1991 (his story was made famous by his memoir, *The Infiltrator*). Mazur, whose firm Chase & Associates works closely with law enforcement and trains officers for bank anti-money-laundering efforts, cast a keen eye over the case against Wachovia and, in an interview, he says now that "the only thing that will make the banks properly vigilant to what is happening is when they hear the rattle of handcuffs in the boardroom."

With the DEA in Miami declining to return calls relating to the Wachovia case, Mazur's view is all the more compelling. "Why did [Wachovia] think they were getting $400 billion from Mexico? Did they really think all that money was coming from family transfers? I mean, that kind of money, even if it was in twenty-dollar bills (and it was probably banked in fives or tens), comes to about *725 tons* of twenty-dollar bills!" Mazur says, "I know a lot of people like Martin Woods, who are very well intentioned. I know three people who worked for Wachovia and were doing the same thing as he was—former law enforcement, brave souls. But ultimately, the bank's actions are determined by the business model— how can the bank ultimately make a profit?—and that will undermine the work that people like Martin are trying to do."

Mazur found that "a lot of the law enforcement people were disappointed to see a settlement" between the administration and Wachovia. "But I know that there were some external circumstances that worked to Wachovia's benefit, not least that the U.S. banking system was on the edge of total collapse."

What concerns Mazur is that what both law enforcement and politicians can hope to achieve against the cartels is limited and falls short of the obvious attack the United States could make in its war on drugs: Follow the money.

"We're thinking way too small," Mazur says. "I train law enforcement officers, thousands of them every year, and they say to me that if they tried to do half of what I did, they'd be arrested. But I tell them, 'You got to think big. The headlines you will be reading in seven years' time will be the result of the work you begin now.' With BCCI, we had to spend two years setting it up, two years doing undercover work, and another two years getting it to trial. If they want to do something big, like go after the money, that's how long it takes."

But, says Mazur, "If you look at the career ladders of law enforcement, there's no incentive to go after the big money. People move every two to three years. The DEA is focused on drug trafficking rather than money laundering. You get a quicker result that way—they want to get the traffickers and seize their assets. But this is like treating a sick plant by cutting off a few branches—it just grows new ones.

"Going after the big money is cutting down the plant—it's a harder door to knock on, it's a longer haul, and it won't get you the short-term riches." It is the same for politicians, Mazur adds. "Congressmen and -women have to get elected every two or six years, so they're on the same short-term career ladder, needing to show short-term results."

The office of the comptroller of the currency is still examining whether individuals at Wachovia are criminally liable. Sources at Fin-CEN say that, as directed by the settlement and agreed to by Wachovia, a look back is in process into the $378.4 billion that was not directly associated with the aircraft purchases and cocaine hauls, but neither subject to the proper anti-laundering checks. A FinCEN source says that $20 billion already examined appears to have "suspicious origins." But this is just the beginning.

Antonio Maria Costa, executive director of the UN's Office on Drugs and Crime from May 2002 to August 2010, charts the history of the contamination of the global banking industry by drug and criminal money since his first initiatives to try to curb it while at the European Commission during the 1990s. "The connection between organized crime and financial institutions started in the late 1970s, early 1980s," he says, "when the mafia became globalized, with the economy."

Until then, criminal money had circulated largely in cash, with the authorities making the occasional spectacular "sting" or haul. During Costa's time as director for economics and finance at the EC in Brussels, from 1987, inroads were made against penetration of banks by criminal laundering, and "criminal money started moving back to cash, out of the financial institutions and banks. Then two things happened: the financial crisis in Russia, after the emergence of the Russian mafia, and the crises of 2003 and 2007–08.

"With these crises," says Costa, "the banking sector was short of liquidity, so the banks exposed themselves to the criminal syndicates, who had cash in hand. It was pure quid pro quo: Banks needed cash, and criminal syndicates needed somewhere to put their cash. And we are talking about huge amounts of money." Criminal syndicates, he says, "will penetrate where there is least resistance, where the banks' need is greatest. So it was Western Europe in 2003 and the USA and UK in 2007–08. It's not suddenly one moment, one place; they get in progressively and they get in deep, buying up shares, buying up major assets."

Costa questions the readiness of governments and their bank regulatory structures to challenge this large-scale corruption of the global economy: "I wonder to what extent government regulators accepted—for want of a better term—this situation and were aware of what was going on. If money was coming into the banking sector, they seem to have adopted a policy of 'Don't ask, don't tell.' They knew that once the money is in the system, it is in the system—and you do not have the right to ask questions. Governments," he adds, with a perceptive sting, "certainly showed what they were capable of when the issue suddenly changed to laundering money for terrorism. Suddenly they became serious and changed their attitude."

It's hardly surprising, then, that with regard to Mexico, Wachovia does not appear to be the end of the line. In August 2010, it emerged in quarterly disclosures by the giant bank HSBC that the U.S. Justice Department was seeking to fine HSBC for anti-money-laundering compliance problems reported to include dealings with Mexico. On October 7, 2010, Reuters put out the following report:

The Federal Reserve issued an order on Thursday against HSBC North American Holdings Inc, requiring the bank to improve its practices to prevent customers from laundering money . . . through its accounts. The U.S. Office of the Comptroller of the Currency issued a related order against the U.S. subsidiary of HSBC, for violating a law governing how the company reports and assesses suspicious activity around its accounts, including international wire transfers and large cash withdrawals. HSBC is Europe's largest bank.

The regulators have not fined HSBC for the violations, but they could in the future. The OCC said its order "does not preclude" it from assessing a civil money penalty against the bank. The regulators' orders come amid heightened U.S. government attention to how major banks monitor and report suspicious activity, including signs of money laundering, from their accounts. . . .

The OCC said in its complaint that HSBC Bank USA's "compliance program and its implementation are ineffective, and accompanied by aggravating factors, such as highly suspicious activity creating a significant potential for unreported money laundering or terrorist financing." [4]

The regulator cited inadequate staffing, incomplete reviews and reporting of suspected suspicious activity from HSBC accounts, and insufficient monitoring of funds transfers and the financial activities of the bank's "high-risk" customers. HSBC said in a statement it was cooperating fully with its regulators and it was "committed to prompt resolution." [2] Mazur, for his part, says, "My information is that this investigation will go much deeper than the Wachovia case."

"Wachovia had my résumé, they knew who I was," says Martin Woods. "But they did not want to know. Their attitude was, 'Why are you doing this?' They should have been on my side, because they were compliance people, not commercial people. But they weren't, really; they were commercial people all along.

"We're talking about hundreds of millions of dollars," Woods continues, his police officer's mind-set affording him a moment of rage. "This is the biggest money-laundering scandal of our time. In a global context, there has never been anything like this. And we need to ask some fundamental questions: Where does the money come from and what is the message if no one goes to jail? Responsibility for the failures is admitted, but no one is held accountable? Isn't that how the global crisis happened? Because no one at the banks was held accountable?

"These are the proceeds of murder and misery in Mexico, and of drugs sold around the world," he goes on. "All the law enforcement people wanted to see this come to trial. But no one goes to jail. What does the settlement do to fight the cartels? Nothing—it doesn't make the job of law enforcement easier and it encourages the cartels and anyone who wants to make money by laundering their blood dollars. Where's the risk? There is none—there is only an upside.

"Is it in the interest of the American people to encourage both the drug cartels and the banks in this way? Is it in the interest of the Mexican people? It's simple: If you don't see the correlation between the money laundering by banks and the thirty thousand people killed in Mexico, you're missing the point."

Woods feels unable to rest on his laurels. He tours the world for a consultancy he now runs, Hermes Forensic Solutions, counseling and speaking to banks on the dangers of laundering criminal money and how to spot and stop it.

"New York and London," says Woods, "have become the world's two biggest laundries of criminal and drug money, and offshore tax havens. Not the Cayman Islands, not the British Virgin Islands, not the Isle of Man or Jersey. The big laundering is right through the City of London and Wall Street.

"After the Wachovia case, no one in the regulatory community sat down with me and asked, 'What happened?' or 'What can we do to avoid this happening to other banks?'

"In fact, on the face of it they are not interested. They are the same people who attack the whistle-blowers, and this is a position the FSA [the UK's Financial Services Authority] at least has adopted on legal advice: It has been advised that the privacy and confidentiality of banking and bankers take primacy over the Public Information Disclosure Act. That is how the priorities work: secrecy first, the public interest second.

"Meanwhile, the drug industry has two products: money and suffering. On the one hand, you have massive profits and enrichment. On the other, you have massive suffering, misery, and death. You cannot separate one from the other. When I saw what I saw, I wasn't caught between a rock and a hard place; I was in a difficult place, and I only had one honorable option: to speak up.

"What happened at Wachovia was symptomatic of the failure of the entire regulatory system to apply the kind of proper governance and adequate risk management that would have prevented not just the laundering of blood money but also the global crisis."

NOTES

INTRODUCTION: AMEXICA

1. Molly Molloy, New Mexico State University, Las Cruces, "Fronterizo List," December 31, 2009. Molloy's collection of documents is the definitive historical record of the carnage in Juárez.
2. Annual Report, Chamber of Commerce, Laredo, Texas, 2009.
3. A good guide to border Spanglish is *Cabo Bob's Mexican Slang*, slang101.com.
4. Tomás Ybarra-Frausto, "Rasquachismo," in *Puro Border*, ed. Luis Humberto Crosthwaite, John William Byrd, and Bobby Byrd (El Paso: Cinco Puntos Press, 2003), p. 191.
5. Gloria Anzaldúa, *Borderlands*, 3rd ed. (San Francisco: Aunt Lute Books, 2007), p. 25.
6. Bernardino de Sahagún, *A History of Ancient Mexico*, trans. Fanny R. Bandelier (Nashville: Fisk University Press, 1932).
7. Eduardo Matos Moctezuma, *Los Aztecas* (Mexico City: Consejo Nacional para la Cultura y las Artes, 2000), pp. 31–51.
8. Interview with Dr. Miguel Olmos Aguilera. See his "Imaginando Fronteras: Representación y Ficción en la Frontera Norte," paper presented at "La Frontera: Una Nueva Concepción Cultural" conference, Universitad Piloto de Colombia, 2004.
9. See Alejandro Lugo, *Fragmented Lives, Assembled Parts* (Austin: University of Texas Press, 2008), pp. 20–24.
10. The best history of the frontier is Leon C. Metz, *Border: The U.S.-Mexico Line* (El Paso: Mangan Books, 1989), p. 31.

11. Ted Conover, *Coyotes* (New York: Vintage, 1987), p. xviii.

12. Conversation with Roberto Saviano, Rome, 2008.

13. Daniel Borunda, "El Pasoans Stay Uneasy as Slayings Continue," *El Paso Times*, August 17, 2008.

14. Chris Kraul, "'Captain Nemo' Is Grounded," *Los Angeles Times*, December 14, 2008.

15. Laurence Iliff, "Mexico Drug Cartels' Banners Escalate Attacks Against Calderón's Government," *Dallas Morning News*, December 13, 2008.

16. Diana Washington Valdez, "Firearms in Mexico Have Ties to El Paso," *El Paso Times*, December 13, 2008.

17. "Gunmen Kill Family of Mexican Drug Hero," CBS News/Associated Press, December 23, 2008.

18. "TV Station Targeted in Attack," *Los Angeles Times* wire, January 7, 2009.

19. CNN/World Co., February 4, 2009.

20. Dan Glaister, "US Surge Plan to Contain Mexico Drug Violence," *Guardian*, January 10, 2009.

21. Molloy, "Fronterizo List," December 5, 2009.

22. Stewart Powell et al., "Mexico to Begin Receiving Drug-Fighting Aid," *Houston Chronicle*, December 4, 2009.

23. Dudley Althaus, "Zetas Terrorizing Border Outposts," *Houston Chronicle*, December 14, 2009.

24. "Police Arrest Man Linked to Slayings of 2000," *El Paso Times*, December 11, 2009.

25. Committee to Protect Journalists, press release, November 2, 2009.

26. Mark Stephenson, Associated Press bulletin, December 18, 2009.

27. Tracy Wilkinson, "Mexican Drug Raid Hero's Family Slaughtered," *Los Angeles Times*, December 23, 2009.

28. Associated Press, January 8, 2010.

29. Molloy, "Fronterizo List."

30. Ibid.

31. Associated Press, December 31, 2009.

1: LA PLAZA

1. Various articles by Alfredo Corchado in *The Dallas Morning News*, especially May 30, 2008; and Elaine Shannon, *Desperados* (New York: Viking, 1988), pp. 31–42.

2. Dudley Althaus, "Cartels Have Mexican Citizens Trembling," *Houston Chronicle*, July 19, 2008.

3. For a full account of the American secret services' role in cocaine dealing and the contras, see Gary Webb, *Dark Alliance* (New York: Seven Stories Press, 1998); Shannon, *Desperados*; and Michael Levine, *The Big White Lie* (New York: Thunder's Mouth Press, 1993).

4. Don Winslow, *The Power of the Dog* (New York: Knopf, 2005), p. 103.

5. See Terence E. Poppa, *Drug Lord* (El Paso: Cinco Puntos, 2010), pp. 135–238.

6. Statement by Anthony Placido, assistant administrator for intelligence, U.S. Drug Enforcement Administration, before the U.S. Senate Judiciary Committee on Crime and Drugs, March 17, 2009.

7. Tony Payan, "The Drug War and the Border," in *The Last Frontier*, ed. Jane Juffer (Durham, NC: Duke University Press, 2006), pp. 864–65.

8. *Proceso*, no headline—part of summary of killings, February 25, 2009; and *Los Angeles Times*, wire service, February 26, 2009.

9. Tracy Wilkinson, "Women Play Bigger Role in Mexico's Drug War," *Los Angeles Times*, November 10, 2009.

10. Marcela Turati, "Chapos Contra Zetas," *Proceso*, June 30, 2009, and various articles by Alfredo Corchado, *Dallas Morning News*, during 2008.

11. Jorge Chabat, op-ed, *El Universal*, December 20, 2009.

12. Ken Ellingwood, "Drug Cartel Boss Arturo Beltrán Leyva and the Luxurious RIPs of Mexico's Narcos," *Los Angeles Times*, December 21, 2009.

13. Tracy Wilkinson, "Mexican Family Slaughtered as Drug Lords Take Revenge," *Los Angeles Times*, December 23, 2009.

14. See full account in Poppa, *Drug Lord*.

15. For a full account of Carrillo Fuentes's takeover and running of the Juárez cartel, see Charles Bowden, *Down by the River* (New York: Simon & Schuster, 2002).

16. Tracy Wilkinson, "'El Chapo' Has Left the Building," *Los Angeles Times*, December 3, 2008.

17. *Los Angeles Times* wire, June 18, 2009.

18. *Corriere della Sera*, Milan, October 2, 2008.

19. Quoted on Fox News/Associated Press, April 3, 2009.

20. Private briefings with Mexican diplomatic sources, London, 2009; UK Interpol sources, London 2009; and U.S. DEA sources, Washington, D.C., 2008. See also Mark Townsend, "How the Liverpool Docks Became a Hub of Europe's Deadly Cocaine Trade," *Observer*, May 16, 2010.

21. Julia Preston and Samuel Dillon, *Opening Mexico* (New York: Farrar, Straus and Giroux, 2004), p. 500.

22. Ibid.

23. Dane Schiller, "DEA: Bribes Taint Late Mexican Drug Czar," *Houston Chronicle*, May 13, 2009.

24. Speaking on MSNBC Television, April 9, 2009.

25. Quoted in Leslie Berenstein and Sandra Dibble, "Border Bloodshed Likely to Worsen," *San Diego Union-Tribune*, October 5, 2008.

26. Ken Ellingwood, "U.S. Shares Blame for Mexico Drug Violence," *Los Angeles Times*, March 18, 2009.

2: AQUÍ EMPIEZA LA PATRIA (HERE BEGINS THE HOMELAND)

1. Pablo Vila, "Identificaciones de Región, Etnia y Nación en la Frontera Entre México-EU" (Universidad Autonóma de Ciudad Juárez, 2004), p. 47.

2. See Luis Alberto Urrea, *Across the Wire* (New York: Anchor, 1993).

3. For a full account of the "Instituto Set" and AFO drug smugglers, see Anne-Marie O'Connor: "Seduction of a Generation," *Los Angeles Times Magazine*, July 28, 2002.

4. For a full account of Alfredo Hodoyán's abduction, and of what the U.S. embassy in Mexico City did and did not know about it, see Julia Preston and Craig Pyes, "Witness to Evil," *New York Times*, August 18, 1997.

5. Redacción, *El Universal*, January 25, 2009; Marc Lacey, "Mexican Man Admits Using Acid on Bodies," *New York Times*, January 26, 2009.

6. Rafael Morales Magaña, "Edecán Era Informante," *El Mexicano*, August 13, 2009.

7. Dudley Althaus, "With Mexico's Violence, Nothing Is Sacred," *Houston Chronicle*, July 2, 2009.

8. See Tim Gaynor, *Midnight on the Line* (New York: St. Martin's Press, 2009), pp. 77–100.

9. See Alfonso A. Cortez Lara, Megan K. Donovan, and Scott Whiteford, "The All-American Canal Lining Dispute: An American Resolution over Mexican Groundwater Rights?" *Frontera Norte* 21, no. 41 (Enero–Junio 2009).

3: EL CAMINO DEL DIABLO (THE DEVIL'S HIGHWAY)

1. Pinau Merlin, *Desert Holes* (Tucson: Arizona-Sonora Desert Museum Press, 1999), pp. 51–53.

2. Stephen Trimble, *The People* (Santa Fe: School of American Research Press, 1993), p. 131.

3. Luis Alberto Urrea, *The Devil's Highway* (New York: Little, Brown, 2004), p. 85.

4. Richard Felger and Bill Broyles, eds., *Dry Borders* (Salt Lake City: University of Utah Press, 2007), p. xiii.

5. For full accounts of the Wellton disaster, see Ken Ellingwood, *Hard Line* (New York: Pantheon, 2004); and Urrea, *Devil's Highway*.

6. See Metz, *The Border*, pp. 385–95.

7. Quoted in Urrea, *Devil's Highway*, p. 12.

8. Josh Meyer, "Sinaloa Cartel May Resort to Deadly Force in U.S.," *Los Angeles Times*, May 6, 2009.

9. Interviewed in Salt Lake City, November 2009 (real name withheld).

10. Joel Millman, "Immigrants Become Hostages as Gangs Prey on Mexicans," *Wall Street Journal*, June 10, 2009.

11. Ibid.

12. For a history of Pitiquito and its mission and church, see Claudio Murrieta, "Las Paredes Hablan" (Pitiquito, 2004).

13. Redacción, *L'Expreso* (Hermosillo), October 30, 2009; and Tracy Wilkinson, "Mexican Farm-Workers Activist, 14 Others Slain," *Los Angeles Times*, November 1, 2009.

14. Winston P. Erickson, *Sharing the Desert: The Tohono O'odham in History* (Tucson: University of Arizona Press, 1994), p. 25.

15. Ibid., pp. 69–70.

16. Ruth M. Underhill et al., *Rainhouse and Ocean: Speeches for the Papago Year* (Tucson: University of Arizona Press, 1997), pp. 17–37.

17. Ralph Vartabedian, "US Soldiers, Law Officers Snared in Border Drug Sting," *Los Angeles Times*, May 13, 2005. Also Brenda Norrell, "US Soldiers Ran Border Cocaine Operation," Censored News, July 23, 2007, and "Army Soldiers Sentenced in Drug Sting," *Arizona Daily Star*, December 17, 2006.

18. Carol Ann Alaimo, "FBI: Military Recruiters Ran Cocaine," *Arizona Daily Star*, December 17, 2006, and Narcosphere.com, "FBI: Recruiters Caught in Drug Probe," www.unsolvedmysteries.com/usm469076.html?t=Conspiracy.

19. For a history of the narcocorrido genre and Los Tigres' career, see Elijah Wald, *Narcocorrido* (New York: Harper, 2001).

20. Randal Archibold, "Mexican Drug Cartel Violence Spills Over, Alarming U.S.," *New York Times*, March 22, 2009.

21. Interviewed by Martin Hodgson, "Death in the Midday Sun," *Observer*, London, September 19, 2004.

22. Tracy Wilkinson, "Song Banned, Band Pulls Out," *Los Angeles Times*, October 29, 2009.

23. Dudley Althaus, "Singer Shot to Death After Surgery in Matamoros ER," *Houston Chronicle*, December 4, 2007.

INTERMISSION: THE BUSINESS END OF A 12-GAUGE—BARRETT AND MORGAN'S WAR

1. Miriam Davidson, *Lives on the Line* (Tucson: University of Arizona Press, 2000), p. 13.
2. Lee Morgan II, *The Reaper's Line* (Tucson: Rio Nuevo, 2006).
3. Interview with former agent Jaime González, Austin, 2009.
4. Quoted in Sebastian Rotella, "Mexican American Former Anti-Drug Chief's Reputation on Trial," *Los Angeles Times*, November 22, 2009.
5. Stan Tekiela, *Mammals of Arizona* (Cambridge, MN: Adventure Publications, 2008).
6. Associated Press, September 18, 2009.

4: URBAN FRANKENSTEIN

1. Associated Press, February 24, 2009.
2. CCPSSJ report, quoted in *El Diario de Juárez*, January 11, 2010.
3. For an excellent discussion of the city's origins and name, see Lugo, *Fragmented Lives*.
4. Quoted in Metz, *Border*, pp. 168–69. The book also contains a detailed account of the development of the twin cities, Juárez and El Paso.
5. Charles Bowden, *Murder City: Ciudad Juárez and the Global Economy's New Killing Fields* (New York: Nation Books, 2010).
6. Redacción, *El Diario de Juárez*, November 14, 2008.
7. See various entries by Bill Conroy on Narcosphere.com. Search "Ramirez" or click on Conroy byline.
8. Alicia Caldwell, Associated Press, September 9, 2009.
9. See *Guillermo Eduardo Ramirez-Peyro, Petitioner v. Alberto Gonzales, Attorney General of the United States*. United States Court of Appeals for the Eighth Circuit, no. 06-1569, January 12, 2007.
10. U.S. Department of Justice, Executive Office of Immigration Review, in the matter of Espino-Ledezma, Martin. File no. 074-876-432 (lead).
11. Lugo, *Fragmented Lives*, p. 119.

12. *El Diario de Juárez*, July 17, 2009.

13. For a full account of troops dressing up as criminals, and vice versa, see Ignacio Alvarado Álvarez, "Desapariciones y Masacres," *El Universal*, April 8, 2008.

14. Ken Ellingwood, *Los Angeles Times*, February 27, 2009.

15. Steve Fainaru and William Booth, "An Army Takeover Quells Violence in Mexico," *Washington Post*, April 21, 2009.

16. Ibid.

17. *Proceso*, no byline, June 15, 2009.

18. Ramon Bracamontes, "Mexican Cartel Battle Shifts," *El Paso Times*, June 23, 2009; see also Howard Campbell, *Drug War Zone* (Austin: University of Texas Press, 2009), pp. 96–107.

19. Molloy, "Fronterizo List," December 31, 2009.

20. Redacción, *El Diario de Juárez*, February 9–11, 2009; and Associated Press, February 11, 2009.

21. Alejandro Salmon and Orlando Chávez, "Ejecutados son un delincuente menos," *El Diario de Juárez*, April 4, 2008.

22. Jo Tuckman, "At Least 20 Dead in Mexican Prison Riot," *Guardian*, London, March 5, 2009.

6: THE WIND OF KNIVES

1. *Proceso*, various articles in special edition, December 9, 2009.

2. The articles were part of a series over many years by Diana Washington Valdez, in *The Killing Fields: Harvest of Women* (Los Angeles: Peace at the Border, 2006).

3. Ken Ellingwood, "Court Cites Rights Failure by Mexico in Juárez Killings of Women," *Los Angeles Times*, December 12, 2009.

4. Ibid.

INTERMISSION: THE ROAD IT GIVES, AND THE ROAD IT TAKES AWAY

1. Don Henry Ford, *Contrabando* (El Paso: Cinco Puntos, 2005).

2. Alicia Caldwell, Associated Press, various reports during December 2009.

7: "EAT OFF THE FLOOR"

1. *San Antonio Standard*, March 10, 1996.
2. See Enrique Krauze, *Mexico: Biography of Power*, trans. Hank Heifetz (New York: Harper, 1997), pp. 526–600.
3. Lugar, *Assembled Parts, Fragmented Lives*, pp. 148–52.
4. Altha J. Cravey, *Women and Work in Mexico's Maquiladoras* (Lanham, MD: Rowman and Littlefield, 1998), p. 49.
5. Krauze, *Mexico*, pp. 697–98.
6. Todd Gillman, "Obama Talks of 'Upgrade' to NAFTA with Mexico's Calderón," *Dallas Morning News*, January 13, 2009.
7. Reglamento Interior del Trabajo, Article 13, 1980.
8. Quoted by Diana Washington Valdez, *El Paso Times*, February 2, 2009.

8: GATEWAY TO THE AMERICAS/PAX MAFIOSA

1. Ginger Thompson, "Rival Drug Gangs Turn the Streets of Nuevo Laredo into a War Zone," *New York Times*, December 4, 2005.
2. Sara A. Carter, "Here We Are Prisoners," *San Bernardino Sun*, December 28, 2006.
3. Ricardo Ravelo, "Los Zetas: Ejército de Osiel," *Proceso*, September 15, 2005; and Dudley Althaus and James Pinkerton, "Violence in Nuevo Laredo," *Houston Chronicle*, August 7, 2005.
4. Susana Hayward, "Drug War Rages in Border Town," *Miami Herald*, July 31, 2005.
5. Ravelo, "Los Zetas"; and Manuel Roig-Franzia, *Washington Post*, May 7, 2008.
6. *Frontera NorteSur* website, May 15, 2004.
7. Alicia Caldwell, Associated Press, January 28, 2010.
8. Committee to Protect Journalists, Mexico Annual Country Report for 2008.
9. See Cecilia Ballí, "Ropa Usada," in Crosthwaite, Byrd, and Byrd, *Puro Border*, pp. 183–90.

10. Ibid., p. 187.

11. Keith Bowden, *The Tecate Journals* (Seattle: Mountaineers Books, 2007), pp. 219ff.

12. Dudley Althaus and James Pinkerton, "River to Ruin: Descent of the Rio Grande," *Houston Chronicle* special supplement, October 17, 1993.

9: IRON RIVER/TELL THEM WHO YOU ARE

1. Tracy Wilkinson, "Mexico Drug Gangs Turn Weapons on Army," *Los Angeles Times*, March 15, 2009.

2. Thomas Koch, *The Militia Battle Manual* (El Dorado, AZ: Desert Publications, 1996).

3. *Full Auto Volume One: AR-15 Modification Manual* (El Dorado, AZ: Desert Publications, 1981).

4. *Select Fire AK-47 Gilil and Valmet Conversion Manual* (El Dorado, AZ: Desert Publications, 1994).

5. Lora Lumpe, "The US Arms Both Sides in Mexico's Drug War," *Covert Action Quarterly* 61, Summer 1997.

6. Richard A. Serrano, "Guns from U.S. Equip Drug Cartels," *Los Angeles Times*, August 10, 2008.

7. United States Government Accountability Office, "Firearms Tracking: U.S. Efforts to Combat Arms Trafficking to Mexico Face Planning and Coordination Challenges," Report no. GAO-09-709, June 2009.

8. FBI press release, May 2, 2009.

9. Tracy Wilkinson, "Ex-General, 2 Others Found Shot to Death Near Cancún," *Los Angeles Times*, February 4, 2009.

10. Dudley Althaus, "Cancún's Top Cop Is Grilled in Retired General's Killing," *Houston Chronicle*, February 9, 2009.

11. Ken Ellingwood, "Killings Uncover Seamier Side of Cancún," *Los Angeles Times*, March 2, 2009.

12. Dudley Althaus, "Beheadings Shake W. Mexico Town," *Houston Chronicle*, March 15, 2009.

13. Tracy Wilkinson, "Mexico Sees Inside Job in Prison Break," *Los Angeles Times*, May 18, 2009.

14. Ken Ellingwood, "Drug Violence Spilling into Guatemala," *Los Angeles Times*, June 7, 2009.

15. Tracy Wilkinson, "Mexican Cartel Weapons from Central America," *Los Angeles Times*, March 15, 2009.

16. Dudley Althaus, "Gunfight Near Mexican School Leaves Pupils Traumatized," *Houston Chronicle*, February 21, 2009.

17. Lynn Brezosky and Dudley Althaus, "Blood Flows in Streets of Reynosa," *Houston Chronicle*, February 19, 2009.

18. Marc Lacey, "Drug Tie Seen to Protests in Mexico," *New York Times*, February 18, 2009.

19. Tracy Wilkinson, "Mexican Cartels Buying Public Support," *Los Angeles Times*, March 13, 2009.

20. Dane Schiller, "Drug Cartel May Be Using Bogus 'FBI' Vests," *Houston Chronicle*, April 1, 2009.

21. Milo Kearney and Anthony Knopp, *Boom and Bust: The Historical Cycles of Matamoros and Brownsville* (Austin: Eakin Press, 1991), pp. 106–30.

22. Antonio Zavaleta and Alberto Salinas, Jr., *Curandero Conversations* (Bloomington, IN: AuthorHouse, 2009).

23. For a discussion of the competing influences of Mexican and Irish Catholicism in the United States, see Manuel G. Gonzales, *Mexicanos: A History of Mexicans in the United States* (Bloomington: Indiana University Press, 1999), p. 241.

24. See Katherine Boo, "Letter from South Texas," *New Yorker*, March 29, 2004.

25. For an analysis of high school football and Latino identity in the Rio Grande Valley, see Joel Huerta, "Red, Brown, and Blue: A History and Cultural Poetics of High School Football in Mexican America," Ph.D. diss., University of Texas at Austin, 2005.

26. For an analysis of Los Angeles as style capital for Mexican narcos, see Sam Quinones, *True Tales from the Other Mexico* (Albuquerque: University of New Mexico Press, 2001).

27. Tim Rutten in the *Los Angeles Times*, February 28, 2009, discusses Quinones's theory.

28. U.S. District Court, Southern District of Texas, *USA v. Hernandez*, case H-08-317M, filed April 24, 2008.

29. Dane Schiller, "Windshield Repairman Admits Gun-Smuggling," *Houston Chronicle*, November 21, 2009.

30. Dane Schiller, "Suspected Drug Boss 'Taunting' Feds," *Houston Chronicle*, July 12, 2009.

31. Dane Schiller, "Mexican Cartels Infiltrate Houston," *Houston Chronicle*, October 17, 2009.

32. Dane Schiller and Jacquee Petchel, "Drug Cartel Chief Sentenced in Secrecy," *Houston Chronicle*, February 24, 2010.

AFTERWORD: BLOOD MONEY

1. *United States of America V. Wachovia Bank*, N.A., United States District Court S.D. Fl., no. 10-20165, March 12, 2010.

2. David Voreacos, "Wachovia to Pay $160 Million to End Money Laundering Probe," Bloomberg, March 18, 2010.

3. Michael Smith, "Banks Financing Mexico Gangs Admitted in Wells Fargo Deal," Bloomberg news wire, June 29, 2010.

4. Maria Aspan and Glenn Somerville, "Fed Orders HSBC to Improve Anti-Fraud Controls," Reuters news wire, October 7, 2010.

BIBLIOGRAPHICAL NOTE

Books and newspaper articles used for reference in this book are annotated and numbered at the appropriate points in the text. But some guide to sources and further reading may be useful, arranged roughly in accordance with the chapters in this book. Some are referred to in the text and notes, others not, but all the following have been useful to this endeavor in one way or another.

By far the best general histories of Mexico are *Mexico: Biography of Power* by Enrique Krauze (New York: Harper, 1997) and *The Oxford History of Mexico*, a collection of essays edited by Michael C. Meyer and William H. Beezley (New York: Oxford University Press, 2000). The story of the U.S.-Mexican war, the plunder of Indian lands, and raids by the Indians as a border narrative is nowhere better told than in the epic *War of a Thousand Deserts*, by Brian DeLay (New Haven: Yale University Press, 2008). A very useful recent history is *Opening Mexico* by Julia Preston and Samuel Dillon (New York: Farrar, Straus and Giroux, 2004).

There are innumerable books on ancient Mexican and Aztec lore, of which the best (in Spanish) is Eduardo Matos Moctezuma's *Los Aztecas*, published by Mexico's National Council for the Arts, 2000. Bernardino de Sahagún's definitive *Historia General de las Cosas de Nueva España* is available in English as *A History of Ancient Mexico*, trans. Fanny R. Bandelier (Nashville: Fisk University Press, 1932). For those wanting an English translation of Bernal Díaz's *The Conquest of New Spain*, that by J. M. Cohen (New York: Penguin, 1963) has yet to be rivaled. The University of California Press at Berkeley publishes a reprint of T. T. Waterman's famous book, *Bandelier's Contribution to the Study of Ancient Mexican Social Organization* (1917). *The Mexican Dream* is a famous meditation by J.M.G. Le Clézio on what he calls "The Interrupted Thought of Amerindian Civilizations," translated by Teresa Lavander Fagan (Chicago: University of Chicago Press, 1993). *Aztec and Maya Myths* by Karl Taube is an excellent introduction (London: British Museum, 1993).

There are many books on the U.S.-Mexican border generally. The best history of the frontier itself is *Border: The U.S.-Mexico Line* by Leon C. Metz (El Paso: Mangan Books, 1989), who has written many other books about the wars and personalities that make up the border's eventful history. Of the many collections of academic essays on the border, these have proved useful: *U.S.-Mexico Borderlands: Historical and Contemporary Perspectives*, edited by Oscar J. Martínez (Wilmington, DE: Scholarly Resources, 1996); *The Last Frontier: The Contemporary Configuration of the U.S.-Mexico Border*, edited by Jane Juffer (Durham, NC: Duke University Press, 2006); *Crossing Borders, Reinforcing Borders: Social Categories, Metaphors, and Narrative Identities on the U.S.-Mexico Frontier*, edited by Pablo Vila (Austin: University of Texas Press, 2000); "Identifaciones de Región, Etnia y Nación en la Frontera Entre Mexico-EU" by Pablo Vila (Universidad Autonóma de Ciudad Juárez, 2004). There is also *Life, Death and In-Between on the U.S.-Mexico Border*, edited by Martha Oehmke Loustaunau and Mary Sánchez-Bane (Westport, CT: Bergin & Garvey, 1999), which is specifically about health issues, and the very readable collection of journalism *Puro Border*, edited by Luis Humberto Crosthwaite, John William Byrd, and Bobby Byrd (El Paso: Cinco Puntos Press, 2003). A good study of Mexicans living in the United States is *Mexicanos* by Manuel G. Gonzales (Bloomington: Indiana University Press, 1999).

Three main books have been written on the history of U.S. covert involvement in narco trafficking, the most famous of which is *Dark Alliance* by Gary Webb (New York: Seven Stories Press, 1998). Also the excellent *Desperados* by Elaine Shannon (New York: Viking, 1988) and *The Big White Lie* by Michael Levine (New York: Thunder's Mouth Press, 1993).

The best book on Tijuana is Luis Alberto Urrea's *Across the Wire* (New York: Anchor, 1993). Much has been written on migration, the original of which is *Coyotes* by Ted Conover (Vintage, 1987), after which came, notably, *The Devil's Highway* by Luis Alberto Urrea (New York: Little, Brown, 2004), about the tragedy in 2001 mentioned in chapter 3 of this book, and *Hard Line* by Ken Ellingwood (New York: Pantheon, 2004). There are also *Lives on the Line* by Miriam Davidson (Tucson: University of Arizona Press, 2000); *No One Is Illegal* by Justin Akers Chacón and Mike Davis (Chicago: Haymarket Books, 2006); *Cutting for Sign* by William Langewiesche (New York: Vintage, 1993); and Tim Gaynor's *Midnight on the Line* (New York: St. Martins Press, 2009). *Exodus* is a collection of poignantly evocative photographs by Julián Cardona, with a text by Charles Bowden (Austin: University of Texas Press, 2008).

Bowden is *the* writer on the border, and his work centers mainly on Ciudad Juárez. *Juárez: The Laboratory of Our Future* (New York: Aperture, 1988) is probably the most terrifyingly insightful book ever written on the city and what it means. Bowden also gave us many great works of part fiction, including *Down by the River* (New York: Simon & Schuster, 2002) and *Murder City* (New York: Nation Books, 2010)—the only book apart from this one about the current stage of the drug war. Also useful is the excellent academic study *Drug War Zone* by Howard Campbell (Austin: University of Texas Press, 2009). Campbell's colleague at UTEP Tony Payan has written *The Three U.S.-Mexico Border Wars* (Westport, CT: Praeger, 2006).

The first book on a cartel chief—and the only time one was interviewed for the purpose—was *Drug Lord* by Terence Poppa (El Paso: Cinco Puntos, 2010). Two great memoirs and one great "novel" followed Poppa's landmark book: *Contrabando* by Don Henry Ford is the autobiography of a drug smuggler (El Paso: Cinco Puntos, 2005) and *The Reaper's Line* is that of customs special agent Lee Morgan, who tried to stop people like Ford (Tucson: Rio Nuevo, 2006). Both Ford and Morgan are featured in this book, and I'll wager they'd get along just fine. Don Winslow's *Power of the Dog* (New York: Knopf, 2005) is fiction—but it all happened for real. Another lovely memoir is of the Rio Grande, navigated by kayak, Keith Bowden's *The Tecate Journals* (Seattle: Mountaineers Books, 2007).

Books on the Tohono O'odham Native American tribe are harder to come by than general histories of other tribes. The best is Winston P. Erikson's *Sharing the Desert: The Tohono O'odham in History* (Tucson: University of Arizona Press, 1994), while *Rainhouse and Ocean* by Ruth Underhill et al. (Tucson: University of Arizona Press, 1979) gives a poetic account of O'odham rituals and speeches. Frank Russell's *The Pima Indians* was recently republished in paperback (Nabu Press, 2010). There are innumerable books on the Arizona desert landscape and natural life—too many to list here—but none are as informative as *Dry Borders*, edited by Richard Felger and Bill Broyles (Salt Lake City: University of Utah Press, 2007). As a literary meditation, Edward Abbey's *Desert Solitaire* (New York: Simon & Schuster, 1990) stands alone, and there is also Charles Bowden's *Desierto* (New York: Norton, 1993).

Elijah Wald wrote *Narcocorrido* (New York: Harper, 2001), and the best book on maquiladoras is *Fragmented Lives, Assembled Parts* by Alejandro Lugo (Austin: University of Texas Press, 2008), focused on Ciudad Juárez. There are also *Women and Work in Mexico's Maquiladoras* by Altha J. Cravey (Lanham, MD: Rowman and Littlefield, 1998) and *NAFTA from Below*, edited by Martha A. Ojeda and Rosemary Hennessy (Missouri City, TX: Coalition for Justice in the Maquiladoras, 2007). Ciudad Juárez itself has commanded much attention, and the best sociological study is *La Realidad Social de Ciudad Juárez*, coordinated by Clara Jusidman (Universidad Autónoma de Ciudad Juárez, 2008), and a companion statistical volume and DVD, both compiled by Hugo Almada Mireles. On the mass murder of women in Juárez, there is *The Killing Fields* by Diana Washington Valdez (Los Angeles: Peace at the Border, 2006) and *Desert Blood: The Juárez Murders* by Alicia Gaspar de Alba (Houston: Arte Público Press, 2005). Others include *Daughters of Juárez* by Teresa Rodriguez, Diana Montané, and Lisa Pulitzer (New York: Atria, 2007), and *If I Die in Juárez* by Stella Pope Duarte (Tucson: University of Arizona Press, 2008).

There are few histories of the Rio Grande Valley as such, but *Boom and Bust: The Historical Cycles of Matamoros and Brownsville* by Milo Kearney and Anthony Kopp (Austin: Eakin Press, 1991) will do. An excellent academic study in Spanish only is *Estructura Urbana en Ciudades Fronterizas* by Eduardo Alarcón Cantú (Tijuana: Colegio de la Frontera del Norte, 2000). A detailed book on patrolling the valley border is *Patrolling Chaos* by Robert Lee Maril (Lubbock: Texas Tech University Press, 2004). *Brownsville* by Oscar Casares (Boston: Little, Brown, 2003) is fiction, but it speaks volumes about reality. From Laredo come three books: *Nuevo Laredo: A Prelude to War* by Dan Robinson (Fort Lee, NJ: Shotmakers, 2009), *Laredo Stories* by Tony Rauch (Portland, OR: Eraserhead Press, 2008), and *My Border Patrol Diary* by Dale Squint (Bloomington, IN: AuthorHouse, 2007). There exist two books in Spanish on Los Zetas: *Crónicas de Sangre: Cinco Historias de los Zetas* by Ricardo Ravelo (Mexico: Random House Mondadori, 2007) and *De Los Maras a Los Zetas* by Jorge Fernández Menéndez and Víctor Ronquillo (Mexico: Grijalbo Mondadori, 2007).

So much has been written on Mexican "folk Catholicism" as explored in chapter 9. It would be hard to improve on D. A. Brading's *Mexican Phoenix: Our Lady of Guadalupe—Image and Tradition Across Five Centuries* (New York: Cambridge University Press, 2001). The fascinating *Curandero Conversations* by Antonio Zavaleta and Alberto Salinas, Jr. (Bloomington, IN: AuthorHouse, 2009) is discussed in chapter 9.

ACKNOWLEDGMENTS

This book would not have been considered or written without my dear friend David Rieff, whose idea of a holiday way back was to go looking for cowboy boots in El Paso and Del Rio, and stories in Ciudad Juárez and Acuña. David later introduced me to Tracy Bohan at the Wylie Agency, who many, myself included, would call a wonderful literary agent, but who I also regard as something between having one's own military wing and a sports coach with that canny enthusiasm that motivates the final extra sprint. There are three colleagues without whom the book would also not have happened: Julián Cardona, the bravest reporter I have ever met, who profoundly influenced the ensuing arguments and who remains, defying all, in Ciudad Juárez; Cecilia Ballí, whose family history is in many ways that of the border, and whose compassion for its people and their lives, and keen eye across its atrocities, likewise charge this text; and Dudley Althaus, whose generosity, commitment, and expert company on the road knew no bounds. It was, sadly and belatedly, only in researching this paperback edition that I came upon a journalist covering this war like none other, a striking role model for any reporter and humbling in her courage: Sandra Rodriguez of *El Diario* in Ciudad Juárez, whose arguments and insight also infuse this latest version of the book.

These are times when good reporting is under siege from mediocrity, blog, and Twitter—but some fight on the ramparts of quality, and there remain moments in American journalism when a cluster of exceptional talent forms in one place. Mexico City is experiencing one such fortunate era, thanks to correspondents from whose work and in many cases company

I have had the honor to benefit: above all, the great Tracy Wilkinson of the *Los Angeles Times*, who also kindly amended the draft. Also Marc Lacey of *The New York Times*, Alfredo Corchado of *The Dallas Morning News*, the photographer David Rochkind and Ken Ellingwood of the *Los Angeles Times*, William Booth of *The Washington Post*—plus the inimitable Dudley, as above, of the *Houston Chronicle*, and *The Guardian* and *The Observer*'s Jo Tuckman. They are the visitors. Among the Mexicans, I owe thanks to the best of those who do the difficult, right thing: in Tijuana, Jorge Fregoso of Síntesis TV; in Mexico City, to the rising star León Krauze; to Alejandro Páez and Ignacio Álvarez Alvarado of *El Universal*; and in Hermosillo to Juan Carlos Zúñiga and Marco Mendoza. Thanks to those who chronicle Juárez for *El Diario* and *El Norte*. And in terrifying Tamaulipas, you know who you are.

In Nuevo León, with their works of art, Francisco Benítez, Tomás Hernández, and Jessica Salinas break new ground of resistance, humor, courage, and even hope.

North of the border, these folks are supplemented—and this book enhanced—by the personalities and committed work of two great heretics: Dane Schiller of the *Houston Chronicle* and Brenda Norrell of the Censored News and Narcosphere websites. Also Jesse Bogan, whose fine work *Forbes* magazine rewarded with a layoff (and they're supposed to be the smart guys?—no wonder the economy's down the pan), and Sacha Feinman, who writes on Sonora (and boxing) better than anyone else but has difficulty getting hired by a two-bit sports mag—God help journalism.

I am grateful for hospitality along the way: in GHQ Tucson, to Debra May and Phreddie and Olivia Bartholomaei; Trudy Duffy, Elaine Mauriole, Joan and Jen at the ranch, Anne and Eddie, James Romero and Rene Escalante, and Bob and Peggy Feinman. In Mexico City, to León, as above, and to Marco and Juan Carlos in Hermosillo. To Charles Bowden in Patagonia, Tom and Nadine Russell in El Paso, Don Henry and Leah Ford in Belmont, Raymundo Ramos in Nuevo Laredo, Mario Treviño in Reynosa, Cecilia Ballí in Brownsville, and Lisa Hilton in Houston. Among these are the authors of two of five great border books to which I am indebted: C. Bowden's *Juárez: The Laboratory of Our Fu-*

ture, and Ford's *Contrabando*. The other three are K. Bowden's *The Tecate Journals*, Lee Morgan's *The Reaper's Line*, and Don Winslow's *Power of the Dog*. Thanks to Molly Molloy in Las Cruces, for hospitality but even more so for the tenacious tracking of deaths and narco violence that makes her "Fronterizo List" the most reliable regular source of information by far, as well as an embarrassment for the amount of monitoring work we reporters could and should be doing ourselves. Other books and sources are listed in the notes and bibliography.

There are good and brave people in this book who will claim their acknowledgments through the narrative, but Mike Flores, Angelita Ramón, Pastor José Antonio Galván, Josué Rosales, Norma Andrade, Marisela Ortiz, Rosario Acosta, Paula González, and Julia Quiñones need special thanks for their company, courage, and the influence they had on things.

I owe perennial thanks to John Mulholland, editor of *The Observer*, for commissioning some of the articles that gave way to all this, and to Paul Webster, my main editor for two and a half decades at *The Observer* and *The Guardian*. Also thanks at *The Guardian* to Holly Bentley for her assiduous research across the archives, Arnel Hecimovic for the picture research, and Finbarr Sheehy for drawing the map. There are debts and thanks due to the main editor of the British edition of this volume, Will Sulkin, and his American counterpart, Eric Chinski, for terrifying faith at the outset and subsequent and invaluable guidance on the text. Also to Kay Peddle and Eugenie Cha for their kind efficiency and patience, to Chris Peterson, to Cynthia Merman and Alison Tulett for copyediting, and to Laura Mell and Laurel Cook. Thanks also to Elena Cosentino of the BBC, Ginerva White, and to Philip Breeden at the U.S. embassy in London. Any undertaking of journalism by me will owe a debt in origin to my teachers John Ware, Duncan Campbell, and Dan Morgan.

Some precious friends propelled this book and its background: John Cale with a steady stream of information and his own caustic but always velvet observations; Paul Gilroy and Vron Ware without whose wisdom, company, and friendship over four decades I would have been locked away; Marco "el Sexto Sol" Roth with his irrepressible faith in uprising and complicated love for his native Mexico; Mark Dowie and Wendy

Schwarz, in the most beautiful place on earth; and Tom Rhodes, who I met in the storm of another war. Deep thanks to Josh Lord at East Side Ink, grand master of the chisel, for our mutual design, and his execution with painless finesse of the Guadalupe/Coatlicue/Amexica protective tattoo. It was a joy to find in Toronto a precious friend from another war, Erica Zlomislic, whose deep and intelligent Catholic faith was a guiding hand through the riptide of religiosity that cuts beneath this book.

There are deepest personal thanks too, for this has not always been easy: to lovely Elsa and Claudia for being who they are and putting up with me (if they do); to Victoria for the desert and for bearing with it all so kindly (if she did); to Louisa and to Mum, Tom, and Clara. In New York, thanks to Roger Cohen, to Stacy and Leslie the propeller girls, and to Nebojsa Shoba Serić. There was a lot of tiring and miserable hobbling on crutches getting ready, during which many thanks to Hawkwind, Fairport, and the LSO for music of delight and encouragement; to Angela, Kate, and Thomas Turley-Mooneyham in Chicago; to the Uxbridge Arms and Torriano pubs; to the Frontline Club; the Tavola Calda "da Maria" for *vera cucina casalinga*, even in Notting Hill Gate; and to the Kop on the lock at the Constitution for never having to walk alone, even on crutches. For repairing the damage and getting me mobile, thanks initially to Tamara Cilliers, then Kerry Dowson, and everyone that morning at Royal Liverpool Infirmary—but no thanks at all to the Paterson wing at St. bloody Mary's hospital in Paddington, which did its best to stop the whole thing happening.

Crucially, thanks to Echols the Arizona alley cat.

INDEX